INDIGENOUS HOMELESSNESS

INDIGENOUS HOMELESSNESS

Perspectives from Canada, Australia, and New Zealand

Edited by Evelyn J. Peters and Julia Christensen

UMP

University of Manitoba Press

University of Manitoba Press
Winnipeg, Manitoba
Canada R3T 2M5
uofmpress.ca

Printed in Canada
Text printed on chlorine-free, 100% post-consumer recycled paper

20 19 18 17 16   1 2 3 4 5

Interior design: Karen Armstrong
Cover design: Jess Koroscil
Cover image: Glenna Matoush, *Untitled*, 2009

Library and Archives Canada Cataloguing in Publication

Indigenous homelessness : perspectives from Canada,
Australia, and New Zealand / edited by Evelyn J. Peters, Julia
Christensen.

Includes bibliographical references and index.
Issued in print and electronic formats.
ISBN 978-0-88755-826-9 (pbk.)
ISBN 978-0-88755-528-2 (pdf)
ISBN 978-0-88755-526-8 (epub)

1. Indian homeless persons—Canada. 2. Homeless persons—Canada.
3. Homeless persons—Australia. 4. Homeless persons—New Zealand.
5. Native peoples—Canada—Social conditions. 6. Aboriginal Australians—
Social conditions. 7. Maori (New Zealand people)—Social conditions.
8. Homelessness—Canada. 9. Homelessness—Australia.
10. Homelessness—New Zealand. I. Peters, Evelyn J. (Evelyn Joy),
1951–, editor II. Christensen, Julia, 1978–, editor III. Title.

HV4493.I53 2016   362.5'92089   C2016-903136-5
                                              C2016-903137-3

This book has been published with the help of a grant from the Federation for the
Humanities and Social Sciences, through the Awards to Scholarly Publications Program,
using funds provided by the Social Sciences and Humanities Research Council of Canada.

The University of Manitoba Press gratefully acknowledges the financial support
for its publication program provided by the Government of Canada through the Canada
Book Fund, the Canada Council for the Arts, the Manitoba Department
of Culture, Heritage, Tourism, the Manitoba Arts Council,
and the Manitoba Book Publishing Tax Credit.

FSC
www.fsc.org
MIX
Paper from
responsible sources
FSC® C016245

Contents

Illustrations

Introduction

JULIA CHRISTENSEN

Canada, Australia, and New Zealand share a common creation story as now-sovereign states within the Commonwealth of Nations. Ironically, the Commonwealth was formed through the decolonization of the British Empire and the granting of self-governance to its former colonies. This is ironic because many of the Indigenous[1] peoples whose territories were dispossessed and whose cultures were desecrated through the "taking" of these new worlds are still calling for recognition and decolonization in their own right. Though definitions and legal statuses differ between these three contexts, as the self-identified descendants of the original inhabitants of those colonized territories, Indigenous peoples today are at various points in processes of self-determination, self-governance, and reclaiming of ancestral lands.

Yet despite many significant advances in the political and economic clout of some Indigenous peoples, overall they continue to experience a higher rate of social, economic, and health inequalities. These inequalities explain in part the disproportionate number of Indigenous people affected by homelessness in both rural and urban settings in Canada, Australia, and New Zealand (see Anderson, Tayler, and Collins 2014; Beavis et al. 1997; Belanger, Awosoga, and Weasel Head 2013; Collins 2010; Memmott and Chambers 2008). These disparities are in many ways bound up in, and representative of, long-standing colonial processes of social, cultural, economic, and physical marginalization (of Indigenous peoples) on what remain their traditional homelands. Though the particular experiences of Indigenous homelessness reflect their unique geographic contexts, they share the story they tell about the social and systematic vulnerability of Indigenous peoples in settler colonial societies.

How and why homelessness amongst Indigenous peoples occurs, and most importantly, what can be done to alleviate the ill effects of homelessness in culturally relevant and respectful ways, are the timely and significant questions that have compelled us to write this book. Chronic housing need, inappropriate architecture and planning, and other socio-structural disparities exist in rural Indigenous communities that contribute to hidden forms of homelessness as well as rural-urban migration (Kearns, Smith, and Abbott 1991; Peters and Robillard 2009). However, the high number of Indigenous people facing homelessness is most visible in urban settings (Belanger, Awosoga, and Weasel Head 2013; Cardinal 2006; Collins 2010). While the shifting dynamics of the housing and job markets, as well as those of neo-liberal social policy, can be linked to Indigenous homelessness just as they can be to homelessness among other demographic groups, only a small body of work has explored the particular reasons why Indigenous people are so highly overrepresented in the homeless populations of settler societies (see Menzies 2009; Peters 2012; Peters and Robillard 2009).

The dominant understanding of homelessness in the academic literature is informed by "broadly white Western conceptions of home [that] privilege a physical structure or dwelling" (Mallett 2004, 65). The reductionism of housing-as-home "glosses over cultural, spiritual, and ideational meanings of 'home' as a secure place to be" (Geisler and George 2006, 26). Meanwhile, the emphasis on absolute homelessness in urban settings in both popular and academic discourse neglects the often less visible forms of homelessness that take place in rural or reserve settings (see Peters 2012; Tester 2009), while at the same time obscuring linkages between urban "street" homelessness and dynamics of the rural community or the reserve (see Christensen 2012; Peters and Robillard 2009).

As a result, research on Indigenous homelessness has focused predominantly on social pathologies and the higher rates of poverty, addiction, and poor mental and physical health amongst Indigenous peoples, particularly in urban settings. Relatively little attention has been given to the specific ways in which such alarming social outcomes can occur within the settler colonial context, the broader spatialities of Indigenous homelessness across diverse scales (rural, urban, homeland, nation), or the phenomenology of Indigenous homelessness.

However, several scholars have recently suggested that colonialism has particular, ongoing effects on the lives of homeless Indigenous people (Menzies 2009; Peters and Robillard 2009). Moreover, others have found homelessness among Indigenous people to be qualitatively distinct (Christensen 2013; Memmott and Chambers 2008). A narrow view of homelessness as predominantly (1) a lack of shelter; (2) an urban phenomenon; and (3) a matter of social pathologies, effectively detaches Indigenous experiences of homelessness from the overall socio-spatialization of settler colonial societies. In other words, Indigenous homelessness cannot be decontextualized from the uneven economic and community development, institutionalization, landlessness, and cultural genocide experienced in different degrees and scales across Canada, Australia, and New Zealand. What this means in terms of understanding the meaning and scope of Indigenous homelessness, as well as the potential for effective policy and support programs, is the focus of this book.

Defining Indigenous Homelessness

Definitions of homelessness have proved both useful and problematic for researchers and policy makers. Definitions are never trivial, for they can have "profound consequences for policy, resource allocation, and parameters used to evaluate the success of homeless initiatives" (Frankish, Hwang, and Quantz 2005, s24). The categories and definitions commonly used to categorize homelessness differ across Canada, Australia, and New Zealand. In an effort to build a standard vocabulary across the chapters in this book, we suggest the following loose definitions, with the understanding that of course many experiences and assessments of homelessness will surely fall outside, or blur the lines between, these categories.

Most homelessness and housing studies scholars conceptualize homelessness as existing along a spectrum. At one end of the spectrum are those "sleeping rough," for example, living outdoors and in other places not intended for human habitation. Then there are those living in emergency shelters. In this book, we refer to individuals experiencing these forms of homelessness as "absolutely homeless." The spectrum of course also includes people who are staying with friends or family on a temporary basis (i.e., "couch surfing"), which we refer to, in this book, as "hidden homelessness." It is necessary to underline that rarely, if ever, does one exclusively experience one form of homelessness. The main objective in conceptualizing homelessness as a spectrum is to convey that there is considerable movement between the different points. For example, someone sleeping rough may also occasionally sleep in an emergency shelter. Likewise, someone who was precariously housed may stay at an emergency shelter before once again finding accommodation.

A third and final category, "at risk of homelessness," refers to those individuals who are living in situations of domestic violence, living in substandard or unsafe housing, and persons who are spending a very large proportion of their monthly income on housing. While some scholars might include this third category under hidden homelessness, highlighting the ontological aspects of feeling tenuously housed, we chose to keep these categories separate to reflect the particular vulnerability of being insecurely housed. Similarly, as the chapters in the volume demonstrate, these definitions fall far short of adequately describing and conceptualizing Indigenous homelessness. In response, some scholars, such as Greenop and Memmott in Chapter 13, necessarily problematize such definitions as they seek to uncover and analyze the geographies of homelessness specific to their geographic context. Not only are such definitions ill-fitting for Indigenous peoples' ideas of how to live "properly," they also keep the focus squarely on occupation of a dwelling, with little to no regard for the socio-cultural dimensions of Indigenous homelessness. As a result, these definitions effectively obscure homelessness as experienced by Indigenous peoples, as well as create homelessness through ineffective public policy.

Overview of the Book

The chapters in this volume explore the culturally and geographically distinct aspects of Indigenous homelessness across and within Canada, Australia, and New Zealand, with a particular emphasis on the Canadian context. Altogether, they position Indigenous homelessness in the wake of historic Commonwealth colonialisms and contemporary neo-liberal policies. Moreover, the scholars who have contributed to this volume have long-standing engagements with culturally sensitive research processes and university-community collaborations.

The book is organized into three sections. Each focuses on a specific country and each begins with a short introductory chapter to describe the colonial, socio-economic, and political context for Indigenous homelessness in that country. Following brief introductions, subsequent chapters explore various aspects of Indigenous homelessness across diverse, and yet in many ways similar, geographical contexts. In a final chapter, we bring together several key themes that emerge across these varied settings and analyses, as well as set out future research directions.

In the first section and the first chapter, we introduce the Canadian context. In Chapter 2, Christensen and Andrew examine the role of social policy in (re) producing Indigenous homeless geographies in the Canadian North. Taking up Mallett's (2004) concept of "home/journeying," they argue that many Indigenous pathways to homelessness are efforts at home-building that come into direct conflict with social policy. The condition of literal homelessness, they suggest, is in many ways the result of a clash between Indigenous cultural values and dominant social policy paradigms. In particular, the complex intersections between housing policy, income support, corrections, and child welfare present critical gaps in support for northern Indigenous men and women seeking to exit homelessness. Reflecting on the recent Northwest Territories Minister's Forum on Addictions and Community Wellness, they explore how these gaps are broadened by the northern mental health and addictions treatment, which serves to undermine culturally rooted, community- and family-based supports. They argue that, to meaningfully address Indigenous homelessness across settler societies, decolonizing agendas must reorient social policy interventions away from the management of "deficiencies" or "deviance" towards culturally relevant, community- and family-based programming based on Indigenous values and focused on supports for home-building.

In the third chapter, Peters and Kern explore the housing strategies of low-income First Nations migrants to Winnipeg, Manitoba. They argue that it is housing services, and not employment or other factors critical to urban survival, that are the most important, and often the most problematic, when attempting to start a life in the city. In particular, their chapter focuses on the housing strategies of low-income First Nations migrants who accessed housing counselling services at the Eagle Urban Transition Centre. Peters and Kern's study focuses on the mobility patterns of these individuals as they attempt to meet their housing needs in the city. Peters and Kern problematize the emphasis in current research and policy on absolute homelessness and alternatively propose that there are distinctive features of First Nations homelessness that need to be understood in order to provide services for this population. They suggest that hidden forms of urban First Nations homelessness remain poorly understood in policy and housing service areas due to a lack of understanding of the cultural values that often underlie strategies such as couch surfing, the many challenges and strains that efforts to care for homeless family and friends can place on a host family, and finally the particular vulnerabilities of hidden homeless people. Peters and Kern illustrate the necessity for increased research into the housing strategies of hidden homeless First Nations migrants in order to create responses that respond sensitively to their particular needs.

Freistadt begins the fourth chapter with a story of three police officers in Edmonton, Alberta, who, in May 2005, took nine Indigenous panhandlers from a popular commercial strip in the city's core, drove them around in a hot van for an hour and a half, and dropped them off half-clothed in a distant neighbourhood. During a disciplinary hearing, police officials insisted that race was not a factor in their actions, and instead argued that this practice was meant to protect homeless people and help them access social services. Freistadt examines such informal police responses to Indigenous homelessness in Edmonton, documenting how the police practice of "dumping"—where officers remove individuals from spaces in which they generate complaints and drop them off in other locations—contributes to and reflects the racialization of marginalized inner cities. Furthermore, he suggests that such practices reinforce long-standing colonial controls that dangerously tie Indigenous people to marginalized spaces, while at the same time preserving ideal notions of prime space as white space. He then uses these observations to discuss how responses to the racialized policing of homelessness must look beyond the potential racial prejudices of individual officers and instead focus on some of the larger processes by which policing and space are racialized.

In Chapter 5, Klodawsky, Cherner, Aubury, Farrell, Parrell, and Smith move into a decisively different direction by examining quantitative data through an intersectional lens in an effort to understand the health and housing experiences of Indigenous peoples. In this chapter, the authors reflect on findings from the health and housing in transition (HHiT) study, a longitudinal cohort study that aims to track the health and housing status of a representative sample of homeless and vulnerably housed single adults in three Canadian cities (Toronto, Ottawa, and Vancouver) over a four-year period. They examine matched samples of Indigenous and non-Indigenous respondents to explore changes in health status and housing outcomes over a two-year period and to determine whether Indigenous identity has an impact on health and housing outcomes.

Bonnycastle, Simpkins, and Siddle and Thurston, Turner, and Bird take a united approach across Chapters 6 and 7 in their privileging of the knowledge and lived experiences of homeless Indigenous men and women. In soliciting such first-hand insight, the authors insist that it is critical to the development of meaningful and robust policy interventions. Using participatory photography, the authors draw on Friere's critical pedagogy to determine how the knowledge of homeless people living in Thompson, Manitoba, can be incorporated into policy interventions. Meanwhile, reflecting on their work in Calgary, Alberta, Thurston and co-authors discuss the need for community-engaged scholarship to inform policy development vis-à-vis Indigenous homelessness. They make the pointed argument that community-engaged scholarship is the only appropriate approach to working with populations facing social exclusion and discrimination.

Linking back to Christensen's and Andrew's earlier reflections, in Chapter 8 Belanger and Lindstrom not only contemplate the qualitative distinctiveness of Indigenous homelessness but also the broader significance of Indigenous homelessness in cities located on the traditional lands of Indigenous peoples. Taking up Blackfoot conceptions of land, and understanding their centrality to individual Blackfoot people, Belanger and Lindstrom explore the experiences of Blackfoot homelessness in the city of Lethbridge, Alberta. In their discussion, they consider how homelessness influences one's relationship with the land and, just as importantly, how one's relationship with the land influences one's homeless experience.

Academic literature tends to frame the issue of Indigenous homelessness as an urban phenomenon, neglecting rural, and less visible, experiences. However, several smaller studies have attempted to understand the scope and scale of homelessness and housing insecurity in specific rural areas across Canada. In Chapter 9, Schiff, Turner, and Waegemakers Schiff engage in a comprehensive review of these case studies in order to establish several overarching themes that describe the current landscape of rural homelessness and housing insecurity for Indigenous peoples. The authors also provide a number of new insights into the nature and dynamics of this significant, yet often hidden issue. In particular, they point to the current popularity of the Housing First model and suggest several alterations that must be made for the model to be effective in rural Indigenous community settings.

In the second section of the book, in Chapter 10, we move to Australia, with an introduction by Memmott and Nash. In Chapter 11, Prout Quicke and Green discuss Indigenous "fringe dwelling" in Geraldton, Western Australia, as being symptomatic of a larger colonial legacy in Australia. Living, literally and figuratively, on the edges of town life/urban society, Indigenous fringe dwellers have largely been constructed through scholarly and literary accounts as having abandoned, or been dislocated from, their customary moorings and attachment to country, while being simultaneously unwilling or unable to become immersed within the socio-spatial systems and norms of settler society. However, Prout Quicke and Green suggest an alternative reading, namely that fringe dwelling may also be read as a means of tempered (and in some cases highly strategic) engagement with the colonial frontier. Today, the authors suggest, fringe locations are often preferred sites of residence and gathering for many Indigenous people fostering complex feelings regarding their dwelling and belonging. Relating such historical narratives of contested Indigenous presence is, Prout Quicke and Green argue, critical to understanding the drivers of contemporary Indigenous "homelessness" in all its forms and critical to assessing the capacity of towns and cities to accommodate Indigenous presence.

In Chapter 12, Memmott and Nash (with Willetts and Frank) address the dynamics of support services in framing Indigenous pathways to homelessness in regional and remote Australia, where necessary support services are under tremendous pressure as a result of high demand compounded by a chronic lack of housing. The Jimaylya Topsy Harry Centre, in Mount Isa in northwestern Queensland, and the Tennant Creek Women's Refuge, in the Barkly region of the Northern Territory, are two examples of support services offering critical resources to Indigenous people in crisis and at risk of homelessness. However, in their analysis, Memmott and Nash find that the Centres both enable and constrain the lives of Indigenous people in these regional towns, complicating the goal of social inclusion sought by state and federal Australian governments. Memmott and Nash argue that a nuanced understanding of the social and cultural constraints on Indigenous people's paths into and out of homelessness can valuably inform policy.

In Chapter 13, Greenop and Memmott tackle the definitional dilemmas of crowding and homelessness in urban Indigenous Australia. Indeed, the authors' reflections in this chapter inform similar definitional dilemmas in Canada and New Zealand, as well as in other contexts. Specifically, the authors are interested in how current measures of homelessness and crowding in the Australian Indigenous and Torres Strait Islander context are premised on culturally specific, Anglo-Australian norms of home, house, sedentariness, and sociality. As a point of departure, Greenop and Memmott analyze the circumstances that affect crowding and homelessness in the state's capital city of Brisbane and in the regional, remote city of Mount Isa. They then uncover the important links between "hidden homelessness" and crowding and relate them to important modes of Indigenous sociality and mobility. In a provocative discussion, the authors suggest that current approaches to housing, including the metrics used to measure crowding and homelessness, are part of the long-standing attempts to assimilate Indigenous people into Western patterns of housing use. Such approaches, they contend, should be replaced with evidence-based policies that assist people to stay in housing, within their own persisting cultural values.

Birdsall-Jones is also interested in challenging the ways in which the dominant policy terminology classifies and categorizes Indigenous homelessness. One of the most strongly held features of Australian Indigenous culture and identity is the obligation of kinfolk to look after one another, a significant cultural value that is also strongly represented among diverse Indigenous cultures in Canada and New Zealand. In Chapter 14, Birdsall-Jones explores the role of kinship in shaping the mobility patterns of Indigenous homeless people. In particular, she is interested in how the role of the family in caring for homeless kin effectively "hides" the houselessness of those kin, leaving them outside the purview of most policy interventions. Moreover, she suggests that there are important differences among types of homelessness and associated mobility patterns that may be culturally or socially legitimized or not legitimized at all within Indigenous societies. Through an examination of the ways in which kin relationships structure the management of housing the homeless in Indigenous households in Broome, Carnarvon, and Perth in Western Australia, Birdsall-Jones distinguishes the role of Indigenous culture from the role of mainstream society in shaping the homeless behaviour of Australian Indigenous people.

In Part 3, with Chapter 15, Groot and Peters introduce the topic of Indigenous homelessness in New Zealand. In Chapter 16, Brown explores *tūrangawaewae*, or having an ancestral "place to stand," a concept that is central to individual and collective Māori identities and is strongly associated with contemporary notions of "home." While colonization is often cited in New Zealand homelessness literature as the mechanism for estranging Māori from their tūrangawaewae, the processes by which this has happened are not often described in detail. In this chapter, Brown identifies the key historical moments at which Māori have experienced the loss of tribal lands and explains the effect that this had on specific communities and families, leading to a sense of spiritual homelessness, if not actual loss of housing. All of these events have contributed to a loss of spiritual identification with ancestral landscapes and collective identities. To conclude, Brown proposes that long-term, large-scale strategies for restoring these identities go hand in hand with the decolonization of national policy as it applies to Māori housing and homelessness in tandem with the restoration of Māori constitutional authority.

In Chapter 17, King, Hodgetts, Rua, and Te Whetu take us to a key site of Māori resistance to colonialism, Ōrākei marae (communal complex used by everyday Māori), which is found at the heart of Takaparawhau (Bastion Point in central Auckland). This contested site became a national focal point for Māori protests over land confiscations by the Crown, culminating in a mass occupation of the site for 504 days between 1977 and 1978 that ended with 222 arrests prior to the land being returned to its rightful owners, Ngāti Whātua (a local tribal group in the Auckland area). King and co-authors' chapter begins in present day, where they explore the involvement of a group of older, homeless Māori men who work at Ōrākei marae, though this is not the ancestral *marae* or meeting grounds of the homeless participants themselves. King and colleagues consider the significance of such culturally patterned space to interrelated questions of place, homelessness, and Māori ways of being. In particular, they explore the importance of maintaining cultural spaces, such as marae, in preserving associated Māori practices and thereby building or maintaining a sense of home among homeless Māori men.

Altogether, the chapters in this volume push back against the commonplace assumption that Indigenous homelessness is qualitatively indistinct and, worse still, against the prevalence of apathy and even passive acceptance of Indigenous homelessness in Canada, Australia, and New Zealand. Not only do we set out to trace the colonial roots of contemporary Indigenous homelessness, we also seek to explore diverse Indigenous cultural perspectives in order to understand the scope and significance of Indigenous experiences of homelessness in settler colonial societies. Finally, by situating Indigenous homelessness within both colonial and Indigenous cultural contexts, our intention is to inform scholars, policy makers, and wider publics about the need for a decolonization of discourse and policy in order to meaningful alleviate Indigenous homelessness.

Notes

1   Though there is no universal definition for Indigenous peoples, the Martinéz Cobo Report to the UN Sub-Commission on Prevention of Discrimination and Protection of Minorities (United Nations 1987, paras. 379–82) offers some useful, clear identification criteria: "Indigenous communities, peoples and nations are those which, having a historical continuity with pre-invasion and pre-colonial societies that developed on their territories, consider themselves distinct from other sectors of the societies now prevailing in those territories, or parts of them. They form at present non-dominant sectors of society and are determined to preserve, develop and transmit to future generations their ancestral territories, and their ethnic identity, as the basis of their continued existence as peoples, in accordance with their own cultural patterns, social institutions and legal systems."

References

Anderson, Jalene Tayler, and Damian Collins. 2014. "Prevalence and Causes of Urban Homelessness among Indigenous Peoples: A Three-Country Scoping Review." *Housing Studies* 29 (7): 959–76.

Beavis, Mary Ann, Nancy Klos, Thomas Carter, and Christian Douchant. 1997. *Literature Review: Aboriginal Peoples and Homelessness.* Ottawa: Canada Mortgage and Housing Corporation.

Belanger, Yale D., Olu Awosoga, and Gabrielle Weasel Head. 2013. "Homelessness, Urban Aboriginal People, and the Need for a National Enumeration." *Aboriginal Policy Studies* 2 (2): 4–33.

Cardinal, Nathan. 2006. "The Exclusive City: Identifying, Measuring, and Drawing Attention to Aboriginal and Indigenous Experiences in an Urban Context." *Cities* 23 (3): 217–28.

Christensen, Julia. 2012. "'They Want a Different Life': Rural Northern Settlement Dynamics and Pathways to Homelessness in Yellowknife and Inuvik, Northwest Territories." *The Canadian Geographer/Le Géographe Canadien* 56 (4): 419–38.

_____.2013. "'Our Home, Our Way of Life': Spiritual Homelessness and the Sociocultural Dimensions of Indigenous Homelessness in the Northwest Territories, Canada." *Social and Cultural Geography* 14 (7): 804–28.

Collins, Damian. 2010. "Homelessness in Canada and New Zealand: A Comparative Perspective on Numbers and Policy Responses." *Urban Geography* 31 (7): 932–52.

Frankish, C. James, Stephen W. Hwang, and Darryl Quantz. 2005. "Homelessness and Health in Canada: Research Lessons and Priorities." *Canadian Journal of Public Health/Revue Canadienne de Santé Publique* 96 (Supplement 2): S23–S29.

Geisler, Charles, and Lance George. 2006. "Homeless in the Heartland: American Dreams and Nightmares in Indian Country." In *International Perspectives on Rural Homelessness*, edited by Paul Cloke and Paul Milbourne, 25–44. Abingdon, Oxon: Routledge.

Kearns, Robin A., Christopher J. Smith, and Max W. Abbott. 1991. "Another Day in Paradise? Life on the Margins in Urban New Zealand." *Social Science and Medicine* 33 (4): 369–79.

Mallett, Shelley. 2004. "Understanding Home: A Critical Review of the Literature." *The Sociological Review* 52 (1): 62–89.

Memmott, Paul, and Catherine Chambers. 2008. *Homelessness amongst Aboriginal People in Inner Sydney.* Brisbane: University of Queensland.

Menzies, Peter. 2009. "Homeless Aboriginal Men: Effects of Intergenerational Trauma." In *Finding Home: Policy Options for Addressing Homelessness in Canada*, ch. 6.2, edited by J. David Hulchanski, Philippa Campsie, Shirley. B.Y. Chau, Stephen W. Hwang, and Emily Paradis. Toronto: Cities Centre Press.

Peters, Evelyn. 2012. "'I Like to Let Them Have Their Time'. Hidden Homeless First Nations People in the City and Their Management of Household Relationships." *Social and Cultural Geography* 13 (4): 321–38.

Peters, Evelyn, and Vince Robillard. 2009. "'Everything You Want Is There': The Place of the Reserve in First Nations' Homeless Mobility." *Urban Geography* 30 (6): 652–80.

Tester, Frank J. 2009. "Iglutaasaavut (Our New Homes): Neither 'New' nor 'Ours': Housing Challenges of the Nunavut Territorial Government." *Journal of Canadian Studies/Revue d'études canadiennes* 43 (2): 137–58.

United Nations. 1987. *Sub-Commission on Prevention of Discrimination and Protection of Minorities: Study of the Problem of Discrimination against Indigenous Populations.* New York: United Nations.

Part I

CANADA

CHAPTER I

Indigenous Homelessness: Canadian Context

JULIA CHRISTENSEN

Recent years have brought about a growing call to political action from Indigenous governments, non-governmental organizations (NGOs), and researcher-academics alike. They recognize that the overrepresentation of Indigenous peoples among Canada's homeless is a matter of urgent concern, and a matter that represents the significance of colonial continuities in the social, health, and material aspects of Indigenous peoples' lives. This brief overview can in no way do justice to the diversity of Indigenous peoples in Canada, nor to the many social, economic, cultural, political, and health issues bound up within Indigenous geographies of homelessness. Nevertheless, by way of introduction and context, it offers the key threads necessary to understand the current landscape of Indigenous homelessness in Canada.

Indigenous peoples in Canada include the First Nations, Inuit, and Metis.[1] There are approximately 1,400,685, Indigenous people in Canada today, accounting for 4.3 percent of the total population. This number includes 851,560 First Nations people, 451,795 Metis, and 59,445 Inuit (Statistics Canada 2011). The legal identities and rights of the First Nations, Inuit and Metis peoples are set out in the repatriated Canadian Constitution of 1982.[2] Each Indigenous group in Canada is unique in terms of its history of European contact, as well as its historical and contemporary relations with the state.

Several treaties between First Nations and the Crown were signed after the Royal Proclamation of 1763 and before Confederation in 1867. However, after Confederation, a series of eleven treaties (known as "numbered treaties") were signed between First Nations and the Crown from 1871 to 1921. Under the treaties, First Nations gave up large areas of their traditional homelands to the Crown. In exchange, the treaties were meant to provide First Nations with such things as reserve lands, annual treaty payments, and certain hunting and fishing rights. However, systemic failures of the government to live up to their agreements, evidenced by chronic housing need and widespread issues with water quality and sanitation, as well as policy that relinquishes treaty rights when one leaves the reserve, have led to poverty and dependency among many Indigenous peoples on- and off-reserve.[3]

Where numbered treaties were not signed, or where it has otherwise been proven in court that traditional Indigenous land rights were not extinguished, comprehensive (or "modern") land-claims agreements may be negotiated. These modern land claims encompass a much broader range of rights and benefits, and are negotiated directly between Indigenous and Canadian governments. Modern land claims have been settled, or are still under negotiation, in many parts of British Columbia and across most of northern Canada. Some, but not all, claims include self-government responsibilities.

Residential School and Child Welfare Systems

Many scholars have argued that intergenerational trauma resulting from such colonial practices as Indigenous displacement and dispossession is indelibly tied to Indigenous experiences of homelessness in Canada (see Belanger, Awosoga, and Weasel Head 2013; Berman et al. 2009; Leach 2010; Menzies 2009). The Indian Residential School System was one of the most tragic, destructive, and defining moments of colonial intervention in Canada (Milloy 1999; Thornton 2008). Beginning in the nineteenth century, the Canadian government developed a policy of aggressive assimilation to be implemented by residential schools, which were church-run but funded by the federal government. A parallel objective of this system was to facilitate the displacement of Indigenous people from their lands (De Leeuw 2009). Attendance at the schools was mandatory, and strictly enforced by government agents. Once in the schools, few children received an adequate education. Instead, many were taught to be ashamed of their languages and cultural identities. Indigenous families were delegitimized, and the knowledge of parents and grandparents was undermined by teachers and administrators (Lavallee and Poole 2010; Ruttan, LaBoucane-Benson, and Munroe 2010). Many children were also physically and sexually abused, and the rates of disease and mortality at the schools were also extremely high (Brasfield 2001; DeGagné 2007).

A second "phase" in the assimilation of Indigenous children began in the 1960s, as large numbers of Indigenous children across Canada were removed from their families and placed up for adoption with non-Indigenous families in Canada, the United States, and Europe (Kirmayer, Simpson, and Cargo

2003). This period lasted three decades, but was termed "the Sixties Scoop." Though the practice of removing Indigenous children from their families for the explicit purpose of cultural assimilation has now ceased, the legacy of this period is alive and well: there are currently more than three times the number of Indigenous children in state care than there were at the height of the residential school system (Blackstock 2008). Experience in the child welfare system figures prominently as a contributing factor to homelessness among Indigenous youth (Baskin 2007) and is often highlighted by homeless Indigenous adults as integral to their homelessness (see Christensen 2013; Menzies 2009).

Poor mental health, substance abuse, violence, and other risk factors for homelessness are linked to intergenerational trauma resulting from colonial policies like the Indian Residential School System (Brasfield 2001; Hawkeye Robertson 2006). Likewise, the disproportionately high number of Indigenous people in Canadian prisons is tied to intergenerational trauma and institutionalized racism (LaPrairie 1997; Waldram 1997), and explains well-documented prison-to-homelessness pathways (Gaetz and O'Grady 2009; Walsh et al. 2011). Though factors like crime, violence, and substance abuse are framed by neo-liberal policy as matters of individual agency, scholars have argued that for Indigenous homeless men and women in Canada, and across settler societies, individual traumas are bound up in, and further complicated by, the broader dynamics of collective, intergenerational trauma (Belanger, Awosoga, and Weasel Head 2013; Christensen 2013).

The Extent of the Knowledge on Indigenous Homelessness in Canada

Across Canada, Indigenous people are overrepresented among rural and urban homeless populations (see Beavis et al. 1997; Belanger, Awosoga, and Weasel Head 2013; Christensen 2012; Golden et al. 1999). While there are no official data on the national state of Indigenous homelessness, the Native Counselling Service of Alberta estimates the rate of Indigenous homelessness to be "about 40 percent [of the total homeless population] Canada wide" (NCSA 2000, 3). Further complicating the lack of enumeration is the prevalence of hidden homelessness and high mobility in Indigenous homeless people's experiences (Distasio, Sylvestre, and Mulligan 2005). After combing through data collected by researchers in cities across Canada, Belanger, Awosoga, and Weasel Head (2013) calculated that on any one night in Canada, 6.97 percent of the urban Indigenous population is homeless, compared to the national average of 0.78 percent. Many community-based support providers and researcher-academics in Canada have called for a more expansive definition that accounts for the

multi-dimensionality in Indigenous homeless experiences, including the role
of colonialism, intergenerational trauma, and the socio-cultural and material
conditions of "being displaced from critical community social structures and
lacking in stable housing" (Menzies 2005, 8).

The history of settler and Indigenous relations and the resulting settlement
patterns frame the social and material inequalities that drive the high mobility of homeless Indigenous people. In 2009, Peters and Robillard illustrated
the socio-spatial tensions between rural reserve life and urban life, and the
movement between them. In particular, they found that certain circumstances
experienced by interviewees (i.e., lack of social and economic opportunities,
strained personal relationships) often motivated them to leave rural reserves
for urban areas. However, once in the city, interviewees were confronted by
a lack of economic, social, and cultural resources as well as a longing for the
important social networks left at home on the reserve. Christensen (2012) examined similar geographies in the homeless pathways of Indigenous homeless
people in northern Canada, where chronic housing need and unemployment
motivates or forces already-vulnerable people to leave smaller settlements for
larger centres. Social networks are also key to rural-urban movement among
Indigenous populations and in the experiences of Indigenous homeless people
in the city (Bruce 2006; Christensen 2012; Peters and Robillard 2009). In
some cities, the urban spatialization of such social networks has resulted in
ghettoization (see Belanger 2007; Cohen and Corrado 2004; Walker 2005).

Hidden Homelessness and Core Housing Need

The high levels of hidden homelessness characteristic of Indigenous homelessness in Canada makes an accurate assessment of and effective response to the
phenomenon very difficult (Distasio, Sylvestre, and Mulligan 2005). Hidden
homelessness is a sweeping category and includes those who are in transition homes, jails, and detoxification centres; living in overcrowded, unstable,
or inadequate housing; "couch surfing"; and at risk of becoming homeless.
Overcrowding is a particularly common experience among the Indigenous
hidden homeless, and is associated with social strain, poor mental health,
domestic violence, and acute respiratory diseases such as tuberculosis (Clark,
Riben, and Nowgesic 2002; Tester 2006, 2009; Kovesi et al. 2007; Orr 2007).
Indigenous people experiencing hidden homelessness comprise a demographi-
cally diverse group, ranging from families (especially single-parented ones)
to youth and elders. Nevertheless, hidden homelessness among Indigenous
people in Canada remains distinctly gendered. According to Hulchanski and
co-authors, Indigenous women are more likely to be single parents, and almost

half (47 percent) of Indigenous single parent families experience core housing need.[4] Moreover, for Indigenous women, violence, poverty, and poor housing are often closely interlinked (Hulchanski et al 2009).

Overall, roughly 20 percent of Indigenous households in Canada experience core housing need, compared to 13.5 percent of non-Indigenous Canadians. Rates of Indigenous core housing need exceed those of non-Indigenous households in every province and territory (CHFC 2007). The numbers tell a story that is even more dire for those Indigenous people living on-reserve or in Arctic Canada: 24 percent of Indigenous households on-reserve nation-wide and 40 to 50 percent of households in Nunavut and Nunavik are in core housing need (CMHC 2006).

Key Areas of Focus in Community-Based Advocacy on Indigenous Homelessness in Canada

Key areas of focus for Indigenous communities, community-based advocates, and policy makers around Indigenous homelessness concern intergenerational trauma, homelessness, and supportive housing initiatives. Indigenous communities and support organizations are working together to implement healing knowledges, found in Indigenous cultural and spiritual frameworks, into programs and services for the homeless and at-risk-of-homelessness Indigenous population. Examples can be found in several Canadian prisons (Waldram 2007) and substance-abuse programs geared specifically towards Indigenous peoples, such as Poundmaker Lodge near Edmonton, Alberta.

Community-based approaches that embrace recovery-oriented or other supportive and/or transitional housing models and include Indigenous wellness approaches are also cropping up across Canada. For example, Homeward Trust Edmonton works closely with Indigenous stakeholders and community members. It maintains a majority Indigenous board membership and an Aboriginal Advisory Council in its effort to address Indigenous homelessness in the city. The Vancouver Native Housing Society offers similar supportive housing programs, and is also engaged in social enterprise.

Conclusion

While the trend in Canadian social policy responses has been to understand Indigenous homelessness in terms of poverty, housing needs, and social exclusion, in recent years several researcher-academics have argued that Indigenous homelessness must be situated within the context of colonialism. This literature has collectively identified two key factors that frame the landscape of Indigenous homelessness in Canada. The first is intergenerational trauma resulting from colonialism and present-day colonial continuities. Such trauma contributes to the high rates of mental health complications, substance abuse, violence, and other risk factors for homelessness. The second is the structural inequality that frames the social and material life of Indigenous peoples. This inequality is represented in the high rates of core housing need and poverty in Indigenous households both on- and off-reserve, in high rates of Indigenous children living in poverty and/or in the child welfare system, and in the high rates of Indigenous men and women incarcerated in the criminal justice system. Yet while these factors are widely recognized among Indigenous governments, NGOs, and researcher-academics, they have yet to be fully recognized and addressed by policy makers. However, recent government efforts to collaborate with Indigenous communities and other community-based agencies show significant potential in implementing culturally relevant support strategies for Indigenous homeless people.

Notes

1   Though "Aboriginal" is a widely accepted term for these three groups, the term "Indigenous" has gained prominence in recent decades to describe Aboriginal peoples in both a Canadian and an international context.

2   While the term "Indian" has legal status in the Canadian Constitution, the term "First Nations" has gained significant currency as a more respectful replacement for "Indian." "Inuit" means "people" in the Inuktitut language and refers to a specific ethnic and linguistic group living across the Canadian Arctic and parts of the Subarctic. "Indian" and "Metis," on the other hand, are both terms with a complex and contentious history. A "status Indian" is someone who is registered as an Indian under the federal Indian Act and/or is registered to a band which has signed a treaty with the Crown. A "non-status Indian" is a legal term referring to any First Nations individual who for whatever reason is not registered with the federal government, and/or is not registered to a band which has signed a treaty with the Crown. This legal term also includes the Metis, which is a contentious inclusion and explains in part why the Metis have struggled so much in Canada to have their traditional rights recognized. The Metis have a unique culture of mixed First Nations and European heritage, derived mainly from intermarriages during the fur trade of Scottish, French, Ojibwe and Cree peoples. They are distinct from First Nations people, Inuit, or non-Aboriginal people.

3   A reserve is a tract of land, the legal title to which is held by the Crown, set apart for the use and benefit of an Indian band.

4   According to the Canada Mortgage and Housing Corporation (CMHC), a household is in core housing need if its housing falls below at least one of the adequacy, affordability, or suitability standards (as defined by CMHC) and if in order to pay the median rent of alternative local housing (deemed acceptable according to CMHC standards) the occupants would have to spend 30 percent or more of their total before-tax income (CMHC 2014).

References

Baskin, Cyndy. 2007. "Aboriginal Youth Talk about Structural Determinants as the Causes of Their Homelessness." *First Peoples Child and Family Review* 3 (3): 31–42.

Beavis, Mary Ann, Nancy Klos, Thomas Carter, and Christian Douchant. 1997. *Literature Review: Aboriginal Peoples and Homelessness.* Ottawa: Canada Mortgage and Housing Corporation.

Belanger, Yale D. 2007. *Assessing Urban Aboriginal Housing Needs in Southern Alberta.* Regina: Saskatchewan Institute on Public Policy.

Belanger, Yale D., Olu Awosoga, and Gabrielle Weasel Head. 2013. "Homelessness, Urban Aboriginal People, and the Need for a National Enumeration." *Aboriginal Policy Studies* 2 (2): 4–33.

Berman, Helene, Gloria Alvernaz Mulcahy, Cheryl Forchuk, Kathryn Ann Edmunds, Amy Haldenby, and Raquel Lopez. 2009. "Uprooted and Displaced: A Critical Narrative Study of Homeless, Aboriginal, and Newcomer Girls in Canada." *Issues in Mental Health Nursing* 30 (7): 418–30.

Blackstock, Cindy. 2008. "Reconciliation Means Not Saying Sorry Twice: Lessons from Child Welfare in Canada." In *From Truth to Reconciliation: Transforming the Legacy of Residential Schools*, edited by Marlene Brant Castellano, Linda Archibald, and Mike DeGagné, 163–78. Ottawa: Aboriginal Healing Foundation.

Brasfield, Charles R. 2001. "Residential School Syndrome." *BC Medical Journal* 43 (2): 78–81.

Bruce, David. 2006. "Homelessness in Rural and Small Town Canada." In *International Perspectives on Rural Homelessness*, edited by Paul Cloke and Paul Milbourne, 63–78. Abingdon, Oxon: Routledge.

CHFC (Co-operative Housing Federation of Canada). 2007. *Dimensions of Core Housing Need in Canada.* Toronto: Co-operative Housing Federation of Canada.

Christensen, Julia. 2012. "'They Want a Different Life': Rural Northern Settlement Dynamics and Pathways to Homelessness in Yellowknife and Inuvik, Northwest Territories." *The Canadian Geographer/Le Géographe canadien* 56 (4): 419–38.

____.2013. "'Our Home, Our Way of Life': Spiritual Homelessness and the Sociocultural dimensions of Indigenous homelessness in the Northwest Territories (NWT), Canada." *Social and Cultural Geography* 14 (7): 804–28.

Clark, Michael, Peter Riben, and Earl Nowgesic. 2002. "The Association of Housing Density, Isolation and Tuberculosis in Canadian First Nations Communities." *International Journal of Epidemiology* 31 (5): 940–45.

CMHC (Canada Mortgage and Housing Corporation). 2006. *2006 Census Housing Series Issue 9 – Inuit Households in Canada.* Ottawa: Canada Mortgage and Housing Corporation.

Cohen, Irwin M., and Raymond R. Corrado. 2004. "Housing Discrimination among a Sample of Aboriginal People in Winnipeg and Thompson, Manitoba." In *Aboriginal Policy Research: Setting the Agenda for Change*, edited by Jerry P. White, Paul Maxim, and Dan Beavon, 113–26. Toronto: Thompson Educational Publishing.

de Leeuw, Sarah. 2009. "'If Anything Is to Be Done with the Indian, We Must Catch Him Very Young': Colonial Constructions of Aboriginal Children and the Geo-Graphies of Indian Residential Schooling in British Columbia, Canada." *Children's Geographies* 7 (2): 123–40.

DeGagné, Michael. 2007. "Toward an Aboriginal Paradigm of Healing: Addressing the Legacy of Residential Schools." *Australasian Psychiatry* 15 (S1): 49–53.

Distasio, Jino, Gina Sylvestre, and Susan Mulligan. 2005. *Home Is Where the Heart Is and Right Now That Is Nowhere—: An Examination of Hidden Homelessness among Aboriginal Peoples in Prairie Cities*. Winnipeg, University of Winnipeg: The Institute of Urban Studies.

Fournier, Suzanne, and Ernie Crey. 1997. *Stolen from Our Embrace: The Abduction of Indigenous Children and the Restoration of Aboriginal Communities*. Vancouver: Douglas and McIntyre.

Gaetz, Stephen, and Bill O'Grady. 2009. "Homelessness, Incarceration and the Challenge of Effective Discharge Planning: A Canadian Case." In *Finding Home: Policy Options for Addressing Homelessness in Canada*, edited by J. David Hulchanski, Philippa Campsie, Shirley B.Y. Chau, Stephen W. Hwang, and Emily Paradis, 672–93. Toronto: Cities Centre Press.

Golden, Anne, William H. Currie, Elizabeth Greaves, and E. John Latimer. 1999. *Taking Responsibility for Homelessness: An Action Plan for Toronto*. Toronto: City of Toronto.

Hawkeye Robertson, Lloyd. 2006. "The Residential School Experience: Syndrome or Historical Trauma." *Pimatisiwin* 4 (2006): 2–28.

Hulchanski, J. David, Philippa Campsie, Shirley B.Y. Chau, Stephen W. Hwang, and Emily Paradis, eds. 2009. *Finding Home: Policy Options for Addressing Homelessness in Canada*. Toronto: Cities Centre Press.

Kirmayer, Laurence J., Cori Simpson, and Margaret Cargo. 2003. "Healing Traditions: Culture, Community and Mental Health Promotion with Canadian Aboriginal peoples." *Australasian Psychiatry* (S1): S15–S23.

Kovesi, Thomas, Nicholas L. Gilbert, Corinne Stocco, Don Fugler, Robert E. Dales, Mireille Guay, and J. David Miller. 2007. "Indoor Air Quality and the Risk of Lower Respiratory Tract Infections in Young Canadian Inuit Children." *Canadian Medical Association Journal* 177 (2): 155–60.

LaPrairie, Carol. 1997. "Reconstructing Theory: Explaining Aboriginal Over-Representation in the Criminal Justice System in Canada." *Australian and New Zealand Journal of Criminology* 30 (1): 39–54.

Lavallee, Lynn F., and Jennifer M. Poole. 2010. "Beyond Recovery: Colonization, Health and Healing for Indigenous People in Canada." *International Journal of Mental Health and Addiction* 8 (2): 271–81.

Leach, Andrew. 2010. "The Roots of Aboriginal Homelessness in Canada." *Parity* 23 (9): 12–13.

Macdonald, David, and Daniel Wilson. 2013. *Poverty or Prosperity: Indigenous Children in Canada*. Ottawa: Canadian Centre for Policy Alternatives.

Menzies, Peter. 2005. "Orphans within Our Family: Intergenerational Trauma and Homeless Aboriginal Men." PhD diss., University of Toronto.

_____.2009. "Homeless Aboriginal Men: Effects of Intergenerational Trauma." In *Finding Home: Policy Options for Addressing Homelessness in Canada*, ch. 6.2, edited by J. David Hulchanski, Philippa Campsie, Shirley B.Y. Chau, Stephen W. Hwang, and Emily Paradis. Toronto: Cities Centre Press.

Milloy, John S. 1999. *A National Crime: The Canadian Government and the Residential School System, 1879 to 1986*. Winnipeg: University of Manitoba Press.

NCSA (Native Counselling Service of Alberta). 2000. *Community Consultation on Homelessness Report*. Edmonton: NCSA.

Orr, Pamela H. 2007. "Respiratory Tract Infections in Inuit Children: 'Set Thine House in Order.'" *Canadian Medical Association Journal* 177 (2): 167–68.

Peters, Evelyn. 2002. "Aboriginal People in Urban Areas." In *Urban Affairs: Back On the Policy Agenda?*, edited by Caroline Andrew, Katherine A. Graham, and Susan D. Phillips, 45–70. Montreal: McGill-Queen's University Press.

Peters, Evelyn, and Vince Robillard. 2009. "'Everything You Want is There': The Place of the Reserve in First Nations' Homeless Mobility." *Urban Geography* 30 (6): 652–80.

Ruttan Lia, Patti LaBoucane-Benson, and Brenda Munroe. 2010. "'Home and Native Land': Aboriginal Young Women and Homelessness in the City." *First Peoples Child and Family Review* 5 (1): 67–77.

Statistics Canada. 2011. *2011 National Household Survey: Aboriginal Peoples in Canada: First Nations People, Métis and Inuit*. Ottawa: Statistics Canada.

Tester, Frank J. 2006. "Iglu to Iglurjuaq." In *Critical Inuit Studies: An Anthology of Contemporary Arctic Ethnography*, edited by Pamela Stern and Lisa Stevenson, 230–52. Lincoln: University of Nebraska Press.

_____.2009. "Iglutaasaavut (Our New Homes): Neither 'New' nor 'Ours' Housing Challenges of the Nunavut Territorial Government." *Journal of Canadian Studies/ Revue d'études canadiennes* 43 (2): 137–58.

Thornton, Thomas F. 2008. *Being and Place among the Tlingit*. Seattle: University of Washington Press.

Waldram, James B. 1997. "The Aboriginal Peoples of Canada: Colonialism and Mental Health." In *Ethnicity, Immigration, and Psychopathology*, edited by Ihsan Al-Issa and Michel Tousignant, 169–87. New York: Springer, 1997.

Walker, Ryan C. 2005. "Social Cohesion? A Critical Review of the Urban Aboriginal Strategy and its Application to Address Homelessness in Winnipeg." *Canadian Journal of Native Studies* 25 (2): 395–416.

Walsh, Christine A., Paula MacDonald, Gayle E. Rutherford, Kerrie Moore, and Brigette Krieg. 2011. "Homelessness and Incarceration among Aboriginal Women: An Integrative Literature Review." *Pimatisiwin: A Journal of Aboriginal and Indigenous Community Health* 9 (2): 363–86.

Warry, Wayne. 1998. *Unfinished Dreams: Community Healing and the Reality of Aboriginal Self-Government*. Toronto: University of Toronto Press.

CHAPTER 2

"They Don't Let Us Look after Each Other Like We Used To": Reframing Indigenous Homeless Geographies as Home/Journeying in the Northwest Territories, Canada

JULIA CHRISTENSEN WITH PAUL ANDREW

> *Another event that Ayah predicted was that the Dene way of life would change. Some kind of power would come from somewhere and people would listen to it. Their lifestyle would change and they would be affected by the change. "I see that in the future," said Ayah. "Whatever you do, do not change your lifestyle. If you do, you will be sorry later." He said that to the people, but the people did not listen.*
>
> *In 1940, the federal government started to develop the Northwest Territories. They began to improve government services in the North by introducing education, health care and welfare. These services really altered the Dene way of life. Dene children learned to speak English and there was a change in languages spoken by the children. Kids did not listen to their parents anymore. Adults spent less time trapping and hunting. Pretty soon, nobody used the land anymore.*
>
> —George Blondin, in *Legends and Stories from the Past*

Change is a constant thread woven throughout considerations of contemporary Indigenous life in Canada. Researchers in particular tend to be preoccupied with the concept of change and the ways in which it affects Indigenous cultures, livelihoods, and health. It is true that the scope and scale of change that Indigenous peoples have experienced as a result of colonialism and paternalism are unprecedented, and continue to have profound and far-reaching impacts on families and communities through the dynamics of intergenerational transmission. As George Blondin, the late Dene storyteller and respected Elder, describes above, one of the most powerful drivers of change for Indigenous peoples in the Canadian North was the extension of the Canadian welfare state into that region in the mid-twentieth century.

In the Canadian North, the introduction of the Canadian welfare state transformed the Indigenous-State relationship from the economic exchange and laissez-faire attitude that had characterized the fur trade to one that actively sought to assimilate northern Indigenous people into Canadian modes of citizenship by *changing* Indigenous homes and ways of life. This was accomplished through policies that moved Indigenous peoples off the land and into settlements, separated children from their families, and enforced the adoption of Euro-Canadian cultural and societal norms through social policy and strategic modes of penalization (see Chapter 16 in this volume for Brown's description of similar experiences in the New Zealand context). The settlements also became distribution points for medical care, income support, and government-provided housing (Condon 1990; Tester and Kulchyski 1994; Damas 2002). Consequently, the government increased the vulnerability of northern Indigenous peoples by creating a relationship of dependency on the state for shelter and other basic needs (Tester and Kulchyski 1994; CMHC 1997; Tester 2006). The result, according to Alfred (2009, 42), has been the entrenchment of Indigenous people in colonial societies as "dependencies, in physical, psychological and financial terms, on the very people and institutions that have caused the near erasure of [their] existence and who have come to dominate [them]."

The Canadian welfare state established a relationship between Indigenous peoples and the state that can be understood as welfare colonialism, a concept first articulated by Paine (1977) to describe the uneven political and economic landscape for Indigenous peoples in the Canadian North. Since then, the term has been taken up to describe more widely the policies and practices through which liberal democratic (settler) governments both *recognize* the citizenship of Indigenous peoples vis-à-vis access to welfare benefits, and at the same time effectively *deny* their citizenship by nurturing their dependency on the state (Tyler 1993). As Paine (1977, 43) writes: "any decision taken by the colonizers has a basic flaw: a decision made for the material benefit of the colonized at the same time can be construed as disadvantaging them; a 'generous' or 'sensible' decision can at the same time be morally 'wrong.' This is because it is the colonizers who make the decisions that control the future of the colonized; because the decisions are made (ambiguously) on behalf of the colonized, and yet in the name of the colonizers' culture (and to her administrative, political, and economic priorities)."

However, colonial geographies are resisted and altered in many deliberate ways by the very people colonizers attempt to oppress. Resistance to welfare colonialism can be found in the examples of "home/journeying" first discussed by Mallett in 2004 and revealed through the pathways to home and homelessness described in this chapter. The experiences detailed in this chapter provide insight into efforts to find or return home, the ways in which these efforts come into direct conflict with social policy, and how these efforts are consequently implicit in pathways through homelessness. Moreover, the concept of "home/journeying" offers a productive and meaningful way of recognizing many important acts of agency that may otherwise be lumped together with contributing factors to homelessness. For example, in Christensen (2013), actions within individual pathways to homelessness that might be interpreted as resulting in or perpetuating homelessness may in fact be better understood as being in pursuit of a sense of home and of family. These may include rural-urban migration to leave a violent relationship or tent camping in order to gain a sense of independence from the rules of a homeless shelter. Attending to examples of home/journeying allows for the identification of new areas for policy and program interventions to support the alleviation of homelessness. Moreover, the inclusion of home/journeying in our conceptualization of homeless pathways places an emphasis on efforts to find or create home by men and women experiencing homelessness, and provide important insight into the ways in which we might support homeless people as they transition into homed lives.

Drawing on other scholars like Ahmed (1999), Massey (1992) and hooks (1990), Mallett (2004, 79) suggests that:

> Home is not necessarily a singular place or state of being rather it may be one's country, city or town, where one's family lives or comes from and/or where one usually lives. It may be other places or relationships. These homes hold differing symbolic meaning and salience. It is possible to be homeless in one, some or all of these categories at the same time. This view resonates with Mary Douglas's (1991) view of home as a "kind of space" or "localizable idea." "Home is located in space, but it is not necessarily a fixed space…home starts by bringing some space under control" (289). It cannot be simply equated with shelter, house or household.

Mallett's dynamic definition of home, in turn, contributes to an understanding of Indigenous homelessness as "multi-scalar, and occur[ing] both collectively (as a community, as a nation) and individually" (Christensen 2013, 18). A similar argument is made by Belanger and Lindstrom (see Chapter 8 in this volume), who suggest that a loss of family, identity, community, and trust are core elements of Indigenous homelessness. As such, the examples of home/journeying described in this chapter demonstrate the myriad ways in which the meaning and pursuit of home extends beyond shelter to include familial, spiritual, and cultural connections. By understanding Indigenous homelessness as qualitatively distinct, as more than absolute homelessness, but also a matter of spiritual homelessness, we recognize that practical approaches to home-building must address not only basic social and material needs, but also "individual and collective needs for self-determination, cultural emplacement and socio-economic inclusion" (Christensen 2013).

We argue in this chapter that Indigenous homelessness in Canada can be traced directly to the dynamics of welfare colonialism and the resulting relationships of dependency. These relationships of dependency exist not only at the personal or individual level, but also have consequences in terms of collective experiences of Indigenous homelessness (see Christensen 2013), or "spiritual homelessness" (Keys Young 1998). The central tension between northern Indigenous socio-cultural values and needs, the imposition of neo-liberal, Euro-Canadian societal norms through northern social policy, and the failure of such policy to meaningfully and effectively address Indigenous values and concerns, is a shared narrative throughout the life experiences of homeless Indigenous men and women in the Canadian North. In many ways, Indigenous homelessness is the outcome of a self-fulfilling prophecy; set into motion when the first federal agents arrived in the North and saw Indigenous lifestyles as deficient and disorderly (see De Leeuw, Greenwood, and Cameron 2010). This prophecy is perpetuated today as experiences of Indigenous homelessness are complicated by a clash in values, and a refusal on the part of state-sponsored social services to recognize and support home/journeying.

Background

Absolute homelessness has been a significant social concern in Canada's Northwest Territories since the late 1990s, particularly in the territorial capital, the city of Yellowknife, as well as in the town of Inuvik. Yellowknife and Inuvik are the two key centres in the territory for administration, transportation, and economic development (see Figure 2.1). In both communities, the emerging population of homeless northerners is disproportionately Indigenous, with estimates that 90 to 95 percent of the visible homeless population is Dene, Inuit, or Metis (Christensen 2011).

Public housing in the Northwest Territories (NWT) is administered through twenty-three local housing organizations (LHOs), each of which is accountable to the Northwest Territories Housing Corporation (NWTHC), a branch of the territorial government. In Inuvik and Yellowknife, the LHOs are known as Housing Authorities. The NWTHC serves the entire population of the NWT, both Indigenous and non-Indigenous. It also receives substantial funding from Canada Mortgage and Housing Corporation (CMHC). The NWT has no on-reserve housing administered by Aboriginal Affairs and Northern Development Canada (AANDC). This is a significant distinction because federal initiatives that fund Indigenous housing tend to be geared towards Indigenous people living on-reserve, leaving northern Indigenous people out of federal Indigenous housing initiatives. Instead, northern housing is provided through special pockets of funding established on a case-by-case basis.

The high cost and inadequate supply of housing in the Canadian North is accentuated by the decrease in government funding for housing over the past two decades. In 1993, the federal government froze new spending on social housing, stopped its off-reserve, Indigenous-specific housing assistance, and has been gradually phasing out funding for public housing maintenance since 2004.

Access to public housing is further complicated by chronic housing shortages, high construction costs, and high rates of "core housing need"[1] in the vast majority of settlement communities. In an effort to alleviate core housing need across the Canadian North, in 2006 the federal government allocated $300 million for northern public housing. The NWT received $50 million, which was matched by the territorial government (NWTHC 2009). However, these funds were used to increase the number of privately owned homes as well as to replace aging public housing stock, instead of increasing the actual number of public housing units (Falvo 2011).

For twenty-nine of the thirty-three communities in the NWT, public housing makes up the majority of housing stock. However, in Yellowknife, Inuvik, and the three other "market" communities, the housing stock is more diverse. In Yellowknife and Inuvik especially, much of the housing is either privately rented or owned. Public housing, meanwhile, is diminishing in both locales. The limited number of public housing units is especially dire for single adults: the public housing stock in both communities is largely comprised of family-sized units, and what units do exist for singles are prioritized for those over sixty years old and with disabilities (Falvo 2011).

This chapter results from a combination of in-depth ethnographic research, mutual experience and learning, and conversation and friendship between the two authors. Julia Christensen is a non-Indigenous scholar, born and raised in Yellowknife, NWT. This chapter is grounded primarily in more than seven years of ethnographic research she has conducted on geographies of Indigenous home and homelessness in the NWT. This research was accomplished through a collaborative, community-based research process with Indigenous governments, NGOs, and homeless men and women in the communities of Inuvik and Yellowknife.[2]

Paul Andrew is Tulita Dene, born and raised in the Sahtu region of the NWT, and he has had a long career in community leadership, broadcasting, storytelling, and writing. He is frequently called upon to offer his experience, knowledge, mentorship, and understanding in discussions of key northern and Indigenous issues. He most recently chaired the NWT Minister's Forum on Addictions and Community Wellness, the dynamics of which are highly relevant to the understanding of northern Indigenous homelessness we articulate here. The analysis in this chapter is informed by the knowledge Paul has gathered through his own personal life experiences as a young child and adult on the land, as a listener of the Elders' stories, and for over thirty years as a reporter with CBC North, speaking with northerners across the territory about the issues that matter to them.

In this chapter, we examine the intersections between Indigenous homelessness, welfare colonialism, and contemporary northern social policy. Building on a multi-dimensional understanding of Indigenous home and homelessness (see Christensen 2013), we take up both "spiritual homelessness" (Keys Young 1998) and "home/journeying" (Mallett 2004) in our reading of the scale and scope of homelessness among northern Indigenous people, and of the role northern social policy plays in (re)producing these geographies. In particular, we argue that many pathways to homelessness are comprised of home/journeying efforts and are demonstrative of the ways in which these efforts come into direct conflict with northern social policy. Through our explorations in this chapter, we seek to expand the definition of literal and spiritual homelessness to include conflicts in Indigenous cultural values and dominant social policy paradigms.

Drawing on personal narratives of homelessness, we explore several key areas of conflict between social policy and home/journeying in the Canadian North. In particular, we look at the complex intersections between public housing policy, child welfare, intergenerational trauma, and dependency which present critical gaps in social support for northern Indigenous men and women

Figure 2.1. Map of the Northwest Territories.

seeking to exit homelessness and in many ways undermine culturally rooted community- and family-based supports. We examine this conflict in values, and the ways in which narratives of home/journeying arise in response.

Moreover, we consider how home/journeying can be supported through social policy. In this vein, we discuss recent developments in the Northwest Territories that respond to community health needs through the provision of wellness-oriented services and reflect Indigenous values. One of the principal needs highlighted through the Northwest Territories Minister's Forum on Addictions and Community Wellness was a community-based, on-the-land mental health and addictions programming. This outcome, we argue, speaks to the need for community-scale supports in combination with individual-scale interventions. While the outcomes of the Northwest Territories' Minister's Forum on Addictions and Community Wellness are a significant step toward embracing Indigenous cultural frameworks in northern healthcare, there is an urgent need for similar transformations in other areas of care such as housing, income support, child and family services, and the criminal justice system, all of which feature prominently in individual pathways to homelessness. In other words, to meaningfully address Indigenous homelessness across settler societies, decolonization agendas must be adopted to reorient social policy interventions away from the management of perceived "deficiencies" or "deviance" (see De Leeuw, Greenwood, and Cameron 2010) toward culturally relevant, community- and family-based programming focused on supports for home-building.

Geographies of Indigenous Home and Homelessness

The call for a greater recognition of "home as place" (see May 2000b) in cultural geography implies an emotional, spiritual, or psychological attachment to place as intrinsic to a sense of home. For Indigenous cultures across Canada, land and family are inextricable from "home." Moreover, "family" extends beyond the nuclear unit to include all members of a community.

However, this sense of home was not understood by the early government agents who came to the Canadian North to bring health care and housing to the people who lived there. Motivated by colonial ideology and other national paternalistic interests, outsiders disrupted Indigenous peoples' relationship to place; both through the dispossession of land and territory as well as through displacement from family and culture (see Easthope 2004). The result has been the widespread destruction of Indigenous homes and the rendering of many Indigenous peoples "homeless in their own lands" (Baskin 2007, 33).

Many scholars, including those contributing to this volume, argue that Indigenous homelessness in settler colonial societies must be situated within the larger context of colonialism (Cedar Project Partnership et al. 2008; Christensen 2013; Peters and Robillard 2009). Geisler and George (2006) echo this broad and comprehensive approach, referring to the myriad colonial interventions experienced by Indigenous people collectively as "the other homelessness." In their view, Indigenous homelessness "is not an either-or binary of shelter versus no shelter. Such reductionism confuses housing with home and thereby glosses over cultural, spiritual, and ideational meanings of "home" as a secure place to be" (2006, 26). This same profound and deep-seated displacement is found at the heart of the concept "spiritual homelessness," a concept to explain the broader ontological significance of being disconnected from traditional homelands and community, cultural identity, and spirituality in relation to homelessness in the Australian Aborigine and Torres Strait Islander context (Keys Young 1998). The individual experiences of homeless Indigenous men and women cannot therefore be considered separately from collective experiences of colonialism, paternalism, and the intergenerational impacts of trauma (Christensen 2013).

Though intergenerational trauma is a persistent thread in the discourse around Indigenous health and homelessness in Canada, the general literature on homelessness in the highlights *individual* trauma as playing a more critical role in shaping homeless experiences across rural and urban settings (Kim and Ford 2006; Robinson 2005; Stewart et al. 2004; Taylor and Sharpe 2008). However, to understand the complexities of Indigenous homelessness, a strict focus on *individual* trauma does not suffice (Kirmayer, Brass, and Tait 2000), for individual traumas implicated in Indigenous homeless experiences are inextricably linked to collective experiences of colonization (Belanger, Awosoga, and Weasel Head 2013; Cedar Project Partnership et al. 2008) and the cumulative impact of government policies on Indigenous peoples (Menzies 2009).

The causes of intergenerational trauma among Indigenous people are not situated solely in the past. Colonial continuities "[spill] over into the present" (Warry 1998, 84), as evidenced by the persistent health, economic, political, and social inequalities experienced by Indigenous peoples. Canadian social policy has served to eradicate "value systems that existed for thousands of years, replacing them with doctrines that continue to disrupt life for Aboriginal peoples and creating a legacy of trauma" (Menzies 2009, 2).

Intergenerational trauma can be found in the disruption of Indigenous families. Colonial policies have consistently resulted in the removal of Indigenous children from their homes, be it to place them in residential schools, foster care and group homes, or non-Indigenous adoptive families (Fournier and Crey 1997). As described in the introductory section to the Canadian chapters, there are now more Indigenous children in the Canadian child welfare system than there ever were at the height of the residential school system (CBC 2011). The institutionalization of Indigenous children in the child welfare system is a testament to the profound degree of structural violence enacted on Indigenous children and the persistent failure on the part of the state to meaningfully and productively care for the needs of Indigenous families and communities. The high rates of family violence and child abuse in many Indigenous communities, conditions that are widely linked to the intergenerational impacts of colonialism (Fournier and Crey 1997; Warry 1998), also attest to the pervasiveness of the trauma. Many Indigenous children in Canada are effectively rendered homeless at an early age by these conditions, or put into the child welfare system, and often experience both (Menzies 2009).

The prevalence and (re)production of intergenerational trauma is one reason why colonialism persists as a significant social determinant to Indigenous health (Czyzewski 2011). Intergenerational trauma also continues to play an enormous role in the homelessness pathways of Indigenous men and women (Menzies 2009; Wente 2000). In the Canadian North, the history of colonization has additional effects on Indigenous homelessness by shaping geographies of economic and social disparity between regional, urbanizing centres and rural settlement communities (Christensen 2012). Thus, the dynamics of welfare colonialism have both social and spatial outcomes, both of which guide individual homeless experiences.

Narratives of Home/Journeying in Pathways to Homelessness

Throughout this research, homeless Indigenous men and women living in the NWT described their personal experiences with homelessness. Several Indigenous support providers had themselves been homeless previously and were therefore able to reflect on their pathways out of the homelessness and the factors that aided their journey. In the following sections, we share some of these personal accounts and highlight the home/journeying strategies conveyed within them. The particular stories shared here were selected because they each represent a journey or experience commonly shared by other research participants. However, in order to illustrate the multidimensional nature of these personal experiences, and also to demonstrate the ways in which home/journeying efforts come into conflict with policy on many different occasions across time and space, it is important to provide significant detail while still maintaining the anonymity of individual research participants. For this reason, all participant-identifying features were changed.

Public Housing Provision

There are several key areas of northern social policy and programming that clash with the home/journeying efforts of northern families and, in so doing, directly contribute to individual pathways to homelessness. One area is the regulation and surveillance of public housing provision. In response to decreasing supply of public housing, and growing demand in northern urban centres, local Housing Authorities have implemented increasingly strict policies around tenancy and outstanding payments or rental arrears. One such policy concerns the length of time adult guests may stay with friends or family who live in public housing. In both Inuvik and Yellowknife, an unofficial limit of two weeks is imposed on adult guests over nineteen years of age.

A government administrator working in public housing emphasized that the two-week time limit on adult guests is largely an effort to cut down on the number of people living in a unit who can afford to contribute to the rent (either through employment or income support) but do not. The two-week limit is also in place to ensure that no one with arrears or an otherwise poor record with the NWTHC is staying in a public housing unit. An individual who is not paying his/her arrears or who has a poor housing record is ineligible to have his/her name on the lease. In fact, such offences usually result in an eviction of that person well before the two-week limit has passed.

Housing Authority representatives in both Inuvik and Yellowknife communities emphasized time and again that above all else, the two-week limit was implemented in order to protect tenants. Administrators offered a number of accounts of single mothers and Elders who had been in situations where a disruptive family member would not leave the housing unit, or refused to contribute financially to the household. One Housing Authority representative spoke of several instances where public housing tenants contacted the Authority to request an eviction notice be sent to the guest in question because it was not appropriate within the cultural norms of sharing and reciprocity to tell a family member to leave. The Housing Authorities in general expressed a desire to not only protect the housing they provide, but also the tenants. The alternative, they believe, would be to let the tenant have the guest over until problems occurred and the tenant, him or herself, was evicted. For example, one homeless Elder in Inuvik had been evicted twice from public housing on account of the destructive actions of his adult children. Several homeless women in Yellowknife also described being evicted after allowing violent partners to stay with them in public housing. Their accounts were further complicated by the presence of children and the loss of those children to foster care following eviction.

Though the regulation of public housing is clearly nuanced and complex, it ultimately eliminates a housing option for those who cannot, for any number of reasons, contribute to the rent but also have no other place to stay. For instance, a homeless woman in Inuvik had been staying with her sister after being evicted from her unit because of domestic violence. She had arrears owed to the Housing Authority, and because she could not pay them was not eligible to be put on her sister's lease. At the same time, she had nowhere else to go. Two men staying at the shelter in Yellowknife described how they had tried to stay with friends in public housing following their release from prison. Without any money, and with debts they had accumulated in housing prior to their incarceration, they were told to leave by the Housing Authority.

Indeed, there are also examples of the ways in which this policy can help a family in public housing. Some public housing tenants described times when a family member wanted to stay, but their presence was deemed undesirable due to substance abuse, violence, or simply because they were a drain on precious household resources. In these cases, a notice from the Housing Authority was welcomed because it provided the institutional muscle necessary to ask a family member to leave, especially where cultural norms of reciprocity and sharing dictate that one should look after family in need. Housing Authority staff also described instances where they would receive a call from a tenant requesting a notice in advance of two weeks so that they could ask their guest to leave.

However, there were far more examples of this policy being applied in cases where public housing tenants wanted to provide shelter to a family member or a friend for longer than two weeks, and where having their name put onto the lease was not possible due to life crises, unemployment, or outstanding arrears. Anne's story below is an example of how the two-week limit serves both to help a tenant by forcing the eviction of a violent partner, and to hinder her by forcing the eviction of a son or daughter in need.

Anne has been a single mother since she was pregnant with her first child. Her on- and off-again boyfriend, a man she refers to as her "ex-common law" lived with her from time to time, but "when things were good, they were really good; when things were bad, he'd go on a drunk, come home, and beat me up." Anne lived in public housing and after one too many blow-ups from her ex-common law, the Housing Authority in Inuvik brought by a letter telling her she would be evicted if he even came to stay with her again. This was the push she needed to split-up with him for good: "I had three kids by then, all under five years old. I couldn't afford to get kicked out of housing. Where else would I go?" Today, Anne doesn't know where her ex is: "He went to jail, I know that," she says. "The last I heard, he was staying at a shelter in Edmonton."

Anne never finished high school, but she was able to pick up work from time to time working in one of the three local hotels housekeeping, or working as a cashier at a local grocery store. After a brief relationship with a new boyfriend, Anne had a fourth child. Despite working when she could, and being on income support, "it was always a struggle." When her children were older, Anne started to take classes at Aurora College, working toward her General Educational Development (GED) accreditation. She currently aspires to become an office manager or an executive assistant.

When Anne's eldest son reached high school, he was barely attending class. He refused to go, and Anne felt there was little she could do to make him: "He saw his Dad be violent a lot when he was little, so I think he learned to be that way, too. I couldn't make him do anything, because he would get angry and push us all around." Anne was upset and frustrated when her son was charged with several breaking and entering incidents in Inuvik. He ended up at the youth detention centre in Inuvik for several months. When he got out, he told Anne he wanted to move to Yellowknife to live with her sister and have a fresh start. Anne was worried that the big city would be a challenging place for him to be, but nevertheless she arranged with her sister to have him stay with her.

A few weeks after Anne's son arrived in Yellowknife, he was charged with several breaking and entering crimes and was once again sentenced to youth detention in the city. By the time he got out, he was almost an adult. He had started drinking in Inuvik, and the problem grew much worse while he was living in Yellowknife. Eventually, he found his way into the detoxification program at the Salvation Army. The program lasts two weeks. During this time he phoned Anne and asked her to help him get back to Inuvik when he finished the program. She called around to family and was able to get the money together for airfare. However, just a few days after her son arrived back home, a rental officer from the Inuvik Housing Authority came by to say that her son would have to get his name on the lease and start paying for rent, or they would all be evicted. Anne tried to argue with the Authority, explaining that her son had just left a detoxification program, but they reminded her of the rules on adult guests: two-week maximum stay or the guest must be named on the lease. Anne knew her son wouldn't be able to contribute to the rent, and she couldn't afford to pay for his share. There was nowhere else for him to go—all of her extended family members also lived in public housing. In the end, Anne's son went to live at the Inuvik homeless shelter. At the time of our interview, he had been there for a week and had started to drink again.

Staying with family or friends for short periods of time offers an important coping strategy for homeless men and women. However, housing policy often comes into direct conflict with local cultural values, which prioritize caring for extended family. For example, one woman in Inuvik whose brother had been forced to leave her public housing unit after two weeks complained that "there are so many rules that prevent people from being able to help others or help themselves.... People used to live in sod houses, like my grandparents. Nowadays, we think that sounds crazy, like it must have been so tough, but that was home for them. They felt at home and they felt good about themselves because they could care for their families and that was most important. Now there are so many rules that prevent people from being able to look after themselves."

Public housing rules and enforcement policies such as those discussed here also demonstrate how matters of shelter are media through which broader social and cultural issues play out. Some families wish to care for family members who may be vulnerable to homelessness. In these cases, this desire comes in conflict with the limits the Housing Authorities place on adult guests. Ironically, when someone becomes homeless as a result of public housing policy, policy makers and implementers either naively expect that this person will be taken care of by family who do not live in public housing, or accept that this person will simply be homeless. Yet as illustrated here, there are few supports for families who wish to care for vulnerable adult family members, whether in public or private housing, and therefore the outcome more often than not appears as passive acceptance of homelessness. The result is a more profound sense of homelessness through not only a lack of shelter but also through disconnection from family.

Not only do housing policies often clash with important cultural values and family wishes, but the punitive nature of enforcement is an inappropriate response to the trauma that underlies many of the life experiences of northern homeless men and women. Moreover, these enforcement strategies are implemented despite the total lack of alternative shelter options, save emergency shelters, which are only located in Inuvik and Yellowknife. There is therefore a direct and immediate connection between the increasing implementation of such policies and rising homelessness in the territory.

Child Welfare and the Trauma of Uprooting

Like public housing policy, the child welfare system plays a profound and immediate role in individual pathways to homelessness, both for parents and children. For homeless parents, relationships with their children were repeatedly cited as integral to their sense of home. The loss of children to the child welfare system is a deeply traumatic and uprooting experience for parents. Furthermore, many of the young adults who are homeless in the Northwest Territories grew up in and out of the child welfare system, and speak about their separation from family and community as early experiences of homelessness and uprooting. The role of the northern child welfare system in the homelessness of young adults has been documented elsewhere (see Christensen 2012, 2013), in addition to the wider literature on Indigenous youth, child welfare, and homelessness in Canada (see Baskin 2007; Menzies 2009). However, comparatively little has been written on the homelessness of parents that also relates to the child welfare system.

In the NWT, foster parents tend to be concentrated in the territorial capital, Yellowknife, which means that many children placed in care are not only separated from their family homes, but also separated from their communities. The physical distance only intensifies the sense of uprooting and detachment that occurs as a result of child removal. The individual pathways to homelessness of women in this study were almost always bound up within the broader, complicated geographies of the northern child welfare system. Like for Mona, whose story we introduce below, for many women the apprehension of their children and subsequent placement with Yellowknife foster families led to their parallel rural-urban migration. They often followed their children in an effort to remain geographically close to them and in hope that they would regain custody.

Julia first met Mona at the women's shelter in Yellowknife. Mona was quiet and shy, but told Julia she wanted to be interviewed. "Tomorrow, though," she said. "Not today. I'm not having a good day today." The next day, Julia returned to the shelter to find Mona on the phone, crying. Julia left, and weeks later the two women ran into each other on the street. "I could talk now," Mona said, so they went for coffee. The day Julia had seen her crying on the phone, Mona said that she had been talking to her mother. Her mother lived "back home" in a small community in the high Arctic. A family member died, Mona said, and she didn't take it very well. "I'd been really good for while," she told Julia, "but I'm so lonely here, away from my family, so when my [family member] died I started drinking again."

Mona is in her early thirties. She moved to Yellowknife from her home community ten years ago to get away from family members who she said were violent when they drank, which was often. Back home, she and her two small children lived with her parents and several family members, ten in total, in a two-bedroom house. Like her family members, she too had troubles with alcohol. Over time, her problems worsened and a social worker visiting her community threatened to remove her children. Mona made the decision to move to Yellowknife to help her deal with her problems. She also hoped life would be more affordable there, and that she would be able to find a job and her own place to live.

When they first arrived in Yellowknife, Mona and her two children moved in with friends while they waited six months to get on the public housing waiting list. Mona's friends didn't party, and so she managed to avoid drinking for the most part while staying with them. However, not long after she and her children were finally matched with a public housing unit, Mona met a man named Harry, who soon moved in with them. Harry worked and took care of most of the bills. But he also drank heavily on occasion, and when he did, he persuaded Mona to drink with him. Harry was physically abusive while drunk and he beat Mona many times when they had both been drinking.

Mona had two more children with Harry, but over time their drinking worsened. After neighbours complained, social services visited the apartment. After this visit, Harry beat Mona so badly that she was hospitalized. He was arrested and a social worker placed the children in foster care. Mona stopped drinking for a time so she could work to get her children back while Harry was in jail. When he was released a few months later, however, Harry came to live with her again and the drinking and violence resumed. Following another particularly violent episode, Harry was once again arrested. It was at this point that the Housing Authority notified Mona she would be evicted from her family-sized public housing unit because her children were no longer in her custody. Furthermore, because the unit had been damaged during her fights with Harry, she now had arrears to pay to the Housing Authority.

Evicted and heartbroken at the loss of her children, Mona slept on a friend's couch for a couple of weeks until she outstayed her welcome. She then went to the women's shelter, where she had been on and off for five years before she and Julia first met. Due to her ongoing struggles with alcohol, and her homelessness, she has been unable to regain custody of her children. In the meantime, her family members back home have sobered up and asked her to move home. "I don't want to move back there, because my children are here," she says. In Yellowknife, Mona is also able to access some counselling resources for her addictions and has become a part of a church community that she tells me provides her with strength and support. "I want to get my kids back," she says, wiping tears from her eyes. "When I lost them was when things really hit rock bottom for me."

The child welfare system plays a complex role in the reproduction of homelessness. The concentration of Northwest Territories foster families in Yellowknife motivates some parents to stay in the city in spite of not having housing or stable employment. Some parents also move from their communities to Yellowknife to be closer to children in care; this behaviour was used strategically by the federal government during the days of residential school to encourage centralization (Tester and Kulchyski 1994). The willingness to move in order to remain close to children is demonstrative of the home/journeying efforts of many homeless parents and is a profound testament to the significance of family in the lives of many research participants.

However, the dearth of public housing available to single adults makes it difficult for parents to work to regain custody of their children. The women who follow their children to Yellowknife move out of the public housing they hold in their home communities. In Yellowknife, where public housing is more regulated and competition for units is higher, once children are apprehended by social services the parent loses the right to stay in a family-sized dwelling. With very few single adult dwellings, when the parents in this study were evicted, they had nowhere else to stay but at emergency shelters. A parent needs to be in secure housing, among other requirements, to regain custody of her children. The road from the shelter back into housing is fraught with challenges, especially in Yellowknife where the options for affordable, accessible housing are so limited. Several women also spoke of racial discrimination in the private rental market and offered stories in which they had felt doubly judged for being Indigenous and not having custody of their children.

Two important issues are present here. First, the child welfare system continues to act in a reactive sense toward the legacies of the social, cultural, and spiritual damage inflicted through the colonization process. Second, the present-day context of welfare colonialism continues to erode the security of those Indigenous northerners who experience socio-economic marginalization. To date, there are no programs or resources in place in the NWT to assist families and communities in dealing with the root causes leading to the apprehension of children through the child welfare system, such as intergenerational trauma. Though it may indeed be that in some cases a family cannot be reunited, it is clear from the accounts in this research that there are many examples where parents' desire to remain close to their children is resisted by social services. Secondly, once children are removed, there are very few programs or resources in place to support parents in their efforts to regain custody. The programs and resources that do exist do not address the housing needs of a parent seeking to regain custody of her children. This gap is institutionalized through the separation of social services from housing. In other words, there are no commitments on the part of the Housing Authority to support parents seeking to regain custody of their children, and this is deeply problematic. The negligible transitional housing available through the Young Women's Christian Association (YWCA) and the Centre for Northern Families has long waiting lists. Greater coordinated efforts are needed to recognize the home/journeying efforts of homeless parents and to support them in the process of regaining custody of their children.

Conclusion

While popular discourse would have one believe that northern homeless men and women are complacent in their circumstances, numerous life stories shared during this research suggested that in fact many homeless men and women make concerted efforts to resist dependency through home/journeying strategies. Camping out, going out onto the land, or spending time with Elders were some of the home/journeying strategies used by homeless men and women in an effort not only to resist dependency, but also as expressions of self-determination and home-building.

The critical role that family and community play in Indigenous homes, and the deep wounding that results from their loss, highlights the distinct nature of Indigenous homelessness. Similarly, Belanger and Lindstrom (Chapter 8 in this volume) argue for a new definition of Indigenous homelessness that emphasizes the significance of loss of family and community. A disruption of the social fabric of Indigenous families and communities goes hand-in-hand with a fractured sense of belonging and connection to place. Yet the profound significance of family and community, and the sense of rootedness sought from these relationships, can also be read in the many strategies of home/journeying documented here. More than a site of collective wounding, families and communities are also "the source of restoration and renewal" (Kirmayer, Simpson, and Cargo 2003, 21).

Paul Andrew, one of this chapter's authors, is also a residential school survivor. He worked hard for years to find his place back in his community once he had completed school, struggling to relearn his language and the skills required for life on the land. Similarly, Ruth is a support provider who described *feeling* homeless years after returning to her home community from residential school, despite the fact that she had a job, housing, and a close-knit family. This story of spiritual homelessness is very common, shared with us both (Paul and Julia) time and again by colleagues, friends, and family members who have felt disconnected from place, a sense of belonging, and Indigenous identity. These stories also foreground in clear and undeniable ways the colonial context within which geographies of Indigenous homelessness must be understood (Christensen 2013).

One of the objectives we set out to realize in this chapter was to expand the definition of spiritual homelessness to include conflicts in cultural values and social policy paradigms. It is clear from the personal narratives shared here that social policy, and the value framework it embodies, plays a critical role in the reproduction of spiritual homelessness. While public housing policy resulted in the immediate material homelessness of many homeless men and women in this study, it also intensified the disconnection from family and community by preventing some research participants from staying with relatives, or in their home communities. Meanwhile, interactions between public housing policy and the child welfare system resulted in the immediate, literal homelessness of many parents. At the same time, the particular geography of the northern children welfare system served to disconnect parents not only from their children, but also from important social networks in their home communities.

In this chapter, we have further argued that one of the key driving forces behind Indigenous homelessness is the welfare colonialism implicit in northern social policy. The narratives of homelessness explored here illustrate the ways in which key social policies and programs reinforce dominant norms and penalize those who do not comply. They also illustrate the many ways in which home/journeying efforts are implicit in many research participants' experiences of homelessness. Yet a contributing factor to the self-fulfilling prophecy of welfare colonialism is blindness to these efforts, to their strength, and to the potential for meaningful change that could come from social policy that better recognized and supported home/journeying efforts.

The 2012 Minister's Forum on Addictions and Community Wellness, however, suggests that there is a growing awareness in the NWT that culturally relevant responses are needed in order to effectively address the high rates of trauma and substance abuse in the territory. The forum's final report and recommendations appear promising for the delivery of health and wellness programs in the Northwest Territories. One of the main outcomes of the report is a call for an improved understanding of "how colonization, residential schools and rapid socio-economic change have shaped the mental wellness of NWT residents" (GNWT 2012, 18). There is significant potential for these changes to bring about positive impacts on the lives of northern homeless men and women. Similar efforts at developing culturally relevant approaches to Indigenous homelessness are discussed in Memmott and Nash's chapter, also in this volume.

However, alongside these promising changes is an increasingly punitive northern housing market, one where private housing rises in unaffordability and public housing units deplete in number. The globalizing northern economy also brings with it higher competition and greater requirements in terms of education, certification, and security clearance to access employment (Christensen 2009). Rates of Fetal Alcohol Spectrum Disorder (FASD) (Badry and Wight Felske 2013) and suicide (Tester and McNicoll 2004) all continue to rise across the Canadian North, and disproportionately among Indigenous northerners. At the same time, the removing and placing of Indigenous children into the child welfare system is at a historical high across Canada, and the situation is no different in the North.

Bureaucratic practices fragment home and homelessness, reinforcing false divisions between inextricably linked elements like health, housing, and social security. This categorization makes it difficult to resist the structural elements that drive homelessness. The dynamics of welfare colonialism have fragmented Indigenous homes and now act as both a significant cause of Indigenous homelessness and an obstacle in its alleviation. Significantly, the Minister's Forum recognized this, arguing that "there is a need to increase awareness that mental health and addictions are related to other problems and can be improved by addressing basic quality of life issues such as housing, income support and education" (GNWT 2012, 18). These factors are integral to a sense of home and in this way play a significant role in the geographies of homelessness among northern Indigenous men and women.

One of the ways in which contemporary northern social policy perpetuates pathways to homelessness is by failing to recognize the home/journeying strategies of homeless men and women, many of which reflect the diverse cultural value frameworks of northern Indigenous communities. Herein lie some important clues about the places where additional supports are necessary to build upon the strength and agency of homeless men and women. In order to achieve marked improvements in health and wellness, there need to be parallel improvements in family support, housing, and income security for individuals and families across the territory. However, the approach by government is to fragment and compartmentalize aspects of life that would be seen as fitting together by northern Indigenous knowledge. The findings of the Northwest Territories Minister's Forum are a huge step in the right direction. Yet to truly address the role of health and to rebuild from trauma in geographies of Indigenous homelessness requires the support of home/journeying efforts and the addition of a range of housing options, social programs, education initiatives, and employment strategies to an overall wellness plan.

Notes

1   Core housing need is a phrase used by both the federal and territorial governments to refer to housing that does not meet adequacy, suitability, and affordability norms. According to the Northwest Territories Bureau of Statistics (GNWT 2010), 35.5 percent of households experience core housing need in the rural settlement communities. In fact, some communities report that as many as 77 percent of households are in core housing need (GNWT 2010).

2   Between 2007 and 2010, as part of her doctoral research in Inuvik and Yellowknife communities (Christensen 2011), Julia Christensen conducted ninety-five interviews with homeless men and women using a biographical interview approach (May 2000a). This approach involves the use of in-depth, semi-structured conversational interviews to "map" an individual's experiences with homelessness and housing insecurity over time. Importantly, biographical interviews both compliment and facilitate the pathways to homelessness approach by illustrating "the factors shaping a person's movements in and out of homelessness" (May 2000a, 615). Christensen also conducted six focus groups, three in each study community, with groups of either homeless men or women, ranging from four to twelve participants each. Four of the focus groups were conducted at shelters in each community. The remaining two focus groups included community members who identified housing insecurity and homelessness as pertinent issues in their lives. Christensen also conducted fifty-five in-depth, semi-structured interviews with representatives from the territorial and Indigenous governments, representatives of non-governmental organizations, and support providers working in shelter provision, social work, and homeless advocacy. Participants were selected in order to get a solid representation of people who interact with homeless people from all angles: lending support, implementing programs, and through governance.

References

Adelson, Naomi. 2000. "Re-imagining Aboriginality: An Indigenous Peoples' Response to Social Suffering." *Transcultural Psychiatry* 37 (1): 11–34.

Ahmed, Sara. 1999. "Home and Away Narratives of Migration and Estrangement." *International Journal of Cultural Studies* 2 (3): 329–47.

Alfred, Gerald Taiaiake. 2009. "Colonialism and State Dependency." *Journal of Aboriginal Health* 5 (2): 42–60, http://www.naho.ca/documents/journal/jah05_02/05_02_02_Colonialism.pdf (accessed 17 April 2010).

Andrews, Thomas D. 2004. "'The Land Is Like a Book': Cultural Landscapes Management in the Northwest Territories, Canada." In *Northern Ethnographic Landscapes: Perspectives from Circumpolar Nations*, edited by Igor Krupnik, Rachel Mason, and Tonia Woods Horton, 301–22. Washington: Arctic Studies Center.

Badry, Dorothy, and Aileen Wight Felske. 2013. "An Examination of Three Key Factors: Alcohol, Trauma and Child Welfare: Fetal Alcohol Spectrum Disorder and the Northwest Territories of Canada." *First Peoples Child and Family Review* 8 (1): 130–43.

Baskin, Cyndy. 2007. "Aboriginal Youth Talk about Structural Determinants as the Causes of Their Homelessness." *First Peoples Child and Family Review* 3 (3): 31–42.

Belanger, Yale D., Olu Awosoga, and Gabrielle Weasel Head. 2013. "Homelessness, Urban Aboriginal People, and the Need for a National Enumeration." *Aboriginal Policy Studies* 2 (2): 4–33.

Blondin, George. 1997. *Yamoria the Lawmaker: Stories of the Dene.* Edmonton, AB: NeWest Press.

_____. 2000. "The Making of a Prophet When the World Was New." In *Legends and Stories from the Past*, 19–20. Yellowknife: Government of the Northwest Territories.

Blunt, Alison, and Robyn Dowling. 2006. *Home.* London: Routledge.

Bone, Robert M. 2003. *The Geography of the Canadian North: Issues and Challenges.* Oxford: Oxford University Press.

Case, Duncan. 1996. "Contributions of Journeys Away to the Definition of Home: An Empirical Study of a Dialectical Process." *Journal of Environmental Psychology* 16 (1): 1–15.

CBC (Canadian Broadcasting Corporation). 2011. "First Nations Children Still Taken from Parents." CBC North, 2 August, http://www.cbc.ca/news/politics/story/2011/08/02/pol-first-nations-kids.html (accessed 14 September 2012).

Cedar Project Partnership, Margo E. Pearce, Wayne M. Christian, Katharina Patterson, Kat Norris, Akm Moniruzzaman, Kevin J.P. Craib, Martin T. Schechter, and Patricia M. Spittal. 2008. "The Cedar Project: Historical Trauma, Sexual Abuse and HIV Risk among Young Aboriginal People Who Use Injection and Non-Injection Drugs in Two Canadian Cities." *Social Science and Medicine* 66 (11): 2185–94.

Christensen, Julia. 2009. "'Everyone Wants to Have a Place': Homelessness, Housing Insecurity and Housing Challenges for Single Men in the Northwest Territories, Canada." In *Proceedings of the International Congress on Circumpolar Health*, vol. 14, 56–60.

_____. 2011. "Homeless in a Homeland: Housing (In)security and Homelessness in Inuvik and Yellowknife, Northwest Territories, Canada." PhD diss., McGill University.

_____. 2012. "'They Want a Different Life': Rural Northern Settlement Dynamics and Pathways to Homelessness in Yellowknife and Inuvik, Northwest Territories." *The Canadian Geographer/Le Géographe Canadien* 56 (4): 419–38.

_____. 2013. "'Our Home, Our Way of Life': Spiritual Homelessness and the Sociocultural Dimensions of Indigenous Homelessness in the Northwest Territories (NWT), Canada." *Social and Cultural Geography* 14 (7): 804–28.

CMHC (Canada Mortgage and Housing Corporation). 1997. *Housing Need among the Inuit in Canada, 1991.* Ottawa, ON: Canada Mortgage and Housing Corporation.

Condon, Richard G. 1990. "Adolescence and Changing Family Relations in the Central Canadian Arctic." *Arctic Medical Research* 49 (2): 81–92.

Czyzewski, Karina. 2011. "Colonialism as a Broader Social Determinant of Health." *The International Indigenous Policy Journal* 2 (1): Article 5.

Damas, David. 2002. *Arctic Migrants/Arctic Villagers: The Transformation of Inuit Settlement in the Central Arctic.* Montreal: McGill-Queen's University Press.

de Leeuw, Sarah, Margo Greenwood, and Emilie Cameron. 2010. "Deviant Constructions: How Governments Preserve Colonial Narratives of Addictions and Poor Mental Health to Intervene into the Lives of Indigenous Children and Families in Canada." *International Journal of Mental Health and Addiction* 8 (2): 282–95.

Douglas, Mary. 1991. "The Idea of a Home: A Kind of Space." *Social Research* 58 (1): 287–307.

Eades, Gwilym. 2011. *Northwest Territories with Inuvik and Yellowknife Highlighted* [map]. 1:9,000,000. [Base data from Statistics Canada].

Easthope, Hazel. 2004. "A Place Called Home." *Housing, Theory and Society* 21 (3): 128–38.

Falvo, Nick. 2011. *Homelessness in Yellowknife: An Emerging Social Challenge.*
Ottawa, ON: The Canadian Homelessness Research Network Press.

Fournier, Suzanne, and Ernie Crey. 1997. *Stolen from Our Embrace: The Abduction of Indigenous Children and the Restoration of Indigenous Communities.* Vancouver, BC: Douglas and McIntyre.

Geisler, Charles, and Lance George. 2006. "Homeless in the Heartland: American Dreams and Nightmares in Indian Country." In *International Perspectives on Rural Homelessness*, edited by Paul Cloke and Paul Milbourne, 25–44. Abingdon, Oxon: Routledge.

GNWT (Government of the Northwest Territories). 2010. *2009 NWT Community Survey.* Yellowknife: GNWT, Northwest Territories Bureau of Statistics.

GNWT (Government of the Northwest Territories). 2012. *A Shared Path Toward Wellness: Mental Health and Addictions Action Plan.* Yellowknife: GNWT, Department of Health and Social Services.

hooks, bell. 1990. *Yearning: Race, Gender, and Cultural Politics.* Boston: South End Press.

IIC (Inuvik Interagency Committee). 2003. *Inuvik: Homelessness Report.* Inuvik, Northwest Territories: Inuvik Interagency Committee.

Keys Young Firm. 1998. *Homelessness in the Indigenous and Torres Strait Islander Context and Its Possible Implications for the Supported Accommodation Assistance Program (SAAP).* Final Report, prepared for Department of Family and Community Services. Canberra: Commonwealth Department of Health and Aged Care and Department of Family and Community Services.

Kim, Mimi M., and Julian D. Ford. 2006. "Trauma and Post-Traumatic Stress among Homeless Men: A Review of Current Research." *Journal of Aggression, Maltreatment and Trauma* 13 (2): 1–22.

Kirmayer, Laurence J., Gregory M. Brass, and Carolyn L. Tait. 2000. "The Mental Health of Aboriginal Peoples: Transformations of Identity and Community." *The Canadian Journal of Psychiatry/La Revue canadienne de psychiatrie* 45 (7): 607–16.

Kirmayer, Laurence J., Cori Simpson, and Margaret Cargo. 2003. "Healing Traditions: Culture, Community and Mental Health Promotion with Canadian Aboriginal peoples." *Australasian Psychiatry* 11 (S1): S15–S23.

Mallett, Shelley. 2004. "Understanding Home: A Critical Review of the Literature." *The Sociological Review* 52 (1): 62–89.

Massey, Doreen. 1992. "A Place Called Home." *New Formations* 17 (7): 3–15.

May, Jon. 2000a. "Housing Histories and Homeless Careers: A Biographical Approach." *Housing Studies* 15 (4): 613–38.

———. 2000b. "Of Nomads and Vagrants: Single Homelessness and Narratives of Home as Place." *Environment and Planning D*, no. 18, 737–60.

Menzies, Peter. 2009. "Homeless Aboriginal Men: Effects of Intergenerational Trauma." In *Finding Home: Policy Options for Addressing Homelessness in Canada*, ch. 6.2, edited by J. David Hulchanski, Philippa Campsie, Shirley B.Y. Chau, Stephen W. Hwang, and Emily Paradis. Toronto: Cities Centre Press.

NWTHC (Northwest Territories Housing Corporation). 2009. *2009/10 Annual Business Plan.* Yellowknife, NWT: Northwest Territories Housing Corporation.

National Round Table on Aboriginal Health and Social Issues. 1993. *The Path to Healing: Report of the National Round Table on Aboriginal Health and Social Issues.* Ottawa: Royal Commission of Aboriginal Peoples.

Paine, Robert. 1977. "The Path to Welfare Colonialism." In *The White Arctic: Anthropological Essays on Tutelage and Ethnicity*, edited by Robert Paine, 7–28. St. John's: ISER (Institute of Social and Economic Research), Memorial University of Newfoundland.

Peters, Evelyn, and Vince Robillard. 2009. "'Everything You Want Is There': The Place of the Reserve in First Nations' Homeless Mobility." *Urban Geography* 30 (6): 652–80.

Robinson, Catherine. 2005. "Grieving Home." *Social and Cultural Geography* 6 (1): 47–60.

Somerville, Peter. 1992. "Homelessness and the Meaning of Home: Rooflessness or Rootlessness?" *International Journal of Urban and Regional Research* 16 (4): 529–39.

Stewart, Angela J., Mandy Steiman, Ana Mari Cauce, Bryan N. Cochran, Les B. Whitbeck, and Dan R. Hoyt. 2004. "Victimization and Posttraumatic Stress Disorder among Homeless Adolescents." *Journal of the American Academy of Child and Adolescent Psychiatry* 43 (3): 325–31.

Taylor, Kathryn M., and Louise Sharpe. 2008. "Trauma and Post-Traumatic Stress Disorder among Homeless Adults in Sydney." *Australian and New Zealand Journal of Psychiatry* 42 (3): 206–13.

Tester, Frank J. 2006 "Iglu to Iglurjuaq." In *Critical Inuit Studies: An Anthology of Contemporary Arctic Ethnography*, edited by Pamela Stern and Lisa Stevenson, 230–52. Lincoln: University of Nebraska Press.

Tester, Frank J., and Peter K. Kulchyski. 1994 *Tammarniit (Mistakes): Inuit Relocation in the Eastern Arctic, 1939–63.* Vancouver: UBC Press.

Tester, Frank J., and Paule McNicoll. 2004. "Isumagijaksaq: Mindful of the State: Social Constructions of Inuit Suicide." *Social Science and Medicine* 58 (12): 2625–36.

Tyler, William. 1993 "Postmodernity and the Aboriginal Condition: The Cultural Dilemmas of Contemporary Policy." *Journal of Sociology* 29 (3): 322–42.

UNNS (United Native Nations Society of British Columbia). 2001. *Aboriginal Homelessness in British Columbia.* Vancouver, BC: United Native Nations Society of British Columbia.

Warry, Wayne. 1998. *Unfinished Dreams: Community Healing and the Reality of Aboriginal Self-Government.* Toronto: University of Toronto Press.

Webster, Andrew. 2006. *Homelessness in the Territorial North: State and Availability of the Knowledge.* Ottawa, ON: Housing and Homelessness Branch, Human Resources and Social Development Canada.

Wente, Maggie. 2000. "Urban Aboriginal Homelessness in Canada." PhD diss., University of Toronto.

CHAPTER 3

The Importance of Hidden Homelessness in the Housing Strategies of Urban Indigenous People

EVELYN J. PETERS AND SELENA KERN

Urban Indigenous (First Nations, Metis, and Inuit)[1] people often face signifi-cant challenges in finding affordable, suitable, and adequate housing in urban centres, and First Nations people are the most likely of all urban Indigenous people to be living in inadequate, unsuitable, or unaffordable housing (Belanger, Awosoga, and Weasel Head 2013; Carter and Polevychok 2004). Distasio, Sylvestre, Jaccubucci, Mulligan, and Sargent (2004, 19) found that for 70 percent of First Nations migrants to the city, housing was the single most important service needed upon arrival, rating it higher than finding employ-ment. Humphreys (2006, 7) estimates that only one half of First Nations people migrating to cities are able to find housing and this was also a finding of Distasio and co-authors (2004). Indigenous peoples are overrepresented in the urban homeless population across Canada (Belanger, Awosoga, and Weasel Head 2013; Leach 2010). At the same time, there is relatively little research on the nature of urban Indigenous homelessness.

This chapter contributes to an understanding of the housing strategies of low-income Indigenous migrants to the city who accessed housing counselling services at the Eagle Urban Transition Centre in Winnipeg, Manitoba. The study focuses on the mobility patterns of these individuals as they attempted to meet their housing needs in the city. The analysis raises questions about the emphasis in current research and policy on absolute homelessness and suggests that there may be distinctive features of Indigenous homelessness that need to be understood in order to provide services for this population. The follow-ing two sections review the literature on definitions of homelessness and the nature of Indigenous homelessness. A methods section describes the data and analysis on which this chapter is based. The analysis of mobility follows, with a concluding section that raises some policy questions.

Defining Homelessness

Defining homelessness is contentious. The particular definition used affects the number of people categorized as homelessness and shapes the nature of research, services, and policy interventions. Earlier studies such as Rossi's (1989, 10) defined homelessness relatively simply as "not having customary and regular access to a conventional dwelling." This definition refers to people who are now often categorized as absolutely homeless, living on the street or in a shelter. More recently researchers have expanded the definition of homelessness to include "relative homelessness," where individuals have access to housing but it lacks security and quality (Eberle, Kraus, and Serge 2009). An understanding of what constitutes homelessness also varies across cultures and geographic locations, and individuals can define their dwelling as "home" even though society labels them as homeless (Moore 2007; Veness 1993).

"Hidden homelessness," where people live with friends or family because they cannot afford shelter for themselves, is a part of relative homelessness. It is difficult to estimate the size of the hidden homeless population because it is not enumerated in most censuses or homeless counts, and many individuals living in hidden homelessness appear not to use existing services for homeless people. Nevertheless some researchers have suggested that the hidden homeless population is probably much larger than the population living on the streets or in shelters at any point in time. Based on surveys with households contacted through random digit dialing, Eberle, Kraus, and Serge (2009, 13) suggested that hidden homeless individuals comprised more than 70 percent of the homeless population in Metropolitan Vancouver in 2007. Research in other countries similarly suggests that the size of the hidden homeless population is larger than the absolutely homeless population (see Amore et al. 2013; New Policy Institute 2004).

Most research and policy in Canada continues to focus on absolute homelessness. For example, the *2013 Canadian Report on the State of Homelessness in Canada* included in its definition of homelessness unsheltered people, and people living in emergency shelters, in provisional housing, and at risk of homelessness (including hidden homelessness). However counts were only available for the first three categories. The large, multi-year, and multi-city research project *At Home/Chez Soi* focused primarily on absolutely homeless people (Mental Health Commission of Canada 2012), as did the Canadian government's homelessness initiative (ESDC 2016).

At the same time existing studies suggest that a significant proportion of the absolutely homeless population also experience hidden homelessness. May (2000) found that homeless men's residential histories included staying with friends and family, in addition to staying in shelters and rough sleeping. Cloke, May, and Johnsen (2008, 26) noted the "ability [of some homeless people] to access practical help through…local support networks of family and friends." Robinson and Coward's (2003) research with 164 homeless individuals in London, Craven, and North Yorkshire found that 72 percent had stayed with family and friends on a temporary basis since becoming homeless. A Prince Albert study of hidden homeless Indigenous people found that participants had stayed in a variety of places in the previous eighteen months (Peters 2012). While they had stayed with friends or family for more than half of the previous eighteen months (53.9 percent of the time), they also spent time on the street (4.8 percent of the time), in a shelter (2.8 percent of the time), in jail (9.6 percent of the time), and in their own apartment with a partner, roommate, or children (29.0 percent of the time). The implication is that an individual categorized as experiencing a particular type of homelessness at one point in time could be categorized differently at another time.

Nevertheless, there is very little research on these homeless dynamics. May (2000, 616) notes that homeless histories "have remained extremely schematic" giving little indication of the shape of housing careers or how different categories of homelessness relate to each other. Similarly, Cloke, May, and Johnsen (2008, 21) point out that there is limited information about the scale and nature of homeless mobility. The result is that researchers' understanding of the context and dynamics of homeless mobility is incomplete (Meert and Bourgeois 2005, 123). Understanding homeless peoples' mobility patterns is an important component in providing a variety of services and in making positive interventions in homeless peoples' lives.

The lack of research and statistics on hidden homelessness may also mean that particular experiences of minority groups may be under-represented in our knowledge about homelessness. There is a small body of research that suggests that some groups are more likely than others to access their personal networks in order to avoid staying in shelters or rough sleeping. Molina's (2000) study of African American, English, and Latin-speaking homeless men found that some networks were more likely to provide temporary housing than others. Working on immigrant homelessness in Vancouver and Toronto respectively, Heibert and co-authors (2005) and Preston and colleagues (2009) found that few immigrants used shelters and other homeless services, relying instead on their social contacts for temporary and precarious housing. In New Zealand, Amore and co-researchers (2013) found that most Māori homeless people were staying with friends and family. DeVerteuil's (2003) research on the mobility of homeless women in Los Angeles similarly found that the few immigrant women in the study avoided mainstream shelters and spent their time near their community areas and support networks. Thus, in their work, DeVerteuil, May, and von Mahs (2009, 659) call for additional research on how race and ethnicity shape experiences of homelessness.

The existing focus of research and policy makers on the absolutely home-less population may limit our understanding of the homeless experiences of significant numbers of homeless people. This study is an attempt to provide some insight into the residential histories of a marginalized urban Indigenous population.

Indigenous People and Homelessness

Since the early 1950s, increasing numbers of Indigenous people have migrated to cities in Canada (Kalbach 1987, 102). According to the 2006 Census, about 45 percent of Indigenous people lived in cities (Statistics Canada 2008). Their movement to cities coincided with state cutbacks to social housing and related programs beginning in the 1980s. Hulchanski (2009) has associated these cutbacks with the emergence of the "homelessness problem" in Canadian public policy.

Indigenous people share some of the personal characteristics that put them at risk of being homeless with other marginalized groups in Canadian society (Leach 2010). These include low levels of human capital and personal disabilities (Beavis et al. 1997). However, additional factors identified in work on homeless Indigenous people include the intergenerational effects of fam-ily violence, lack of housing on reserves, racism, and rural-urban transition (Beavis et al. 1997; Brant Castellano and Archibald 2007; Peters and Robillard 2009). Researchers emphasize that the challenges facing urban Indigenous people need to be situated within the larger context of colonization, includ-ing the effects of residential schools (Cedar Project Partnership et al. 2008; Silver 2006). State definitions of crowding and homelessness and strategies to manage housing provision often reflect non-Indigenous cultural norms and practices. As a result, like Indigenous people's practices in other countries, First Nations' attempts to manage kin relationships and cultural obligations come into conflict with social policies (in this volume see Birdsall-Jones; Christensen and Andrew; Greenop and Memmott). All of these factors contribute to

Indigenous homeless people being overrepresented in Canada's major cities (Belanger, Awosoga, and Weasel Head 2013; Leach 2010).

For Indigenous populations, hidden homelessness or couch surfing appears to be an important strategy for coping with homelessness. A 2000 study of 472 homeless First Nations people living in Prince Albert, Saskatoon, and Regina, Saskatchewan, found that only 5 percent were living on the streets or in shelters; the remainder lived with friends or family (SIIT 2000). Sharing accommodations may be a coping mechanism for dealing with the high costs of housing for both Indigenous hidden homeless individuals and the households in which they live. Research in Winnipeg suggests that the transition from reserves to cities is often accompanied by living with friends and family for periods of time in order to manage housing costs (Distasio et al. 2004). While this strategy can assist new migrants, it can also place a burden on friends' and families' budgets and privacy. A study of hidden homeless First Nations people in Prince Albert found that they constantly monitored the mood of their host(s), moved frequently so that they did not outstay their welcome, attempted to find their meals somewhere else, and left during the day to maximize the privacy of their host(s). These strategies were stressful, and they also interfered with activities individuals needed to accomplish to find their own housing, such as look for work, deal with addictions, or improve education and training (Peters 2012).

The available data shows that many Indigenous urban residents have high rates of intraurban and interurban mobility (Norris and Clatworthy 2003). Many First Nations people move from their home communities to the city and then back and forth between urban centres and smaller communities (Carter and Polevychok 2004). A study of recent Indigenous migrants to Winnipeg found that a substantial number had moved out of Winnipeg and back in again within a six-month period (Distasio et al. 2004). Skelton's (2002) more qualitative study of the movement of single-parent families in inner-city Winnipeg found that parents often moved in an attempt to provide better housing and neighbourhood conditions for their children, but that these attempts were not usually successful. Homeless Indigenous people also seem to be highly mobile. Research on hidden homeless First Nations people in Prince Albert shows that their movement patterns are extremely complex and that poor housing conditions on both urban and reserve sites contributed to high mobility patterns (Peters and Robillard 2009).

This paper explores a subset of marginally housed First Nations occupants' mobility patterns by exploring their movement between different types of residence in Winnipeg during a twelve-month period.

Methods

Indigenous people have challenged geographers and other researchers to decolonize their research processes so that academic research can begin to meet the needs and priorities of Indigenous people themselves (Hodge and Lester 2005; Pualani Louis 2007). Collaborative research practices involving Indigenous organizations may begin to address some of these concerns (Howitt 2001). This research represents a collaboration between Selena Kern, Adult Housing Transition Counsellor at the Eagle Urban Transition Centre (EUTC) in Winnipeg and Dr. Evelyn Peters at the Department of Urban and Inner City Studies, University of Winnipeg.

The Eagle Urban Transition Centre (EUTC) has operated since 2005 under the umbrella of the Assembly of Manitoba Chiefs (AMC). It was established to address the needs of First Nations people migrating to the City of Winnipeg. The EUTC operates cooperatively with other AMC client-focused programming including the Patient Advocate Unit, the Youth Department, and the Eagle's Nest project. Each area has a specific focus, strategy, and resources to respond to Indigenous people's common needs. The EUTC is centrally located in Winnipeg's downtown. It offers access to culturally appropriate transitional supports in a wide variety of areas (Table 3.1), providing direct assistance to 1,700 Indigenous families each year and walk-in services to 8,000 individuals each year. Approximately 90 percent of people using EUTC services are Indigenous and most are First Nations.

Table 3.1. Services and Programs Offered at EUTC

- Referrals to housing resources, emergency shelters, and food banks
- Access to traditional and contemporary spiritual healing
- Counselling and referrals to treat addictions
- Access to on-site resources including telephone, internet, and a resource library
- Advice and referrals on justice related matters
- Referral and access to youth programs and resources
- Access and referral to employment and training service organizations (resume writing, interview skills, and job search techniques)
- Advocacy in the areas of employment, education, justice, family, and housing

EUTC database describing adults who accessed EUTC services for housing related issues between January and December 2013 was analyzed for this chapter. A collaboration agreement was signed with EUTC and AMC representatives, and EUTC personnel collaborated on the study.

There were 601 housing counselling sessions described in the database. For each session the database listed name, gender, name of First Nation, the place the individual was staying at the time, source of income, and services received. The housing counsellor edited the data to substitute numbers for client names, and the researchers tracked the individuals' movements in the twelve-month period. Almost all of the individuals in the database were First Nations. Almost three quarters (72.9 percent) were living on social assistance of one kind or another, and 15.3 percent indicated they had no income. The database therefore documented the housing and mobility strategies of a group of marginalized First Nations urban dwellers as they attempted to find housing over a period of twelve months. Clearly these findings are not representative of the entire urban First Nations population.[2] However, they do provide some insight into mobility patterns of marginalized Indigenous urban migrants.

Five residence categories were coded. The first was individuals renting their own unit (the database did not differentiate between apartments or houses), including individuals living in public housing. The second category referred to individuals living with friends or family. The third category encompassed a variety of institutional settings including homeless shelters, transitional housing, supportive housing, and halfway houses. The fourth category was living on the streets, and the final category was living with a roommate or a partner. We recognize that each of these categories covers a number of different living situations, but it was necessary to simplify in order to identify mobility patterns.

While the database contained a limited amount of information about individuals, males and females were identified. A number of studies have suggested that gender affects experiences of homelessness (see Klodawsky 2006). The analysis therefore compared mobility patterns of male and female participants. The analysis focused on the number of moves individuals made, and the residence categories they moved to and from. Some of the moves could not be classified because either origin or destination was missing. Nevertheless the database described 148 non-movers and eighty-eight movers in the twelve-month period.

While individuals were classified as movers and non-movers and these groups were compared, it is important to note some of the limitations of the database in describing these groups and differentiating between them. Categories were created on the basis of information in the database. "Non-movers" could have moved during the twelve-month period but if they had not contacted the EUTC again, this information would not be reflected in the database. Similarly the location of movers was based on where individuals were located when they contacted the EUTC and the database did not trace their movements between contacts. Finally the database recorded the type of residence an individual was staying at, at the time of the interview, and it may be, for example, that an individual staying with friends was staying with different friends than he or she was staying with at previous contact. However their category of residence remained the same. As a result, the number of moves is almost certainly underestimated. Nevertheless, the data provide a glimpse into the housing strategies employed by these First Nations urban residents.

The analysis focused on three main questions. The first question was: What were the main mobility patterns employed by individuals in their attempt to remain housed in Winnipeg? The second question was: Are particular mobility (or stability) patterns associated with particular residence patterns? The final question was: Are there mobility patterns differentiated by gender?

Analysis of Mobility Patterns

Table 3.2 describes individuals' place of residence when they first made contact with the EUTC in the twelve-month period of the study. The main differences between individuals who did and did not move in the study periods was that non-movers were more likely to be renting their own place, and movers were more likely to report being on the street or in an institutional setting. Two-thirds as many movers (83 percent) as non-movers (59.5 percent) were homeless at their first contact with the EUTC. It is important to note, though, that this still means that over half of non-movers were homeless when they used EUTC services, including 34 percent who were hidden homeless, 21.7 percent who were absolutely homeless, and 4.1 percent who lived with roommates or a partner in order to find shelter. Living with family and friends represents the single largest category of residence when the mover and non-mover data are aggregated.

Table 3.2. First Residence of Non-Movers and Movers

	Non-Movers	Movers
Own Place	40.5%	17.0%
Family or Friends	33.8%	40.9%
Institution	20.3%	28.4%
Streets	1.4%	9.1%
Roommate	4.1%	4.5%
Observations	n=148	n=88

Table 3.3. Type of Moves (n = 167)

	Own Place	Family or Friends	Institution	Streets	Roommate	Total
Own Place	0.7%	13.9%	1.3%	3.7%	3.1%	22.7%
Family or Friends	20.6%	11.6%	6.7%	1.3%	1.8%	42.0%
Institution	7.1%	8.4%	4.3%	0.7%	0.7%	21.2%
Streets	1.3%	2.5%	4.3%			8.1%
Roommate	1.3%	3.7%				5.0%
Total	30.6%	40.1%	16.6%	5.7%	5.6%	

Table 3.3 describes the types of moves made by movers in the database. The left-hand column represents the residence category individuals moved from, and the rows at the top represent where they moved to. (Note that totals on the right do not match Table 3.3 because many individuals moved more than once.) The eighty-eight mobile individuals in the study moved 167 times during the twelve months of the study. Several patterns are evident in these data. The first is that having their own place did not necessarily represent stability for this population. Over one-fifth (22 percent) of participants moved from their own place to another place of residence, and only one participant moved from their own place to another rental place. Instead of moving to their own rental unit, participants moved to friends or family (13.9 percent), an institutional setting (1.3 percent), the streets (3.7 percent), or a roommate (3.1 percent). Fewer than one-third (30.6 percent) lived in their own rental place at some time during this period, suggesting that many of these individuals do not find stable housing, or stay put, as a result of their search for housing (to the extent that renting represents a stable residence for these participants). An exploration of the reasons for moves away from a rented unit is beyond the data set, but other sources suggest that landlord issues, poor quality housing, conflicts with public housing regulations, or addictions are factors (Christensen and Andrew, this volume; Kern 2014; Skelton 2002).

A second observation is that living with family and friends represented the single largest origin for moves (20.6 percent) and the single largest destination (40.1 percent). What these data may be showing is that networks of friends and family represent the main source of housing security for this population, even if these networks do not produce stability. In other words, friends and family can be counted on to provide shelter in a pinch, but due to a variety of reasons (e.g., crowding, budgets, and public housing regulations) these did not appear to be long-term residency options for participants.

A third observation is that this population is not what is known in the literature as "institutional cyclers" (DeVerteuil 2003). Most participants did not stay in institutions. Individuals moved from institutions to other places of residence and from other places of residence to institutions rather than between institutions. Clearly this is not a representative sample and it may be that the individuals using EUTC services represent only a particular segment of the homeless or marginally housed urban Indigenous population. However McCallum and Isaac suggested in their BC study that "Aboriginal peoples who are homeless are not accessing services at the same rates as their non-Aboriginal counterparts...This finding suggests that Aboriginal peoples who are homeless either avoid shelters, that shelters do not service this population as well, or that they are under-reported in the sheltered homeless data provided by the shelters" (2011, 21).

Finally, staying with friends and family is not a stage in finding their own place for most participants. About one-fifth of participants (20.6 percent) moved from friends and family to a place of their own, but almost the same proportion (21.4 percent) moved to other types of residence.

Table 3.4. Moves of Multiple Movers

	Own Place	Family or Friends	Institution	Streets	Roommate	Total
Own Place		17.0%		3.8%	1.9%	22.7%
Family or Friends	18.9%	22.6%	7.4%	1.9%		50.8%
Institution	3.8%	8.9%	3.8%			16.5%
Streets	1.9%	1.9%	1.9%			5.7%
Roommate		3.8%				3.8%
Total	24.6%	54.2%	13.1%	5.7%	1.9%	99.5%

The strategies of highly mobile participants are similar to less mobile ones. Table 3.4 presents mobility data for individuals who moved four or more times during the study year. Thirteen participants (seven men and six women) moved a total of fifty-three times. The mobility strategies of multiple movers are very similar to the movement patterns of the larger group, where occupying a rental unit did not represent stability, and friends and family were the most common origin and destination.

Table 3.5. Male and Female Movers and Non-Movers

	Male	Female
Non-movers		17.0%
Movers	18.9%	22.6%
Average moves	3.8%	8.9%
% Multiple Movers	15.2%	14.0%

Male and female movers are compared in Table 3.5. They were very similar in terms of numbers of movers and non-movers, proportion of multiple movers, and average number of moves in this period.

Table 3.6. Residence of Male and Female Non-Movers

	Male Non-Movers	Female Non-Movers
Own Place	27.1%	52.7%
Friends or Family	40.0%	28.9%
Institution	25.7%	10.8%
Streets	2.9%	
Roommate	4.3%	8.1%
Total	100.0%	100.5%*

Resulting from rounding up of percentages to one decimal point.

Table 3.6 begins to show some differences between men and women, with women who did not move during the study period most likely to be living in their own place (52.7 percent) and men most likely living with friends or family (40.0 percent). At the same time it is important to note that only slightly more than half of women were living in their own place, and that many still relied on friends and family.

Table 3.7. Moves of Male and Female Movers

	Own Place	Family or Friends	Institution	Streets	Roommate	Total
Male Movers						
Own Place		9.3%	1.1%	2.3%	4.7%	17.4%
Family or Friends	15.1%	15.0%	9.3%	2.3%	3.5%	45.2%
Institution	8.1%	8.1%	5.8%			22.0%
Streets	1.1%	3.5%	5.8%			10.4%
Roommate	2.3%	1.1%	2.3%			5.7%
Total	26.6%	37.0%	24.3%	4.6%	8.2%	100.7%*
Female Movers						
Own Place	1.6%	13.1%	1.6%	1.6%	3.3%	21.2%
Family or Friends	32.8%	14.8%	4.9%			52.5%
Institution	9.8%	4.9%	1.6%			16.3%
Streets	1.6%	1.6%				3.2%
Roommate		6.6%				6.6%
Total	45.8%	41.0%	8.1%	1.6%	3.3%	99.8%

Resulting from rounding of percentages to one decimal point.

Table 3.7 compares male and female movers. Women were more likely to have their own place as one of their places of residence, and to move from friends and family and other residences to their own place. However the differences are not very great, keeping in mind that this is a relatively small data set. It is also important to note that the majority of moves for both men (74.1 percent) and women (54.0 percent) were to residences other than those they rented. Males appear to be slightly less likely to live in their own rental unit, but it seems likely that this reflects housing priorities given to women with dependent children. While there are some differences by gender, there are also many similarities.

Conclusion

This is by no means a representative sample nor a large database, but it does reveal some of the housing strategies of a marginalized group of urban Indigenous people. The following paragraphs highlight the main findings of this study, namely the high mobility rates and the importance of hidden homelessness (staying with friends and family), as well as some implications for research and policy.

The mobility rates of this population are very high. More than one-third (37.3 percent) moved in the year of the study and this is almost certainly an underestimation of moves, given the source of the database. Moves are between different types of residences including rented units, dwellings of family or friends, institutions, the street, and roommates. Only a small number of participants could be classified as absolutely homeless at any point in time, and even when they were absolutely homeless, many subsequently moved into other housing categories. The creation of homelessness categories can take on a life of its own and definitions suggest that there are different types of homeless people rather than, as this database shows, recognizing that some homeless populations use a wide variety of strategies to gain and maintain access to shelter. Because we know so little about the housing histories of homeless people, we don't know to what extent these patterns represent unique strategies or whether other homeless groups have similar strategies.

The data raise questions about the extent to which a focus on absolute homelessness in research and policy addresses the larger issue of homelessness as experienced by the urban Indigenous population. Hidden homeless people represent a high need population. Yet the existing emphasis in academic research on absolute homelessness means that the necessary services for hidden homeless people have not been adequately documented. They may or may not have similar needs to absolutely homeless individuals—we don't know. We also don't know whether people staying with friends and family know about or can access programs for absolutely homeless individuals, and whether these programs are geared to their needs. We also don't know very much about households that provide shelter to homeless friends and family, and whether there are initiatives available to reduce the challenges they face without creating new challenges.

The large number of people staying with friends and family almost certainly reflects the norms of many Indigenous people—those of taking care of family and community (Christensen and Andrew, this volume). It is important to understand the cultural values underlying these strategies in order to create responses that respond sensitively to these beliefs. Staying with friends and family can have positive results for both householders and the individuals staying with them. It can help make ends meet, and provide child and elder care as well as company. However it can also be challenging. For householders (people responsible for renting the unit), hidden homelessness can exacerbate crowding, strain household budgets, generate tension because of lack of privacy, create conflicts with landlord and public housing administrators, and jeopardize household stability. People living with family and friends can face insecurity of tenure, lack of privacy and sometimes even a bed, and experience tension in managing household relationships. In the worst situation, hidden homeless people can be vulnerable to sexual exploitation. We know from other studies that many First Nations hidden homeless individuals leave the house during the day in order to reduce the pressure on the household, which means that they may not have phone access to look for a place, employment, or services (Peters 2012; Robinson and Coward 2003). We hear provincial governments suggesting that the poor housing conditions on reserves are one way that the federal government is shifting costs for Indigenous people to provincial governments. Reserve housing conditions encourage Indigenous people to move to cities where provincial governments become responsible for their needs. But the data analyzed in this study reveal another set of costs, and that is costs to the Indigenous social networks which are taking up the slack in providing vulnerable community members with suitable, affordable, and adequate housing. Staying with friends and family can have positive aspects, but this approach to housing provision eventually hurts householders and hidden homeless individuals.

The overrepresentation of Indigenous people in the urban homeless population and the patterns found in these data (especially the reliance on friends and family and the low levels of shelter use) emphasize the need for culturally supportive service provision. The importance of providing culturally appropriate support services has been identified in other research on Indigenous homelessness (Beavis et al. 1997; SIIT 2000). In their Winnipeg study, Deane and co-authors (2004) found that Indigenous residents considered mainstream organizations to practice values based on charity, which created indignity for Indigenous residents. Alternative Indigenous values of reciprocity and giving back led Indigenous residents to rely, instead, on their own social networks. Webster (2007) suggests that Indigenous homeless people are more underserved than other homeless populations in terms of having Indigenous shelters and suggested that it was important to provide services within traditional Indigenous environments (see also Jim Ward Associates 2008). Based on their interviews, McCallum and Isaac found that many Indigenous people felt uncomfortable in existing shelters, especially those operated by faith-based agencies (2011, 21). Thurston, Oelke, Turner, and Bird's (2011) study of organizations that offered services and programs to homeless people in the Western provinces recommended that cultural safety should be a foundation for providing services to Indigenous people, that Indigenous governance be supported, and that cultural reconnection was important in addressing the needs of Indigenous people who were homeless. Strategies for addressing the needs of this segment of the urban homeless population must have the strong support and participation of Indigenous organizations.

Acknowledgements

We express our appreciation to the AMC and EUTC staff who supported this research. The Canadian Centre for Policy Alternatives (CCPA) including researcher Josh Brandon partnered with us on an earlier project related to this study. The support of the Social Sciences and Humanities Research Council (SSHRC) through the Canada Research Chair (CRC) program is gratefully acknowledged.

Notes

1 While the Canadian Constitution Act (1982 as amended) uses the term "Aboriginal Peoples" to refer to the Indian, Metis, and Inuit peoples of Canada, I prefer to use the term "Indigenous." Most contemporary writers use the term "First Nations" instead of "Indian." While I use the term "First Nations" to refer to an aggregate of these people in Winnipeg, I recognize that many Indigenous people prefer to identify with a specific First Nations community, for example Mi'kmaq, Cree, or Ojibway.

2 Against public perceptions that homogenize urban Indigenous populations as uniformly socio-economically disadvantaged and concentrated in inner-city ghettos it is important to emphasize that, as Peters pointed out, there is a growing middle class in the urban Indigenous community (Peters 2010; Wotherspoon 2003; Urban Aboriginal Task Force 2007).

References

Amore Kate, Helen Viggers, Michael G. Baker, Philippa Howden-Chapman. 2013. *Severe Housing Deprivation: The Problem and Its Measurement.* University of Otago: Department of Public Health.

Beavis, Mary Ann, Nancy Klos, Thomas Carter, and Christian Douchant. 1997. *Literature Review: Aboriginal Peoples and Homelessness.* Ottawa: Canada Mortgage and Housing Corporation.

Belanger, Yale D., Olu Awosoga, and Gabrielle Weasel Head. 2013. "Homelessness, Urban Aboriginal People, and the Need for a National Enumeration." *Aboriginal Policy Studies* 2 (2): 4–33.

Brant Castellano, Marlene, and Linda Archibald. 2007. "Healing Historic Trauma: A Report from the Aboriginal Healing Foundation." In *Aboriginal Policy Research Volume IV: Moving Forward, Making a Difference,* edited by Jerry P. White, Susan Wingert, Dan Beavon, and Paul Maxim, 69–92. Toronto: Thompson Educational Publishing.

Carter, Tom, and Chesya Polevychok. 2004. *Literature Review on Issues and Needs of Aboriginal People*. Prepared for the Federation of Canadian Municipalities. Winnipeg. http://www.urbancentre.utoronto.ca/pdfs/elibrary/Carter_Aboriginal-Issues-Li.pdf.

Cedar Project Partnership, Margo E. Pearce, Wayne M. Christian, Katharina Patterson, Kat Norris, Akm Moniruzzaman, Kevin J. P. Craib, Martin T. Schechter, and Patricia M. Spittal. 2008. "The Cedar Project: Historical Trauma, Sexual Abuse and HIV Risk among Young Aboriginal People Who Use Injection and Non-Injection Drugs in Two Canadian Cities." *Social Science and Medicine* 66 (11): 2185–94.

Clatworthy, Stewart J., and Mary Jane Norris. 2007. "Aboriginal Mobility and Migration in Canada: Trends, Recent Patterns and Implications, 1971–2001." In *Aboriginal Policy Research Volume IV: Moving Forward, Making a Difference*, edited by Jerry P. White, Susan Wingert, Dan Beavon, and Paul Maxim, 207–34. Toronto: Thompson Educational Publishing.

Cloke, Paul, Jon May, and Sarah Johnsen. 2008. "Performativity and affect in the homeless city." *Environment and Planning D: Society and Space* 26 (2): 241–63.

Deane, Lawrence, Larry Morrissette, Jason Bousquet, and Samantha Bruyere. 2004. "Explorations in Urban Aboriginal Neighbourhood Development." *The Canadian Journal of Native Studies* 24 (2): 227–52.

DeVerteuil, Geoffrey. 2003. "Homeless Mobility, Institutional Settings, and the New Poverty Management." *Environment and Planning A* 35 (2): 361–79.

DeVerteuil, Geoffrey, Jon May, and Jürgen von Mahs. 2009. "Complexity Not Collapse: Recasting the Geographies of Homelessness in a 'Punitive' Age." *Progress in Human Geography* 33 (5): 646–66.

Distasio, Jino, Gina Sylvestre, Christa Jaccubucci, Susan Mulligan, and Kurt Sargent. 2004. *First Nations/Métis/Inuit Mobility Study: Final Report*. Winnipeg: Institute of Urban Studies.

Eberle, Margaret, Deborah Kraus, and Luba Serge. 2009. *Results of a Pilot Study to Estimate the Size of the Hidden Homeless Population in Metropolitan Vancouver*. Ottawa: Homeless Partnering Secretariat, Human Resources and Skills Development Canada (HRSDC).

ESDC (Employment and Social Development Canada). 2016. *Homelessness Strategy*. http://www.edsc.gc.ca/eng/communities/homelessness/index.shtml.

Gaetz, Stephen, Jesse Donaldson, Tim Richter, and Tanya Gulliver. 2013. *The State of Homelessness in Canada 2013*. Toronto: Canadian Homelessness Research Network Press.

Hiebert, Daniel, Silvia D'Addario, and Kathy Sherrell, with Sherman Chan. 2005. *The Profile of Absolute and Relative Homelessness among Immigrants, Refugees, and Refugee Claimants in the GVRD*. Vancouver: MOSAIC.

Hodge, Paul, and John Lester. 2006. "Indigenous Research: Whose Priority? Journeys and Possibilities of Cross-Cultural Research in Geography." *Geographical Research* 44 (1): 41–51.

Howitt, Richard. 2001. "Constructing Engagement: Geographical Education for Justice within and beyond the Tertiary Classroom." *Journal of Geography in Higher Education* 25 (2): 147–66.

Homelessness Partnering Strategy. 2014. *Supporting Families and Communities.* http://actionplan.gc.ca/en/initiative/homelessness-partnering-strategy.

Hulchanski, J.David. 2009. *Homelessness in Canada: Past, Present, Future.* Ottawa, Canadian Policy Research Networks.

Humphreys, David. 2006. *Aboriginal Housing in Canada: Building on Promising Practices.* Ottawa, ON: International Housing Coalition (IHC) and The Canadian Real Estate Association (CREA).

Jim Ward Associates. 2008. *Dealing Effectively with Aboriginal Homelessness in Toronto: Final Report.* Toronto, ON: Toronto Shelter, Supported Housing Administration.

Kalbach, Warren E. 1987. "Growth and Distribution of Canada's Ethnic Populations, 1871–1981." In *Ethnic Canada. Identities and Inequalities*, edited by Leo Dreidger, 82–110. Toronto: Copp Clark Pitman.

Kern, Selena. 2014. Personal communication.

Klodawsky, Fran. 2006. "Landscapes on the Margins: Gender and Homelessness." *Gender, Place and Culture* 13 (4): 365–81.

Leach, Andrew. 2010. "The Roots of Aboriginal Homelessness in Canada." *Parity* 23 (9): 12–13.

May, Jon. 2000. "Housing Histories and Homeless Careers: A Biographical Approach." *Housing Studies* 15 (4): 613–38.

McCallum, Katie, and David Isaac. 2011. *Feeling Home: Culturally Responsive Approaches to Aboriginal Homelessness.* BC: Social Planning and Research Council of British Columbia (SPARC BC) and the Centre for Native Policy and Research (CNPR).

Meert, Henk, and Marie Bourgeois. 2005. "Between Rural and Urban Slums: A Geography of Pathways through Homelessness." *Housing Studies* 20 (1): 107–25.

Mental Health Commission of Canada. 2012. *At Home/Chez Soi Early Findings Report*, vol. 2. http://www.mentalhealthcommission.ca/sites/default/files/Housing_At_Home_Early_Findings_Report_Volume%2525202_ENG_0_1.pdf.

Molina, Edna. 2000. "Informal Non-Kin Networks among Homeless Latina and African American Men: Form and Functions." *American Behavioral Scientist* 43 (4): 663–85.

Moore, Jeanne. 2007. "Polarity or Integration? Towards a Fuller Understanding of Home and Homelessness." *Journal of Architectural and Planning Research* 24 (2): 143–59.

New Policy Institute. 2004. *Estimating the Numbers of People in Housing Need and at Risk of Homelessness in London: A Report for the GLA.* London: New Policy Institute.

Norris, Mary Jane, and Stewart Clatworthy. 2003. "Aboriginal Mobility and Migration within Urban Canada: Outcomes, Factors and Implications." In *Not Strangers in These Parts: Urban Aboriginal Peoples*, edited by David Newhouse and Evelyn J. Peters, 51–78. Ottawa: Policy Research Initiative.

Peters, Evelyn J. 2010. "Aboriginal People in Canadian Cities." In *Canadian Cities in Transition: New Directions in the Twenty-First Century*, edited by Trudi E. Bunting, Pierre Filion, and Ryan Walker, 375–90. Don Mills, ON: Oxford University Press.

_____. 2012. "'I Like to Let Them Have Their Time.' Hidden Homeless First Nations People in the City and Their Management of Household Relationships." *Social and Cultural Geography* 13 (4): 321–38.

Peters, Evelyn J., and Vince Robilland. 2009. "'Everything You Want Is There': The

Place of the Reserve in First Nations' Homeless Mobility." *Urban Geography* 30 (6): 652–80.

Preston, Valerie, Robert Murdie, Jane Wedlock, Sandeep Agrawal, Uzo Anucha, Silvia D'Addario, Min J. Kwak, Jennifer Logan, and Ann M. Murnaghan. 2009. "Immigrants and Homelessness—At Risk in Canada's Outer Suburbs." *Canadian Geographer* 53 (3): 288–304.

Pualani Louis, Renee. 2007. "Can You Hear Us Now? Voices from the Margin: Using Indigenous Methodologies in Geographic Research." *Geographical Research* 45 (2): 130–39.

Robinson, David, and Sarah Coward. 2003. *Your Place, Not Mine: The Experiences of Homeless People Staying with Family and Friends*. London: Crisis and the Countryside Agency.

Rossi, Peter H. 1989. *Down and Out in America: The Origins of Homelessness*. Chicago: University of Chicago Press.

SIIT (Saskatchewan Indian Institute of Technologies). 2000. *Urban First Nations People without Homes in Saskatchewan: Final Report*. Saskatoon: SIIT. http://www.ywcaregina.com/Programs/HomelessnessPoverty/Homeless%20Urban%20First%20Nations.pdf.

Silver, Jim. 2006. *In Their Own Voices: Building Urban Aboriginal Communities*. Halifax: Fernwood.

Skelton, Ian. 2002. "Residential Mobility of Aboriginal Single Mothers in Winnipeg: An Exploratory Study of Chronic Moving." *Journal of Housing and the Built Environment*, 17 (2): 127–144.

Statistics Canada. 2008. *Aboriginal Peoples in Canada in 2006*. (accessed 15 May 2008). http://www12.statcan.ca/english/census06/analysis/aboriginal/decade.cfm#01.

Thurston, Wilfreda E., Nelly D. Oelke, David Turner, and Cynthia Bird. 2011. *Final Report: Improving Housing Outcomes for Aboriginal People in Western Canada: National, Regional, Community and Individual Perspectives on Changing the Future of Homelessness*. Prepared for Human Resources and Skills Development Canada, National Housing Secretariat. http://www.ucalgary.ca/wethurston/FinalReport-Improving%20housing%Aboriginal%20people.pdf.

Urban Aboriginal Task Force. 2007. *Urban Aboriginal Task Force: Final Report*. Toronto, ON: Ontario Federation of Indian Friendship Centres.

Veness, April R. 1993. "Neither Homed nor Homeless: Contested Definitions and the Personal World of the Poor." *Political Geography* 12 (4): 319–40.

Webster, Andrew. 2007. *Sheltering Urban Aboriginal Homeless People: Assessment of Situation and Needs*. Ottawa, ON: National Association of Friendship Centres (NAFC).

Wotherspoon, Terry. 2003. "Prospects for a New Middle Class among Urban Aboriginal People." In *Not Strangers in These Parts. Urban Aboriginal Peoples*, edited by David Newhouse and Evelyn J. Peters, 147–66. Ottawa: Policy Research Initiative.

CHAPTER 4

No Dumping: Indigenousness and the Racialized Police Transport of the Urban Homeless

JOSHUA FREISTADT

On 20 May 2005 three Edmonton Police Service (EPS) officers removed nine Indigenous homeless persons from Whyte Avenue, a pedestrian-oriented commercial strip in the south-side Old Strathcona neighbourhood, and dropped them off in a north-side residential community. The transport infamously became known as the "sweatbox incident" because the homeless men and women were cramped inside a police van designated for only six persons and several spent up to an hour and a half in these stuffy conditions ("Edmonton Police Guilty" 2010; EPS 2010a). When they were let out in a distant parking lot, some of the men were half-clothed and dripping with sweat (Simons 2007, B1). One individual immediately sought water from a local resident who was tending to his yard (EPS 2010a; Warnica 2010). Community members soon reported the presence of visibly homeless Indigenous persons to their local police detachment and eventually relayed the story to media outlets (Simons 2007, B1; EPS 2010a). Some homeowners in the area were upset that their community was used as a "dumping ground for derelicts from Whyte Avenue" (Simons 2007, B1) and several news reports suggested that the incident was "racially motivated" ("Edmonton Police Guilty" 2010; EPS 2010a, 2010b; Sands 2010; Wittmeier 2010).

During the police disciplinary hearing into the incident five years later, two of the senior officers involved were sanctioned for discreditable conduct and insubordination because they did not follow police protocol requiring them to take notes on all investigations and to ensure that intoxicated persons were either transported into the care of a responsible adult or taken to a local shelter (EPS 2010a). The presiding officer, alongside the defence counsel for the accused EPS members, proclaimed that there was "no evidence whatsoever" to support allegations that the event was racially motivated (Sands 2010, n.p.; EPS 2010a, 43). They stressed that the officers came from teaching and social work backgrounds, held positive rapport with the homeless outside this incident, wanted to transport the individuals to protect them from intoxicated young persons who frequent the Avenue's bars and came "from diverse ethnic and cultural roots," which "in the case of one individual" included being "part Aboriginal" (EPS 2010a, 43).

Questions concerning race thus revolved around whether or not the individual officers were prejudiced. The investigators concluded that given each officer's own racial identity and prior dealings with Indigenous homeless persons, the sweatbox incident did not involve malice toward the individual homeless persons or their race (EPS 2010a; Sands 2010, n.p.). The fact that all nine homeless persons were Indigenous was considered irrelevant to explanations of why the event occurred. In fact, the presiding officer felt public accusations that the event was racially motivated unduly damaged the reputations of the officers. Consequently, he considered these accusations to be mitigating factors that lessened the disciplinary sanctions the officers received (EPS 2010b).

For police officials involved in the disciplinary hearing, the sweatbox incident was an isolated, albeit serious, case of poor judgement. The seriousness stemmed primarily from the officers' failure to follow police protocol and the negative public reaction that stemmed from this transgression (EPS 2010a). Apparently, had police policy prevailed, the reputation of the EPS would not have fallen into disrepute. Indeed, despite the fact that the level of intoxication among the nine homeless persons was never established, investigators held that had the officers simply taken the group to an inner-city shelter as they claimed to be doing, then their actions would have been acceptable insofar as they aligned with the EPS protocol concerning the transport of adult inebriates to shelters (EPS 2010a).

Transports to shelters were both encouraged and common. The staff sergeant for Old Strathcona, for example, explained during the disciplinary hearing that the usual practice at the start of a weekend night shift was to "round-up" the homeless and relocate them to shelters. These move outs were apparently so frequent that the homeless would "casually...load themselves" anytime the police van pulled up and opened its doors (EPS 2010a, 8). Furthermore, police officials claimed that transports to local shelters occurred out of "compassion," constituted a genuinely benevolent effort to protect the homeless from other residents, and intended to help the homeless by linking them with social services (EPS 2010a; Pierce 2010, n.p.). Officers explicitly denied that the purpose of the sweatbox incident and similar transports was "to get them [the homeless] off Whyte Avenue" (EPS 2010a, 26).

In this chapter I seek to unsettle some of the claims police officials make about transports of homeless persons. First, I challenge the idea that these types of police transports, which policing scholars King and Dunn (2004) refer to as "police dumping," are unproblematic so long as they deliver homeless persons to inner-city shelters.[1] Second, I counter the position that the racial identities of the homeless persons involved in such transports are unimportant. To do so I draw on twenty-two ethnographic interviews with street-involved Edmontonians to show how Indigenousness and the police dumping of homeless persons intersect.[2] I argue that transporting homeless persons to shelters (or distant neighbourhoods) is not as benevolent as the police suggest and is in fact implicated in issues of racialization. In particular, I contrast the stories of differently racialized homeless adults to demonstrate how police dumping is racialized in ways that reinforce prime consumer spaces as "white spaces" and dangerous inner-city spaces as "spaces of Indigenousness."

By using a lens of "racialized policing" (Comack 2012), my analysis moves beyond concerns over the possible presence of racial prejudice among individual police officers to highlight how responses to homelessness must also address the ongoing socio-economic, spatial, and colonial processes that policing both reflects and perpetuates. Using Edmonton as a backdrop to illuminate the intersections between policing, homelessness, and Indigenousness is particularly relevant because it is the Canadian metropolis with the second highest urban Indigenous population (Environics Institute 2010).

Racialized Policing

Attention to the racialized policing of homelessness is long overdue. Although a considerable amount of scholarship documents the growing dependencies of governments on law or police action to respond to visible homelessness (Beckett and Herbert 2009; Berti and Sommers 2010; Blomley 2007, 2011; Collins and Blomley 2003; Duneier 2001; Ellickson 1996; Feldman 2004; Gordon 2006, 2010; Hermer and Mosher 2002; McNeil 2010; Parnaby 2003; Schafer 1998, 2007), few of these analyses examine how the policing of homelessness intersects with race. Given the vast overrepresentation of Indigenous persons among the homeless in Canada (Belanger, Weasel Head, and Awosoga 2012; Hulchanski et al. 2009; Lenon 2000), this oversight severely truncates knowledge of Indigenous homelessness and its relationship to state institutions of social control. Of course, Herbert and Brown (2006), alongside O'Grady, Gaetz, and Buccieri (2011), note that persons of non-white racial identity are more likely to be homeless and so are more often subject to the policing of homelessness. Although this observation points to how homelessness is "raced," it does not highlight how the policing of homelessness is "racialized." Discussing how policing is racialized means outlining the ways that persons with different racial identities have qualitatively different experiences of policing.

If the analysis of the intersections between Indigenousness and the policing of homelessness ends at the observation that homelessness is raced, the claims of police investigators that attention to racial identity is unimportant are easily justified. The frequent occurrence of police encounters, benevolent or harmful, with Indigenous persons is apparently simply a product of statistics beyond police control. As in the disciplinary hearing to the sweatbox incident, the only pertinent question is whether or not individual officers hold racial prejudice and so are unfairly targeting (i.e., racially profiling) those homeless persons they identify as Indigenous.

Focusing on individual officers' biases, however, easily reduces concerns about the policing of Indigenous homeless persons to the actions of a "few bad apples" and so overlooks systemic racism and the various ways policing, intentionally or otherwise, draws on and reinforces racial inequalities (Comack 2012). In contrast, to adopt a lens of racialized policing is to discuss how police action creates and reinforces differences along socially constructed racial lines (Comack 2012; Razack 2002a, 2002b; Goldberg 1993). This view acknowledges that race is a social construct rather than a biological trait (Blackburn 2000; Green 2006) and that racialization is "the process through which groups come to be designated as different and on that basis subjected to different and unequal treatment" (Block and Galabuzi 2011, 19). The production of differences according to racial identity is not, in and of itself, a problem because such differences can and should be celebrated. However, racialization is problematic and develops into a form of racism when the creation of differences establishes a hierarchy that disadvantages some groups (Comack 2012; Green 2006).

Policing contributes to racialization, and embodies a form of racism, whenever it serves as "one of the projects through which race is interpreted and given meaning" in a way that the inequitable "racialized order of a society is reproduced" (Comack 2012, 60). While the presence of racial profiling and the actions of individual police officers are relevant considerations (James 2002; Tanner 2009), analyses of racialized policing in Canada demonstrate the much more nuanced ways in which police action contributes to racial inequality and the subordination of Indigenous persons (Comack 2012). For instance, Comack (2012), Mawani (2002, 2012), Gordon (2006), and Nettelbeck and Smandych (2010) separately document how policing contributes to racialization whenever colonial states use police forces (such as the North West Mounted Police) to settle regions and dominate Indigenous persons. It is also well documented that police have paved paths for the "white settler society" (Gordon 2006; Razack 2002a) by displacing and confining Indigenous persons to ostensibly "degenerate spaces" (Razack 2002a) such as the reserve, the residential school, the inner city, or the prostitution-laden "stroll" (Comack 2012; Goldberg 1993; Hogeveen and Freistadt 2013; Razack 2002a, 2002b; Mawani 2002, 2012). Moreover, as Razack (2002a, 2002b) observes, this confinement not only associates Indigenousness with spaces of danger and vice, it also privileges individuals who are racialized as white because they see prime spaces as their own and can more freely move in and out of spaces of their choosing. The racialization of space and policing, in fact, become mutually reinforcing when officers view the spaces in which they help concentrate Indigenous persons as dangerous and therefore patrol them more frequently (Comack 2012).

Analyses of the racialized policing of Indigenous persons in Canada thus draw attention to processes beyond individual officers and toward considerations of colonialism and spatial regulation. Nevertheless, how contemporary urban policing of the visibly homeless is similarly racialized has yet to be documented. The discussion that follows therefore brings together literature on racialized policing and that on the policing of homelessness. It grounds this merger in qualitative analyses of the lived experiences of twenty-two visibly homeless adult Edmontonians. Interviews were held over the spring and summer of 2011 and were collected in the same consumption-oriented areas the EPS identified as "hot spots" for complaints about homeless persons: Old Strathcona and Downtown (Elanik 2009). Eight of the respondents identified as Indigenous, one as East Asian, and the remainder as white. Contrasting the stories of these participants highlights that colonialism and racialization are processes that continue through specific practices (Samuelson and Monture-Angus 2002; Mawani and Sealy 2011), including the ostensibly non-racial and benevolent act of police dumping.

Indigenousness and Racialized Police Dumping

Although interview respondents and secondary news data confirmed the existence and seriousness of police transports to desolate distant locales within or near Edmonton (Rusnell 2007, B1), these forms of police dumping were rare. Investigations into the infamous "Starlight Tours" in Saskatoon (Comack 2012; Green 2006; Reber and Renaud 2005; Wright 2004) have made officers and the public aware of the potentially deadly consequences of this type of police transport. Aside from the sweatbox incident, only one research participant mentioned an occasion in which police dropped him off in a remote area. Rather, the accepted police protocol of transporting the homeless to local shelters was by far the most frequent type of transport encounter that homeless persons had with officers. These police-sanctioned transports most often displaced homeless persons to shelters in Edmonton's McCauley and Boyle Street neighbourhoods, where the vast majority of homeless-serving agencies in the city exist. Debrah,[3] for instance, explained that police often pick her up from Whyte Avenue on the south-side of the North Saskatchewan River and take her "all the way down to the Hope"—an inner-city shelter in the McCauley-Boyle region. Russ relayed a similar occurrence: he said that when police saw him panhandling in Old Strathcona, "They said they would take [him] up to the Hope Mission and drop [him] off there. And that is what they did." Darlene likewise explained that police frequently "pick [her] up" and "drop [her] off at Spady's," which is the colloquial term the street-involved use to refer to a shelter (the George Spady Centre) in the McCauley-Boyle region. The area was so familiar to homeless persons that participants who spent most of their time in Old Strathcona often referred to McCauley-Boyle simply as the "north-side."

This McCauley-Boyle "north-side" sharply contrasts with the consumer-oriented areas of Downtown and Old Strathcona. The two abutting communities of McCauley and Boyle Street lie in the heart of the inner city just northeast of Downtown and are among the city's most impoverished and dangerous neighbourhoods (Hogeveen and Freistadt 2013). In 2010 McCauley and Boyle Street witnessed violent crime rates that were over ten times the average rate for Edmonton (City of Edmonton 2010a, 2010c). Both neighbourhoods have median incomes that are less than half of the city-wide median, with McCauley and Boyle Street posting the lowest and the third-lowest median incomes of all Edmonton neighbourhoods (Edmonton Social Planning Council 2011). Unsurprisingly, the region also contains a disproportionately high percentage of Edmonton's subsidized housing. While 4.8 percent of the housing across Edmonton is subsidized, 61 percent of housing in the McCauley neighbourhood falls into this category (Kleiss 2010, A1). Moreover, while city officials have plans to redevelop both Downtown (City of Edmonton 2010b) and Old Strathcona (City of Edmonton 2011) into even greater pedestrian-led and consumer-oriented locales, areas like Boyle Street are slotted for redevelopments that further concentrate poverty. In particular, the City of Edmonton, in what it terms the "Boyle Renaissance," plans to build an additional 550 low-income housing units. This redevelopment includes a "mega-complex" that combines 150 units of affordable housing with rental spaces for more social services (Kent 2010, B3; McKay, Finnigan and Associates 2010; O'Donnell 2012)

Although many residents take great pride in these neighbourhoods and are working hard to improve their reputation (Filipski 2001; Kent 2009; Loyie 1997; Retson 1998), interview respondents confirmed the dangerousness of this inner-city district. Many tried to avoid the area as much as possible. Stan described the constant threat of victimization he felt in the vicinity:

> Fuck, I lock my window. I put a blanket up and everything, I keep my lights on most of the time. People lurk around all night. They do, man. People lurk around all night and day.... Oh, robberies and everything, man. There are just so many people that hang around in front of the liquor store, they are all alcoholics, they are all drug addicts, they are hanging out in front of the liquor store. You know what they do...? They wait for people to come out of the liquor store and even though they got one little bottle or six pack, they will grab it and fucking run.

Stan's rooming house was in McCauley, yet the dangers of the neighbourhood led him to remain on the street. He avoided the area, which he referred to as a "ghetto," as much as he could "because there is crime everywhere." Instead he spent most of his time Downtown where he felt safer. Keith also explained that he avoided the McCauley-Boyle area as a means of ensuring safety. When asked if he felt safe on the streets, he replied, "Oh yeah. I don't make a habit of going down around the Bissell or the Co-op [two adult drop-in centres in the McCauley and Boyle Street neighbourhoods] or any place where there is high crime rate."

Most participants recounted stories of victimization they witnessed or endured in the locality or outside the region's homeless-serving agencies. Many had their few belongings stolen from them in the neighbourhood. Several had been physically assaulted. Jason, for example, explained: "It is not safe...I hate going too near the [inner-city shelters]. You see this mark here? [He takes off his hat to reveal a scar]. A guy cut me with a razor. I was in line, talking with a buddy of mine. We were waiting for lunch I think.... A guy comes along, tells my friend to move, elbows me...and says, "This is not a good spot, bugger off you guys." And he took our place in line. My friend turns around and because of that out comes the razor and swish, swish [gesturing that he was cut]."This attack, alongside other victimizations he witnessed, led Jason and many other interview respondents to avoid inner-city agencies altogether and live outside in consumer spaces. Although remaining on the street in consumer spaces does not remove the homeless from a high likelihood of victimization (Gaetz 2004), within these spaces they felt safer and frequently developed "street families" that helped reduce the everyday precariousness of their lives (Beckett and Herbert 2009; Tanner 2009).

While police officials frame the practice of police dumping to the shelters as an act of compassion meant to help the homeless utilize the available social services, the dangers of this area are a real concern for the homeless. Few of the respondents actually remained at the services police dropped them off at and so eventually had to venture through the McCauley-Boyle district to make their way back to the consumer spaces in which they lived. For instance, after Darlene explained that police routinely picked her up from Downtown or Whyte Avenue and dropped her off at the George Spady Centre, she laughingly added, "And I go right back." Stan likewise reported that after police escort him out of Old Strathcona, he simply turns around and returns. He chuckled, "You go to Whyte Avenue and panhandle, they [the police] throw you in the van and take you [to a shelter] and say, 'Don't come back.'....Oh yeah, I go back there again." Indeed, all the research participants said that when they were left at inner-city shelters, they typically waited a brief period of time for the police to leave and then returned to the spaces from which officers had ejected them.

That many individuals do not remain inside the agencies to which police deliver them must be known to officers because they eventually come back into contact with the same homeless persons. In fact, EPS officials unwittingly admitted that they were aware transports to shelters did not result in service use for many homeless persons. Testifying at the disciplinary hearing for the sweatbox incident, the Acting Supervisor for the officers involved explained that members of the EPS did not formally record these transports "because the drop-offs were so frequent" and "police would often have to transport the same individual two to three times in a single shift." He further explained that the homeless often saw the transports as "a game" and that when police would complete these escorts, most homeless persons would simply laugh and tell the officers, "See you in a few hours" (EPS 2010a, 8; Pierse 2010, n.p.).

This admission that police dumping seldom results in service use undercuts claims that service integration is the primary objective of the transports. Rather, if police know that few homeless people use the inner-city agencies to which they are transported, then police dumping to these locations is less of an effort to find homeless persons help than it is an act (intentional or otherwise) to displace the homeless into the dangerous inner city region of McCauley-Boyle.

That displacement is among the primary concerns of officers who employ police dumping is evident in the descriptions of how these transports unfold. For instance, the following description by one homeless male was representative of stories involving police transports to shelters: "They [the police] drive me to the Spady Centre. Drop me off and say, 'We don't want to see you down here [Downtown] no more. You are banned off Jasper Avenue and you are not allowed to be down here no more panhandling because that is what you do all day.'" The actions of the officers in this typical transport emphasize that their dominant concern is not to integrate the homeless individual into the services that the George Spady Centre offers. They do not remain at the facility to ensure the homeless secure assistance with income, personal traumas, or addictions. Rather, police simply leave homeless persons with the direction that they are "banned off Jasper Avenue." This valediction stresses where the homeless ought not to be—prime consumer spaces like Jasper Avenue or Whyte Avenue—not what they ought to do to access help. For the homeless, escorts to the shelters hardly appear as compassionate or benevolent as police officials suggest. Rather, the homeless experience police dumping primarily as an act of dislocation. It demonstrates to the homeless that they are not welcome in spaces of affluence and ostensibly belong in spaces of poverty, danger, and vice.

Research participants also demonstrated that, despite police claims to the contrary, race clearly shaped practices of police dumping to shelters within the dangerous "north-side" McCauley-Boyle region. Certainly, police transports to local shelters occasionally involve non-Indigenous homeless persons. Nevertheless, these policing measures were racialized insofar as police more readily displaced Indigenous respondents to the inner city. In fact, only one Indigenous participant, Carl, reported that police had never transported him to inner-city shelters. Carl, however, regularly spent the time when he was not busking Downtown on the streets of the McCauley-Boyle region, thus making it rather unnecessary to transport him. All other Indigenous participants recounted at least one incident, often many more, where police dropped them off outside or near inner-city shelters. In contrast, only one white male, Rick, reported being taken to the shelters by police. This exception might reflect the fact that, although most research participants preferred to avoid McCauley-Boyle, Rick often wanted to go to the region. He declared that he "would have went regardless of whether they [police] took [him] or not" because he did not "mind going to the Spady's...or Hope Mission just to get off the streets, take a break once in a while."

Although this small sample of participants means we must be cautious making generalizations, the role race plays in police dumping is obvious in the preferential treatment white homeless persons received compared to Indigenous homeless persons. It was common for officers to permit homeless white persons to remain in prime consumer spaces like Old Strathcona or Downtown so long as they did not cause disturbances along the busy strips of Whyte Avenue or Jasper Avenue. For instance, Jason, a white homeless man, conveyed how police allowed him to stay in the area of Whyte Avenue: "I said [to the officers waking him up in an alley behind Whyte Avenue], 'Guys give me a break, at least let me sleep a couple hours.' He [the police officer] said, 'I would if I could, but I can't. If we get a complaint, it goes on our system, we have to do something about it and chase you out.' He says, 'I will tell you what, though, between you and me, go a couple blocks that way away from Whyte and find a place to go to sleep.'" Many other white interview participants reported similar treatment.

In stark contrast, Indigenous participants reported being continually re-moved from these spaces and taken to inner-city shelters regardless of their actions or level of intoxication. For example, Darlene, an Indigenous woman, explained how she and her Indigenous partner, Keith, are quickly and com-monly stopped by police on Whyte Avenue and escorted to the shelters: "Well...for example...one time, [Keith] and I, we weren't panhandling at the time. I had gone to work and we were sitting on the street bench off Whyte Avenue. We ordered up [a] slice of pizza each. And the police van drove, comes storming right in, started accusing us of panhandling and drinking. And I said that wasn't what was going on. They threw [Keith] in the van, handcuffed him, threw him in, and they said, 'Come on, you too.' That was me. I got in and helped [Keith].... Well anyways, they brought us there...to Spady's."

Police allowed Jason—a white homeless male whose behaviour drew an official complaint—to remain in Old Strathcona, yet they quickly accused Darlene and Keith—Indigenous homeless persons eating in a public space and not obviously drawing public complaints—of engaging in social disorder and so they took the pair to the McCauley-Boyle region. Darlene and Keith were neither intoxicated nor committing any illegal acts, suggesting that police dumping displaces those who are simply guilty of being homeless and Indigenous in prime consumer spaces.

In some cases this disparity in treatment between white and Indigenous homeless persons was apparent within a single police encounter. For instance,

Debrah, an Indigenous homeless woman, and Kyle, her homeless white male partner, explained that despite the fact they were often together and engaging in the same activities, officers would frequently escort Debrah out of Old Strathcona but allow Kyle to stay in the area:

> Debrah: They [police] give us a ticket or then they drive me downtown....

> Kyle: No, not me, I don't go.... [Police] give us a ticket and tell us to go on our own.... I tell them "no" [when they say they are taking him to the inner city]....

> Debrah: Well they take me downtown. I got to go to Hope Mission.

Neither Debrah nor Kyle wanted to go to the inner-city shelters or the McCauley-Boyle region and both would have preferred to stay together. Nonetheless, Debrah is not permitted to remain in the vicinity of Old Strathcona. Debrah explained that she once lived in McCauley and still held a bad reputation such that she faced high likelihood of victimization anytime she returned to the neighbourhood or went to the shelters. The transports, however, were so common for Debrah that she no longer tried to protest. She saw her removal as dangerous but inevitable and simply explained that she has "got to go." Yet as soon as police dropped her off she invariably began what she described as "the long" and "dangerous" walk through the inner city and "across the bridge" back to the Old Strathcona neighbourhood where her social circle and safety network existed. While the police indulge her white male partner's requests to remain in Old Strathcona, they pay less attention to her desires and safety.

Police Dumping Both Reflects and Reinforces Processes of Racialization

The contrasting stories between white and Indigenous homeless persons show that officer discretion obviously plays a role in the racialized nature of police dumping, but there is more at work here than a "few bad apples" who choose to respond inequitably to Indigenous homeless persons. In particular, it is important to understand that policing itself unfolds in a social context beyond the control of individual officers. While the police might have constructed questionable narratives of compassion and service use to justify police dumping, their central task is to reproduce social order (Ericson 1982) and they face immense pressures from business leaders to deal with the presence of visible homelessness in consumer spaces (Beckett and Herbert 2009). Investigations into the sweatbox incident revealed that concerns from area businesses about the homeless were so frequent that Whyte Avenue businesses had a hotline they could use to bypass the regular complaint procedure and to phone the beat officers directly (Pierse 2010). Moreover, shortly after the sweatbox incident EPS authorities and local businesses joined forces to develop an integrated response to the homelessness and panhandling in the Old Strathcona and the Downtown regions, part of which included the development of an anti-aggressive panhandling bylaw (Ho 2010; Larson 2011).

Beat officers, then, faced intense pressures from both business leaders and their supervisors to crack down on the visibly homeless in spaces of consumption. The tools at their disposal, however, included tickets—which often lead to cumbersome paperwork and additional processing since the fines are seldom paid (Beckett and Herbert 2009; O'Grady, Gaetz, and Buccieri, 2011; King and Dunn 2004)—or the use of police dumping under the EPS's policy for the transport of adult inebriates. The pressure to do something about the visibly homeless, combined with the limits of effective tools to deal with homelessness, results in significant frustration for front-line officers (Beckett and Herbert 2009). One of the officers involved in the sweatbox incident described his conundrum as follows: "Yeah, I could just leave them [the homeless] where they are and then let the stakeholders continue to complain about them, but then I'm looked at doing neglective [*sic*] duty, so the choice really is...neglect our duty or to find a solution. And this is a community problem that has been placed upon us and we are the ones to blame, but nobody gives us the right options.... [W]e're the ones that are left with no choice" (EPS 2010a, 23).

Faced with limited tools and continual demands from powerful "stakeholders," officers often choose police transports as the most expedient and efficient way to deal with complaints (Beckett and Herbert 2009; Comack 2012; King and Dunn 2004). It is troubling that police would see the primary "stakeholders" they are responsible to as being business leaders and not other members of the community, including the homeless. Nevertheless, given these pressures, it is perhaps understandable that for some officers the decision to either instigate the arduous process of ushering the homeless through the criminal justice system, via the issuance of tickets, or engage in police dumping to inner-city shelters appears as "no choice" at all. Moving the street-involved into less desirable spaces relays the message to the business actors, who constitute the visibly homeless as a problem, that the police are doing something. It is easier to displace the homeless than it is to solve homelessness (Beckett and Herbert 2009).

That these police transports most often drop the homeless off in the dangerous inner-city McCauley-Boyle region is also not entirely in the control of officers and is partly a product of Edmonton's pre-existing urban design and ongoing redevelopment agendas. Specifically, the concentration of social services and poverty in the McCauley-Boyle region and the city administration's drive to constitute larger sections of Old Strathcona and Downtown as bastions of consumption help split the city into two symbiotic parts. Areas of consumption and leisure are being fashioned to attract footloose capital and consumers; yet doing so requires the expulsion of visible reminders of poverty that undercut the excitement of unbound recreation and spending (Mitchell 2003). Those persons unable to uphold the celebrated image of consumption are shunted into marginalized spaces where they remain hidden from the consciousness of the privileged (Martin 2002; Mosher 2002). The consequence is that officers seeking to remove the homeless from consumer spaces, or even genuinely hoping to help them by linking them with social services, have few options as to where to place them. The McCauley-Boyle region is the area that has already been designated as the appropriate receptacle for the marginalized (Hogeveen and Freistadt 2013).

However, while the reasons for police dumping to the McCauley-Boyle inner city might be understandable from the perspective of officers, the dangers of casting the homeless into inner-city spaces are real. Moreover, the reasons this practice is so highly racialized require further consideration. In this vein, it is pertinent to note that police officers draw on the cultural frames of reference available to them when they complete their work (Comack 2012). Samuelson and Monture-Angus (2002), as well as Razack (2002a, 2002b), remind readers that stereotypes perpetuated by colonial processes continue to encourage many non-Indigenous persons to conceive Indigenous persons as lazy, drunk, disorderly, criminal, and dangerous. Sadly, many individuals continue to equate Indigenous persons (especially marginalized Indigenous persons, like women and the homeless) with these characteristics and therefore see them as most appropriately belonging in spaces of danger and disorder (Razack 2002a, 2002b).

These negative stereotypes about Indigenousness help justify the police displacement and confinement of Indigenous persons to marginalized spaces rife with poverty, drinking, and crime. Darlene and Keith's story, for example, reveals how police simply "started accusing [them] of panhandling and drinking" even though "that wasn't what was going on." Assuming the two are intoxicated allows the police to quickly remove them from Whyte Avenue and take them to the inner city. This stereotype of the "drunken Indian" (Comack and Balfour 2004) also comes to the fore in the investigation of the sweatbox incident. The presenting officer in the investigation notes that according to the testimonies of the officers and homeless persons involved, "many of the people that were picked up were not intoxicated" (EPS 2010a, 30), but he then assumes repeatedly that all nine Indigenous persons placed in the van must have been "in various states of intoxication" (EPS 2010a, 31). Similarly, the defence counsel for the officers involved and the presiding officer hearing the case continually stressed that some of the persons involved in the transport were "chronic alcoholics and substance abusers" (EPS 2010a, 38). Assuming that Indigenous homeless persons are inebriates allows the EPS to dodge questions about unlawful confinement and defer to the EPS-approved policy concerning the transport of intoxicated adults. The standard operation procedures of the EPS are thus racialized, insofar as they help tether Indigenous homeless persons to the spaces into which police usher them whether they are drunk or not. In particular, the dangerous and disorderly McCauley-Boyle area, where street drinking is plainly visible (Bouw 1997; Gelinas 2008), appears as a legitimate container for marginalized Indigenous persons who are racialized in ways that reproduce the stereotype of the "drunken Indian" (Comack and Balfour 2004).

Adding to the apparent grafting of Indigenousness onto dangerous spaces like the McCauley-Boyle area is the fact that these districts are also being explicitly crafted into Indigenous spaces. The McCauley and Boyle Street neighbourhoods are home to many racialized groups and encompass Edmonton's Chinatown and Little Italy, but the communities contain a vastly disproportionate number of the city's Indigenous population. Although only 5 percent of housed Edmontonians listed Aboriginal as part of their heritage in the 2006 Census, the percentage of census respondents who identified with these backgrounds in the McCauley and Boyle Street neighbourhoods were 11 and 8 percent, respectively (City of Edmonton 2006a, 2006b). Moreover, the disadvantaged region's designation as a space of Indigenousness is growing. Many of the low-income units and social service spaces being built as part of the Boyle Renaissance are reserved for Indigenous clients and organizations. Additionally, the middle of the Boyle Renaissance redevelopment will feature an urban park that is inspired by Indigenous symbols and will have a designated "Aboriginal quadrant" with a "First Nations Welcoming Centre" (McKay, Finnigan, and Associates 2010, n.p.).

The construct of the McCauley-Boyle area as a space of dangerousness, disadvantage, and Indigenousness helps to justify the displacement of homeless Indigenous persons to the region. The area has already been constituted as a space of Indigenousness through urban planning and through socio-economic processes that concentrate poverty and specific racial identities in the inner city. Thus, in contrast to drop offs (like the sweatbox incident) that involve more affluent communities where Indigenous persons are less concentrated, these displacements are unlikely to generate further demands for police action given that Indigenousness and homelessness are already normalized features of the streetscape. The constitution of dangerous inner-city spaces as spaces of Indigenousness shapes police practices of dumping Indigenous homeless persons outside of shelters in the region. Simultaneously, however, the racial-ized police practice of dumping perpetuates the racialization of space and its attendant racial hierarchies. The repeated displacement of Indigenous homeless persons to the McCauley-Boyle reinforces the ties that these spaces have to Indigenousness while concurrently helping to establish the consumer spaces of Old Strathcona and Downtown as ideally white spaces.

Indeed, the construction of consumer spaces like Whyte Avenue as white spaces and dangerous spaces like the McCauley-Boyle "north-side" as Indigenous spaces was apparent to several white homeless persons that police permitted to stay in Old Strathcona. For example, Dan, a white recycler who worked the alleys behind Whyte Avenue, demonstrated how he—and the EPS—tied Indigenousness to crime and dangerous "north-side" space. He declared:

> Yeah, we [his street associates who are white bottle pickers] are probably some of the better guys in Edmonton. On the south side, you don't get the rowdies. But we are becoming a minority now. We are getting taken over by the Natives. There is getting to be too many of them.... They are gonna form a union and take over our routes.... I have informed the police already of it and told them what is coming down. They said, "Don't worry about it, we know who all the north-side guys are, and if we see too many of them over here causing problems, we will send them back where they come from...." They know we don't hurt anybody. We don't break into peoples' garages and stuff like that. But those people will, I know they will.

Despite the fact that many of the Indigenous people Dan referred to lived on the south-side, Dan labelled all Indigenous homeless persons as "north-side guys" and blamed them for most of the problems in the Old Strathcona neighbourhood. To him, "those people" resorted to crime, unjustifiably invaded his bottle-picking territory, and did not belong in his neighbourhood. He had good relationships with local police officers and when he expressed concern to them about the "Natives" they too apparently felt these Indigenous homeless persons did not belong in Old Strathcona and promised to "send them back where they came from." The inner-city space of McCauley-Boyle was, according to the police and Dan, a space of Indigenousness, and Indigenous homeless persons were criminals who belonged in that dangerous and crime-ridden space. Meanwhile, the prime spaces of Old Strathcona and Whyte Avenue were ideally white spaces and any ills within these spaces were apparently caused by Indigenous outsiders.

Dan's comments suggest that Indigenous homeless persons in consumer spaces, by being both poor and having a racialized identity, threaten the white domination of these spaces and so face greater chances of being "dumped" by police into dangerous, crime-ridden inner-city areas that allegedly reflect their assumed characteristics. This clearly demonstrates how police dumping further racializes already-racialized consumer spaces and inner-city spaces. The racialized practice of police dumping thus both reflects the already-existing racialization of space and helps solidify the racial boundaries of these spaces. In so doing, it underlines Razack's (2002a) observation that race and space are central to policing and that racialized policing reproduces a long-standing hierarchy in which white persons can more easily enjoy, and exist within, prime consumer spaces, while Indigenous persons are confined to dangerous and marginalized spaces. Confining homeless persons, especially Indigenous homeless persons, to inner-city spaces allows prime consumer spaces to be represented as devoid of poverty, inequality, and racism without having to address the underlying causes of these issues. Accordingly, the status quo of consumption, investment, and white ownership in consumer spaces can continue unabated.

Among the many problems of this racialized police dumping is that it denies the legitimate claims Indigenous homeless persons have to white consumer spaces. Interview respondents strongly identified areas like Old Strathcona's Whyte Avenue and Downtown's Jasper Avenue as their home. For instance, when asked what he considered his home, Keith replied, "Right here, Jasper Avenue." Although Keith was an Indigenous man without shelter and slept in alleyways Downtown, he viewed his home, as many homeless persons do (Beckett and Herbert 2009; Mayers 2001; Pratt, Gau, and Franklin 2011; Tanner 2009), as the space in which he struggled to meet his daily needs. He relied on the familiar pattern of office workers going to and from work to sell his newspapers at prominent intersections along Jasper Avenue. He claimed a niche in a local alleyway as his own spot, referring to it possessively as "[his] cubbyhole"—a sort of semi-private bedroom where he was hidden from view within his Downtown home. Repeatedly removing homeless persons like Keith from consumer areas denies that they have already established these spaces as home. It suggests that they do not, or should not, live there and constitutes these spaces as devoid of inhabitants in ways that allow redevelopment plans aimed at consumption and leisure to unfold uncontested (Beckett and Herbert 2009; Hayward 2004).

Of course, denying the legitimate claims Indigenous persons have to desirable spaces is not new. Police dumping must therefore be further situated beyond the actions of individual officers and alongside historical colonial controls used to affirm white ownership of prime spaces. Just as colonial administrators claimed that the lands in which Indigenous persons lived were a *terra nullius* or "empty land" in order to support arguments that white settlers could claim these lands as their own (Goldberg 1993; Mawani 2005; Razack 2002b), police dumping removes Indigenous homeless persons from the desirable spaces in which they live so that new capitalist developments can lay claim to these spaces. Furthermore, the constant transport of Indigenous homeless persons to inner-city spaces attempts to confine Indigenousness to marginalized spaces of danger in ways somewhat reminiscent of how Canadian colonists set aside lands for Indigenous settlement and then guarded entry and exit from these reserve lands through white Indian agents and the pass system (Goldberg 1993; Lawrence 2002; Mawani 2005; Razack 2002a, 2002b; Samuelson and Monture-Angus 2002). Indeed, when Indigenous homeless persons refuse to remain in marginalized spaces, police agents quickly send them back to the McCauley-Boyle inner city. Consequently, Indigenous homeless persons struggle to achieve a sense of permanent home and belonging within spaces set aside for consumer capitalism. Constantly escorting Indigenous homeless persons out of consumer spaces ensures that if they want to settle in city spaces, they can do so only in the inner-city spaces *reserved* for them.

The Challenges a Lens of Racialized Policing Brings into View

The long-standing role that policing plays in perpetuating racial inequalities and grafting racial hierarchies onto particular geographies becomes apparent once we look beyond individual officers' potential prejudice and instead focus on and contextualize the experiences of those subject to this policing. This broader view shows that race is, indeed, an important consideration when examining the relationship between homeless persons and state institutions of control. Moreover, foregrounding the experiences of those subject to the racialized practice of police dumping challenges existing police policy that unquestioningly encourages officers to transport homeless adults to inner-city spaces. Indeed, interviews with homeless individuals reveal that police dumping to inner-city shelters reflects and reinforces racial hierarchies that constitute prime consumer spaces as white spaces and marginalized spaces as spaces of Indigenousness. The stories of interview participants clearly show that Indigenous homeless persons have been more readily ushered into dangerous settings through police dumping.

Analyzing the policing of homelessness through a lens of racialized policing—wherein policing is understood as both unfolding in a context of existing racial inequalities and as a practice that helps produce these inequalities—demonstrates the limits of searching for and sanctioning individual racial prejudice among officers. Rather, this view demands consideration of the systemic racism found in the concentration of Indigenousness in inner cities, in wider cultural beliefs about Indigenous persons and the spaces they ought to inhabit, and in ongoing colonial processes that constitute prime spaces as devoid of legitimate Indigenous claims and so available for white settlement.

These considerations do not completely dissolve the importance of attending to the actions of individual officers, but they do highlight that attending to the disadvantages Indigenous homeless persons face requires acknowledging the larger racialized and colonial conditions that policing both reflects and reinforces. As in the investigation of the sweatbox incident, many police agencies have concentrated on implementing individual cultural sensitivity training or have focused on trying to root out officers who hold racial prejudice (Comack 2012; Green 2006). The larger view of policing as racialized, however, shows that we must also confront the damaging ways in which Indigenous persons are perceived as dangerous and disorderly and, as a consequence, are seen to fit more readily in spaces with similar characteristics. The normalized practice of police dumping through which Indigenous homeless persons are escorted to such spaces must be questioned. The EPS policy of transporting homeless persons to shelters without assessing their true sobriety and without considering their preferences to remain in public spaces must cease. These transport policies will continue to contribute to racial inequalities and racialized spaces so long as Indigenous persons continue to be unfairly constructed as disorderly drunkards and so long as addiction and homelessness disproportionately affect Indigenous persons.

At the same time, the urban planning processes that concentrate Indigenous persons in marginalized inner-city spaces and so legitimize Edmonton's racialized police dumping must be challenged. In this context, the constitution of prime spaces as white spaces and the ongoing redevelopment of city spaces in ways that exacerbate racial and class inequalities cannot continue unquestioned. Of course, identity groups ought to have their own spaces to celebrate their differences. Such spaces, however, ought to be spread throughout the city, should not relegate certain people to dangerous areas, and must not reinforce negative stereotypes of any group. The ongoing efforts of many inner-city residents to turn their communities into safer and less stigmatized spaces must receive the same level of support as efforts to redevelop consumer spaces. Urban development must enable the creation of neighbourhoods of diversity and inclusion rather than the continued bifurcation of city spaces.

The recommendations that follow from adopting a view of policing as racialized highlight the weighty challenges that face those who wish to address detrimental state responses to Indigenous homelessness. The complexity of the issue defies simple answers. It is certain, however, that race is an important consideration in police interactions with the homeless. Considerations of the importance of Indigenousness should not be simply swept under the rug by framing concerns about race in terms of individual prejudice. Rather, a view of policing as racialized is required. Such a view brings into sight different systemic forms of racism and the social, spatial, and colonial contexts through which racial inequalities and their geographies both shape, and are shaped by, policing. Understanding these contexts and identifying how the policing of homelessness is racialized further highlights that addressing Indigenous homelessness is primarily a social justice issue, and not simply a criminal-justice problem.

Notes

1   Adopting King and Dunn's (2004) term "dumping" is not intended to reify the notion that homeless persons are waste, but to highlight how the homeless are constituted as waste by some authority figures and to underline the discourses of "civic sanitation" that apparently operate through these transportations (see Berti and Sommers 2010; Collins and Blomley 2003; Feldman 2004; Mitchell 1997, 2003; Mosher 2002).

2   "Street-involved" refers to persons who are absolutely homeless or persons who might have housing but continue to spend significant amounts of time on the street engaging in activities like panhandling.

3   All participants have been assigned pseudonyms.

References

Beckett, Katherine, and Steve Herbert. 2009. *Banished: The New Social Control in Urban America*. Oxford: Oxford University Press.

Belanger, Yale D., Gabrielle Weasel Head, and Olu Awosoga. 2012. *Assessing Urban Aboriginal Housing and Homelessness in Canada*. Ottawa: National Association of Friendship Centres and the Office of the Federal Interlocutor for Métis and Non-Status Indians.

Berti, Mario, and Jeff Sommers. 2010. "'The Streets Belong to People that Pay for Them': The Spatial Regulation of Street Poverty in Vancouver, British Columbia." In *Poverty, Regulation and Social Justice: Readings on the Criminalization of Poverty*, edited by Diane Crocker and Val Johnson, 60–74. Halifax: Fernwood.

Blackburn, Daniel G. 2000. "Why Race Is Not a Biological Concept." In *Race and Racism in Theory and Practice*, edited by Barry Lang, 3–16. New York: Rowman and Littlefield Publishers.

Block, Sheila, and Grace-Edward Galabuzi. 2011. *Canada's Colour Coded Labour Market: The Gap for Racialized Workers*. Ottawa: Canadian Centre for Policy Alternatives.

Blomley, Nicholas. 2007. "How to Turn a Beggar into a Bus Stop: Law, Traffic and the 'Function of the Place.'" *Urban Studies* 44 (9): 1697.

_____. 2011. *Rights of Passage: Sidewalks and the Regulation of Public Flow*. New York: Routledge.

Bouw, Brenda. 1997. "These Alcoholics Aren't Going Away." *Edmonton Journal*, 11 May.

City of Edmonton. 2006a. *Boyle Street: Neighbourhood Profile*. Edmonton: City of Edmonton.

_____. 2006b. *McCauley: Neighbourhood Profile*. Edmonton. City of Edmonton.

_____. 2010a. *Boyle Street Neighbourhood Indicators*. Edmonton: City of Edmonton.

_____. 2010b. *Capital City Downtown Plan*. Edmonton: City of Edmonton.

_____. 2010c. *McCauley Neighbourhood Indicators*. Edmonton: City of Edmonton.

_____. 2011. *Strathcona Area Redevelopment Plan*. Edmonton: City of Edmonton.

Collins, Damian, and Nicholas Blomley. 2003. "Private Needs and Public Space: Politics, Poverty, and Anti-Panhandling By-Laws in Canadian Cities." In *New Perspectives on the Public-Private Divide*, edited by Law Commission of Canada, 40–67. Vancouver: UBC Press.

Comack, Elizabeth. 2012. *Racialized Policing: Aboriginal People's Encounters with the Police.* Halifax: Fernwood.

Comack, Elizabeth, and Gillian Balfour. 2004. *The Power to Criminalize: Violence, Inequality and the Law.* Halifax: Fernwood.

Duneier, Mitchell. 2001. *Sidewalk.* Photographs by Ovie Carter and foreword by Hakim Hasan. New York: Farrar, Straus and Giroux.

"Edmonton Police Guilty in 'Sweatbox' Case: Presiding Officer Finds Constables' Actions Not Racially Motivated." 2010. *CBC News Online,* 5 November. http://www.cbc.ca/news /canada/edmonton/edmonton-police-guilty-in-sweatbox-case-1.901510.

EPS (Edmonton Police Service). 2010a. *Decision.* Edmonton: Edmonton Police Service. Obtained through freedom of information request and on file with the author.

_____. 2010b. *Penalty Decision.* Edmonton: Edmonton Police Service. Obtained through freedom of information request and on file with the author.

Edmonton Social Planning Council. 2011. *Tracking the Trends: Edmonton's Increasing Diversity.* Edmonton: Edmonton Social Planning Council.

Elanik, Dave. 2009. *Public Safety Concerns Related to Panhandling.* Edmonton: Edmonton Police Service. http://webdocs.edmonton.ca/OcctopusDocs/Public/Complete /Reports/CC/CSAM/2009-02-04/2009PCS2006 Attach 1.doc. (accessed 8 February 2011).

Ellickson, Robert. 1996. "Controlling Chronic Misconduct in City Spaces: Of Panhandlers, Skid Rows and Public-Space Zoning." *The Yale Law Journal* 105 (5): 1165–1248.

Environics Institute. 2010. *Urban Aboriginal Peoples Study: Edmonton Report.* Toronto: Environics Institute.

Ericson, Richard V. 1982. *Reproducing Order: A Study of Police Patrol Work.* Toronto: University of Toronto Press.

Feldman, Leonard C. 2004. *Citizens without Shelter: Homelessness, Democracy, and Political Exclusion.* Ithaca: Cornell University Press.

Filipski, Gerald. 2001. "Little Plots of Earth Grow Communities as well as Food." *Edmonton Journal,* 19 April.

Gaetz, Stephen. 2004. "Safe Streets for Whom? Homeless Youth, Social Exclusion, and Criminal Victimization." *Canadian Journal of Criminology and Criminal Justice* 46 (4): 423–55.

Gelinas, Ben. 2008. "Disorder Sparks Crackdown: Police to Increase Presence in North-Central Neighbourhood of Boyle-McCauley." *Edmonton Journal,* 15 May.

Goldberg, David Theo. 1993. *Racist Culture: Philosophy and the Politics of Meaning.* Malden, Massachusetts: Blackwell.

Gordon, Todd. 2006. *Cops, Crime and Capitalism: The Law and Order Agenda in Canada.* Halifax: Fernwood.

_____. 2010. "Understanding the Role of Law-and-Order Policies in Canadian Cities," In *Poverty, Regulation & Social Justice: Readings on the Criminalization of Poverty,* edited by Diane Crocker and Val Marie Johnson, 33–42. Halifax: Fernwood.

Green, Joyce. 2006. "From *Stonechild* to Social Cohesion: Anti-Racist Challenges for Saskatchewan." *Canadian Journal of Political Science* 39 (3): 507–27.

Hayward, Keith. 2004. *City Limits: Crime, Consumer Culture and the Urban Experience.* London: GlassHouse Press.

Herbert, Steve, and Elizabeth Brown. 2006. "Conceptions of Space and Crime in the Punitive Neoliberal City." *Antipode* 38 (4): 755–77.

Hermer, Joe and Janet Mosher. 2002. "Introduction." In *Disorderly People: Law and the Politics of Exclusion in Ontario*, edited by Joe Hermer and Janet Mosher. Halifax: Fernwood.

Ho, Clara. 2010. "Edmonton Wants Task Force to Deal with Panhandlers." *Edmonton Sun Online*, 15 April 2010, http://www.edmontonsun.com/news/edmonton/2010 /04/15/13600786.html.

Hogeveen, Bryan, and Joshua Freistadt. "Hospitality and the Homeless: Jacques Derrida in the Neoliberal City." *Journal of Theoretical and Philosophical Criminology* 5 (1): 39–63.

Hulchanski, J. David, Philippa Campsie, Shirley B.Y. Chau, Stephen W. Hwang and Emily Paradis. 2009. "Homelessness: What is in a word?" In *Finding Home: Policy Options for Addressing Homelessness in Canada*, edited by J. David Hulchanski, Philippa Campsie, Shirley B.Y. Chau, Stephen W. Hwang and Emily Paradis. Toronto: Cities Centre Press.

James, Carl. 2002. "'Armed and Dangerous': Racializing Suspects, Suspecting Race." In *Marginality and Condemnation*, edited by Bernard Schissel and Carolyn Brooks. Halifax: Fernwood.

Kent, Gordon. 2009. "Housing plan 'against the grain.'" *Edmonton Journal*, 15 January.

_____. 2010. "Boyle Street Begins Renaissance: 550 Units of Social Housing Slated for Downtown Project." *Edmonton Journal*, 25 November.

King, William R, and Thomas M. Dunn. 2004. "Dumping: Police-Initiated Transjurisdictional Transport of Troublesome Persons." *Police Quarterly* 7 (3): 339–58.

Kleiss, Karen. 2010 "Housing Dollars Fuel Social Chaos, Residents." *Edmonton Journal*, 11 October.

La Prairie, Carol. 2002. "Aboriginal Over-Representation in the Criminal Justice System: A Tale of Nine Cities." *Canadian Journal of Criminology and Criminal Justice* 44 (2): 181–208.

Larson, Jackie L. 2011. "Aggressive Panhandling Still Common Despite Bylaw." *Edmonton Sun Online*, 13 October, http://www.edmontonsun.com/2011/10/13 /aggressive-panhandling-still-common-despite-bylaw.

Lawrence, Bonita. 2002. "Rewriting Histories of the Land: Colonization and Indigenous Resistance in Eastern Canada." In *Race, Space and the Law: Unmapping a White Settler Society,* edited by Sherene H. Razack, 21–46. Toronto: Between the Lines.

Lenon, Suzanne. 2000. "Living on the Edge: Women, Poverty and Homelessness in Canada," *Canadian Women Studies* 20 (3): 123–26.

Loyie, Florence. 1997. "Waking Up the Neighbourhood: Former Hawaii Cop Helped Take McCauley Back from Pushers, Prostitutes." *Edmonton Journal*, 5 October.

Martin, Dianne. 2002. "Demonizing Youth, Marketing Fear: The New Politics of Crime." In *Disorderly People: Law and the Politics of Exclusion in Ontario*, edited by Joe Hermer and Janet Mosher, 91–104. Halifax: Fernwood.

Mawani, Renisa. 2012. "Racial Violence and the Cosmopolitan City." *Environment and Planning D: Society and Space* 30 (6): 1083–1102.

———. 2005. "Genealogies of the Land: Aboriginality, Law, and Territory in Vancouver's Stanley Park." *Social and Legal Studies* 14 (3): 315–39.

———. 2002. "'The Iniquitous Practice of Women': Prostitution and the Making of White Spaces in British Columbia, 1898–1905." In *Working through Whiteness: International Perspectives*, edited by Cynthia Levine-Rasky, 43–68. Albany: State University of New York.

Mawani, Renisa, and David Sealy. 2011. "On Postcolonialism and Criminology." In *Criminology: Critical Canadian Perspectives*, edited by Kirsten Kramar, 159–72. Toronto: Pearson.

Mayers, Marjorie. 2001. *Street Kids and Streetscapes: Panhandling, Politics, and Prophecies.* New York: Peter Lang Publishing.

McKay, Finnigan, and Associates for the City of Edmonton. 2010. *Final Report of the Boyle Renaissance Advisory Committee II.* Edmonton: McKay, Finnigan and Associates.

McNeil, Claire. 2010. "Homeless in Halifax: The Criminal Justice System Takes Aim at the Poor." In *Poverty, Regulation & Social Justice: Readings on the Criminalization of Poverty,* edited by Diane Crocker and Val Marie Johnson, 150–162. Halifax: Fernwood.

Mitchell, Don. 1997. "The Annihilation of Space by Law: The Roots and Implications of Anti-Homeless Laws in the United States." *Antipode* 29 (1): 303–35.

———. 2003. *The Right to the City: Social Justice and the Fight for Public Space.* New York: Guilford Press.

Mosher, Janet. 2002. "The Shrinkage of the Public and Private Spaces of the Poor." In *Disorderly People: Law and the Politics of Exclusion in Ontario,* edited by Joe Hermer and Janet Mosher, 37–53 . Halifax: Fernwood.

Nettelback, Amanda, and Russell Smandych. 2010. "Policing Indigenous Peoples on Two Colonial Frontiers: Australia's Mounted Police and Canada's North West Mounted Police." *Australia and New Zealand Journal of Criminology* 43 (2): 356–75.

O'Donnell, Sarah. 2012. "Melcor Backs YMCA's Affordable Housing Initiative." *Edmonton Journal Online*, 17 April, http://www.edmontonjournal.com/business/Melcor +backs+YMCA+affordable+housing+initiative/6475317/story.html (accessed 30 April 2012).

O'Grady, Bill, Stephen Gaetz, and Kristy Buccieri. 2011. *Can I See Your ID? The Policing of Youth Homelessness in Toronto.* Toronto: Justice for Children and Youth and the Homeless Hub.

Parnaby, Patrick. 2003. "Disaster through Dirty Windshields: Law, Order and Toronto's Squeegee Kids." *Canadian Journal of Sociology* 29 (3): 281–307.

Pierse, Conal. 2010. "Edmonton Police Had Hotline to Roust Homeless: Transportation to Shelters Preferred Option to Arresting Intoxicated Vagrants, Hearing Told." *Edmonton Journal*, 16 June.

Pratt, Travis, Jacinta Gau, and Travis Franklin. 2011. "Key Idea: The Police Can Control Crime." In *Key Ideas in Criminology and Criminal Justice*, edited by Travis Pratt, Jacinta Gau, and Travis Franklin, 103–20. Thousand Oaks, CA: Sage.

Razack, Sherene. 2002a. "Gendered Racial Violence and Spatialized Justice: The Murder of Pamela George." In *Race, Space and the Law: Unmapping a White Settler Society*, edited by Sherene Razack, 121–56. Toronto: Between the Lines.

_____. 2002b. "Introduction: When Place Becomes Race." In *Race, Space and the Law: Unmapping a White Settler Society*, edited by Sherene Razack, 1–22. Toronto: Between the Lines.

Reber, Susanne, and Robert Renaud. 2005. *Starlight Tour: The Last, Lonely Night of Neil Stonechild*. Toronto: Random House.

Retson, Don. 1998. "In League to Keep Their Neighbourhood Thriving; Boyle Street in Brief." *Edmonton Journal*, 21 July.

Rusnell, Charles. 2007. "'It Sure as Hell Happened to Me.'" *Edmonton Journal*, 2 February.

Samuelson, Les, and Patricia Monture-Angus. 2002. "Aboriginal People and Social Control: The State, Law, and 'Policing.'" In *Marginality and Condemnation*, edited by Carolyn Brooks and Bernard Schissel. Halifax: Fernwood.

Sands, Andrea. 2010. "Edmonton Police Officers Found Guilty in Homeless Roundup: Two of Three Constables Charged Found Guilty." *Edmonton Journal Online*, 6 November. http://www.edmontonjournal.com/news/Edmonton+police+officers +found+guilty+homeless+roundup/3784388/story.html (accessed 15 November 2011).

Schafer, Arthur. 1998. *Down and Out in Winnipeg and Toronto: The Ethics of Legislating Against Panhandling*. Ottawa: Caledon Institute of Social Policy.

_____. 2007. *The Expressive Liberty of Beggars: Why It Matters to Them, and to Us*. Ottawa: Canadian Centre for Policy Alternatives.

Simons, Paula. 2007. "So Maybe You're Not Outraged by the Catch and Release of Street People." *Edmonton Journal*, 3 February.

Tanner, Julian. 2009. *Teenage Troubles: Youth and Deviance in Canada*. Oxford: Oxford, 2009.

Warnica, Richard. 2010. "Witness Recounts Drop-Off of Homeless in Balwin." *Edmonton Journal*, 17 June.

Wittmeier, Brent. 2010. "Two Cops Suspended and Fined: Place Group of Homeless in Hot Van." *Edmonton Journal Online*, 20 December. http://www.edmonton-journal.com/news/Edmonton+cops+suspended+fined/4005542/story.html (accessed 4 January 2011).

Wright, David H. 2004. *Report of the Commission of Inquiry into Matters Relating to the Death of Neil Stonechild*. Regina: Government of Saskatchewan.

CHAPTER 5

Indigenous and Non-Indigenous Respondents to the *Health and Housing in Transition (HHiT) Study*: An Intersectional Approach

FRAN KLODAWSKY, REBECCA CHERNER, TIM AUBRY, SUSAN FARRELL, JULIE PARRELL, AND BARBARA A. SMITH

As noted in this section's opening essay, scholarship has begun to identify Indigenous-specific[1] pathways and experiences in relation to housing and homelessness in urban centres (Belanger, Awosoga, and Weasel Head 2013; Belanger, Weasel Head, and Awosoga 2012, 2011; Freistadt, this volume; Menzies 2009; Peters and Robillard 2009; Peters 2012; Thurston, Turner, and Bird, this volume). Belanger and co-authors (2011) drew on Statistics Canada data to examine "the current state of urban Aboriginal housing in Canada" (iv), shedding new light on the extent to which home ownership had impacts on core housing need among various Indigenous groups. They also explored gaps between Indigenous and non-Indigenous households with the former reporting levels of core housing need that were significantly higher than those of the latter (20.4 percent as opposed to 12.7 percent). In another recent publication, Belanger, Awosoga, and Weasel Head estimated that "more than one in fifteen urban Aboriginal people are homeless, compared to one out of 128 non-Native Canadians...[and that] urban Aboriginal people are more than eight times likely to be or become homeless than non-Native urban individuals" (2013, 14). They also acknowledged the particular and challenging circumstances faced by many Indigenous women and girls who they recognize as having been particularly "disadvantaged by social factors and structural inequalities" (2013, 20).

The recent Homeless Hub publication, *The State of Homelessness in Canada in 2013* (Gaetz et al. 2013), has highlighted the ground breaking research of such scholars, for providing "the historical, social and economic context in which [Indigenous homelessness] has emerged" (3). Importantly, the report reinforced Belanger and co-authors' (2011) findings as well as acknowledging the overrepresentation of homeless Indigenous peoples in urban areas. The document also recognized that addressing the "historical, experiential and cultural differences, as well as experiences of colonization and racism" is fundamental, and that "Aboriginal peoples must be part of any solutions to homelessness" (Gaetz et al. 2013, 7).

The objective of this paper is to contribute to and provide further insights about the specific health and housing situations of Indigenous peoples who have been homeless or vulnerably housed, in comparison to non-Indigenous Canadians in similar circumstances. Our goal is to assess whether quantitative survey data about a "general" representative sample of homeless and vulnerably housed adults in three Canadian cities is able to provide insights into the following question: Among an already marginalized population of homeless and vulnerably housed adults, does Indigenous identity impact health and housing outcomes? We ask this question while fully acknowledging that "the urban Aboriginal homeless experience differs from that of mainstream Canadians due to a convoluted policy environment predicated on assumptions of cultural inferiority and forced societal participation.... An additional aggravating factor is the connection...to colonization" (Belanger, Awosoga, and Weasel Head 2013, 15).

Our exploration of the links between complex social identities, health, and homelessness has been inspired by recent discussions about how best to incorporate intersectionality into empirical studies (Scott and Siltanen 2012; Veenstra 2011, 2013). Although Canadian researchers have greatly expanded the array of topics and groups under their purview, only a few studies have attempted to examine social identities in ways that reflect peoples' complex realities and acknowledge that gender, race/ethnicity, and class are not additive or independent characteristics but are integrally implicated in each person's life chances and circumstances. Intersectionality is a concept that promotes such recognition and encourages analysis that addresses social inequalities by looking beyond broad and often misleading categories. As Hankivsky and colleagues (2010) have noted in the area of women and health:

> the traditional foci of Canadian health research on women tends
> to essentialize the category of women (that is, assumes that all

women, regardless of age, cultural background, geographic location, socio-economic status, religion, sexual orientation and other categories of difference), share exactly the same experiences, views, and priorities, and further, gives too much primacy to gender over other key determinants and does not adequately address the interactions among all determinants of health. Consequently, the issues and priorities of many vulnerable women, including members of ethnic, racial and linguistic minorities, Aboriginal women, low-income women, lesbians, and women with disabilities are usually excluded from mainstream women's health research (1).

The concept of intersectionality was articulated in the 1990s by Kimberle Crenshaw in the context of black women's experiences of both racism and sexism in the American legal system (1991). Since that time, its theoretical and methodological implications have been the focus of growing interest among feminist and other social science scholars. Although most of intersectionality analysis has been in the context of relatively small-scale, in-depth qualitative studies (Scott and Siltanen 2012), scholarship that draws on large scale, quantitative data sets is a growing trend.

Few scholars have used an intersectional lens to examine the interactions between housing and homelessness, health, and complex social identities, but the studies that have used this approach have yielded insightful albeit sometimes contradictory results. Benoit, Carroll, and Chaudhry (2003) explored the reflections of marginalized Indigenous women in Vancouver's Downtown Eastside and concluded that various efforts to provide appropriate health care services to these women had not been successful. Thurston, Soo, and Turner (2013), among other characteristics, compared the health conditions of Indigenous and non-Indigenous homeless individuals in Calgary, and found no statistically significant differences regarding the majority of health conditions except substance abuse. They found Indigenous respondents were more likely to report this as an issue than their non-Indigenous peers. In this volume, Thurston and co-authors highlight the extent to which homeless Indigenous women in Calgary are "overrepresented among the homeless served by the domestic violence sector" (150). Monette and co-researchers (2011) examined longitudinal data collected in Ontario through the *Positive Spaces, Healthy Places* study and concluded that "compared to Caucasian participants living with [Human Immunodeficiency Virus] HIV, Aboriginal participants were more likely to be younger, female or transgender women, less educated, unemployed, and homeless or unstably housed. They were also more likely to have low incomes and to have experienced housing-related discrimination" (215). Also drawing on data from *Positive Spaces, Healthy Places,* Greene and co-authors (2013) investigated the housing experiences of African and Caribbean mothers with HIV. They demonstrated that this group of women "have intersecting identities that result in multiple sites of marginalization and oppression and that this can have a detrimental impact on their housing experiences… [and that] policy interventions need to take such insights into account in how services are coordinated and delivered" (130). Mair (2010) explored the intersections between "race" (Black/White), social ties, and depression for older American adults, using the most recent Health and Retirement study. She concluded that "[there were] pronounced differences between Black women's and White women's friend and kin ties…[noted] the potential vulnerability of older Black men…[and] highlight[ed] the importance of catering community-based elder care support towards diverse aging populations" (667). Benbow, Forchuk, and Ray (2011) examined "the structural forces shaping the health of mothers with mental illness experiencing homelessness as well as their individual acts to overcome existing barriers" (687). They found the "complex and compounding nature of social locations as intersecting sites of discrimination" (2011, 692) and considered their implications for nursing practice. Marshall and co-authors (2008) explored the prevalence of HIV and associated risk factors in street-involved Indigenous and non-Indigenous youth in Vancouver. Unfortunately, other than the first five studies listed above, we were unable to identify other studies that examined links between Indigenous health and housing or homelessness using an intersectional lens.

The absence of additional literature relating health to housing is a noteworthy gap, especially given the numerous Canadian studies that focus on Indigenous health (Bombak and Bruce 2012; Lix, Metge, and Leslie 2009; Senese and Wilson 2013; Gionet and Roshanafshar 2013; Snyder and Wilson 2012; Tjepkema 2002; Veenstra 2009, 2011; Wilson, Rosenberg, and Abonyi 2011). A few of these studies have adopted an intersectional approach, including Veenstra (2009) who found that when socio-demographic variables and health behaviours were accounted for, the odds of Indigenous Canadians reporting poor health outcomes compared to non-Indigenous Canadians was reduced, although the odds of poor health were still greater for the Indigenous group. Similarly, Tjepkema (2002) noted that when Indigenous and non-Indigenous Canadians with high incomes were compared, they had similar numbers of chronic conditions, whereas Indigenous people with low- and middle-income households had more chronic conditions that other Canadians with similar incomes. Socio-economic status has also been found to account for some of the risk of diabetes and poor health ratings for Indigenous people (Veenstra 2009). In their examination of data drawn from rural and urban settings in Manitoba, Canada, Lix, Metge, and Leslie (2009) reported that Indigenous and non-Indigenous women did not differ in the prevalence of osteoporosis.

Generally though, within the Canadian population, off-reserve Indigenous Canadians have been found to report poorer health outcomes than non-Indigenous Canadians on a range of variables (Tjepkema 2002), including rating their health status as lower (O'Donnell and Tait 2003) and having a lower life expectancy (Statistics Canada 2003). In addition to reports of poorer overall health, off-reserve First Nations (56 percent) and Metis (55 percent) reported being diagnosed with one or more chronic conditions more frequently than non-Indigenous people (48 percent) (Gionet and Roshanafshar 2013). Specific health conditions that have been reported more frequently by Indigenous individuals included diabetes (Tjepkema 2002; Veenstra 2009), high blood pressure (Tjepkema 2002; Veenstra 2009), arthritis/rheumatism (Tjepkema 2002), HIV/AIDS in injection drug users (Wood et al. 2008), and a strain of *Streptococcus pneumonia* (Vanderkooi et al. 2011). Indigenous individuals were also more likely to report symptoms of a major depressive episode in the previous twelve months (Tjepkema 2002).

With respect to gender differences within Indigenous populations, in the 2001 and 2006 "Aboriginal Peoples Survey" Canadian Indigenous women were less likely to describe their health as excellent or very good compared to Indigenous men (O'Donnell and Tait 2003; O'Donnell and Wallace 2011). Indigenous women were also more likely to report being diagnosed with a chronic health condition compared to Indigenous men (O'Donnell and Wallace 2011). Also, the gender distribution of HIV/AIDS patients is such that women make up a greater proportion of individuals with HIV or AIDS in the Indigenous population compared to women in the non-Indigenous (Public Health Agency of Canada 2010).

The Study

Our exploration is based on data from the *Housing and Health in Transition (HHiT) Study*, an ambitious longitudinal initiative wherein homeless and vulnerably housed adults living on their own were interviewed at three different points in time between 2009 and 2011 in Toronto, Ottawa, and Vancouver.[2] At baseline (January 2009), 1,192 individuals were interviewed in the three study sites. Overall, about 18 percent (n = 205) of the respondents indicated an Indigenous affiliation. The HHiT study was motivated by three main objectives:

1. To determine the incidence of housing transitions...defined as (a) the rate at which homeless individuals exit homelessness, (b) the rate at which vulnerably housed individuals become homeless, and (c) the rate at which vulnerably housed individuals attain residential stability by the end of the follow-up period;

2. To identify risk factors and individual, interpersonal, and community-level resources associated with (a) the attainment of residential stability among homeless individuals, (b) the onset of homelessness among vulnerably housed individuals, and (c) the attainment of residential stability among vulnerably housed individuals; and

3. To ascertain whether changes in housing status are associated with subsequent changes in physical and mental health functioning and major health determinants (including access to health care, alcohol and drug use, food security, and social supports). (Hwang et al. 2011, 610)

While a comparison of Indigenous and non-Indigenous respondents was not a primary goal of HHiT, the study does provide a unique opportunity to further explore the similarities and differences of these populations' experiences over time. In this chapter, we examine health status and housing outcomes on the basis of self-reported ethnic affiliation/ancestry and country of birth. We compare three groups of respondents on the basis of self-reported identity: a) those who reported as Indigenous, b) those who were Canadian-born and non-Indigenous, and c) those who were not born in Canada and were not Indigenous. The decision to distinguish the non-Indigenous participants on the basis of country of origin was made due to demonstrated differences between Canadian-born and foreign-born respondents to the Ottawa-based Panel Study on Homelessness (Klodawsky, Nemiroff, and Aubry 2014).

Participants, Recruitment, and Sampling Design

Individuals who were eligible to participate in HHiT included single adults over eighteen years of age who were not living with a partner or a dependent child at the time of the baseline survey. The goal of the recruitment strategy was to capture a broadly representative sample of equal numbers (two hundred each) of single adults who were homeless and who were vulnerably housed at the onset of the study in each of the three study sites. Wherever possible, random samples were used at places such as shelters, rooming houses, and meal programs, following guidelines developed by Ardilly and Le Blanc (2001). Participants were categorized as either homeless or vulnerably housed according to the following criteria:[3]

> Participants were considered homeless if they were currently living in a shelter, public place, vehicle, abandoned building, or someone else's place and did not have their own place. Participants were considered vulnerably housed if they reported living in their own room, apartment, or place and had been homeless in the past twelve months and/or had two or more moves in the past 12 months. Participants who were temporarily living with friends and family and were paying rent were considered vulnerably housed, while those who were not paying rent were considered homeless. Full-time students and individuals who were visiting the city for less than or equal to 3 months were excluded. (Hwang et al. 2011, 614)

Further details about the recruitment strategy as well as follow-up procedures have been reported in Hwang et al. (2011).

The study was structured around the concept of housing transition because housing transitions were viewed as "a valuable opportunity to better understand the complex connections between housing and health, and to answer certain intriguing and policy-relevant questions" (Hwang 2008, 12a). In each city, a similar sampling design and sets of survey questions were used. In addition to information about housing histories (where respondents had lived since the previous interview), social networks, health status, and health and social service utilization, the baseline surveys collected a wealth of demographic data. Given the study's aim to recruit a representative population, substantially more men (n = 781, 65.7 percent) than women (n= 389, 32.7 percent) were enrolled in the study. In response to a question about ethnic background, 17.7 percent of the overall sample self-identified as Indigenous. Unique among all racial/cultural groups in the study, Indigenous respondents were almost twice as likely to be vulnerably housed as to be homeless in contrast to the study respondents overall, for whom the proportions of being housed or homeless were much more similar (Hwang et al. 2011, 620).

Study Setting

Toronto, Vancouver, and Ottawa are Canada's first-, third-, and fourth-largest cities with 2011 populations of about 5,841,000; 2,426,200; and 1,255,900 in their metropolitan areas respectively (Statistics Canada 2013). While Toronto and Ottawa are both located in the province of Ontario in eastern Canada,

Vancouver is located on the west coast and in the province of British Columbia. In all three cases, homelessness and risk of homelessness have been issues of growing severity since the early 1990s.

The profile and size of Indigenous peoples in each of these cities vary, as is the case more generally. As Norris, Clatworthy, and Peters (2013) noted, "The significance of various factors affecting Aboriginal population growth varies between different cities and for different subgroups of the Canadian Aboriginal population" (30). In 2006, Indigenous peoples were estimated to be 1.8 percent (20,590) and 1.9 percent (40,310) of the urban population in Ottawa-Gatineau and Vancouver respectively and 0.5 percent (26,575) in Toronto (Norris, Clatworthy, and Peters 2013). Based on a review of various homeless counts over the last decade, about 18 percent, 25 percent, and 30 percent of the homeless populations of Toronto, Vancouver, and Ottawa, respectively, are estimated to be Indigenous (Belanger, Awosoga, and Weasel Head 2013).

Measures

This study examined the results from five sets of measures/questions. For further details about the types of questions used in each measure, see Hwang et al. 2011. The SF-12 is a twelve-item measure of health status that includes the Physical Component Summary (PCS) score and the Mental Component Summary (MCS) score (Ware, Kosinski, and Keller 1996). The scales for the items of the SF-12 vary. For example, participants are asked to rate their health in general from 1 (*excellent*) to 5 (*poor*), and to indicate how much their health limits them from performing different types of activities, such as climbing several flights of stairs on a scale from 1 (*yes, limited a lot*) to 3 (*no, not limited at all*). The measure also includes four yes or no questions regarding whether physical and mental health have interfered with activities during the past four weeks. There was one item regarding how much pain interfered with work (inside and outside the home) during the past four weeks, from 1 (*not at all*) to 5 (*extremely*). Three items (feeling calm, having energy, and feeling down in the past four weeks) were rated on a scale of 1 (*all of the time*) to 6 (*none of the time*). The final item asked how often physical or emotional problems interfered with social activities in the past four weeks, from 1 (*all of the time*) to 5 (*none of the time*). Scores on the PCS and MCS range from 0 to 100 with a higher score representing better health. For the PCS and the MCS, a score of 50 represents the mean for the general American population (Ware, Kosinski, and Keller, 1998). Normative SF-12 data for the Canadian population have not been established.

In the study, another measure, the EQ-5D, was included in addition to the SF-12. Both measures involve different timelines, with the EQ-5D focusing on "your own health state today" versus health over the past four weeks, which is the timeline of 75 percent of the SF-12 items. First, in measuring the EQ-5D index score, participants are asked to "Please let me know which of the statements I read to you best describes your own health state today." The five areas that are explored in the EQ-5D include mobility, self-care, usual activities, pain/discomfort, and anxiety/depression. For each aspect of health, participants indicate the level of difficulty they experience on a scale of 1 (e.g., *I have no problems walking about*) to 3 (e.g., *I am confined to bed*). Second, the EQ-5D visual analogue scale score is a self-reported one-item measure of current health status ("your own state of health today") (The EuroQol Group 1990). The score ranges from 0 (*worst imaginable state of health*) to 100 (*best imaginable state of health*). In another part of the study, participants were surveyed about their experiences with various chronic health conditions over the past year. They were asked to identify whether they had experienced any of the medical conditions that were on a list provided to them, and to identify other relevant medical conditions as well. Finally, Toro's Housing Quality Instrument, a six-item measure of housing quality, was used as part of the study (Toro et al. 1997). Participants rated six aspects of their housing, comfort, safety, spaciousness, privacy, friendliness, and overall quality, on a seven-point scale from 1 (*very bad*) to 7 (*very good*): (e.g., "How would you rate the place where you currently live in terms of comfort?").

Data Analysis and Results

Given our interest in intersectional analysis as discussed above, we decided to compare Indigenous and non-Indigenous respondents on the basis of matched identity groups (Indigenous, non-Indigenous and Canadian-born, and non-Indigenous and foreign-born). At baseline, these matched sets consisted of 330 participants in total, with 110 participants in each group. Participants were matched on city (Ottawa, Toronto, or Vancouver), gender (woman or man—unfortunately, the eighteen transgender respondents could not be included because of their very small numbers across identity groups), housing status (vulnerably housed or homeless), and age group (<30, 30–49, ≥50). Forty-eight (48.2) percent of the participants were from Toronto, 28.2 percent from Vancouver, and 23.6 percent from Ottawa. The majority of participants were men at 70.9 percent and 29.1 percent were women. At baseline 55.5 percent were homeless and 44.5 percent vulnerably housed. There were no group differences on age; the average age of the participants across all three groups was approximately forty-two.[4] Two hundred and sixty-seven participants from these matched groups completed the second annual follow-up interview (in the third year of data collection). Participants who were homeless at baseline were less likely to complete the follow-up, and Indigenous participants were more likely to complete the follow-up. There were no gender or age differences in completing the follow-up interview.

Multivariate analyses of variance were used to look at group differences on health variables and housing quality, at baseline and at the second follow-up interview. Follow-up univariate analyses were used to identify significant group differences. Repeated measures statistical models to look at differences among and between groups (Analysis of Variance) were used to explore changes on health variables and housing quality from baseline to follow-up. Interactions between change over time and identity group, change over time and gender, and the three-way interaction between change over time, gender, and group were explored for each variable. Chi-square analyses were used to explore differences in chronic health conditions, health conditions within the past twelve months, housing outcomes, and changes in housing status. Fisher's Exact Test was used when assumptions for chi-square analyses were not met. Baseline housing status was used as a covariate in the analyses of follow-up data where it demonstrated an effect on the dependent variables. Partial eta squared (n_p^2) is presented as a measure of effect for ANOVA results, Cohen's *d* is used as a measure of effect size for *t*-tests, and Cramer's V is reported for chi-square analyses.

Health Differences between Identity Groups

To begin, it is important to acknowledge that each of the identity groups reported significantly poorer physical health[5] and mental health[6] than a normative sample of the general American population. Within this already marginalized population of homeless and vulnerably housed adults, the scores illustrated a consistent trend of group differences on physical health,[7] with the Indigenous respondents reporting poorer physical health functioning compared to the non-Indigenous groups at both baseline (non-Indigenous, foreign-born: $p < .01$; non-Indigenous, Canadian-born: $p < .05$) and follow-up ($p \le .01$). Mental health functioning was similar for all three identity groups at baseline and follow-up. However, mental health functioning scores increased significantly from baseline to follow-up[8] indicating improvements in mental health functioning for all the groups at follow-up.

The groups also differed on the EQ-5D[9] Index score, indicating differences in their health[10] on the day of the interview. The Indigenous participants had a lower score than the non-Indigenous, foreign-born participants at baseline ($p < .01$), but, at follow-up, the EQ-5D Index score was similar for all three groups. The ratings on the EQ-5D visual analogue scale (state of your health today) at baseline did not differ by identity group. However, at follow-up, there was a group difference on the visual analogue scale[11] and the Indigenous group had a lower score, and thus a lower rating of their health on that day, than did both non-Indigenous groups. EQ-5D visual analogue scores did not change significantly over time.

Gender and Health

When comparisons were made at baseline and then at follow-up on the basis of gender, there were no significant differences in physical health or mental health functioning between men and women. The same was the case for the EQ-5D visual analogue scale. Intriguingly though, the results of the EQ-5D index score indicated a significant gender difference,[12] with women having a significantly lower EQ-5D index score than did men.

T-tests were used to explore gender differences within each identity group and several gender differences were found within the Indigenous ancestry group (see Table 5.1). Indigenous women reported significantly lower physical health[13] and mental health[14] at baseline and follow-up compared to Indigenous men. Indigenous women also had significantly lower EQ-5D index scores compared to Indigenous men on both occasions.[15] Although there was no gender difference in the Indigenous group on the visual analogue scale (state of your health today) at baseline, women had a significantly lower score at follow-up.[16] Indigenous women also reported a greater number of chronic conditions compared to Indigenous men.[17] This was also the case within the non-Indigenous, Canadian-born group,[18] whereas within the non-Indigenous, foreign-born group, the only significant gender difference was that women reported a greater score on the visual analogue scale (state of their health today) compared to men at follow-up.[19]

Table 5.1. Health Functioning and within Group Gender Differences on Health Variables at Baseline and Follow-Up

Measure	Indigenous M (SD)		Non-Indigenous and Canadian-born M (SD)		Non-Indigenous and non-Canadian born M (SD)	
	Women	Men	Women	Men	Women	Men
Baseline						
SF-12 Physical Component Summary	**38.63 (9.60)**[a]	**43.97 (10.14)**[a]	44.03 (11.31)	47.55 (10.66)	47.37 (10.11)	46.37 (11.55)
SF-12 Mental Component Summary	**34.94 (12.58)**[b]	**40.25 (12.36)**[b]	35.43 (10.93)	39.87 (13.08)	41.25 (14.62)	38.68 (13.04)
EQ-5D Index Score	**0.64 (0.22)**[c]	**0.77 (0.19)**[c]	0.73 (0.24)	0.78 (0.21)	0.79 (0.22)	0.79 (0.20)
ED-5D VAS (State of health today)	56.25 (21.39)	60.33 (20.97)	60.86 (21.91)	63.46 (21.28)	68.13 (22.11)	62.68 (24.85)
Number of chronic conditions	**4.47 (2.34)**[b]	**3.35 (2.17)**[b]	**3.41 (2.73)**[d]	**2.10 (1.80)**[d]	1.81 (1.66)	1.94 (1.83)
Follow-up 2						
SF-12 Physical Component Summary	**37.49 (10.24)**[a]	**43.77 (12.46)**[a]	47.30 (10.26)	46.93 (11.87)	48.63 (9.31)	47.30 (10.74)
SF-12 Mental Component Summary	**37.38 (10.99)**[b]	**43.37 (12.59)**[b]	39.31 (10.73)	42.95 (12.66)	46.86 (10.71)	43.14 (13.19)
EQ-5D Index Score	**.64 (.24)**[c]	**.77 (.20)**[c]	.72 (.24)	.78 (.22)	.79 (.25)	.77 (.22)
ED-5D VAS (State of health today)	**50.23 (30.84)**[b]	**63.95 (22.02)**[b]	64.85 (21.54)	66.13 (22.03)	79.25 (19.75)[e]	64.60 (24.25)[e]

Note. Bold face indicates significant gender differences within an identity group. Indigenous: baseline n = 110, follow-up n = 101; non-Indigenous, Canadian-born: baseline n = 110, follow-up n = 82; non-Indigenous, foreign-born: baseline n = 109, follow-up n = 80.

[a] p = .01 gender difference for Indigenous participants. [b] p < .05 gender difference for Indigenous participants. [c] p < .01 gender difference for Indigenous participants. [d] p < .05 gender difference for non-Indigenous, Canadian-born participants. [e] p < .05 gender difference for non-Indigenous, foreign-born participants.

Chronic Health Conditions and Health Conditions within the Past Twelve Months at Baseline[20]

The extent of frequently reported chronic health conditions differed between the identity groups.[21] The Indigenous group reported significantly more chronic health conditions than the other identity groups (p < .001), and the non-Indigenous, foreign-born participants had fewer chronic conditions than non-Indigenous, Canadian-born participants ($p = .01$). We explored identity group differences on individual health conditions. The findings on health conditions that were identified by a minimum of 20 percent of the Indigenous sample are included in Tables 5.2 and 5.3.[22] More Indigenous participants reported the following health conditions than expected: bronchitis, hepatitis B or C, arthritis, back problems, migraine headaches, head injury, and hearing problems. Non-Indigenous, non-Canadian born participants reported fewer of the following conditions than expected: hepatitis B and C, arthritis, back problems, migraine headaches, head injury, and hearing problems. In terms of health conditions within the past twelve months, Indigenous participants were also more likely to report pneumonia, and non-Indigenous, foreign-born participants were less likely to report pneumonia.

Table 5.2. Chronic Conditions Reported at Baseline by Group

Health Condition	Indigenous (in percentages)	Non-Indigenous and Canadian-born (in percentages)	Non-Indigenous and non-Canadian born (in percentages)
High blood pressure	20.4	18.4	18.7
Asthma	28.2	19.3	17.4
Chronic bronchitis[a]	**27.4**	15.6	4.6
Hepatitis B or C[b]	**40.4**	22.2	**12.1**
Arthritis[c]	**44.9**	30.8	**20.4**
Back problems[d]	**53.2**	41.7	**25.2**
Problems walking, lost limb, other physical handicap	31.2	22.7	24.1
Migraine headaches[e]	**33.0**	19.6	**12.8**
Head injury[f]	**69.1**	59.1	**44.0**
Hearing problems[g]	**24.5**	15.4	**4.6**
Mood disorder	38.5	39.8	40.6
Anxiety disorder	27.8	23.1	30.2

Note. Significant differences are indicated in bold.

[a]χ^2 (2, $N = 324$) = 21.01, $p < .001$, Cramer's V = .26. [b]χ^2 (2, $N = 324$) = 23.60), $p < .001$, Cramer's V = .27. [c]χ^2 (2, $N = 322$) = 14.91, $p = .001$, Cramer's V = .22. [d]χ^2 (2, $N = 324$) = 17.75, $p < .001$, Cramer's V = .23. [e]χ^2 (2, $N = 325$) = 13.46, $p = .001$, Cramer's V = .20. [f]χ^2 (2, $N = 329$) = 14.24, $p = .001$, Cramer's V = .21. [g]χ^2 (2, $N = 323$) = 17.27, $p < .001$, Cramer's V = .23.

Table 5.3. Health Conditions within Past Twelve Months By Group

Health condition	Indigenous (in percentages)	Non-Indigenous and Canadian-born (in percentages)	Non-Indigenous and non-Canadian born (in percentages)
Bed bug bites	48.1	40.6	45.9
Pneumonia[a]	22.2	13.9	6.4
Foot problems	41.3	28.2	31.8

[a]χ^2 (2, N = 325) = 11.16, p = .003, Cramer's V = .19.

Housing Status, Changes in Housing Status, and Housing Quality at Follow-Up

Given the HHiT study's interest in housing transitions and health, we investigated three characteristics of the participants' housing situations over time. The first had to do with housing status at follow-up, the second reflected changes in housing status between baseline and follow-up, and the third depicted the perceived quality of the place in which the respondent was living at baseline and at follow-up.

On the basis of the statistical analyses performed on these data, the participants in each identity group were equally likely to be housed at follow-up[23] (see Table 5.4). When the identity group differences were examined separately for men and women (e.g., women were compared across identity groups and so were men) using Fisher's Exact Test, there were no significant identity group differences in whether participants were housed at follow-up (see Table 5.4). However, when men and women within each identity group were compared, more non-Indigenous, foreign-born women were housed compared to non-Indigenous, foreign-born men (p = .05). There were no differences in housing status between men and women for the Indigenous group or for non-Indigenous, Canadian-born participants. When group differences on housing outcome were explored by city, there were no differences between the housing statuses of the Indigenous identity groups in each city at follow-up. However, when scanning across the results, it is noteworthy that in each case investigated, the proportion of Indigenous identity group participants who were housed was lower than was the case for the other groups, although not in a manner that was deemed to be statistically different. In other words, in a statistical sense, there is no expectation that the reported differences are likely to happen again. The difference is one that might have occurred by chance.

Table 5.4. Housing Status at Follow-Up

Group	Indigenous (N = 97) (in percentages)		Non-Indigenous and Canadian-born (N = 78) (in percentages)		Non-Indigenous and non-Canadian born (N = 78) (in percentages)	
	Housed	Homeless	Housed	Homeless	Housed	Homeless
All	72.2	27.8	80.8	19.2	80.8	19.2
Women	72.4	27.6	84.6	15.4	95.5	4.5
Men	72.1	27.9	78.8	21.2	75.0	25.0
Vancouver	69.6	30.4	85.0	15.0	88.9	11.1
Toronto	74.5	25.5	80.0	20.0	80.5	19.5
Ottawa	69.6	30.4	77.8	22.2	73.7	26.3

Note. Groups did not differ on housing outcomes in a statistically significant manner.

In addition, group differences in housing status between the baseline interview and the follow-up interview were explored (see Table 5.5). It is important to note that in this analysis we were not able to include information about changes in housing status between these two interviews (e.g., a respondent who became homeless for a period between the interview dates, but was housed on the interview dates). There were no statistically significant group differences in changes of housing status for the three identity groups. When identity group differences were examined separately for men and women using chi-square analysis, no identity group differences were found. When gender differences for each identity group were explored using Fisher's Exact Test, women in the non-Indigenous, foreign-born group were more likely to have been housed compared to men in that group ($p < .05$). There were no other gender differences within the three identity groups. Identity group differences were also examined within each city using Fisher's Exact Test. No statistically significant differences were found. However, while scanning across the results, it is noteworthy that when comparing the outcomes for Indigenous and non-Indigenous Canadians, the proportion of Indigenous participants that stayed or became homeless was always higher, and the proportion of Indigenous group that stayed or became housed was always lower than was the case for non-Indigenous Canadians.

Table 5.5. Changes in Housing Status from Baseline to Follow-Up

Group	Indigenous (N = 97)				Non-Indigenous, Canadian-born (N = 78)				Non-Indigenous, foreign-born (N = 78)			
	Homeless		Housed		Homeless		Housed		Homeless		Housed	
	Stayed %	Became %	Stayed %	Became %	Stayed %	Became %	Stayed %	Became %	Stayed %	Became %	Stayed %	Became %
All	19.6	8.2	39.2	33.0	12.8	6.4	39.7	41.0	14.1	5.1	43.6	37.2
Women	24.1	3.4	27.6	44.8	15.4	0	30.8	53.8	4.5	0	31.8	63.6
Men	17.6	10.3	44.1	27.9	11.5	9.6	44.2	34.6	17.9	7.1	48.2	26.8
Vanc.	21.7	8.7	30.4	39.1	10.0	5.0	40.0	45.0	11.1	0	33.3	55.6
Tor.	13.7	11.8	49.0	25.5	10.0	10.0	47.5	32.5	12.2	7.3	58.5	22.0
Ottawa	30.4	0	26.1	43.5	22.2	0	22.2	55.6	21.1	5.3	21.1	52.6

Note. Groups did not differ on changes in housing status in a statistically significant manner.

A repeated measures ANOVA found that mean ratings of housing quality on Toro's Housing Quality Instrument did not differ significantly between Indigenous identity groups, or men and women at baseline or follow-up (see Table 5.6). There was no significant interaction between identity group and gender on housing quality ratings. However, the ratings of housing quality increased overall from baseline to follow up,[24] indicating greater self-reported housing quality at the time of the follow-up interview compared to baseline.

Table 5.6. Housing Quality by City and Gender

Group	Housing Quality					
	Indigenous		Non-Indigenous and Canadian-born		Non-Indigenous and non-Canadian born	
	Baseline M (SD)	Follow-up M (SD)	Baseline M (SD)	Follow-up M (SD)	Baseline M (SD)	Follow-up M (SD)
Vancouver	24.47 (7.74)	29.41 (8.18)	28.52 (7.59)	30.29 (8.59)	26.00 (8.27)	29.09 (9.91)
Toronto	27.83 (8.73)	28.02 (8.58)	27.15 (7.84)	30.13 (8.32)	29.09 (9.25)	29.90 (7.63)
Ottawa	26.31 (6.78)	29.35 (9.04)	27.54 (7.65)	30.26 (7.51)	26.96 (7.48)	28.79 (9.20)
Men	25.97 (8.18)	28.59 (8.04)	28.03 (7.45)	30.23 (8.13)	26.77 (8.73)	28.43 (8.53)
Women	27.88 (7.81)	28.94 (9.65)	26.66 (8.25)	30.15 (8.26)	30.03 (8.01)	32.18 (8.27)

Note. Groups did not differ on housing quality in a statistically significant manner.

Discussion

This study contributes to knowledge about the health of homeless and vulnerably housed Indigenous peoples in Ottawa, Toronto, and Vancouver, in comparison to those without Indigenous ancestry. It also provides information about differences in gendered health status within the Indigenous population. In the analyses discussed above, physical health status was poor for all groups, but it was particularly poor for the Indigenous identity group. This was not the case with regard to mental health status where all of the identity groups exhibited relatively similar poor mental health in comparison to a normative sample. Notably though, when gender differences were explored within each identity group, Indigenous women exhibited poorer physical health status and mental health status than did their male peers. Comparisons among the identity groups about specific health conditions provided further insights: in many cases the Indigenous group reported higher rates of and significantly more chronic health conditions than the other groups. The findings that non-Indigenous, foreign-born participants reported fewer health conditions than the non-Indigenous, Canadian-born participants was consistent with the results reported in Klodawsky, Nemiroff, and Aubry (2014) where foreign-born respondents to the Panel Study on Homelessness in Ottawa reported significantly fewer chronic health conditions than did their matched, Canadian-born peers.

These results reinforce some other studies about the health of Indigenous peoples. Various evidence has already been presented about off-reserve First Nations, Metis, and Inuit peoples' poorer physical health, although typically these analyses have not focused specifically on homeless or vulnerably housed populations nor gender differences among them (Gionet and Roshanafshar 2013; Tjepkema 2002; Veenstra 2009; Vanderkooi et al. 2011). We are not aware of studies other than HHiT that have used the SF-12 or EQ-5D in interviews with Indigenous Canadians, so it is not possible to compare the scores from this study to those of other scholars. More generally, evidence about gender differences in health status or chronic health conditions within Indigenous populations has been limited (Veenstra 2009; Wilson, Rosenberg, and Abonyi 2011; O'Donnell and Wallace 2011).

Some of our findings on specific chronic conditions were consistent with previous research whereas others were not. Like Wood and co-authors (2008), this study found a higher rate of HIV/AIDS among Indigenous participants. Similar to our research, Thurston, Soo, and Turner (2013) reported no significant differences in mobility limitations, brain injuries, or mental health when they compared Indigenous and non-Indigenous homeless individuals.

The conclusion of no group differences with regard to asthma in our work was consistent with Thurston, Soo, and Turner (2013), but these findings conflict with the higher rates of respiratory conditions in the Indigenous population reported in other research (Gionet and Roshanafshar 2013). One respiratory condition that was more prevalent in the Indigenous group in our study was chronic bronchitis. So too was the reporting of hepatitis B or C. Yet, Thurston and colleagues (2013) did not find such differences in relation to hepatitis C. Tjepkema's (2002) conclusion that arthritis was more common among Indigenous groups also was consistent with our findings. However, the lack of difference in the prevalence of hypertension or mood disorder among the groups in our study did not reflect other research.

One possible reason that our study did not find group differences in the prevalence of certain chronic conditions might be due to the extent to which the whole of the HHiT study population was low-income and thus likely to be in relatively poor health overall. Although Tjepkema (2002) found that low income was related to greater health differences between Indigenous and non-Indigenous individuals, perhaps at very low levels of income some health differences are less noticeable Thurston, Soo, and Turner (2013) focused on a similar population to our study but found fewer differences in chronic conditions between Indigenous and non-Indigenous respondents. One possible reason why our study did find some group differences on health might be the inclusion of vulnerably housed as well as homeless respondents: the participants in HHiT study sample might have had slightly more access to financial resources relative to Thurston, Soo, and Turner's sample overall.

The study also highlights the particularly poor mental health and physical health status of Indigenous women as compared to Indigenous men in Canada. The finding of a greater number of chronic conditions in Indigenous women compared to Indigenous men is consistent with other research (O'Donnell and Wallace 2011). The poorer health outcomes of women provide additional support for the growing calls to urgently address this group's complex and multiple unmet health needs within a framework that also addresses the particular situations of marginalized Indigenous peoples more generally (Belanger, Awosoga, and Weasel Head 2013; Thurston, Turner, and Bird in this volume).

Another, albeit very preliminary, contribution of this article is the examination of interactions between identity group and housing outcomes over time. Our analyses were unable to discern any statistically significant trends between identity group and housing status, changes in housing status, and changes in perceived housing quality over time, despite the evidence that the Indigenous homeless and vulnerably housed respondents had poorer physical health and more chronic health conditions than their non-Indigenous peers.

A third contribution is methodological and has to do with an approach to intersectional analysis that is quantitative but does not require the very large sample sizes needed to explore complex social identities through regression analysis (Scott and Siltanen 2012). This study's approach to analysis has demonstrated the utility of examining similarities and differences between carefully matched samples that take into account multiple aspects of identity (such as age, country of origin, and locale) within a study population.

Limitations

In his landmark article on intergenerational trauma among homeless Aboriginal men, Menzies (2009) asserted that: "I did not use a non-Aboriginal comparison group to identify differences in their experiences. My concern with research on homelessness is the assumption of a generalized 'homeless' population. I wanted this study to focus on the experience of Aboriginal men, as I believe their issues should not be compared to those of another group. I believe their experiences warrant singular attention and should not be weighed against the experiences of other 'subpopulations'" (20). Menzies's approach certainly raises important questions about the utility of investigating Indigenous/non-Indigenous differences in the context of the HHIT study. Comparative studies may lead to implicit and unwarranted assumptions about what similarities or differences may or may not mean. For example, the outcome reported above about similar low levels of mental health functioning among Indigenous and non-Indigenous Canadian participants in HHIT should not be taken as an indication that the mental health challenges of these populations are the same or that they stem from similar histories, experiences, and policy contexts. However, drawing informed and circumspect inferences from comparative quantitative studies is an important strategy for linking such results to policy implications.

With regard to the HHiT study in particular, reflecting on the centrality of the concept of "transition" does provide an opportunity to assess the potential challenges involved in comparative studies of homelessness and housing vulnerability. As Christensen has noted in this volume: "the emphasis on absolute homelessness in urban settings in both popular and academic discourse neglects the often less visible forms of homelessness that take place in rural or reserve settings…while at the same time obscuring linkages between urban 'street' homelessness and dynamics of the rural community or the reserve" (2). The author highlights a unique feature of transitions among Indigenous peoples in Canada, having to do with their movement between reserve and city. This feature raises questions about the appropriate scale of examination as well as the meaning and motivation for participants' transitions (see Christensen and Andrew, this volume). As Peters and Robillard (2009) note, "There is very little work that explores whether First Nations' ability to access housing on reserve affects rates of homelessness in urban areas" (668). These culturally informed insights highlight the limitations of the more typically generic approach to housing in scholarly work on homelessness. "Transition" is used as a code word for instability but not much attention is paid to the particular circumstances and pathways through which vulnerable people move and/or stay in place. Simultaneously though, the open-endedness of HHiT's approach and its efforts to draw upon a broad "representative" sample, does present a unique opportunity for analysis. Interrogating the implicit assumptions in the use of the term transition in HHiT is an entry point for recognizing the critical importance of culture and histories of colonialism. Taking such limitations into account in conjunction with the study's strengths might provide a particularly powerful basis for further analysis.

Another limitation of this study is that the health findings were based on self-reports. The self-reported nature of the data could have adversely affected the reported findings if participants were unaware that they had specific health conditions. Moreover, as noted by Bombak and Bruce in their review of published studies (2012), "differences in how SRH [self-rated health] is assessed by ethnicities have been detected" (1). Their research raises questions about the utility of comparing Indigenous and non-Indigenous respondents with regard to self-reports.

Conclusions and Recommendations

The goal of this paper was to assess whether quantitative survey data about a "general" representative sample of homeless and vulnerably housed adults in three Canadian cities was able to provide insights into the following question: among an already marginalized population of homeless and vulnerably housed adults, does Indigenous ancestry impact health and housing outcomes? This question was investigated through an intersectional lens while recognizing that social identities are complex. To this end, participants were sorted into three equal-size groups based on Indigenous ancestry, country of birth, and also matched on the basis of city, age, and gender. The analyses presented above provide some evidence that Indigenous ancestry does have an impact on health. On measures having to do with physical health status and chronic conditions, there were statistically significant differences between the Indigenous identity group and others, and within the Indigenous identity group, gender differences also were statistically significant with regard to mental health functioning, physical health functioning, and the extent of chronic conditions. With regard to housing outcomes, none of the analyses conducted thus far revealed any statistically significant differences but there were some intriguing trends that warrant further investigation.

The limitations of using a comparative, quantitative approach have been noted as well. Given the breadth of the HHiT study, however, these limitations also point to how further analyses might proceed. For example, it would be productive to explore the detailed housing histories of the matched participants to compare patterns of transitions over time, together with the reasons given for each move. In addition, further insights might be garnered through a comparative examination of the qualitative responses of interviewees, as researchers are doing in a side study now underway with a subsample of HHiT participants (ten women and ten men in each of the three cities).

Notes

1   In this article, the term Indigenous is used to refer to the HHiT study participants who self-identified as Aboriginal in response to the question "To which racial or cultural group(s) do you belong to or identify with?" We have chosen this convention (the term Indigenous) in the context of the terminology favoured by the editors. The term Aboriginal remains when citing secondary sources with this terminology in quotations and titles.

2   The HHiT Study completed its fifth and last iteration of surveys in 2013, together with a sub-study that conducted in-depth qualitative interviews with selected respondents in each of the study sites.

3   In the HHiT study, being vulnerably housed is most similar to the terms the editors of this volume define as being at risk of homelessness OR experiencing hidden homelessness.

4   Indigenous M = 42.21 years old, SD = 9.91; non-Indigenous, Canadian-born M = 41.60, SD = 10.78; non-Indigenous, foreign-born M = 42.49, SD = 10.90.

5   At baseline, Indigenous: $t(109)$ = -7.77, $p < .001$, d = -0.75; non-Indigenous and Canadian-born: $t(109)$ = -3.33, p = .001, d = -0.33; non-Indigenous, foreign-born, $t(109)$ = -3.28, p = .001, d = -0.33.

6   At baseline, Indigenous: $t(109)$ = -9.40, $p < .001$, d = -0.99; non-Indigenous and Canadian-born: $t(109)$ = -9.50, $p < .001$, d = -1.00; non-Indigenous, foreign-born, $t(109)$ = -8.33, $p < .001$, d = -.90.

7   Baseline: $F(2,323)$ = 6.91, p = .001, n_p^2 = .04; Follow up: $F(2,257)$ = 9.72, $p < .001$, n_p^2 = .07.

8   $F(1,257)$ = 11.69, p = .001, n_p^2 = .04.

9   $F(2,323)$ = 5.08, p = .007, n_p^2 = .03.

10 Physical and mental health both included in measure.

11 $F(2, 257) = 7.25, p = .001, n_p^2 = .05$.

12 $F(1, 261) = 4.50, p = .04, n_p^2 = .02$ (result of a repeated measures ANOVA with time, gender, and group as independent variables).

13 Baseline: $t(108) = -2.55, p = .01, d = -0.54$; Follow-up: $t(69.31) = -2.65, p = .01, d = -0.55$.

14 Baseline: $t(108) = -2.04, p = .04, d = -0.43$; Follow-up: $t(99) = -2.29, p = .02, d = -0.51$.

15 Baseline: $t(50.10) = -2.88, p = .006; d = -0.63$; Follow-up: $t(48.48) = -2.65, p = .01, d = -0.59$.

16 $t(44.10) = -2.24, p = .03, d = -0.51$.

17 $t(108) = 2.41, p = .02, d = 0.50$.

18 $t(42.45) = 2.49, p < .05, d = 0.57$.

19 $t(80) = 2.31, p < .05, d = 0.61$.

20 Information about chronic health conditions was not collected in the follow-up survey.

21 $F(2, 323) = 21.06, p < .001, n_p^2 = .12$.

22 In other cases, more Indigenous respondents than those from other groups reported specific health conditions (e.g., HIV/AIDS ($\chi^2 (2, N = 329) = 13.06, p = .001$, Cramer's V = .20), exposure to tuberculosis (TB)/positive TB test ($\chi^2 (2, N = 328) = 9.80, p = .01$, Cramer's V = .17), fetal alcohol syndrome or fetal alcohol spectrum disorder ($\chi^2 (2, N = 316) = 7.48, p = .02$, Cramer's V = .15)); however, when less than 20 percent of Indigenous group reported the condition, it was not included in Table 5.2.

23 $\chi^2 (1, N = 253) = 2.54, p = .28$, Cramer's V = .10.

24 $F(1, 261) = 9.02, p < .01, n_p^2 = .03$.

References

Ardilly Pascal, and David Le Blanc. 2001. "Sampling and Weighting a Survey of Homeless Persons: A French Example." *Survey Methodology* 27 (1): 110–18.

Belanger, Yale D., Olu Awosoga, and Gabrielle Weasel Head. 2013. "Homelessness, Urban Aboriginal People, and the Need for a National Enumeration." *Aboriginal Policy Studies* 2 (2): 4–33.

Belanger, Yale. D., Gabrielle Weasel Head, and Olu Awosoga. 2011. *Assessing Urban Aboriginal Housing and Homelessness in Canada*. Final Report prepared for the National Association of Friendship Centres (NAFC) and the Office of the Federal Interlocutor for Métis and Non-Status Indians (OFI). Ottawa: Urban Aboriginal Network.

_____.2012. "Housing and Aboriginal People in Urban Centres: A Quantitative Evaluation." *Aboriginal Policy Studies* 2 (1): 4–25.

Benbow, Sarah, Cheryl Forchuk, and Susan L. Ray. 2011. "Mothers with Mental Illness Experiencing Homelessness: A Critical Analysis." *Journal of Psychiatric and Mental Health Nursing* 18 (8): 687–95.

Benoit, Cecilia, Dena Carroll, and Munaza Chaudhry. 2003. "In Search of a Healing Place: Aboriginal Women in Vancouver's Downtown Eastside." *Social Science and Medicine* 56 (4): 821–33.

Bombak, Andrea E., and Sharon G. Bruce. 2012. "Self-Rated Health and Ethnicity: Focus on Indigenous Populations." *International Journal of Circumpolar Health*, no. 71, 1–10.

Canada Mortgage and Housing Corporation. 2014. "Housing in Canada online." http://cmhc.beyond2020.com/HiCODefinitions_EN.html#_Core_Housing_Need_Status.

Crenshaw, Kimberle. 1991. "Mapping the Margins: Intersectionality, Identity Politics and Violence against Women in Colour." *Stanford Law Review* 43 (6): 1241–99.

Gaetz, Stephen, Jesse Donaldson, Tim Richter, and Tanya Gulliver. 2013. *The State of Homelessness in Canada in 2013*. Toronto: Canadian Homelessness Research Network Press.

Gionet, Linda, and Shirin Roshanafshar. 2013. "Select Health Indicators of First Nations People Living Off Reserve, Métis and Inuit." *Health at a Glance* (January): 1–14. http://www.statcan.gc.ca/pub/82-624-x/2013001/article/11763-eng.htm#n1.

Greene, Saara, Lori Chambers, Khatundi Masinde, and Doris O'Brien-Teengs. 2013. "A House Is Not a Home: The Housing Experiences of African and Caribbean Mothers Living with HIV." *Housing Studies* 28 (1): 116–34.

Hankivsky, Olena, Colleen Reid, Renee Cormier, Colleen Varcoe, Natalie Clark, Cecilia Benoit, and Shari Brotman. 2010. "Exploring the Promises of Intersectionality for Advancing Women's Health Research." *International Journal for Equity in Health*, no. 9, 1–5.

Hwang, Stephen. 2008. "Research Proposal: The Health and Housing in Transition (HHiT) Study: A Longitudinal Study of the Health of Homeless and Vulnerably Housed Adults in Vancouver, Toronto, and Ottawa." Submitted to Canadian Institute for Health Research.

Hwang, Stephen W., Tim Aubry, Anita Palepu, Susan Farrell, Rosane Nisenbaum, Anita M. Hubley, Fran Klodawsky, Evie Gogosis, Elizabeth Hay, Shannon Pidlubny, Tatiana Dowbor, and Catharine Chambers. 2011. "The Health and Housing in Transition Study: A Longitudinal Study of the Health of Homeless and Vulnerably Housed Adults in Three Canadian Cities." *International Journal of Public Health* 56 (6): 609–23.

Klodawsky, Fran, Tim Aubry, and Rebecca Nemiroff. 2014. "Homeless Immigrants' and Refugees' Health Over Time." In *Homelessness and Health in Canada*, edited by Manal Guirguis-Younger, Ryan McNeil, and Stephen W. Hwang. Ottawa: University of Ottawa Press.

Lix, Lisa M., Colleen Metge, and William D. Leslie. 2009. "Measurement Equivalence of Osteoporosis-Specific and General Quality-of-Life Instruments in Aboriginal and Non-Aboriginal Women. *Quality of Life Research* 18 (5): 619–27.

Mair, Christine A. 2010. "Social Ties and Depression: An Intersectional Examination of Black and White Community-Dwelling Older Adults." *Journal of Applied Gerontology* 29 (6): 667–96.

Marshall, Brandon D.L., Thomas Kerr, Chris Livingstone, Kathy Li, Julio S. G. Montaner, and Evan Wood. 2008. "High Prevalence of HIV Infection among Homeless and Street-involved Aboriginal Youth in a Canadian Setting." *Harm Reduction Journal*, no. 5, 1–35.

Menzies, Peter. 2009. "Homeless Aboriginal Men: Effects of Intergenerational Trauma." In *Finding Home: Policy Options for Addressing Homelessness in Canada*, edited by J. David Hulchanski, Philippa Campsie, Shirley B.Y. Chau, Stephen W. Hwang, and Emily Paradis, 457–81. Toronto: Cities Centre.

Monette, Laverne, Sean B. Rourke, Katherine Gibson, Tsegaye M. Bekele, Ruthann Tucker, Saara Greene, Michael Sobota, Jay Koornstra, Steve Byers, Elisabeth Marks, Jean Bacon, James R. Watson, Stephen W. Hwang, Amrita Ahluwalia, James R. Dunn, Dale Guenter, Keith Hambly, Shafi Bhuiyan, and The Positive Spaces, Healthy Places Study Team. 2011. "Inequalities in Determinants of Health among Aboriginal and Caucasian Persons Living with HIV/AIDS in Ontario: Results from the Positive Spaces, Healthy Places Study." *Canadian Journal of Public Health* 102 (3): 215–19.

Norris, Mary Jane, Stewart Clatworthy, and Evelyn Peters. 2013. "The Urbanization of Aboriginal Populations in Canada: A Half Century in Review." In *Indigenous in the City: Contemporary Identities and Cultural Innovation*, edited by Evelyn Peters and Chris Andersen, 29–45. Vancouver: UBC Press.

O'Donnell, Vivian, and Heather Tait. 2003. "Aboriginal Peoples Survey 2001— Initial Findings: Well-Being of the Non-Reserve Aboriginal Population." Ottawa: Housing and Social Statistics Division, Statistics Canada. http://publications.gc.ca/Collection/Statcan/89-589-X/89-589-XIE2003001.pdf#page=1&zoom=auto,0,800.

O'Donnell, Vivian, and Susan Wallace. 2011. "First Nations, Métis and Inuit Women." In *Women in Canada: A Gender-Based Statistical Report, Sixth Edition*, by Social and Aboriginal Statistics Division of Statistics Canada, 205–49. Statistics Canada. http://www.statcan.gc.ca/pub/89-503-x/2010001/article/11442-eng.htm#a37.

Peters, Evelyn J. 2012. "'I Like to Let Them Have Their Time': Hidden Homeless First Nations People in the City and Their Management of Household Relationships." *Social and Cultural Geography* 13 (4): 321–38.

Peters, Evelyn J., and Vince Robillard. 2009 "'Everything You Want is There': The Place of the Reserve in First Nations' Homeless Mobility." *Urban Geography* 30 (6): 652–80.

Public Health Agency of Canada. 2010. "Population-Specific HIVS/AIDS Status Report: Aboriginal Peoples." http://www.phac-aspc.gc.ca/aids-sida/publication/ps-pd/index-eng.php.

Scott, Nick, and Janet Siltanen. 2012. "Gender and Intersectionality—a Quantitative Toolkit for Analyzing Complex Inequalities." Prepared for Human Resources and Skills Development Canada, December. Ottawa: Employment and Social Development Canada.

Senese, Laura C., and Kathi Wilson. 2013. "Aboriginal Urbanization and Rights in Canada: Examining Implications for Health." *Social Science and Medicine*, no.91, 219–28.

Snyder, Marcie, and Kathi Wilson. 2012. "Urban Aboriginal Mobility in Canada: Examining the Association with Health Care Utilization." *Social Science and Medicine* 75 (12): 2420–24.

Statistics Canada. 2003. "Aboriginal Peoples of Canada: A Demographic Profile." *2001 Census: Analysis Series*.

_____. 2013. "Population of Census Metropolitan Areas."

The EuroQol Group. 1990. "EuroQol—A New Facility for the Measurement of Health-Related Quality of Life." *Health Policy*, no.16, 199–208.

Tjepkema, Michael. 2002. "The Health of the Off-Reserve Aboriginal Population." *Supplement to Health Reports*, no.13, 1–17. http://www.statcan.gc.ca/pub/82-003-s/2002001/pdf/82-003-s2002004-eng.pdf.

Thurston, Wilfreda E., Andrea Soo, and David Turner. 2013. "Are There Differences Between the Aboriginal Homeless Population and the Non-Aboriginal Homeless Population in Calgary?" *Pimatisiwin: A Journal of Aboriginal and Indigenous Community Health* 11 (2): 283–92.

Toro, Paul A., Julie M. Passero Rabideau, Charles W. Bellavia, Chester V. Daeschler, David D. Wall, David M. Thomas, and Sheila J. Smith. 1997. "Evaluating an Intervention for Homeless Persons: Results of a Field Experiment." *Journal of Consulting and Clinical Psychology* 65 (3): 476–84.

Vanderkooi, Otto G., Deirdre L. Church, J. MacDonald, Franziska Zucol, and James D. Kellner. 2001. "Community-Based Outbreaks in Vulnerable Populations of Invasive Infections Caused by Streptococcus Pneumonia Serotypes 5 and 8 in Calgary, Canada." *PLoS One* 6 (12): e28547.

Veenstra, Gerry. 2009. "Racialized Identity and Health in Canada: Results from a Nationally Representative Survey." *Social Science and Medicine* 69 (4): 538–42.

_____. 2011. "Race, Gender, Class and Sexual Orientation: Intersecting Axes of Inequality and Self-Rated Health in Canada." *International Journal for Equity in Health*, no.10, 3-13.

Ware, John E. Jr., Mark Kosinski, and Susan D. Keller. 1996. "The 12-Item Short-Form Health Survey: Construction of Scales and Preliminary Tests of Reliability and Validity." *Medical Care*, no. 34, 220–33.

_____. 1998. *SF-12: How to Score the SF-12 Physical and Mental Health Summary Scales, third edition*. Lincoln: QualityMetric Incorporated.

Wilson, Kathi, Mark W. Rosenberg, and Sylvia Abonyi. 2011. "Aboriginal peoples, Health and Healing Approaches: The Effects of Age and Place on Health." *Social Science and Medicine* 72 (3): 355–64.

Wood, Evan, Julio S. G. Montaner, Kathy Li, Ruth Zhang, Lucy Barney, Steffanie A. Strathdee, Mark W. Tyndall, and Thomas Kerr. 2008. "Burden of HIV Infection among Aboriginal Injection Drug Users in Vancouver, British Columbia." *American Journal of Public Health* 98 (3): 515–19.

CHAPTER 6

The Inclusion of Indigenous Voices in Co-Constructing "Home": Indigenous Homelessness in a Northern Semi-Urban Community in Manitoba

MARLENY M. BONNYCASTLE, MAUREEN SIMPKINS, AND ANNETTE SIDDLE

The dominant strategies to address homelessness often exclude the voices of the homeless people themselves. We argue that without including voices of the homeless, any attempts to design and develop meaningful and long-term initiatives run the risk of failing. Those interventions generally see individuals as the cause of the problem, as individuals who need to be rescued, treated, and supported through individualized social programs such as addictions treatment, mental health programs, food programs, shelters, or cold-weather initiatives. While such immediate survival strategies are a must, little progress has been made in including the voices, experiences, and knowledges of those who are homeless, when analyzing homelessness as a growing social issue, particularly among Indigenous peoples.

A growing literature describes a variety of causes of homelessness, among them socio-economic structural factors. Such factors include the impact of colonization (Baskin 2007; Ruttan, LaBoucane-Benson, and Munro 2010; Alfred 2009), the impact of poverty and racism on accessing and keeping housing (Ruttan, LaBoucane-Benson, and Munro 2010; Kauppi et al. 2013; Gould and Williams 2010), reserve conditions (Peters and Robillard 2009), institutions and social policies (Klodawsky 2009; Whitzman 2006), unemployment and social assistance (Kauppi et al. 2013; Baskin 2007; Gould and Williams 2010; Montgomery, McCauley, and Bailey 2009), as well as the economic impacts of the housing market and affordability (Gaetz 2012, Schiff and Waegemakers Schiff 2010; Tester 2009; Cockell and McArthur-Blair 2012).

Colonization has been, and continues to be, a contest over whose knowledge matters and who counts as an expert in determining this. The importance given to the voices of the homeless in this chapter reflects a concern over the long history of exclusion of the marginalized, in particular the Indigenous peoples in Canada. Our work follows recent trends towards challenging these traditional exclusionist approaches. Hall, Dei, and Rosenberg (2000) explain that Indigenous knowledges are unique to given cultures, localities, and societies, and are "acquired by local people through daily experiences" (19) and Wilson (2008) asserts that the "foundation of Indigenous research lies within the reality of the lived Indigenous experience" (60).

Homelessness affects a significant group of Indigenous people in northern Manitoba communities and in the city of Thompson. City authorities continue to develop strategies to address the problem of homelessness through the creation of the Thompson Homeless Shelter, the Thompson Community Advisory Board for Homelessness, the Downtown Strategy, and through the newest long-term proposal led by the city of Thompson in collaboration with different levels of government, service providers, and community organizations—Project Northern Doorway. For the most part, these strategies have been expert and authority driven.

In contrast, to authority driven and designed programs this chapter is grounded in the stories and knowledge of those who are homeless and living in Thompson, Manitoba, as well as their allies. These stories are the foundation to co-construct the concept of home. Borg and co-authors (Borg et al. 2005, 243) define home as, "a stage for everyday life. Having a home affords a sense of order, identity, connectedness, warmth, haven, and physical protection, which, in turn, provide the means to pattern existence in meaningful ways through, for example, cherished routines or interactions with people one cares about." Such a definition helps us to understand better what is missing from the lives of the homeless. Oliver adds that the "conceptions of homelessness cannot exist without conceptions of home" (Oliver 2013, 113). A lack of control over one's environment, then, poses a risk to one's overall health and well-being. Home is not simply a place of shelter, but also a place of belonging, inclusion, and social support. Mallet (2004) states, "house and home, therefore, are two separate concepts: the architectural structure of a building is but one component of the overall machinery of home, one that varies between societies, cultures, times, and places" (quoted in Oliver 2013, 113).

Homelessness intersects with space, place, gender, and age (Buccieri 2013) and there are several stages of homelessness that affect people differently. Single mothers, for example, are more likely to be in insecure housing and/or depending on others for housing than experiencing rough sleeping, whereas single men are more likely to be rough sleeping (Whitzman 2006; Weber Sikich 2008). Single mothers, youth, single men, those with mental health problems, those with addiction issues, and those who come from overcrowded housing conditions on reserves into Thompson for work, independence, safety, and social reasons are often at risk of various types of homelessness (Qulliit Nunavut Status of Women Council 2007; Kidd et al. 2013; George and O'Neill 2011; Stewart and Ramage 2011).

In exploring homelessness in Thompson, Manitoba, we document our co-constructive process using Freire's "Praxis" (1995) approach of learning, action, and reflection through a community-based research experience that uses photovoice[1] when possible. From the interviews undertaken, we find a number of themes emerge that help us (1) understand the meaning of "home" in a northern context, (2) recognize the reasons for absolute and relative homelessness, and (3) provide some recommendations to the Thompson Downtown Strategy, and other initiatives involving the homeless Indigenous population. This chapter represents our initial research, as this project is still in progress.

First we situate homelessness in the city of Thompson and the greater region. Following our research methodology, we share individual narratives of homelessness from those interviewed. Their voices ground the discussion on northern homelessness and introduce central concerns such as housing conditions on- and off-reserve, domestic violence, mobility, importance of security, and a sense of belonging. This chapter concludes with a discussion of these issues and their significance in conceptualizing home and homelessness from the perspectives of Indigenous homeless people.

Situating Homelessness in Northern Manitoba

The city of Thompson is the largest semi-urban centre in northern Manitoba and is situated 750 kilometres north of Winnipeg. Thompson acts as an economic and service hub for northern Manitoban communities, and includes commercial, educational, recreational, and medical services. Employment opportunities such as the Vale nickel mine or Manitoba Hydro also contribute to inward migration from outlying communities. The city of Thompson services an area that covers 396,000 square kilometres, which includes thirty-two communities and totals approximately 72,000 people (see Figure 6.1). The average age of a Thompson resident is thirty-one, well below the provincial median age

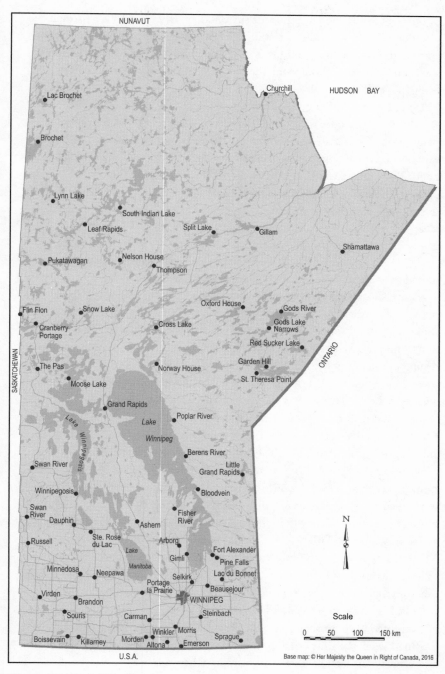

Figure 6.1. Map of Manitoba.

of thirty-eight. Regionally, the area surrounding Thompson has a median age of only twenty-four, and this trend is growing within the region's Indigenous communities. In such communities as Garden Hill and Split Lake, the average age is under twenty. Thompson's current population is estimated as 50 percent Indigenous. The city is located on the territory of the Nisichawayasihk Cree Nation (Thompson Economic Diversification Working Group 2012).

Starting in 1956, the city of Thompson was built by Inco mining company to provide a stable workforce for the nearby nickel mine. The city has experienced wide population fluctuations over the decades, with an all-time population high of over 20,000 in the 1970s (FemNorthNet Project 2012, 5). At present, Thompson's population is estimated at closer to 13,000. The economy, the unique demographic makeup of Thompson, as well as its isolated northern location, presents particular challenges in terms of access to housing and other core social needs for the vulnerable segments of the city's population.

Being homeless in Thompson is often depicted by authorities and service providers as a phenomenon of circular mobility generated by the movement of residents back and forth from outlying communities and reserves to Thompson in need of medical/rehabilitation treatment, education, or other services and supports (Thompson Community Advisory Board for Homelessness 2011). Sometimes it is a matter of survival that brings people to the city, for example, fleeing a violent family member or being kicked out of an overcrowded house on reserve. Lack of resources in the First Nations and northern communities reinforces the need to move to Thompson. Mental health, domestic violence, and social issues intersect with housing needs in northern communities and, in the case of Indigenous people, these issues are often associated with colonization and relocation (Christensen 2012; MacKinnon 2010; Hart 2010; Fernandez, MacKinnon, and Silver 2010). In northern Manitoba, experiences of social disruption can be seen in the residential school experience, where young children were taken away, often for years, and came back not knowing their language and having lost a connection with traditional activities and cultural ways of knowing and understanding (Milloy 1999). Similarly, much social disruption in northern Manitoba can also be attributed to relocations, flooding, and construction due to hydroelectric development from the 1950s onward (Comack et al. 2013). For example, in the case of hydroelectric development in the community of Grand Rapids, McKay states, " When we were kids we didn't know any different we just accepted what was here, we didn't know all the problems that this stuff was causing like all the influx of people looking for work. There was a lot of crime and after when I guess almost right away when the road come the alcohol. And all the violence, you know like I bet you we've seen more violence in those four years than most people will see in a life time. Violence in the community and violence between the workers… they were just harassing the local people [*sic*]" (McKay quoted in Kulchyski and Neckoway 2006, 11). Not only did roads and construction crews contribute to alcohol abuse and violence, but the flooding and the relocation of communities displaced hunters and trappers from their traditional territories, changing economic patterns and family roles and impacting communities for several generations (Tough 1996; Martin and Hoffman 2008). Relocation also caused many people to move to urban centres where, without new skills or resources, they ended up living on the street.

Due to the systemic nature of the social and economic barriers, Indigenous peoples experiencing poverty and homelessness in Thompson are often dismissed as "derelicts" (Barker 2013) by the general public and are treated with particular hostility by a segment of the city's population. While there is an increase in efforts to support Indigenous homeless people, their daily interactions are highly affected by racism and judgments that perpetuate stereotypes and colonial dynamics (Graham 2013). In a 2003 study of 100 Indigenous people in Thompson, 44 percent felt that racial discrimination had limited their housing options at some point over the previous five years (Corrado Research and Evaluation Associates 2003, 44). In this volume, Schiff, Turner, and Waegemakers Schiff also talk about racism in the private rental sector. This perspective is reflected by some of the people we interviewed.

City of Thompson's Homelessness Strategy

For many, the move from reserve communities to Thompson involves many challenges and barriers upon arrival. For example, there is a lack of affordable housing, affordable child care, and accessible job training. Newcomers often arrive lacking life skills and education, and lacking credit and housing references. They often face mental health issues, and within a short period of time become addicted to alcohol and drugs. Recently, positive strategies have been initiated to help with an easier transition to the city.

In 2009, the city of Thompson in collaboration with the Thompson Urban Aboriginal Strategy created the Aboriginal Accord. The Aboriginal Accord is a document that recognizes the role of Indigenous people in the region's history and affirms the city's commitment to strengthen relationships with Indigenous governments and peoples. The Thompson Aboriginal Accord is one of only two agreements of its kind in Canada today. It is a living document where signatories and partners report on the success of the commitment in concrete ways, for example, by observing the progress of new programs and initiatives (City of Thompson 2013b).

In 2012, the city of Thompson, alongside and in collaboration with twenty-five community stakeholders, announced a Downtown Strategy (DS) promoting a safe, clean, and active city for all members in the community. The DS covers primary components such as emergency, transitional, and supported housing, addictions, and mental health. The DS also includes ancillary components such as addressing poverty, domestic violence, unemployment, limited life skills, and gaps in education. The DS encompasses guidelines that include: (1) a proactive rather than punitive approach; (2) using holistic ways to address social issues; (3) enhancing positive relationships; (4) promoting collaborative partnerships with community organizations; and (5) addressing root causes of homelessness and promoting advocacy (Siddle 2013). Contrary to historical strategies, the DS is a long-term commitment that goes beyond band-aid solutions and isolated initiatives to encourage collaboration and mobilization of different sectors, institutions, and communities to contribute to the well-being of Thompson and northern communities.

That said there continue to be struggles for those moving to the city. Thompson's vacancy rate hovers at 0 percent (MacKinnon and Lafreniere 2009), and its young population, combined with an aging/static housing stock and rising prices, together create a major housing crisis (FemNorthNet Project 2012). There are only 144 affordable housing units in Thompson and ninety emergency shelter beds. The emergency shelter beds are split between a homeless shelter, a women's crisis centre, an addiction treatment centre, and transition hostel. The Ma-Mow-We-Tak Friendship Centre and the Addictions Foundation of Manitoba (AFM) also provide transitional and emergency housing (Thompson Economic Diversification Working Group 2012, 15). As a last resort for those who cannot get into the homeless shelter, there are high numbers of people spending days in the Royal Canadian Mounted Police (RCMP) Intoxicated Person Detention cells (Thompson Economic Diversification Working Group 2012, 15). The city of Thompson also has an "Extreme Cold Weather Policy" (City of Thompson 2013a). When the temperatures reach −35°C and lower, the city opens up alternative warm spaces for those who cannot get into the homeless shelter. However, the statistics fail to account for those spending nights with friends and family, those living in bush camps around the city, and those sleeping rough on the street.

In the last year, new housing strategies have been developed in Thompson to respond to the needs of different groups. For instance, MAPS (Men Are Part of the Solution) created a sober living facility for men. This home provides a healing environment for men who have been involved in domestic violence, and encourages them to use holistic approaches to become empowered and practice healthy relationships. Another new initiative is the Project Northern Doorway, which addresses the needs of the chronically homeless people. This is a sixteen-bed supportive (damp housing[2]) personal care home. It follows the Housing First model,[3] to reduce harm and risk to individuals and the community through the provision of programs, services, and supports (City of Thompson 2012). The city of Thompson has also developed a long-term plan to commence a Main Street North Project. This project is also based on the Housing First model and follows a harm reduction and holistic approach by providing a place of respect and non-judgmental care. The Main Street North Project will provide a home for homeless women, men, and youth affected by mental health and addictions issues. They will have not only a roof and a bed but also the resources and supports for treatment and healing, as well as the educational opportunities that will help them to re-establish their lives. The long-term goal is to centralize a number of current resources into one facility, providing wraparound services[4] and a multi-agency approach under one roof. The intent is to be at the forefront of social inclusion, where the conditions will allow people to participate fully in society as valued, respected, and contributing members. This facility will have the physical and human resources to provide individual assistance as well as to develop different kinds of intervention programs for people who are living on the street (Siddle 2013).

As part of the community planning process, the Thompson Community Advisory Board for Homelessness has recommended that homeless people themselves advise the board as it makes recommendations for future programs for the homeless population (Thompson Community Advisory Board for Homelessness 2011). Once open, the Main Street North Project plans to build in a community-based research component with the residents. They will be encouraged to become involved in dialogue and other participatory activities and to work together with staff and allies from different community agencies to make this facility their home and a place that suits their needs. Thus, together, residents, people at risk of homelessness, staff, allies, and researchers will use photovoice, learning circles, and interviews to reflect on their experiences and discuss new developments and initiatives. The information and outcomes of this participatory process will contribute to the inclusion of those without homes and be helpful for the myriad of service providers from both Thompson and other northern communities. Photovoice was chosen because we recently used photovoice to research the life experiences of homeless people in Thompson (Bonnycastle 2013).

Methodology

The major purpose of this research project is to inform the development of sound, meaningful strategies for the alleviation of homelessness in Thompson. To do so, we believe that capturing individual experiences of homelessness is necessary to situate and truly understand what Indigenous homelessness means in the community, the region, and more broadly in the colonial context of northern Manitoba. A community-based participatory research method (CBPR) was chosen as the best approach to our work as it emphasizes collaboration between the researcher and the community (Shdaimah, Stahl, and Schram 2011). CBPR seeks some type of change for those living with problems (Anderson 2006; Paradis and Mosher 2012) and promotes praxis, the combination of action and reflection in which subjects of research have a voice through a participatory and dialogical process of knowledge-action. This follows Dahl's (1970) principle of affected interest, "namely that those who are affected by a policy have a right to participate in its formation and in determining its eventual outcome" (quoted in McKenzie and Wharf 2010, x).

At the beginning of this project, we planned to recruit participants using posters distributed throughout the community, as well as to hold a series of meetings with key community members who had already been working on homeless issues. We defined these contacts as "allies" (Mullaly 2009; Bishop 1994). We hoped that they could provide us with insights into how to recruit participants. During these conversations, we realized that building relationships and trust were key factors when we were recruiting homeless participants. This lead to us reworking our plan for recruitment (see below).

Nine people were invited to participate in the project as allies. Currently there are seven allies taking an active role. They are:

- The resident Elder at the Ma-Mow-We-Tak Friendship Centre. He has been a strong voice in the community on the issue of homelessness. He has also experienced homelessness at a particular time in his life, which gives him increased credibility amongst the homeless population.

- A Cree woman who is the Aboriginal Liaison with the Northern Health Region – Thompson Clinic. Through her work she has fostered strong relationships with the homeless, service providers, and northern communities.

- The executive director of the Thompson Crisis Centre. She not only manages a women's shelter, but is also well-known for her commitment and compassion. She has experience working at a number of agencies across northern Manitoba that work with marginalized populations.

- The coordinator of the Youth Build Program at the Boys and Girls Club. He is deeply committed to supporting youth at risk through training, counselling, and job placements.
- The coordinator of the Thompson Homeless Shelter has shown support for this project by allowing us to conduct interviews at the shelter.
- The director of the Young Women's Christian Association (YWCA) has been open to the possibilities of including women in transitional housing at the YWCA in future interviews. She has also allowed us to use the Women's Centre at the YWCA when a group of women from the homeless shelter did not want to be interviewed at the shelter.
- A mental health worker from the Canadian Mental Health Association has acted as a liaison between some of the people using the homeless shelter and our project. She was also homeless at one time in her life and so has gained the trust of people at the shelter.

The allies primarily participate in two different ways: (1) in individual interviews and (2) by inviting potential participants and sharing information about the project. As stated above, there are other allies that we hope will become involved in the project in the near future.

Participants

A second phase of recruitment consisted of again placing flyers in different public spaces and at agencies serving the homeless population, and using referral or snowball sampling techniques. In addition, we held meetings with potential participants who were contacted by our allies so we could explain the project and invite them to participate. Indigenous women or men, at or above the age of eighteen, who were homeless or at risk of becoming homeless were eligible for the study.

Four groups of participants have taken part in this project. They were recruited at the Friendship Centre, the Thompson Homeless Shelter, the Northern Regional Health Clinic, the Boys and Girls Club, and the Thompson Crisis Centre. The first group we met with included four women and four men who were currently on the street and who sometimes slept at the Thompson Homeless Shelter. The second group was composed of five young men, over eighteen years old, who were attending the Youth Build program at the Thompson Boys and Girls Club. The third group interviewed was made up of eight women living in a transitional home, the Thompson Crisis Centre. The fourth group comprised of five women who are currently using the Thompson Homeless Shelter. That group's interview took place at the Women's Centre at the YWCA, as the women did not want to be interviewed at the shelter. The majority of the participants were homeless at the time of the interviews. As part of our project, we have also interviewed allies. Group and individual interviews as well as research using photovoice will continue over the coming months.[5]

Data Collection

A variety of qualitative and participatory methods were used in this study. Eight men and women participated in one focus group and five women participated in another focus group. Eight participants were engaged in forty-five to sixty minute private interviews using a semi-structured interview guide. Five participants were involved in a photovoice workshop. Similar broad questions were used in the three groups to encourage participants to share their homeless experiences and their meanings of home. Each participant was given an honorarium of ten dollars after informed consent was obtained. Audio-recorded interviews were transcribed verbatim and stored in password-protected electronic files.[6]

Some themes were identified in data collected from twenty-one participants at the Thompson Homeless Shelter (THS) and the Thompson Crisis Centre (TCC), a women's shelter. As a result most of those interviewed were women. Their stories and experiences are captured under two main categories: the meaning of home and pathways to homelessness. Each is then subdivided into a number of subthemes. The first category is loosely organized in chronological sequence: prior to homelessness, and life while experiencing homelessness. We begin with stories regarding the meaning of home.

Meanings of Home

I sleep in the blue boxes, the bush, stairways, laundry rooms...

—Gloria

When participants were asked about the meaning of home, it was difficult for them to imagine home without talking about their struggles and their experience of homelessness. Consequently, this section begins by describing the meanings of home prior to homelessness and then follows with the altered meanings during life while experiencing homelessness.

Prior to Homelessness

For the women interviewed at the TCC, their meaning of home was often negatively influenced by memories of violence, instability, living in precarious conditions, being abused, and enduring poverty. For example, Betty described her situation before coming to the TCC as involving frequent temporary housing in multiple homes.

> I was in a domestic [abuse] relationship and I was tired of moving around every four or five months. Last year I moved four or five times. First I went to my uncle's house, then my cousins' house, then back to mom's, then my sister's.... I thought I would find a place here, but that's not going to happen. I have to go back again to [home community] next week to my parents' house. I've been here about a month. I have been trying to get a house in [home community] and here in Thompson. I have been on a waiting list at Manitoba housing for the past year. In [home community] there are three or four families living in one house. It's really overcrowded. I have to stay with my kids in one room...five kids and me.

Increased mobility and homelessness were the outcomes of ending an abusive relationship. Unfortunately, she was unsuccessful in finding a place to live in Thompson and consequently she believed she had no other choice but to return to precarious housing in her home community.

Glenda talked about being raised by her grandparents; their house was her home until her grandfather passed away. Up to that point, home had meant a sense of security and control. With her grandfather's passing, she and her grandmother lost authority over the house and other family members began making decisions about her housing situation. She explained, "I was getting harassed by my aunties to get out of my granny's house. My granny told me not to leave...but there are already many people living there (four adults and ten children). I have four children and they are here with me. When my grandpa passed away, my aunties start to harass me to leave." She had not only lost her grandfather, but also the security and support of living with her grandmother in her home. She now sees herself and her four children as homeless. She not only struggles to find a place to live but is also dealing with emotions as a consequence of her forced separation from her grandmother.

From the above two cases we find that loss of family and of a permanent place to stay, along with weakened connection to one's hometown, and a loss of security and control, all contribute to a negative meaning of home. These circumstances are further commented on by Florence: "I have nowhere to stay in my hometown. I got kicked out because my brother and I did not get along well. We have different lifestyles, we just didn't see eye to eye. He chose his way I chose mine and we just couldn't work it out. He was the one taking care of us after my mom passed away. Dad isn't in the picture. I was back and forth living at different family members, friends' places, so I just couldn't do it anymore." Such statements often reflected not having options to make choices. Similarly, Doris had to leave an abusive relationship and the only available home in the community was her mom's place, which was already overcrowded. Consequently, the women's shelter in Thompson became her only apparent choice: "I was abused and I didn't have any place to go, only my mom's place but I had to leave. There are twenty-three people already living there, and then me with my six kids. This is the only place I had to go. I chose the TCC because I'm protected here. This is my second time here. Growing up I lived with my granny, and sometimes my parents and sometimes foster homes."

Betty spoke about never truly feeling that she belongs. Her life so far has been a tangle of living arrangements in many different places and institutional settings; she has never truly had her own place. A continuous cycle of struggles and never experiencing what home might mean was a common theme. Now living at the TCC, she reflected on the condition: "I don't feel like I have ever had a home. I have been this way for the past ten years since I started having kids. I think a home should be relaxed and comfortable… a place I would be happy with my kids and not having to move around. My kids could have their friends over. It should be a place where I can make my own decisions."

To the women coming to the TCC, a sense of home is complex; it combines different visible and more elusive factors related to space, time, security, relationships, mobility, loss, and belonging. Home is clearly not a simple binary, of being housed or not. Rather, the meaning of home needs to be seen as a contentious and continuous process of definition and redefinition. We continue this discussion in the next section.

Life while Experiencing Homelessness

This idea that house and home are separate concepts is very much in keeping with our discussions with Elders, Indigenous service supporters, and the participants themselves. We listened to narrative descriptions and experiences of "being at home" that included diverse social, cultural, spiritual, and physical factors. Elder Robinson related that he had once been homeless due to addiction issues. He described that for him, being in the bush and being on the land was "being at home." For him and for many others who have experienced a transient life, the bush is a quiet, private place where one is in control of one's activities. For example, Elder Robinson spoke about the camps on the edge of town, and that some of those who are homeless prefer to stay there rather than in the shelters. These camps enable people to be independent, gain a sense of autonomy, and spend time with their friends and family. This is something they felt that they couldn't do within the restrictive parameters of the shelter (Robinson 2013). In our conversations with homeless people, they expressed that there were too many rules in the shelter, making them feel oppressed and like their sense of freedom was lost. That said there are risks with such housing options primarily due to the weather. Some will come into town to try to get into the shelter when the temperatures are extremely cold; others still prefer to stay in the camps despite the extreme winter temperatures. Elder Robinson takes on the personal responsibility of checking in on people in those camps, particularly when the temperatures get below −35°C.

When participants using the THS were asked what the meaning of home was to them, their responses were often more focused on the immediacy of the current situation and the need to find some form of shelter in order to sleep. For example, due to THS policies and the limited capacity to host all the people who need to find a place to sleep, getting a bed there each day is a continuous challenge. Some participants spoke about having to regularly find alternative places to sleep. For example, Fred stated, "We use the camp even in winter when they don't let us into the shelter. I used to walk ten kilometres to a camp when I couldn't get into the shelter. The shelter is always crowded. Some people can't get in and have to sleep in the doorway or sleep in a tent on the edge of town."

The THS is the city's main resource during the winter season but the blue boxes (dumpsters) are sometimes used as another option for those who are homeless, as Martha explained:

> I have been staying at the shelter off and on for about a year. In the summertime I don't bother with the shelter. I stay in a blue box or in the bush. I just go there [shelter] for meals. Sometimes I sleep outside in the wintertime too. I have been staying here for about ten months now but didn't stay here all summer. I usually sleep outside...in the bush. I have to drink and I can't be with my old man in here so I prefer to stay outside with my old man. You can't drink here. I am a heavy drinker. It's a daily thing for me. I love to drink because it eases my pain...takes all my hurt away. In the summer there is a lot of people living in the bush [on the edge of town]. Nobody hardly stays at the homeless shelter in the summer, only eat there, except when it's raining. When it's cold everyone wants to be inside.

Other options are stairways, laundry rooms, and the Addictions Foundation of Manitoba (AFM). Gloria commented:

I first went to the shelter in 2003. I was in and out. After my ex died of cancer, I lost my kids, and stayed at the homeless shelter. They took my home, my kids...I was homeless in Winnipeg too. I didn't know where to go and friends showed me the shelter...or sleeping outside or in shacks...just to be safe there were a bunch of us...we would walk around all night...stay up all night. Here...the blue boxes, the bush, stairways, laundry rooms, but then I went to the AFM. They put me down [on a list]....when I came back they told me I was evicted. So I went to the homeless shelter again just recently. I plan to go back to the AFM again.

The THS is often not included in the participants' meaning of home as being a safe place in which you can rest and sleep. As described by Evelyn, "You have to straighten out first before you get a home. You go to the treatment centre first and get your life straightened out, then get a place, then go job hunting, or to school. You need somewhere safe. If you were there [in the shelter] right now, you couldn't sleep. People yelling and pounding at the door, snoring. A home is where you have your own key." In this case, home is not associated with the need for temporary or transitional housing such as shelters, but rather with the need for a secure and more permanent condition of being housed. For the female participants, these conditions were often directly associated with living with their children:

"For me it's having my kids with me under the same roof. And having food in the fridge, being able to provide for my kids. That's home for me" (Martha).

"My dream of a home would be to feel safe, and a good environment for me and my baby with a nice backyard where they won't hurt themselves...a nice clean healthy environment" (Ruby).

"Home is a place where you are not being abused, a place where you are encouraged to go forward, not backward. A home is where you can be independent with your children... violence-free is what I consider home" (Florence).

"Home is where you can feel comfortable and be able to breathe and feel free. It's like having a nest with my kids. Home is being content and not threatened. It is to feel love and being wanted... a feeling of confidence in self and growing with possibility. You have to be careful who you bring into the house. Don't bring in trouble" (Roberta).

Having a stable place to go home to and being able to keep that place are important identifiers. Henrietta, who has successfully transitioned into permanent housing, explains: "It feels wonderful when I'm done work and I'm able to go home to a place. But it's a struggle for me too, because I'm a single mom and rent is high. I pay $1,200 a month for my townhouse. I'm barely hanging in but for my kids I'm willing to do anything for them. Now that I have a home, the challenge is keeping it...very high rent." That said, shelters and transitional homes can offer comprehensive services and programs and have the staff and programming to provide more than just a bed to crash for the night. Thompson Crisis Centre (TCC) provides not only a place to stay in flight from domestic violence but also has the supports and resources to help women move forward and acquire the tools needed to regain their stability. For some of those interviewed, the TCC's transitional housing provided a space to build a sense of safety, belonging, and community. They described life at the TCC in very appreciative terms. For example, the TCC can provide counselling and resources to empower women to leave abusive relationships and recover in a safe and secure environment: "I like it here. I like the women and I get counseling. Women here are really nice people and I didn't have this support before" (Glenda).

Although it is a transitional space, the TCC offers protection for extended periods of time. Women appreciate having this option when leaving abusive relationships: "This is the only place I had to go. I chose the TCC because I'm protected here. This is my second time here. I have been here for five months. I have six children here with me" (Doris). From their stories, it was clear that women there receive the support to become empowered, have their needs satisfied, make their own choices, and take control of their lives. Roberta's comments confirm this: "I have these women here to help me, to give me a push... to focus on what I want. They showed me how to be more consistent with my needs. They made me see a difference. They helped me to be good to myself and to be more assertive. I used to think that nobody believed me. I like it here." What often is still missing is the support system for women staying there to transition into affordable and permanent housing once their stay at the TCC is completed.

In conclusion, for people who find themselves homeless and on the street in Thompson, the bush camps have offered, some, a sense of being at home. Others have had to focus on the immediacy of finding temporary shelter on a daily basis in order to survive the night. For the eight women interviewed at the TCC, home includes a greater sense of permanency, and is described as a place where you can live independently and have a sense of control and safety.

Pathways to Homelessness

A homeless pathway has been defined more specifically as the route of an individual or household into homelessness, their experience of homelessness and their route out of homelessness into secure housing.

—Anderson and Tulloch 2000
quoted in Somerville 2013, 39

The stories of those interviewed were similar. Many came to Thompson from their home communities because of overcrowding or behavioural issues. Some came for medical reasons and couldn't get back home. Others fell into addictions due to depression or mental illness. Some went directly from jail to the streets of Thompson. All the women interviewed at the TCC described domestic violence as a major cause of homelessness. They were targets of violence committed by husbands or partners and/or other family members, and their only option was to leave. The following describes some of the participants' pathways to homelessness in Thompson, including such factors such as housing shortages, reserve dynamics, impact of the child welfare system, domestic violence, racism, and exclusion.

Housing Shortage

The lack of opportunities in the reserve communities often pushes Indigenous people to move to Thompson. In addition to poor economic and social conditions, people leave the reserve as a consequence of the housing shortage. Once they are in Thompson, the lack of affordable housing, both in terms of overall numbers of units and cost is a major cause of homelessness. Elder Robinson remarked on this, "There is a lot of overcrowding on reserves, so people come to Thompson to get away. People come to Thompson and don't want to go back to the reserve, but there is a housing shortage here. People can't afford the rent and there are also rent increases."

Henrietta expands on this by adding her experience of the housing shortage after coming to Thompson for a post-secondary education:

> My experience of being homeless began when I came out to go to school. I was a single mom with one daughter. I came out to school when she was six months old. My sister was living here but we didn't get along so well. It was hard to stay in her place... meanwhile I was searching for a place in town. It was hard for me. It took me about a year to get a one bedroom. That's when I went back to school. I started from the bottom and I'm glad I went back

to school. It was hard being a single mom especially when there was no housing in Thompson.

In addition to housing shortage, other obstacles also increase the risk of homelessness. For example, a renter must have a co-signer in order to sign a lease, as was the case with Henrietta: "They [renters] require co-signers and no one wants to co-sign so it gets harder for everyone... I never did find someone to co-sign. At the time I didn't know what a co-signer meant. Finally, someone gave me a place. It worked out. I was lucky at that time. Before that I stayed with my sister but it was crowded. It was a one bedroom and she had her kids too. But she supported me."

Reserve Dynamics

Participants reported different social and individual factors on reserve and in other northern communities that contributed to their pathways to homelessness. These included behavioral issues, limited resources, overcrowding, and accessibility. Some voluntarily moved to Thompson from their reserve with the hope of employment and educational opportunities. Others involuntarily moved after they were forced to leave their reserves through a Band Council Resolution (BCR).[7] Once in Thompson, they often have to deal with issues such as poor health and addictions. This was the case with Fred: "I came to Thompson because I was kicked out of the home for drinking. There was a lot of people living there. I originally got sick so I couldn't work, then I started drinking. I need a letter from the doctor to go back to work...in the meantime I stay at the shelter."

Addictions sometimes force people to leave the reserve and when they arrive in the city, they find that a drug problem can often exclude them from getting a bed in the Thompson Homeless Shelter. There are no resources for treatment in the reserve communities. Addiction can also result because of street life once reserve-leavers get to Thompson. The Aboriginal Liaison for the Northern Health Region talks about such experiences: "People come to Thompson and gradually get addictions. They are often not let into the shelter because of addictions. Communities often BCR a person. The band gives them three chances [drugs or behavioral problems], then eventually they are asked to leave. There are no resources in First Nations communities and no confidentiality." Alcohol consumption, along with mental health issues, and leaving jail without housing in place can lead to further risks of becoming homelessness. For Cheryl, homelessness was also interconnected with her children being taken away by the child welfare system. Cheryl talked about her experience, "I don't get to see my kids... they are all in care. I have alcohol problems. I'm always in and out of jail. I can't stop drinking. I have too much grief. I have tried rehab many times, but go back to drinking. I suffer from depression." Poor housing conditions and accidents on reserve are other pathways to homelessness. This was the case for David and his family: "My home burned down on reserve. My family is at camp in the bush. I'm waiting for them to come and get me. I need to sober up. I want to go back to the bush. Once in trouble, it's hard to get out."

Impact of the Child Welfare System

Some single parents, who lose their children to the child welfare system, find themselves homeless. This was commented on by the Aboriginal Liaison for the Northern Health Region, who works daily with similar issues. She stated, "Often children are apprehended by social services. There is no support for parents such as addictions counselling, literacy training, or counselling to deal with depression after children are apprehended. For a single person with no children they only get about $200.00 a month [on social assistance]. They can't live on that. This in turn causes drinking due to stress, despair, and the influence of others who are also in despair" (Lathlin 2013).

The impact of child welfare cannot be underestimated. Cindy Blackstock (2003) wrote "that there may now be as many as three times more Aboriginal children in the care of child welfare authorities compared to those placed in residential schools at the height of those operations in the 1940's. For Pete Hudson and Brad McKenzie, these figures are not surprising, in that effects of colonization, including underlying socio-economic issues as well as family breakdown and parenting problems, are not erased simply by the creation of community-based child and family services agencies" (quoted in Comack et al. 2013, 16).

Domestic Violence

For the eight women interviewed at the TCC there were some commonalities between their stories about what circumstances brought them to a women's crisis shelter in Thompson. They all identified as Indigenous women, they all had children and some of their children had been apprehended by the child welfare system, the majority had lived in overcrowded housing on their home reserves, and all of them had fled violent domestic situations. Being a resident at the TCC was not new for Edna. Twenty years earlier she had come to this same place as a child, when her mom found herself in a similarly violent situation. Now she too is a direct victim of spousal abuse. She talked about a life of living in an insecure home and in an abusive relationship:

My spouse always locked me out of my house. This is one of the main reasons I am here. I was sick and tired of being locked out of my own home. I would stay home isolated from friends and family and would want to go out and when I did he wouldn't let me back in. I would usually go to my mother's when this happened. I warned him I would leave if he kept on doing this, so finally I left. I have been here for five months now…this is my first time of being here [as an adult].

Pregnancy was mentioned as another reason for coming to the TCC, as in the case of Ruby. She was in a relationship with her partner who became physically abusive when she got pregnant. Ruby commented, "I am here because of my relationship with my ex. He threw me out because I was pregnant and he does not want a child." Domestic violence can cause long-term housing instability and insecurity. Such was the case of the participant mentioned above who has been living on the street, in a tent, at the YWCA, and the TCC. Ruby explained,

I had been living on the street for three months the previous year… in a tent near the hospital for a few weeks. I was a single mother, bouncing from place to place with my baby when I went to the YWCA, things got physical and he knocked me down. After this I lost my child who went into care and my room at the YWCA. Whenever I had a stable place he was there to take me away. I've been here [TCC] for nine months and this is the longest apartment I have ever had of my own. I am always hiding from him, but eventually he finds me out and comes there.

Economic violence was also a cause of homelessness for some of the women at the THS. They reported different experiences in which their partners controlled their money and caused them distress and loss of control, home, children, and health. For instance Martha commented:

Well, what happened was I went for my conference in Edmonton and I found that my husband cashed all my cheques and I was waiting for him to send me money. So I started drinking… went back home for a while. Then we started having problems. I came back out for a medical and I never went back. I left my husband and my kids. My kids got taken away. I didn't feel like going back [to the reserve]…I have five kids…all of them were taken away. I was given chances but I keep messing it up. So I start drinking heavily. My husband was with another woman so I start drinking. He came and got me but he started abusing me. I was scared to go back home with him so I thought I would stick around here. We had opportunities to get our kids back but we didn't get along, we couldn't live under the same roof.

The above stories of domestic violence and physical, emotional, and economic abuse show multiple, complex, and interconnected stressors that increase the likelihood of homelessness for women and children.

Racism and Exclusion

Racism was a common and recurring theme in the daily lives of those we interviewed. Participants told different stories of racism related to housing, for instance, Evelyn described her circumstances:

[Racism is when you] lost your home… lost your apartment… when you can't get along with another person…there is racism… people complaining and complaining about you. The person right next door… when I have friends over, just laughing not partying or anything, and she is constantly knocking at my door. So one day I went to drop off my resumes and all of a sudden they changed the lock on me. They threw all my clothes away… everything. The owner is there and the caretaker. That's how I ended up at the shelter. I was sleeping in the bush. That's where I ended up last year. I couldn't stay with my family. I don't get along with my family.

While there are clear challenges to finding a place to sleep at night, there are additional struggles regarding how to spend the day, especially when it is very cold. When the shelter is closed, there is not an indoor place for the homeless people to congregate and relax during the day. For example, the city malls and businesses have hired security staff specifically to monitor and control the homeless who try to enter such places. When Fred was asked what he does during the day, he commented, "Go out and walk around…talk to friends… no place to go. I can't even go to McDonalds. They ask you to leave. We stay together…safety in numbers. We always walk together especially at night. You get jumped or beat up otherwise. The security guards at the mall poke you or hit you and yell abuse." As previously described, daily life is characterized by a monotonous cycle of wandering to stay safe and warm and have basic needs met.

Immediate and Relative Needs

Kennedy (2013) asserts, "a need implies, that unless it is met, a person will be harmed in some way." Participants in the study expressed different levels of needs when they were asked about their meaning of "home." Their responses can be categorized into two groups: the "immediate and relative needs" (Dean 2010) articulated by those living in absolute homelessness, and "relative needs" articulated by those whose homelessness is more hidden or less visible. The following discussion expands on this difference.

The eight people interviewed at the Thompson Homeless Shelter often focused on more immediate needs. This makes sense considering their precarious situations. For example, they wanted security, comfort, and privacy. When asked what their idea of "home" was, they listed the following basic security needs: "feel safe," "lockers, "even hard to keep clothes here…have to sleep on your shoes." They also talked about comfort needs such as "a warm place in winter," "place to relax," "my own bed," "access to shower and laundry," and "nutritional food." In addition, these participants highlighted the need to have privacy. For example, one participant mentioned, "I need a real home before I can go to school or do training…there is nowhere to do homework here." The participants also discussed relative needs related to ownership and belonging: "a place to eat whenever we want" and "whatever we want and traditional food." Some also expressed occupational and leisure needs such "access to services, advice and training (training such as computer skills and high school upgrading)," "a place to do crafts, beading, and sewing" and "to entertain."

For the women staying at Thompson Crisis Centre, home is a place to embrace changes needed to enhance one's life, thereby reflecting more relative needs. For example, Edna's goal was "to get my own place, that way family can come over and help me out, and continue to go to school…having my children with me. They are the most important part of my life." This goal was reinforced by Betty, "a place to be yourself." Florence added, "I plan on getting my own home one of these days, no abuse, no drugs, it will be mine." All of them include their children in their goals as did Doris, "to find a place to live for me and my kids…a nice clean place…I want a better future…to live healthier. I would like a beautiful house with a roof over our heads…nice background we can call our own…a school close by." Clearly, the stability offered to the women at the TCC provides them with greater opportunities to think about embracing change and more long-term goals. Sadly, that was rarely heard in the voices of those staying at the THS, their meanings of home were often framed around issues of immediacy and survival. Even those using the bush camps offered more optimistic expressions of hope for the future.

Relationships and community were a big part of TCC women's relative needs as Edna explained, "Getting women together, being able to talk together and build relationships." Mary added, "...having somebody here to talk to who knows what you're going through, and having a shelter and food." Such relative needs for support were also expressed by other homeless northern people. For example, Roberta stated that, "We need more people to go out there on the street and talk to people. I am familiar with how they got there. For us northern people, you have to talk to people who are homeless and not in a detrimental way. You need to use the right voice and body skills and to really listen to them. Know where people are from and know their dialect. Give them the time... maybe three or four visits."

In addition to meeting relative needs, women wanted to make sustainable moves away from violence and they did not want their children to continue the same patterns as their fathers. For example, Edna asserted, "I left my spouse in the first place so my children would know it's not right that he was treating me that way." They also commented that women need more support to flee from violence as Ruby said, "I don't feel like there is help for women after violence." One suggestion was for programs that provide a safe place to live for single mothers. Some commented on the need to have better support while living on reserve to be able to make sustainable changes. As Doris explained, "Bands should help their people first. They sent us away. After I left this building last time... I went back to an abusive relationship. They apprehended my kids. I have been working on myself. One day, I just left the relationship and now I'm here." Ruby also highlighted the need to work on herself to achieve goals. She said, "Getting support to help myself... healing myself... I looked for programs to help myself. I'm not leaving this place until I have proper housing for myself and my children. We need our own beds, our own kitchen where we could cook. I want a safe place where there is no drama, no abuse, and no guy coming in to hurt us."

In order to build the bases for a new life, education was often mentioned as being important by the women at the TCC. Edna commented, "I am trying my best to get my GED and would like to one day join the social work program." Mary was also determined to go further in her life, "I'm trying to finish school. I have finished up to grade 10. I applied at UCN, either here or The Pas will work as long as my school gets done. Get a good job, a home." Some were clear about how housing fits in with their future careers. Betty commented, "I want to go back to school when I have a place to stay. I want to finish high school then maybe social work or RCMP. I almost finished grade 12." Glenda also wanted to finish her high school, "I want to finish school. I'm twenty-eight, so I want to get a house. I want a home. I want to go into nursing." Roberta wants to help other women: "I want to go back to my health career. I want to help women out there."

So far we have discussed three main concepts relating to homelessness in northern Manitoba. These were meanings of home, pathways to homelessness, and immediate and relative needs. In the next section we will draw conclusions about these concepts in order to reaffirm the importance of including Indigenous homeless voices in any attempts to design and develop meaningful and long-term initiatives.

Discussion

This study explores the meaning of home as expressed by research participants who are homeless in Thompson, Manitoba, and looks at how their stories can be incorporated into the co-construction of the concept of home. We reaffirm that defining homelessness is a complex matter, as it includes multi-dimensional problems, terms, factors, roots, relationships, and life experiences of those experiencing homelessness. We agree with Clapham (2003) who highlights the "importance of dimensions of home and homelessness other than the physical—for example, ontological, territorial and spiritual" (cited in Somerville 2013, 391). However, some still limit the causes of homelessness to structural and individual attributes (Fitzpatrick, 2005 quoted in Somerville 2013, 398).

We need to move beyond seeing homelessness as a structural matter and beyond blaming the homeless themselves. Particularly in the northern perspective we must face the consequences of colonization. Colonization has had a direct impact on the lives of Indigenous people who experienced residential schools, displacement, and loss of their language and culture. In this regard, Memmott and Chambers (2010) present different categories of Indigenous "homelessness," including spiritual homelessness which they define as "a state arising from separation from traditional land, and from family and kinship networks (noted earlier as a result of historical government policies), and involving a crisis of personal identity wherein a person's understanding or knowledge of how they relate to country, family and Aboriginal identity systems is confused or lacking" (10). Consequences of colonization were ever present as we asked the participants to discuss their meanings of home.

Multi-Dimensional Meaning of Home

This study found that Indigenous participants staying in Thompson's homeless shelters and crisis centres emphasized certain meanings of home prior to homelessness and while experiencing homelessness. Prior to their homelessness, they often associated the meaning of home with structural factors such as poverty, access to housing, patriarchy, domestic violence, lack of appropriate services and inadequate infrastructure leading to overcrowded houses. When participants experienced absolute homelessness, their main meaning of home reflected their immediate need to have a roof over their head and a place to live and sleep. This became their highest priority under such conditions. They often defined home in connection to immediate safety, personal control, and privacy. When reflecting on home during hidden/less visible homelessness, participants often defined home in terms of spiritual and familial meanings of belonging, community, instability for their children and family, and loss. Home also meant a physical and social environment that provides long-term security, allows relationships to build and dreams of the future to take hold. Because of the multiple and changing meanings of home, the participants implied that there were many pathways in and out of homelessness.

Homeless Pathways

In our research the main homeless pathways were heavily influenced by housing shortages, reserve dynamics, the impact of the child welfare, domestic violence, and racism and exclusion. The narratives of our participants in regard to these pathways showed the benefits of including the voices of the homeless in the development and assessment of homeless strategies. In particular, they helped to build a more realistic picture of the route in and out of homelessness. This was especially evident in the stories of the women staying at the Thompson Crisis Centre who shared with us their journey in dealing with domestic violence and the lack of supports in their own communities. In his work, Somerville (2013) provides further insight into such experiences: "the meaning of home is not significantly different for battered women from what it is for women in general, and so similarly with the meaning of homelessness. However, the experience of home for battered women becomes increasingly dangerous as time goes on, and unless the assailant can be successfully excluded from the home, homelessness may come to be seen as safer" (535).

We agree with Groot and co-authors (2011) who assert, "The literature on pathways to homelessness and associated risks does not provide an adequate picture in term of the socio-political context and lived realities of many Indigenous homeless people. Thus, a perspective informed by an Indigenous world view is crucial for developing our understanding of experiences of homelessness among such peoples" (378). Focusing on the stories of Indigenous people experiencing homelessness allowed us to understand the issue within their own contexts, culture, and needs.

Immediate and Relative Needs

Similar to other studies (see Hart 2010) that discuss the poor living conditions on some reserves, most of the participants in this study came to Thompson in search of a better life or to escape the trauma they experienced in their own communities. Their stories spoke of overcrowded housing, behavioural and addictions issues, and domestic violence. Once they arrived in the city, they faced many challenges finding a place to live, due to the chronic shortage in housing, and a lack of facilities to support them. In addition they often experienced racism along with other forms of exclusion that impacted their ability to find adequate housing. Many of these issues are not new. By reaffirming them here, we show a continued need for the inclusion of Indigenous homeless people's voices in defining what is home and what are the options to recover their experiences, to identify their needs, and to satisfy those needs.

Earlier in this chapter, we briefly described the current homeless programs and initiatives being offered or proposed in the city of Thompson. These initiatives are primarily designed to meet short-term palliative strategies that have for the most part been developed by experts and authorities. Under the principle of affected interest, we propose that these programs need to be expanded to include the voices of the homeless. This reflects the premise that collaboration with those affected should occur during any analysis of their needs and in determining how their needs will be satisfied (Dean 2010). Manfred Max-Neef (1991) conceives needs as "deprivation and potential...they reflect a dialectical process in as much as they are in constant movement... better to speak of realizing, experiencing or actualizing needs through time and space." His definition helps us to explain why we argue for the inclusion of Indigenous homeless voices in continuous dialogues on homelessness. Indigenous perspectives aid us to be more inclusive in our reflections on forms of organization, political structures, social practices, subjective conditions, values and norms, spaces, contexts, behaviours, and attitudes that contribute both to stabilization and change. This dialogical process is also an invitation to allies, Indigenous homeless people, service providers, businesses, and the community at large to come together to co-create a space to continue this dialogue. Action is needed to promote change and foster well-being of those northerners who have been excluded from society and have been viewed only as subjects of charity and emergency services, or as negative stereotypes.[8]

To conclude this section, this chapter extends knowledge of homelessness, and echoes some of the existing research on northern and rural homelessness (Peters and Robillard 2009; Christensen 2012; George and O'Neill 2011; Kauppi et al. 2013; Fidler and Bonnycastle 2003). Poverty, instability, relationship breakdown, domestic violence, and a lack of choices precede homelessness for the participants in this study. Additional hardship, anxieties, and suffering result once they fail to find a place, or have to stay in transitional shelters. We also believe that there are factors unique to northern Manitoba and the city of Thompson, particularly its history as a resource-driven and relatively new municipality that affect its homeless population. The city was only built in the 1950s and, like many mining enterprises in that era, there was no consultation with First Nations.

From its beginnings, Indigenous people came to Thompson to try and find work and some ended up living on the edge of town, due to racism and a lack of housing ("Indian May Get Help from Private Industry" 1968). For many Indigenous people in the region, because of a history of colonization, the boom and bust economics of the area, and the relocation and displacement resulting from hydroelectric development, home remains a "contentious and continuous process of definition and redefinition" (McKay quoted in Kulchyski and Neckoway 2006, 11). Some of the experiences of Thompson's Indigenous homeless may be similar to this volume's Prout Quicke and Green's discussion of the Australian "fringe dwellers" or Schiff, Turner, and Waegemakers-Schiff's discussion of the migration and mobility between reserves and urban centres.

Understanding the meanings of home, the pathways to homelessness, and the immediate and relative needs is important to this research process. In the future we will continue engaging Indigenous homeless people in dialogue regarding their knowledge and experiences. In particular, our research plans are to focus more on what strategies the participants may have for addressing their needs and alleviating homelessness in the north. In this way we can move closer to the co-production of solutions and the transformation of services to better meet their needs.

Conclusion

In large part, this research project has been successful in recruiting participants due to the involvement of allies, with whom homeless people have already built trust and relationships. Early on we discovered that homeless-allies and a community-engaged approach was the most effective way to engage more participants in our research. It helped us to build on current relationships that service providers already had with marginalized groups, to eventually achieve larger objectives. The allies who participated in this research project were instrumental in recruiting over twenty-one participants who have been interviewed to date. The waiting list for future participants is very promising and we will continue working together with those who are homeless, with the service providers, and with fellow academics in response to our main questions. To conclude this chapter, we offer the following three recommendations, to feed the dialogue on this issue:

1. As stated in the *Community Plan 2011–2014*, we recommend that the Thompson Community Advisory Board for Homelessness create the space and opportunity for homeless people themselves to advise and make recommendations for future homelessness strategies.

2. That the Main Street North Project incorporates a bush/land component into their strategy in order to create the space for Indigenous people to "be at home."

3. That policy makers incorporate the popular slogan, borrowed from the disability movement, "nothing about us without us" (Charlton 2000) into any decision making process in the future.

We strongly believe that the complexity of homelessness in Thompson and northern Manitoban communities cannot be addressed by isolated solutions without including the voices of Indigenous homeless people and without a coordinated effort on the part of allies and service providers. There is a need and the opportunity to develop programs and solutions that show compassion and justice for those who have been excluded and marginalized.

Acknowledgements

This research is being funded by the generous financial support of the Social Sciences and Humanities Research Council of Canada through the Manitoba Research Alliance grant: "Partnering for Change—Community-Based Solutions for Aboriginal and Inner-City Poverty." We wish to express a sincere thank you to the twenty-one Indigenous women and men for sharing their stories, experiences, and knowledge with us. We would like to extend special thanks to the allies of this research project who shared with us their wisdom, knowledge, and their connection to Indigenous homeless people. We extend thanks to the Thompson Homelessness Shelter, the Thompson Crisis Centre, the Boys and Girls Club, and the YWCA for their help in recruiting participants and providing space for our meetings and interviews. Warm thanks go to Karla Schulz and Melissa Gunn, the research assistants on this project, as well as other students who have worked with us in this and other projects; we value their commitment, knowledge, enthusiasm and support. A special gratitude goes to our friends Colin Bonnycastle, Greg Stott, and Carolyn Creed for taking the time to comment and for editing earlier versions of this paper. Finally, we want to acknowledge the support of our three institutions to conduct this collaborative research: the University of Manitoba, Faculty of Social Work; the University College of the North, Faculty of Arts and Science; and the City of Thompson, Public Safety Department.

Notes

1   Photovoice is an approach that encourages dialogue, storytelling, and the sharing of ideas and has been used in a variety of projects in which participants engage in data collection and analysis (Palibroda et al. 2009; Wang and Burris 1997; Walsh, Rutherford, and Kuzmak 2010; Bonnycastle 2013).

2   "Damp housing" means that people who have been consuming alcohol or who are intoxicated can be accommodated (Project Northern Doorway, 2012).

3   As quoted in Gaetz, Scott, and Gulliver (2013, 2), "Housing First is a recovery-oriented approach to homelessness that involves moving people who experience homelessness into independent and permanent housing as quickly as possible, with no preconditions, and then providing them with additional services and supports as needed."

4   The concept of wraparound services is used to describe any program that is flexible, family or person-oriented and comprehensive – that is, a number of organizations work together to provide a holistic program of supports" (The Homeless Hub http://homelesshub.ca/solutions/tools-and-strategies-support-collaboration-coordination-integration/wrap-around-delivery).

5   Approval for this research study was obtained from the University of Manitoba, Psychology/ Sociology Research Ethics Board. All participants were volunteers and were free to withdraw from the study at any time. Participation, whenever possible, was confidential and participants were able to withdraw from the study without affecting any services they received. All participants completed informed consent forms and were given the choice of individual and group interviews.

6   The actual names of home communities have been left out to ensure confidentiality. Similarly pseudonyms have been used in place of real names of participants. Content-analysis techniques (Smith and Sparkes 2005) were used to identify themes across interviews and focus groups. Using NVIVO qualitative software, transcriptions were analyzed by identifying themes that responded to their meaning of "home" and by determining how the knowledge of those who are homeless living in Thompson, Manitoba, can be incorporated into the co-construction of the concept of home. Data was not included for the photovoice project with the five youth from the Youth Build program. We felt that their needs and experiences were quite different from those living at the Thompson Homeless Shelter and the Thompson Crisis Centre, so we decided to exclude this data until we have done more youth interviews in the future.

7   A written decision made by a (First Nations) band council. The decision is made during a council meeting and must have the support of the majority of council members. A BCR can enable reserve authorities to expel a community member if deemed necessary (https://www.ontario.ca/page/aboriginal-glossary-terms#section-).

8   As quoted in Wilfreda E. Thurston, David Turner and Cynthia Bird's chapter in this book.

References

Ackerly, Brooke, and Jacqui True. 2010. *Doing Feminist Research in Political & Social Science*. New York: Palgrave Macmillan.

Alfred, Gerald Taiaiake. 2009. "Colonialism and State Dependency." *Journal of Aboriginal Health* 5 (2): 42–60.

Anderson, Debra K. 2006. "Mucking through the Swamp: Changing the Pedagogy of Social Welfare Policy Course." *Journal of Teaching in Social Work* 26 (1/2): 1–17.

Barker, John. 2013. "Rick Oberdorfer Letter on Behalf of Thompson Unlimited Board of Directors' Advocates Public Shaming of Intoxicated." *Thompson Citizen*, 9 September.

Baskin, Cyndy. 2007. "Aboriginal Youth Talk about Structural Determinants as the Causes of Their Homelessness." *First People Child and Family Review* 3 (3): 31–42.

Bishop, Anne. 1994. *Becoming an Ally: Breaking the Cycle of Pppression*. Halifax: Fernwood Publishing.

Bonnycastle, Marleny M. 2013. "Homeless not Hopeless: Photographs & Stories from the Street. Thompson, MB: University of Manitoba, Northern Social Work Program.

Borg, Marit, Dave Sells, Alain Topor, Roberto Mezzina, Izabel Marin, and Larry Davidson. 2005. "What Makes a House a Home: The Role of Material Resources in Recovery from Severe Mental Illness." *American Journal of Psychiatric Rehabilitation* 8 (3): 243–56.

Buccieri, Kristy. 2013. "Waldo 101: Mapping the Instersection of Space, Place, and Gender in the Lives of Ten Homeless Youth." In *Youth Homelessness in Canada: Implications for Policy and Practice*, edited by Stephen Gaetz, Bill O'Grady, Kristy Buccieri, Jeff Karabanow and Allyson Marsolais, 425–44. Toronto: Canadian Homelessness Research Network Press.

Charlton, James I. 2000. *Nothing About Us without Us: Disability, Oppression and Empowerment*. Berkeley: University of California Press.

Christensen, Julia. 2012. "'They Want a Different Life': Rural Northern Settlement Dynamics and Pathways to Homelessness in Yellowknife and Inuvik, Northwest Territories." *Canadian Geographer/ Le Géographe Canadien* 56 (4): 419–38.

Christensen, Julia. 2013. "'Our Home, Our Way of life': Spiritual Homelessness and the Sociocultural Dimensions of Indigenous Homelessness in the Northwest Territories (NWT), Canada." *Social and Cultural Geography* 14 (7): 804–28.

City of Thompson. 2012. *Homelessness Proposal: Project Northern Doorway*. Thompson, MB: City of Thompson.

_____. 2013a. "Extreme Cold Weather Policy." In *PD—1.0*, edited by City of Thompson. Thompson, MB: City of Thompson.

_____. 2013b. *The Thompson Aboriginal Accord: Progress Report*. Thompson, MB.

Cockell, Jeanie, and Joan McArthur-Blair. 2012. *Appreciative Inquiry in Higher Education: A Transformative Force*. San Francisco, CA: Jossey-Bass.

Comack, Elizabeth, Lawrence Deane, Larry Morrissette, and Jim Silver. 2013. *"Indians Wear Red": Colonialism, Resistance, and Aboriginal Street Gangs*. Halifax: Fernwood Publishing.

Corrado Research and Evaluation Associates. 2003. *Housing Discrimination and Aboriginal People in Winnipeg and Thompson, Manitoba.* Ottawa: Canada Mortgage and Housing Corporation.

Dahl, Robert. 1970. *After the Revolution? Authority in a Good Society.* New Haven: Yale University Press.

Dean, Hartley. 2010. *Understanding Human Needs: Social Issues, Policy and Practice.* Portland, OR: The Policy Press.

FemNorthNet Project. 2012. *Women, Economic Development & Restructuring in Thompson.* Ottawa: Canadian Research Institute for the Advancement of Women.

Fernandez, Lynne, Shauna MacKinnon, and Jim Silver, eds. 2010. *The Social Determinants of Health in Manitoba.* Winnipeg: Canadian Centre for Policy Alternatives, Manitoba Office.

Fidler, Greg, and Colin Bonnycastle. 2003. "A Search for Understanding Homelessness in Northern Manitoba." *Native Social Work Journal* 5 (November): 261–69.

Freire, Paulo. 1995. *Pedagogy of the Oppressed.* New York: Continuum.

Gaetz, Stephen. 2012. *The Real Cost of Homelessness: Can We Save Money by Doing the Right Thing?* Toronto: Canadian Homelessness Research Network Press.

Gaetz, Stephen, Fiona Scott, and Tanya Gulliver, eds. 2013. *Housing First in Canada: Supporting Communities to End Homelessness.* Toronto: Canadian Homelessness Research Network Press.

George, Serena D., and Linda K. O'Neill. 2011. "The Northern Experience of Street-Involved Youth: A Narrative Inquire." *Canadian Journal of Counselling and Psychotherapy* 45 (4): 365–85.

Gould, Thomas E., and Arthur R. Williams. 2010. "Family Homelessness: An Investigation of Structural Effects." *Journal of Human Behavior in the Social Environment* 20 (2): 170–92.

Graham, Ian. 2013. "KTC Hosts Discussion on Homelessness and Racism." *Thompson Citizen,* 30 October.

Groot, Shiloh, Darrin Hodgetts, Linda Waimarie Nikora, and Chez Leggat-Cook. 2011. "A Māori Homeless Woman." *Ethnography* 12 (3): 375–97.

Hart, Michael Anthony. 2010. "Colonization, Social Exclusion, and Indigenous Health." In *The Social Determinants of Health,* edited by Lynne Fernandez, Shauna MacKinnon, and Jim Silver, 115–25. Winnipeg, MB: Canadian Centre for Policy Alternatives, Manitoba Office.

Hall, Budd L., George Jerry Sefa Dei, and Dorothy Goldin Rosenberg, eds. 2000. *Indigenous Knowledges in Global Contexts: Multiple Readings of Our World.* Toronto: University of Toronto Press.

"Indians May Get Help from Private Industry." 1968. *Ottawa Citizen,* 4 December.

Kauppi, Carol, Henri Pallard, Kathy King, Katrina Srigley, Suzanne Lemieux, Thomas Matukala Nkosi, Arshi Shaikh, and Roger Gervais. 2013. *Homelessness in North Bay.* Sudbury, ON: Laurentian University, Centre for Research in Social Justice and Policy.

Kennedy, Patricia. 2013. *Key Themes in Social Policy.* New York: Routledge.

Kidd, Sean A., Jeff Karabanow, Jean Hughes, and Tyler Frederick. 2013. "Brief Report: Youth Pathways out of Homelessness: Preliminary Findings." *Journal of Adolescence* 36 (9): 1035–37.

Klodawsky, Fran. 2009. "Home Spaces and Rights to the City: Thinking Social Justice for Chronically Homeless Women." *Urban Geography* 30 (6): 591–610.

Kulchyski, Peter, and Ramona Neckoway with Gerald McKay and Robert Buck 2006. *The Town That Lost Its Name: The Impact of Hydroelectric Development on Grand Rapids, Manitoba.* Winnipeg: Canadian Centre for Policy Alternatives.

Lathlin, Cynthia. 2013. "Personal communication." Thompson, MB, 27 November.

MacKinnon, Shauna. 2010. "Housing: A Major Problem in Manitoba." In *The Social Determinants of Health*, edited by Lynne Fernandez, Shauna MacKinnon, and Jim Silver, 139–49. Winnipeg: Canadian Centre for Policy Alternatives, Manitoba Office.

MacKinnon, Shauna, and Charlene Lafreniere. 2009. *Fast Facts: The Housing Crisis in Thompson.* Winnipeg: Canadian Centre for Policy Alternatives.

Martin, Thibault, and Steven M. Hoffman. 2008. *Power Struggles: Hydro Development and First Nations in Manitoba and Quebec.* Winnipeg: University of Manitoba Press.

Max-Neef, Manfred A. 1991. *Human Scale Development: Conception, Application and Further Reflections.* New York: The Apex Press.

McKenzie, Brad, and Brian Wharf. 2010. *Connecting Policy to Practice in the Human Services,* 3rd ed. Don Mills, ON: Oxford University Press.

Memmott, Paul, and Catherine Chambers. 2010. "Indigenous Homelessness in Australia: An Introduction." *Parity* 23 (9): 8–11.

Milloy, John S. 1999. *A National Crime: The Canadian Government and the Residential School System, 1879 to 1986.* Winnipeg: University of Manitoba Press.

Montgomery, Phyllis, Karen McCauley, and Patricia Hill Bailey. 2009. "Homeless, a State of Mind?: A Discourse Analysis." *Issues in Mental Health Nursing* 30 (10): 624–30.

Mullaly, Bob. 2009. *Challenging Oppression and Confronting Privilege.* Don Mills, ON: Oxford University Press.

Norman, Trudy, and Bernadette Pauly. 2013. "Including People Who Experience Homelessness: A Scoping Review of the Literature." *International Journal of Sociology and Social Policy* 33 (3/4): 136–51.

Oliver, Vanessa. 2013. *Healing Home: Health & Homelessness in the Life Stories of Young Women.* Toronto: University of Toronto Press.

Palibroda, Beverly, Brigette Krieg, Lisa Murdock, and Joanne Havelock. 2009. *A Practical Guide to Photovoice: Sharing Pictures, Telling Stories and Changing Communities.* Winnipeg: Prairie Women's Health Centre of Excellence.

Paradis, Emily, and Janet Mosher. 2012. *Take the Story, Take the Needs, and Do Something: Grassroots Women's Priorities for Community-Based Participatory Research and Action on Homelessness.* Toronto: The Canadian Homelessness Research Network Press.

Peters, Evelyn J., and Vince Robillard. 2009. "'Everything You Want Is There': The Place of the Reserve in First Nations' Homeless Mobility." *Urban Geographer* 30 (6): 652–80.

Qulliit Nunavut Status of Women Council. 2007. *The Little Voices of Nunavut: A Study of Women's Homelessness North of 60: A Territorial Report.* Iqaluit, Nunavut: Qulliit Nunavut Status of Women Council.

Robinson, Jack. 2013. "Personal communication." Thompson, Manitoba, 25 November.

Ruttan, Lia, Patti LaBoucane-Benson, and Brenda Munro. 2010. "'Home and Native Land': Aboriginal Young Women and Homelessness in the City." *First Peoples Child and Family Review* 5 (1): 67–77.

Schiff, Rebecca, and Jeannette Waegemakers Schiff. 2010. "Housing Needs and Preferences of Relatively Homeless Aboriginal Women with Addictions." *Social Development Issues* 32 (2): 65–75.

Shdaimah, Corey S., Roland W. Stahl, and Sanford F. Schram. 2011. *Change Research: A Case Study on Collaborative Methods for Social Workers and Advocates.* New York: Columbia University Press.

Siddle, Annette. 2013. "Long-Term Homelessness Strategy—Personal Communication." Thompson, MB, 28 November.

Smith, B., and A. Sparkes. 2005. "Analyzing Talk in Qualitative Inquiry: Exploring Possibilities, Problems, and Tensions." *Quest* 57 (2): 213–42.

Somerville, Peter. 2013. "Understanding Homelessness." *Housing, Theory and Society* 30 (4): 384–415.

Sikich, Keri Weber. 2008. "Global Female Homelessness: A Multi-Faceted Problem." *Gender Issues* 25 (3): 147–56.

Stewart, C.J., and Samantha Ramage. 2011. *A Pan-Northern Ontario Inventory of Homelessness Problems and Practices: A Position Paper.* Thunder Bay, ON: Northern Ontario Service Deliverers Association (NOSDA).

Tester, Frank J. 2009. "Iglutaasaavut (Our New Homes): Neither "New" nor "Ours": Housing Challenges of the Nunavit Territorial Government " *Journal of Canadian Studies* 43 (2): 137–58.

Thompson Community Advisory Board for Homelessness. 2011. *Community Plan 2011–2014.* Thompson, MB.

Thompson Economic Diversification Working Group. 2012. *Housing action plan: Final report.* Thompson, MB: TEDWG.

Tough, Frank J. 1996. *"As Their Natural Resources Fail": Native Peoples and the Economic History of Northern Manitoba 1870–1930.* Vancouver: UBC Press.

Walsh, Christine A., Gayle E. Rutherford, and Natasha Kuzmak. 2010. "Engaging Women Who are Homeless in Community-Based Research Using Emerging Qualitative Data Collection Techniques." *International Journal of Multiple Research Approaches* 4 (3): 192–205.

Wang, Caroline, and Mary Ann Burris. 1997. "Photovoice: Concept, Methodology, and Use for Participatory Needs Assessment." *Health Education and Behavior* 24 (3): 369–87.

Whitzman, Carolyn. 2006. "At the Intersection of Invisibilities: Canadian Women, Homelessness and Health outside the 'Big City.'" *Gender, Place and Culture: A Journal of Feminist Geography* 13 (4): 383–99.

Wilson, Shawn. 2008. *Research Is Ceremony: Indigenous Research Methods.* Winnipeg: Fernwood Publishing.

CHAPTER 7

Community-Engaged Scholarship: A Path to New Solutions for Old Problems in Indigenous Homelessness

WILFREDA E. THURSTON, DAVID TURNER, AND CYNTHIA BIRD

Indigenous peoples face layers of complexity on their pathways into and out of homelessness, in addition to those faced by non-Indigenous peoples. The description of Indigenous peoples' experiences of homelessness in Calgary highlights that there is a pressing need to consider their particular historical experience in Canada when conducting research. We begin with a brief overview of the rates of homelessness among Indigenous peoples in the city of Calgary and stress some gender differences among the Indigenous homeless. The next section places the Calgary Indigenous population within the Alberta context. We then discuss what we have learned through community-based research about the pathways to urban Indigenous homelessness in Calgary and the development of culturally safe services. In closing we propose that community-engaged scholarship, developed from working with oppressed peoples, respects Canadian ethical guidelines for research with Indigenous peoples, is fundamental to Indigenous methodologies, and helps ensure culturally competent recommendations. We argue that such scholarship is the best way to find new solutions to the complex problem of Indigenous homelessness.

Homelessness among Indigenous Peoples in Calgary

Calgary, Alberta, is a city located in western Canada with about 1.2 million residents, a 3 percent annual growth rate, a median age of thirty-six, and one of the lowest unemployment rates in the country at 4.9 percent (City of Calgary 2013). While Calgary has a relatively young population, many of whom make good salaries in the oil and gas and technology sectors, it has been estimated

that 10 percent of Calgarians experience poverty, defined as "as a lack of resources and few opportunities to achieve a standard of living that allows full
participation in the economic, social, cultural and political spheres of society"
(City of Calgary 2014, 4). Furthermore, Indigenous peoples are overrepresented among the poor in Calgary: "While employment rates for Aboriginal
people have improved, the gap in employment rates between Aboriginal and
non-Aboriginal people has not changed much in twenty years and the wage
gap is growing, even for those with relatively high levels of education. In
Calgary, there is an overrepresentation of Aboriginal people living in poverty"
(Pruegger, Cook, and Richter-Salomons 2009, n.p.).

According to the 2006 census, only 2 percent of the Calgary population is
Indigenous. Over half (56 percent) of these identify as Metis, about 40 percent
as First Nations, while only 1 percent are Inuit, and 3 percent report multiple
identities (Statistics Canada 2010).

Indigenous peoples are vastly overrepresented among the homeless on
the streets in Calgary. In one street count of the homeless done in Calgary in
2008, 15 percent were identified as Indigenous (Stroick, Hubac, and Richter-
Salamons 2008). In another study during the same period, the data collected
from 2008 to 2009 to triage the homeless for housing according to their health
needs revealed that 24 percent identified as Indigenous. There were reasons
to suspect, however, that even this was an underestimate (Thurston, Soo, and
Turner 2013). In the most recent count of homeless persons in Calgary, 21
percent of those counted were Indigenous, and a full 38 percent of those found
rough sleeping were Indigenous (Calgary Homeless Foundation 2012). This
highlights the challenges of obtaining accurate estimates of the numbers of
Indigenous homeless peoples, among other research challenges (Thurston,
Oelke, and Turner 2013).

Gender Differences in Urban Indigenous Homelessness

Gendered roles and relationships shape the experiences of Indigenous women
in both the reasons for and experiences of homelessness. Indigenous women
are also overrepresented among the homeless served by the domestic violence
sector. The impact of domestic and other interpersonal violence (IPV) on
homelessness rates is greater for Indigenous people simply because the rates of
violence are greater among Indigenous peoples (J. Bopp, M. Bopp, and Lane
2006). Research conducted over thirty years suggested that Alberta has had one
of the highest rates of violence against women in Canada. One national study
found that Alberta had the second highest rate of violence against women, with
58 percent of the female population over the age of eighteen reporting at least

one form of IPV (Statistics Canada 1993). Another national study confirmed Alberta's high rate of IPV: the *General Social Survey* (GSS) revealed that 10 percent of women in Alberta reported being victims of spousal assault within the past five years, making it the highest rate in the country. The national average was 7 percent (Statistics Canada 1999). Indigenous women were more likely to report the most serious forms of abuse, and more serious injuries (Statistics Canada 2005). Another report highlighted the serious nature of the violence: Alberta had one of the highest rates of female homicide over three decades (FPTMRSW 2002).

The Brenda Strafford Centre, a second-stage shelter for women fleeing domestic violence, opened in Calgary in 1996 with twenty-four apartments. Women were overwhelmingly referred to the centre by first-stage, or emergency shelters. Over the next ten years the centre housed 432 women with their children. About 29 percent of the women were Indigenous. Over that period the centre did not have a specific policy on cultural safety that would attract Indigenous women, although the mission did include provision of a safe community for women and children (Thurston 2006). It is likely, therefore, that the rates they report are an underestimate of the rates of Indigenous women seeking service within the domestic violence sector. Indigenous women experience barriers to personal empowerment and to services, the impacts of colonization and racism that are linked to higher rates of alcohol and substance abuse, and disruption of family systems due to residential school abuse (Perrault and Proulx 2000; Brownridge 2003). The complicated dynamics of racism and discrimination, as well as cultural values and beliefs, frequently make it difficult for Indigenous women to disclose abuse to both formal services (i.e., police, shelters, and health care professionals) and informal supports (i.e., family and relatives). Further, many Indigenous women living in northern and remote communities are faced with limited access to few services, most of which are not designed to recognize Indigenous cultural practices (Thomlinson, Erickson, and Cook 2000, 22).

The above factors, therefore, explain why Indigenous women may be overrepresented among the absolute homeless. Calgary's shelters for women leaving domestic violence consistently have waiting lists. One study found that there were more women among the Indigenous street homeless than the non-Indigenous homeless, and that Indigenous homeless women were more likely to work in the sex trade (Thurston, Soo, and Turner 2013). Indigenous women who are homeless may face some degree of geographic isolation from support networks that may or may not be present in the city. They might also fear loss of confidentiality in urban locations as support workers may in some way be connected to the community they come from and may inadvertently share the circumstances of their clients' personal situation.

The Social Context of Urban Indigenous Homelessness

When Canada was beginning to be populated by English and French settlers, Indigenous peoples had occupied the land for many centuries. Within their nations, they had sophisticated societies, systems of government, traditional territorial land-use treaties, peace alliances, different world views, their own religious systems, art, languages, and sustainable systems for food procurement. In Alberta there is diversity among the Indigenous people in terms of language, ceremonial traditions, and history with settlers (Government of Alberta 2013b). The Crown signed three treaties, Treaty 6, Treaty 7, and Treaty 8, with the Indigenous people of Alberta. Treaty 6 was signed in 1876 and includes sixteen of the forty-five First Nations; Treaty 7, signed in 1877, includes five First Nations; and Treaty 8, signed in 1899, includes twenty-four First Nations. There are also 140 reserves in Alberta scattered from the northernmost to southernmost borders (Indigenous Affairs and Northern Development Canada 2014). Unlike in most Canadian provinces, in Alberta, the Metis were also provided with eight settlements, similar to reserves. About 8,000 Metis occupy these settlements. By contrast there are seventeen cities, 108 towns, and ninety-three villages comprised predominately of non-Indigenous peoples with a population of about 3.8 million compared to 68,000 Indigenous peoples on reserves or similar settlements (Government of Alberta 2013a). There are about 189,000 people in total who identify as Indigenous in Alberta. Thus, about 120,000, or 64 percent of Indigenous people in Alberta do not live on First Nation reserves or in Metis settlements, a trend that is national in scope (Environics Institute 2010). First Nations reserves range in population size from 0 to 8,000. The 0 indicates that everyone has left that community and the 8,000 is the number of the people on a reserve of the Blood Tribe, one of the largest First Nations in Canada, located in southern Alberta (Government of Alberta 2013a). This diversity in history, geography, and general context means that Indigenous peoples cannot be approached with a "one size fits all" policy.

Pathways to Urban Indigenous Homelessness

There is overwhelming evidence in the published literature of long-standing structural inequities that are embedded in Alberta society and experienced in Indigenous communities. The multi-generational poverty and trauma, mass removal of children from homes and families, physical and emotional responses to colonialism, apartheid, cultural genocide policies, and dispossession of lands and property (Valaskakis 2009) all play a role in both reserve and urban Indigenous homelessness.

As described in Chapter 1, systemic abuses of Indigenous peoples are at the root of many contemporary social problems, and Alberta policies were particularly problematic for Indigenous communities. In Canada, the history of government intervention involving Indigenous children can be mapped into three main policy periods: the residential schools period; the "Sixties Scoop" period (from the 1960s to the early 1980s); and the post-Sixties Scoop period in which there has been greater Indigenous control of Indigenous child services (Bennett, Blackstock, and De La Ronde 2005). In the 1880s the federal government adopted a policy of forcing Indigenous children to attend residential schools. In the "Sixties Scoop" large numbers of Indigenous children were apprehended from their parents and moved to towns and cities to be raised by non-Indigenous foster and/or adoptive parents. The pro-assimilatory approach of the first two periods led to harmful effects that continue to impact Indigenous individuals, families, and communities today. With twenty-five residential schools in the province, Alberta had the highest number of residential schools in the country (TRC 2014), which accounts in part for the higher prevalence of domestic violence and homelessness (J. Bopp, M. Bopp, Lane 2003). Residential schools created a generation of people who did not learn parenting at the sides of their parents, and who often felt upon leaving school that they did not belong in either Indigenous or non-Indigenous communities. Inability to form close relationships can result in domestic violence, breakdowns in communication, and choices that lead to homelessness. In Alberta it is still true that a disproportionate number of children in the child welfare systems are Indigenous, comprising 64 percent of the children in care (Alberta Child Intervention Review Panel 2010). The reasons for this over-representation are complex and rooted in the legacy of colonization (Trocmé, Knoke, and Blackstock, 2004). The greater Indigenous control of present-day services for Indigenous children has been a meaningful step toward healing the harms created by the first two policy periods; however, many challenges still face the Indigenous agencies involved in child-welfare work. Adapting Western models of child welfare to Indigenous communities is just one of the challenges. Promoting children's health in a setting where educational opportunities are limited and under resourced is another.

In a study of the pathways from rural to urban homelessness, Thurston, Milaney, Turner and Coupal (2013) asked people what had led them to become homeless in Calgary. The twelve participants were from six Alberta reserves, one Metis settlement, and two reserves in Saskatchewan; their ages ranged from thirty-nine to sixty-eight years old. Seven of the twelve talked about having addiction problems. Their pathways to homelessness revealed life stories of loss, separation from family and community, involvement in the child welfare and justice systems, and unemployment, mixed with a drive for a better life and a hope that the answer was still ahead. Moving to Calgary, where the housing costs were high was done with optimism that employment opportunities would become available and the rest could be worked out. The research found, however, that the pathways to urban homeless were strewn with economic, educational, political, and social inequities on the reserves that were repeated in the cities. The pathways began with historical factors of colonization, including the residential schools, and discriminatory child welfare policies, but the impacts are still felt at present. It is true that anyone who is traumatized in childhood and suffers a loss of identity also may end up homeless, Indigenous peoples additionally face racism from landlords, lack of respect for their traditions and culture, economic and employment discrimination, and cultural alienation.

In moving to the city, Indigenous people are looking for a place to belong and to start over (Turner et al. 2010). The literature suggests that cultural healing and developing a strong identity can restore balance for Indigenous people and provide the capacity to address other challenges such as addictions, mental health, and family relationships. Cultural continuity aids in maintaining an "imagined future," that is, hope for a sustainable and positive community life (Chandler and Lalonde 2009, 221; Kirmayer, Tait, and Simpson 2009, 3).

Ironically, seeking and developing a strong cultural identity can be psychologically healing, but also reinforce "otherness" because of the reactions of other Indigenous people. Otherness can be reinforced during the process of cultural reconnection, for instance, if the approach to teaching and learning is not sympathetic to diversity of background and experience among Indigenous peoples. Anderson writes, "Absurdly, many of us, young and old, have now experienced shame or embarrassment because we are not conversant in the various traditions and ceremonies that have only recently come back to our communities" (2000, 27).

It is more likely, however, that the Indigenous individual will experience stereotyping and racism from non-Indigenous people. A friend, for instance, has described how her Metis background is overlooked and how after the Aboriginal Relations meeting at her place of employment, she is exposed by the non-Indigenous co-workers to hallway denigrations of "those people" (i.e., Indigenous people) when the participants had kept a semblance of concern during the meeting.

Racism and stereotyping are fed by media and other cultural reinforcements depicting one group as the "other" *compared* to the "majority," "mainstream," or "white males." In this chapter, we have presented statistics comparing Indigenous (one diverse group of peoples) to non-Indigenous peoples (another very diverse group that contains a small proportion of people with Indigenous background who either do not know it or do not wish to reveal it) because we believe that the comparison may make sense to many people and possibly help others form a more informed opinion of Indigenous homelessness. It is beyond the scope of this chapter to examine whether that is a justifiable decision when another result is to continue to position Indigenous people as the "other."

Safe Places to Heal

In the western provinces there are few organizations serving Indigenous people that are governed and staffed by Indigenous people, and offer best practices to help Indigenous men and women exit homelessness (Thurston, Oelke, and Turner 2013). There are jurisdictional disputes over which level of government is responsible for the provision of services to Indigenous peoples in Canada, and the issue of homelessness has only gained prominence in social policy in the last decade. It is not surprising, therefore, that few models of Indigenous-run urban services for the homeless exist. Within the homeless sector, however, there has been resistance to acknowledging that Indigenous peoples might need different programs than those needed by their non-Indigenous counterparts (Thurston, Oelke, and Turner 2013). Program directors have been known to respond, "It's not my job," when asked if they were going to introduce cultural safety for Indigenous peoples into their organization.

Opportunities for innovation in a competitive funding environment are limited, and this contributes to the lack of development of safe places strictly for Indigenous peoples who are homeless and want to find cultural reconnection and a sense of belonging. It is, however, possible to create cultural competence in existing programs, if the will exists, as demonstrated by Calgary Alpha House Society, a harm reduction service for the homeless in Calgary. After connecting with the homeless outreach project at the Aboriginal Friendship Centre of Calgary, the staff decided to move forward in building cultural competencies and was supported in this decision by the board of directors (Bird et al. 2013). Oelke, Thurston, and Arthur (2013) describe cultural competencies along a continuum: cultural awareness (getting to know something about another culture); cultural sensitivity (exploring one's own culture and the interacting with other cultures while accepting difference); cultural competence (building on awareness with knowledge and skills that ensure good outcomes in cross-cultural encounters); cultural safety (incorporating collaboration in the creation of culturally safe environments that reduce inequities); and cultural advocacy (promoting social justice). We propose, therefore, that best practice in Indigenous homelessness research is community-engaged scholarship, which requires one to start with the community, to come to understand one's own culture, and to listen when other community members describe their experiences.

Community-Engaged Scholarship and Solutions

Community-engaged scholarship, from an academic perspective, has its roots in the work of underprivileged groups and individuals who were confronting structural inequalities in society. Foundational work came from lower-income countries where political oppression was evident. Working with people who were oppressed by their governments and by other socio-economic forces outside of their immediate control, researchers came to believe that the model of a distant and supposedly objective observer was counterproductive in many cases. Treating the community as a source of valid knowledge and as an equal in the research relationship became the goal of a new model (Wallerstein and Duran 2008, 26).

In a national eight-university project in which the University of Calgary is participating, community-engaged scholarship is defined as encompassing "intellectual and creative activities that generate, validate, synthesize and apply knowledge through partnerships with people and organizations outside of the academy" (CES 2013). It includes "teaching, discovery, integration, application and engagement that involves the scholar (e.g., faculty member, student) in a mutually beneficial partnership with the community and has the following characteristics: clear goals, adequate preparation, appropriate methods, significant results, effective presentation, reflective critique, rigor and peer-review" (CES 2013).

The tri-council policy on research with First Nations, Inuit, and Metis peoples in Canada states that "reciprocity–the obligation to give something back in return for gifts received" is a core value shared by Indigenous peoples in Canada "which they advance as the necessary basis for relationships that can benefit both the Aboriginal and research communities" (CIHR, NSERC, and SSHRC 2010). The First Nations Information Governance Centre (FNIGC) also affirms this principle for research with First Nations peoples. The FNIGC is a national project supported by the Assembly of First Nations to house the First Nations Regional Longitudinal Health Survey (FNRLHS). FNIGC has regional centres and has trademarked OCAP™ (Ownership,

Control, Access and Possession), the principles by which First Nations assess the ethics of research. Their main principle of research is that "communities must be involved as full partners" (FNIGC 2011), a principle that is implemented in the FNRLHS. How the tri-council policy, the FNIGC principles, and the formal ethics review processes at Canadian universities will interface remains to be seen. Alberta First Nations Information Governance Centre (AFNIGC) does not address the Metis, the majority of Indigenous peoples in Alberta living off-reserve, and in urban settings it is often difficult to identify organizations that could or would claim to represent all Indigenous peoples. To abate urban Indigenous homelessness, we agree that community-engaged scholarship is a strong research model that stands up to ethical scrutiny and can be applied with academic rigor. While the foundations of community-engaged scholarship were developed originally by non-Indigenous academics and community partners, the emergence of Indigenous methodologies has strengthened community-engaged scholarship as a method to work with Indigenous populations (Kovach 2009; Tuhiwai Smith 1999).

Community-engaged scholarship is also positioned to address the complexities of a multi-faceted problem such as urban Indigenous homelessness. How such scholarship can benefit the Indigenous homeless depends on the knowledge of the local policy systems, structural barriers to change, and the possible non-Indigenous and Indigenous alliances. Learning to be an ally depends on talking to Indigenous people themselves, and getting information depends on how trustworthy one is perceived to be. In sum, the effectiveness of community-engaged scholarship depends in part on relationships that are built over time and time is often the last resource that an academic possess, especially one competing for promotion and tenure.

Conclusion

Urban research with Indigenous peoples presents challenges, but ending homelessness depends on the success of strategies and methods used to address these challenges. If research is going to help solve the problems of Indigenous homelessness, then it must be rooted in close relationships with Indigenous peoples who can help ensure cultural competence in the methods, in the interpretation of results, and in the proposed solutions. The most effective methodology for ensuring that this happens is community-engaged scholarship. Such research may take more time, and therefore more resources overall than other methodologies but it also may result in innovation and policies needed to end homelessness.

References

Alberta Child Intervention Review Panel. 2010. "Closing the Gap between Vision and Reality: Strengthening Accountability, Adaptability and Continuous Improvement in Alberta's Child Intervention system." Final Report of the Alberta Child Intervention Review Panel. 30 June. http://humanservices.alberta.ca/documents/child-intervention-system-review-report.pdf (accessed 25 March 2014).

Anderson, Kim. 2000. *A Recognition of Being: Reconstructing Native Womanhood.* Toronto: Second Story Press.

Bennett, Marlyn, Cindy Blackstock, and Richard De La Ronde. 2005. *A Literature Review and Annotated Bibliography on Aspects of Aboriginal Child Welfare in Canada,* 2nd ed. Winnipeg: First Nations Research Site of the Centre of Excellence for Child Welfare.

Bird, Cynthia, Wilfreda E Thurston, Nelly D. Oelke, David Turner, and Kathy Christiansen. 2013. *Understanding Cultural Safety: Traditional and Client Perspectives, Final Report for Funder.* Calgary, AB: University of Calgary, Department of Community Health Sciences.

Bopp, Judie, Michael Bopp, and Phil Lane Jr. 2003. *Aboriginal Domestic Violence in Canada.* Ottawa: Aboriginal Healing Foundation.

Brownridge, Douglas A. 2003. "Male Partner Violence against Aboriginal Women in Canada: An Empirical Analysis." *Journal of Interpersonal Violence* 18 (1): 65–83.

Calgary Homeless Foundation. 2012. "Summer 2012 Point in Time Count Report." http://calgaryhomeless.com/wp-content/uploads/2014/06/Summer-2012-Point-In-Time-Count.pdf (accessed 23 January 2014).

Canadian Institutes of Health Research, National Sciences and Engineering Research Council, Social Sciences and Humanities Research Council of Canada. 2010. *Tri-Council Policy Statement: Ethical Conduct for Research Involving Humans.* http://www.pre.ethics.gc.ca/pdf/eng/tcps2/TCPS_2_FINAL_Web.pdf (accessed 23 January 2014).

CES (Community Engaged Scholarship). *Building Capacity for Community Engagement: Institutional Self-Assessment.* 2013. Available by contacting Community-Campus Partnerships for Health. http://www.ccph.info.

Chandler, Michael J., and Christopher E. Lalonde. 2009. "Cultural Continuity as a Moderator of Suicide Risk among Canada's First Nations." In *Healing Traditions: The Mental Health of Aboriginal Peoples in Canada,* edited by Laurence J. Kirmayer and Gail Guthrie Valaskakis, 221–48. Vancouver: UBC Press.

City of Calgary. 2013. "The City of Calgary 2013 Annual Report." http://www.calgary.ca/CA/fs/Documents/Plans-Budgets-and-Financial-Reports/Annual-Reports/Annual-Report-2013.pdf (accessed 22 January 2014).

_____. 2014. "What is poverty?" http://www.calgary.ca/CSPS/CNS/Documents/Social-research-policy-and-resources/What%20is%20Poverty.pdf (22 January 2014).

Environics Institute. 2010. "Urban Aboriginal Peoples Study: Calgary Report." http://uaps.ca/wp-content/uploads/2010/02/UAPS-Calgary-report1.pdf (accessed 14 January 2013).

FNIGC (First Nations Information Governance Centre). 2011. *First Nations Regional Health Survey (RHS): Best Practice Tools for OCAP™ Compliant Research.* Ottawa: FNIGC.

FPTMRSW (Federal/Provincial/Territorial Ministers Responsible for the Status of Women). 2002. *Assessing Violence against Women: A Statistical Profile.* Ottawa: Status of Women Canada.

Government of Alberta. 2013a. *Aboriginal Peoples of Alberta: Yesterday, Today, and Tomorrow.*" http://www.aboriginal.alberta.ca/documents/AboriginalPeoples.pdf (accessed 22 January 2014).

____. 2013b. "Municipal Affairs Population List." http://municipalaffairs.gov.ab.ca/documents/msb/2013_Municipal_Affairs_Population_List.pdf (accessed 22 January 2014).

Indigenous Affairs and Northern Development Canada (formerly Aboriginal Affairs and Northern Development Canada). 2014. "First Nations in Alberta." http://www.aadnc-aandc.gc.ca/eng/1100100020670/1100100020675 (accessed 22 January 2014).

Kirmayer, Laurence J., Caroline L. Tait, and Cori Simpson. 2009. "The Mental Health of Aboriginal Peoples in Canada: Transformations of Identity and Community." In *Healing Traditions: The Mental Health of Aboriginal Peoples in Canada,* edited by Laurence J. Kirmayer, and Gail Guthrie Valaskakis, 3–35. Vancouver: UBC Press.

Kirmayer, Lawrence J. and Gail Guthrie Valaskakis, eds. 2009. *Healing Traditions: The Mental Health of Aboriginal Peoples in Canada.* Vancouver: UBC Press.

Kovach, Margaret E. 2009. *Indigenous Methodologies: Characteristics, Conversations, and Contexts.* Toronto: University of Toronto Press.

Mandell, Deena, Joyce Clouston Carlson, Marshall Fine, and Cindy Blackstock. 2007. "Aboriginal Child Welfare." In *Moving toward Positive Systems of Child and Family Welfare: Current Issues and Future Directions,* edited by Gary Cameron, Nick Coady, and Gerald R. Adams, 115–60. Waterloo, ON: Wilfrid Laurier University Press.

Oelke, Nelly D., Wilfreda E. Thurston, and Nancy Arthur. 2013. "Intersections between Interprofessional Collaborative Practice, Cultural Competency and Primary Healthcare." *Journal of Interprofessional Care* 27 (5): 367–72.

Perrault, Sharon, and Jocelyn Proulx. 2000. "Introduction." In *No Place for Violence: Canadian Aboriginal Alternatives,* edited by Jocelyn Proulx, and Sharon Perrault, 13–21. Halifax: Fernwood Publishing and RESOLVE.

Pruegger, Valerie J., Derek Cook, and Sybille Richter-Salomons. 2009. *Inequality in Calgary: The Racialization of Poverty.* Calgary, AB: City of Calgary, Community and Neighbourhood Social and Research Unit. http://www.calgary.ca/CSPS/CNS/Documents/inequality_in_calgary.pdf (accessed 22 January 2014).

Statistics Canada. 1993. *Violence against Women Survey.* Ottawa: Statistics Canada.

____. 1999. *General Social Survey.* Ottawa: Statistics Canada.

____. 2005. *Family Violence in Canada: A Statistical Profile.* Ottawa: Canadian Centre for Justice Statistics, Statistics Canada.

____. 2010. "2006 Aboriginal Population Profile for Calgary." Component of Statistics. *Canada Catalogue no. 89-638-X no. 201003.* http://www.statcan.gc.ca/pub/89-638-x/2010003/article/11076-eng.pdf (accessed 22 January 2014).

Stroick, Sharon M., Lisa Hubac, and Sybille Richter-Salomons. 2008. *Biennial Count of Homeless Persons in Calgary: 2008 May 14.* Calgary, AB: City of Calgary, Community and Neighbourhood Social and Research Unit.

Thomlinson, Elizabeth, Nellie Erickson, and Mabel Cook. 2000. "Could This Be Your Community?" In *No Place for Violence: Canadian Aboriginal Alternatives*, edited by Jocelyn Proulx, and Sharon Perrault, 22–38. Halifax, NS: Fernwood Publishing and RESOLVE, 2000.

Thurston, Wilfreda E. 2006. *Brenda Strafford Centre: Ten Years of Making a Difference: Report on Goals, 1996–2005*. Unpublished report. Available from the author, Thurston@ucalgary.ca.

Thurston, Wilfreda E., Katrina Milaney, David Turner, and Stephanie Coupal. 2013. *No Moving Back: A Study of the Intersection of Rural and Urban Homelessness for Aboriginal people in Calgary*. Calgary, AB: Calgary Homeless Foundation, and Aboriginal Friendship Centre of Calgary.

Thurston, Wilfreda E., Nelly D. Oelke, and David Turner. 2013. "Methodological Challenges in Studying Aboriginal Homelessness." *International Journal of Multiple Research Approaches* 7 (2): 250–59.

Thurston, Wilfreda E, Andrea Soo, and David Turner. 2013. "Are There Differences between the Aboriginal Homeless Population and a Non-Aboriginal Homeless Population in Calgary?" *Pimatisiwin: A Journal of Indigenous and Aboriginal Community Health* 11 (2): 283–92.

Trocmé, Nico, Della Knoke, and Cindy Blackstock. 2004. "Pathways to the Overrepresentation of Aboriginal Children in Canada's Child Welfare System." *Social Service Review* 78 (4): 577–600.

TRC (Truth and Reconciliation Commission of Canada). "Residential School Locations." http://www.trc.ca/websites/trcinstitution/index.php (accessed 23 January 2014).

Tuhiwai Smith, Linda. 1999. *Decolonizing Methodologies: Research and Indigenous Peoples*. London: Zed Books.

Turner, David, Sharon Goulet, Nelly D. Oelke, Wilfreda E. Thurston, Alanah Woodland, Cynthia Bird, Jack Wilson, Cindy Deschenes, and Mike Boyes. 2010. *Aboriginal Homelessness: Looking for a Place to Belong*. Calgary, AB: The Aboriginal Friendship Centre of Calgary.

Valaskakis, Gail Guthrie. 2005. *Indian Country: Essays on Contemporary Native Culture*. Waterloo, ON: Wilfrid Laurier University Press.

Wallerstein, Nancy, and Bonnie Duran. 2008. "The Theoretical, Historical, and Practice Roots of CBPR." In *Community-Based Participatory Research for Health: From Process to Outcomes, 2nd ed.*, edited by Meredith Minkler and Nina Wallerstein, 25–46. San Francisco, CA: Jossey-Bass.

CHAPTER 8

"All We Need Is Our Land": Exploring Southern Alberta Urban Indigenous Homelessness

YALE D. BELANGER AND GABRIELLE LINDSTROM

Indigenous people[1] in Canada are an inherently mobile group of individuals, whose movement can lead to improved economic and educational opportunities or to economic challenges frequently resulting in homelessness. At least these are the fashionable conclusions mainstream society has determined accurate—beliefs that contradict an increasingly nuanced conception of what Indigenous mobility and homelessness means to those experiencing these trends. Yale and I discussed these and other concerns related to southern Alberta Indigenous homelessness dating to my early days as an undergraduate student, and upon entering graduate school. This prolonged conversation did not help us to quickly generate a thesis topic, for every discussion exploring pathways to Indigenous homelessness inevitably led back to the larger issue of Indigenous mobility. After one particularly frustrating dialogue, I angrily stated, "I don't know where this whole issue of mobility comes from. My people have always been mobile. Why have we become so focused on the negatives?" What I was trying to convey is that mobility, from a Niitsitapi (Blackfoot) perspective, reflects a specific cultural understanding of how to interact with what is today better known as southern Alberta, a traditional Indigenous homeland that snakes along the continental divide and extends south of Edmonton, Alberta, into southern Montana, and east into Saskatchewan.

In the last century the contours of Napi's Land have shifted. The previous territorial map has been overlain with a colonial template that has physically isolated and restricted the people who formerly utilized this once vast territory to small, landlocked islands known as the Blackfeet Reservation in Montana, and the Kainai, Piikani, and Siksika First Nations in Canada. Despite an under-standing that this is how southern Alberta and northern Montana are now to be physically conceptualized, the late Blood (Kainai) elder Narcisse Blood for one challenged this new map's authenticity by reasserting his people's connec-tion to what he described as "a storied landscape, a ceremonial landscape very alive with its spirits and beings" (Savage 2012, 186). It is within this context that mobility emerges as an important channel of spiritual renewal, of (re)as-serting territorial sovereignty, and of ensuring economic reproduction. It is also within this context that ideas such as mobility, home, and land have arguably taken on different meanings. What we see unfolding in southern Alberta, then, is a process prevalent in Canada: homelands mapped by First Nations over centuries of ecological interaction are supplanted by an "authoritative" colonial map that reflects recently introduced, foreign concepts of property ownership and land utilization (McManus 2005).

After reflecting on these and other issues it was evident that his-toric Indigenous processes of mobility within extensive homelands were being downplayed as negative social characteristics as mainstream beliefs in Indigenous-urban incompatibility and innate Indian transiency emerged as normative (i.e., no permanent home could exist if one is always on the move). These tensions demanded clarification prior to determining a thesis topic. As we continued to unpack what mobility meant from the various perspectives, it became apparent that the issue of Indigenous homelessness within this context had also been largely ignored, despite assumptions linking the two. Lack of research into these topics has resulted in: (1) limited availability of data needed to measure the extent of the problem (i.e., what is the extent of Indigenous homelessness nationally); and (2) no real understanding of what it meant to be homeless by those experiencing homelessness.

It was determined that two projects were required. The first was devel-oped to provide a quantitative overview of urban Indigenous homelessness and urban housing issues (see Belanger, Awosoga, and Weasel Head 2013; Belanger, Weasel Head, and Awosoga 2012). The second would be a thesis project exploring the meaning of homelessness (Weasel Head 2011). As our families and work are situated in southern Alberta, we are obligated to explore issues impacting the territory's Indigenous people. We therefore decided to explore what it means to be Niitsitapi and homeless in southern Alberta. We acknowledge the fact that homelessness, conceptualized for this discussion as lacking shelter, did not exist prior to colonial settlement. Many would argue that homelessness in its various configurations could not exist due to the fact that in Creation one is never alone. However, the project in question sought to understand modern Blackfoot homelessness in a particular context, specifically that of being homeless in one's homeland. This chapter expands on these findings and explores: (1) how being and becoming homeless informs one's connection to the land; and (2) whether this connection to a homeland obliges individuals to remain homeless in traditional territories rather than seek shelter in foreign ones.

This chapter unfolds as follows. First we provide a brief overview of the close connection between land and individual and explore how the introduction of new colonial ideas devalued Indigenous regional occupation, resulting in both physical and social marginalization. Then we explain in detail how we chose to formally define homelessness and understand the issues within the context of being and becoming homeless in one's homeland. Following a brief discussion of the methodology employed, we present our analysis of what it means to be Indigenous and homeless in one's homeland. Finally, we wrap up with our conclusions.

Understanding Indigenous Homelessness

Beginning in the 1870s, Canada implemented a series of assimilation policies intended to rid mainstream society of "Indians." This initial foray into Indian administration also demanded an infrastructure of attendant institutions if Canada was to achieve its stated goals. Regrettably, child welfare and in particular residential schooling emerged as the key assimilation tools. They betrayed a bureaucratic ideology that was powerfully influenced by beliefs in Indian inferiority (see Leslie 1999; Titley 1986). Notably, government policies reflected the idea that Indians would remain on reserves anticipating their transition into acceptable citizens. Indian administrators hoped that encouraging Indigenous people to adopt Western-style housing would aid in the process by ensuring sanitary conditions and civility.

Perry (2003) has explored the link between colonial desires to improve Indigenous housing and the corresponding societal diffusion of housing, gender, and family-related ideals, noting that limited federal resources were assigned to facilitate this transition. By 1958, a federally sponsored survey of reserve housing conditions indicated that 24 percent of reserve families required new housing and that a total of 6,999 houses costing $16,796,000[2] were needed to offset impoverished housing conditions among Canada's 560 First Nations.[3] Less than one decade later, media reports in 1966 highlighted what amounted to a full-blown national reserve-housing crisis, and a desperate need for "12,000 new homes over a five-year period to meet a backlog of approximately 6,000 units and to take care of new family formation of about

1,250 a year" (Canada 1966, 59). Sporadic attempts at alleviating the housing crisis characterized the three decades leading up to the Royal Commission on Aboriginal Peoples (RCAP) report (1996), which publicly highlighted the plight of reserve housing. That year First Nations leaders and federal officials agreed that a deficit in reserve housing stock was the culprit, and they prioritized improving housing based on the Indigenous community's projected twenty-five-year growth rate (roughly twice that of non-Indigenous populations) (INAC 2011). Homelessness was not directly mentioned in either of these reports, but inferring its certainty is rational. A lack of attention appears to be the norm, if we accept the limited media coverage of reserve and urban Indigenous homelessness as a guide. By the late 1980s, Indigenous homelessness had, however, suddenly materialized as a source of concern, and was followed with increased academic and political interest in the late 1990s (Beavis et al. 1997).

Indigenous homelessness should have been anticipated when reflecting on the nature of Canadian colonialism and the tremendous intergenerational toll these processes exacted on Indigenous families and communities (Dion Stout and Kipling 2003; McKenzie and Morrisette 2003). Colonial culpability was confirmed by the projected pathways to Indigenous homelessness recently published by Thurston and Mason (2010). They identified the following contemporary drivers of Indigenous homelessness: (1) the Indian Act; (2) inter- and intra-departmental jurisdictional and coordination issues; (3) residential schools; (4) child welfare; (5) social marginalization and isolation, and systemic discrimination and stigmatization within home reserve communities; and (6) individual "ruptures" or impacts and traumas. Additional work by Leach (2010) revealed that territorial displacement, among other risk factors, likewise propels Indigenous homelessness. Historic attitudes about Indigenous mobility (i.e., people aren't homeless *per se*, they are simply passing through town) unfortunately triumph over observed outcomes, and Indigenous homelessness trends are frequently ignored. Or, perhaps more accurately, the issue is that the dimensions of Indigenous homelessness—in this case as understood from a Niitsitapi perspective—are abstract thus hindering our ability to develop promising policy and front-line interventions to combat the situation.

Cultural context speaks in part to the difficulty of defining what homelessness means for the purposes of fashioning intervention strategies. Take, for example, the Canadian Parliamentary Research Branch's (CPRB's) attempts that led it to establish three different meanings for homelessness in 1999 rather than developing one static definition. In doing so CPRB identified people as belonging to a certain class of homeless population (Begin et al. 1999) consisting of chronically homeless, cyclically homeless, and temporarily homeless. Recently the Canadian Homelessness Research Network (CHRN) crafted a working classification of four groups of homeless individuals including those living on the streets, those staying in emergency shelters, those who are temporarily and provisionally accommodated, and those who are insecurely housed and at risk of homelessness (Gaetz 2012). Complicating an already unwieldy task is the centrality of land and how it informs the meaning of home from an Indigenous perspective. For instance, common to the CPRB and CHRN definitions is framing of the homeless experience by a lack of housing, or the belief in shelter as home (Sommerville 1992). Intrinsic to this way of thinking is the belief in the permanency of home, or, that mobility and/or a lack of permanent shelter equates homelessness. Menzies (2005) is critical of this approach and has recommended that scholars and front-line workers alike develop a more nuanced understanding of Indigenous homelessness, one that does not exclusively relate the term to the physical occupation of a shelter. In turn Menzies posits a new definition of homelessness: "the resultant condition of individuals being displaced from critical community social structures and lacking in stable housing" (2005, 8).

Menzies was hinting at what Christensen (2013, 809) would subsequently clarify as our inclination to disregard "the cultural context of home and its meaning" while at the same time focusing on "the central role of place in shaping geographies of home." Most Indigenous peoples embrace a unique relationship to space that is grounded in centuries (or more) of social, spiritual, and economic interaction with landscapes described as points of creation (e.g., Bullchild 1985). Acknowledging this fundamental connection permits us to "begin to understand the profound sense of rootlessness that may come about when a relationship to place, both collectively and individually formed, becomes fragmented or fractured" (Christensen 2013, 809). As a form of homelessness, rootlessness is not confined specifically to living absent from physical shelter but rather reflects the combined impact resulting from a series of physical and psychological displacements described in the Keys Young Report (1998). The report classified homelessness among Australian Aboriginal and Torres Strait Islanders as "spiritual homelessness." Memmott and Chambers (2008) elaborate on this concept to describe spiritual homelessness as "a state arising from: (a) separation from traditional land, (b) separation from family and kinship networks, or (c) a crisis of personal identity wherein one's understanding or knowledge of how one relates to country, family and Aboriginal identity systems is confused." Research participants spoke of common experiences such as poor physical and mental health, violence and crime, racism, intergenerational homelessness, and insecure housing (Memmott and Chambers 2008).

While spiritual homelessness in the Australian and Torres Straight context exposes a collective yet particular experience, the concept itself is pliable thus permitting us to "situate experiences of homelessness within the cultural significance of place and the consequences of socio-cultural upheaval for Indigenous people in settler societies" (Christensen 2013, 810). As a flexible analytic construct, spiritual homelessness allows for the definition of homelessness to encompass personal and collective connections to land. Within such a framework, ideas such as mobility and shelter take on entirely unique meanings, and this informs how to understand reserve and, in particular, urban Indigenous homelessness within homelands that are simultaneously located adjacent to and enclosed by colonial states professing ownership of Napi's Land according to new and foreign land-use protocols and meanings. The next section discusses how the Niitsitapi conceptualize their homeland within historic contexts, and how contemporary challenges are influencing not only how home and land are understood but how Napi's Land is individually and collectively reconfigured by the Niitsitapi.

Conveying and Framing Meaning in Colonially Subsumed Traditional Territories

The land that the city of Lethbridge occupies is known as Sikokotoki, the Kainai wintering grounds. Yet it is rare to find any prolonged discussion of pre-contact Niitsitapi perceptions of land and their role within the city's official history (Weasel Head 2011). Lethbridge, however, is not alone in this regard as it is not uncommon for Canadian city histories to downplay historic Indigenous land use and other contributions. Once vibrant communities—displaced from their lands by settlers citing rightful claims to land—are thus branded by groups of foreigners as lacking comprehensive histories or political agency (e.g., Furniss 1999). General consensus, then, has Indigenous people choosing to remain on reserves in lieu of adopting urban lifestyles due to the evident incommensurability of their culture to the forces of urbanism. Contrary to these values is the reality of Indigenous urbanism in Lethbridge, where roughly 6,000 Indigenous and 87,000 non-Indigenous residents interact to various extents on a daily basis. The accepted incongruity of Indigenous people and urbanism aside, the Kainai philosopher Leroy Little Bear (1996) hints at the reason driving Indigenous urbanism, or, at the very least, he suggests why Indigenous urbanism is not as implausible as previously thought. Sikokotoki, on which Lethbridge is sited, is an element of Creation, "where the continuous and/or repetitive process of Creation occurs. It is on the Earth and from the Earth that cycles, phases, patterns [are] experienced" (Little Bear 1996, n.p.). It is within these and other homelands, Basso (1996, 7) contends, that "social traditions and, in the process, personal and social identities" are constructed, adding we are the "place-worlds we imagine."

In Niitsitapi territory sacred knowledge is derived from *Ihtsipaitapiiyo'pa*, "the great mystery that is in everything in the universe," and is passed on generationally through ceremonies and oral histories that inform traditional ways of knowing (Bastien 2004, 77). Identity, it is important to note, is not entirely dependent upon individual achievement or heroic feats, but is made up of intricate associations with Creation. Bastien (2004, 8) reminds us, however, of a need that arises "to affirm and, as necessary, to reconstruct an identity from the fabric that holds the sacred ways of the ancestors." The Kainai and Piikani in this environment organized into small bands and traversed their territory on foot over five millennia (Bear Robe 1996; Reeves 1988). The mid-eighteenth century introduction of the horse was followed by the development of more efficient hunting techniques and the expansion of Kainai and Piikani territorial claims (Bastien 2004; Binnema 2004; Treaty 7 Elders et al. 1996; Ewers 1955). As the elder Joe Crowshoe explains, irrespective of how well one can hunt or defend, the community peoples would cease to exist in the absence of a connection to and renewal of the relationship with the land (Vest 2005, 580).

Unfortunately, the colonial land utilization schemes and property ownership patterns have compelled Niitsitapi conceptions of land and home to subtly shift. Now, attempts to renew relationships with the land occur within the territory of visible (i.e., fences) and invisible (i.e., property reports indicating ownership) demarcations emphasizing private property claims that limit Niitsitapi access to historically and spiritually important domains (Crowson 2011; Johnston 1997).[4] These shifts were set in motion during the constructed era of the late nineteenth-century frontier, characterized by American and Canadian whisky traders, "drunken Indians," and Canadian or British heroes who defended law and order (Dempsey 2002). Good overcame evil as the whisky trade was stamped out, Indians were sequestered on reserves, and "civilization" took hold with the introduction of coal mining, railways, and agriculture (McManus 2005; Regular 2009). In colonial narratives, Indigenous peoples were effaced as nameless and faceless warriors whose homelands were recast as *terra nullius* sites of nomadic foraging (e.g., Brasser 1982). Banished to the margins by treaties, which ceded their lands to Canada, the regional First Nations played into official and popular histories as dysfunctional and violent, simply victims to be forgotten (Fiske, Belanger, and Gregory 2010).

Notably the Indigenous and settler narratives both demonstrate the importance of place to an individual's sense of identity (Abbott 2008). Moreover, it is a culturally contingent construct as confirmed by First Nations land claims seeking the return of traditional territories from governments that likewise assert legal ownership to the same lands based on a colonial record of settling vacant or legally surrendered lands. Upon possessing Indigenous lands, community-building initiatives commenced, fashioned according to the manifest right to own and develop the contested lands (see Kaye 2011; Owram 1992). Local leaders were quick to deny historic Indigenous contributions, for to do otherwise would weaken local claims to land rights and development. As described by Stanger-Ross (2008), these and other examples of "municipal-colonialism" emphasize a city-planning approach that sought to manage Indigenous peoples in urban settings (Belanger 2013). Indigenous peoples confined to nearby reserves were not easily dissuaded from visiting neighbouring cities that were sited within traditional lands as evidenced by a quick review of the literature exploring municipal development in western Canada. Indigenous city visits to obtain health care and to explore economic opportunities, among others reasons, were frequently discussed. These dispatches also highlighted municipal concern about these visits. It would appear that even at such advanced stage of municipal development the fear of losing everything overwhelmed any desires to reach out to First Nations communities to secure their participation in regional development schemes.

Compounding the self-imposed isolation from orbiting First Nations was municipal-colonialism's belief in the need to physically segregate Indigenous peoples onto reserves as a means of thwarting their potential urbanism. Interestingly, municipal resistance in such instances ran contrary to Canada's implicit goal of relocating to the city those Indigenous individuals who were disinclined to become reserve farmers or ranchers (Belanger 2013). Arguably, these trends endure in the form of municipal resistance to city–First Nations economic agreements, municipal opposition to urban Indigenous development zones, and the presence of NIMBY (Not In My Backyard) attitudes. The resulting feelings of alienation and social dislocation experienced in the city and increasingly in reserve communities commonly lead individuals to try and escape, and this forced or voluntary relocation has been shown to detrimentally impact interpersonal relationships and personal and collective identity development (Windsor and Mcvey 2005). Substantial social upheaval leads to diminished urban Indigenous economic, educational, and health outcomes. The urban Indigenous population is less educated, for instance, and faces higher unemployment rates than non-Indigenous population. It is also overrepresented in terms of homelessness—Indigenous people in major urban centres are as much as eight times more likely to experience homelessness than their non-Indigenous counterparts (Belanger, Awosoga, and Weasel Head 2013)

The already difficult task of urban (and reserve) community building is aggravated by the destabilizing nature of being unwelcome or unwanted in one's own lands (Abele, Falvo, and Haché 2010; Belanger, Awosoga, and Weasel Head 2013; Christensen 2012; Ruttan, LaBoucane-Benson, and Munro 2008; Weasel Head 2011). It is however not uncommon for community leaders, academics, and politicians to highlight urban Indigenous adaptability and the meaningfulness of urban space to Indigenous individuals (Awad 2004; Belanger et al. 2003). As Andersen (2002, 20) notes, Indigenous people "have created new and distinct communities while concomitantly creating new cultural norms, adapting, as we have always done, to the material circumstances around us." Peters (2005, 393) has argued that within the urban Indigenous community exists "a sense of belonging, active household assistance networks, and the growing presence of self-governing institutions" (see also Peters 2004). Within the southern Alberta context, Whittles and Patterson (2009, 97) provocatively suggest that Niitsitapi "stories and storytelling continue to reflect a uniquely Aboriginal sense of the world, even though, to many non-Aboriginal urbanites, the city is a place alien to all things Native." These discussions contest the pervasive literature that asserts, for instance, urban Indigenous peoples' propensity for living in socially and economically poor neighbourhoods (Richards 2001). All positive developments aside, we need to recognize that positive social reproduction is dependent on more than local community support; it is reliant on equitable access to resources and the capacity to participate in local policy development (Belanger and Walker 2009; Prentice 2007; Sookraj et al. 2012).

Arguably, it is within these larger (Canadian) and regional (Niitsitapi) contexts that reserve and urban Indigenous homelessness must be evaluated. Indigenous people nationally are starting to overcome, or are learning to manage, the disparate forces described above while simultaneously (re)establishing unique social and cultural spaces within their traditional lands, which include urban settings. It is therefore imperative that we produce a refined understanding of Indigenous homelessness, including its pathways, if we are to institute effective and responsive intervention and prevention strategies. The following sections explore these and like issues while highlighting the participants' suggested next steps.

Methodology

The Blackfoot elder Percy Bullchild (1985, 2) wrote that retelling stories is a powerful and empowering act that, if properly practised, preserves "our Indian history" by fostering a form of agency that situates the stories within the larger context of Niitsitapi society (see also King 2003). Stories "provide a window to the experiential domain," for humans "interpret experiences as well as make them understood to others through language" (Gregory 1994, 53–54). A focused ethnography method was employed to collect stories and explore chronically homeless Niitsitapi perceptions of, and attachment to, home and land. Knoblauch (2005) has indicated that focused ethnography advocates shorter, more pragmatic researcher field visits thereby ensuring the collection of robust data sets and close analytical scrutiny. Qualitative research is deemed more subjective, allows for a wider range of meaningful data to emerge from the narratives, and is consistent with the Niitsitapi oral tradition.

Preliminary fieldwork for our study began in October 2008 with us participating in the regional homeless census point in time (PIT) count. Then we conducted interviews with six participants (four male, two female) at the Lethbridge Homeless Shelter over a six-month period (October 2009–March 2010). Two interview sessions were conducted at the home of a female participant who had managed to obtain housing with the assistance of the shelter staff. Each of the chronically homeless participants ranged in age from their early thirties to early fifties and had used the local shelter resources for several years. Participants were recruited through the use of plain language, easily accessible and understandable posters displayed in the shelter's high-traffic areas, to draw a purposeful sample. They were selected based on existing information regarding this project's research objectives. Given the time restrictions and the participants' mobile disposition, five narratives were completed with six participants. The data was interpreted and framed through the participants' subjective realties (Kingfisher 2007; Letkemann 2004; Menzies 2007; Sider 2005). Thematic analysis was used for the data analyses because of its emphasis on personal experiences: in this instance, how individuals experience and understand their homeless situation (Bryman and Teevan 2005). Each of the participants was provided with small gifts (i.e., practical clothing items, tobacco/cigarettes) as a token of our appreciation.

Findings

To understand the meaning of homelessness one must first determine the pathways leading to homelessness that are framed within Niitsitapi historic understanding of their traditional homeland. Ultimately the goal was to try and determine how being homeless informs attachment to the land, and whether this connection compels individuals to remain homeless in traditional lands rather than becoming sheltered in foreign territories.

Loss of Family and Identity

Evident in all five narratives is a profound sense of loss related to identity and family, and all of the participants shared experiences that involved losing family members at a very young age. It therefore appears that trauma experienced early on influences pathways to homelessness. Families were frequently split up, leading the participants to develop an incomplete sense of what the land meant from a Niitsitapi perspective. The participants are reminded of this daily due to the fact that Niitsitapi protocols compel individuals to, upon introducing themselves, reveal personal and family connections that shape the participants' identity, for example. Although renewing relationships in this way is a means of reconnecting, being reminded of the historic disconnect from family and territory is psychologically taxing. The participants are phenomenally resilient, but ongoing trauma combined with the impact of residential schools, for example, can eventually overwhelm them. More importantly, resilience alone cannot surmount the effects of profound loss in regards to personal identity development and sense of self. The personal impact is staggering, but these events have also torn the very fabric of Niitsitapi culture, as stated by one participant: "I think it made a hole in the culture. Residential schools came along and broke up the family and family was a big part of the Blackfoot people. Family is the culture... we stick together. Putting the kids in residential schools broke up families and taking away language...all of this trickles down to what we see now...I don't know my culture...maybe a little. I don't know what my grandparents know and they don't always tell me. They don't talk of traditional ways; it's always about what they did in residential schools." What was described as a trickle should more accurately be depicted as a steady stream of loss that is clearly evident upon entering the homeless shelter. One participant noted: "I have never really wondered what profound loneliness looks like or what constant longing feels like until I entered these walls. Depression and loss permeates the air. I wish I didn't have to come back tomorrow."

It is important to note that the deaths of family members usually occurred unnaturally vis-à-vis accidents, addiction, or suicide. The ubiquitous nature of these events led the participants to conclude that they and their families live inherently dysfunctional lifestyles, and this can trigger depression and lead to substance abuse as coping mechanisms. Predictably, participants also felt abandoned by their families, or at the very least that they were turned away, which stripped them of much needed resources and supports. Interestingly, even though the participants sought out familial intimacy, they simultaneously expressed feelings of shame and guilt for past actions that continue to act as barriers to achieving the desired personal contact. The centrality of family to Niitsitapi identity means that family loss exacts tremendous personal impact. The narratives revealed that family support was virtually non-existent in participants' lives, which led them to form bonds with others living on the street in an attempt to fill this void.

Loss of Community

In addition to losing contact with family members, the participants also felt disconnected from what they would describe as traditional community. This included members of the regional First Nations and the local urban Indigenous and non-Indigenous populations. The participants noted that they did not feel like they were contributing members to either of these communities, which resulted in personal alienation from the nearby reserves and the city. The reserves in particular offered them little and being unable to remain on reserve forced many to relocate to the city. As one participant indicated, "it's the transition of coming into town and not knowing what to expect...how to support your family. Finding it hard and tough, you end up drinking because you don't know how to cope." Another added, "When you move to the city, an urban environment, there's certain things you have to comply with that you don't on the reserve." The participants stated that they know many individuals who left the reserve due to feelings of being disconnected from or abandoned by the traditional community. Upon moving into the city, many were confronting similar feelings of disconnection due to a lack of personal contact, which impedes successful urban transition. Moving away from a recognizable landscape and into a largely unrecognizable urban centre amplifies feelings of social disconnection and detachment from the reserve community.

When asked to explain in greater detail what traditional community meant, many of the participants suggested that traditional Niitsitapi community no longer exists. Perhaps more disturbingly, it was suggested that modern Canadian society was forcing Niitsitapi individuals to abandon their traditional values of group support and reciprocity in order to become more economically and socially stable individuals. For example, reciprocity (sharing), in this instance, has the potential to compromise the social stability of those who manage to secure rental housing. In particular, members of their street/shelter family could invariably show up at the new home or apartment, which then directly places the renter at risk of reprimand or eviction. Turning away shelter acquaintances puts the renters in an equally difficult social situation. As most of the chronically homeless individuals had a history of short-term rentals before quickly returning to the street, alienating street family members could lead to stress-filled relationships upon returning to the street.

The centre of this relational network is the local homeless shelter, which is located roughly one kilometre from the city core. The mainstream non-homeless population knows its location and its role in mitigating homelessness and aiding those who are the hardest to house. Yet the shelter is unmistakably separated from local mainstream society: located literally on the north or wrong side of the railway tracks that act as the city's north/south divide, a physical reminder of historic cultural and economic divisions. The building in which the shelter is located is virtually imperceptible to the traffic using a nearby key transportation artery, so in many ways the residents remain hidden there at night. But the shelter users travelling from the city's core at night and who reverse their pilgrimage each morning must nevertheless temporarily put themselves on display twice daily for motorists using this heavily trafficked street. Hearing catcalls and trying to avoid disdainful looks several times a day negatively impacted everyone's self-esteem. The participants endured this ritualized public ridicule before citizens who were at best puzzled at the situation and at worst openly contemptible of urban Indigenous homelessness. The lack of specific, culturally appropriate programming available to the Indigenous homeless population is compounded by the public's unwillingness and/or inability to reconceptualize Indigenous people through a lens of social inclusion (Fiske, Belanger, and Gregory 2010). When mainstream society prefers to rely on narratives stressing settler heroism of taming a wild frontier and ignores pre-contact Indigenous contributions and regional social and economic complexity, it becomes clear why the participants we spoke with feel like strangers in their homeland.

Loss of Trust

Having endured substantial historic and contemporary trauma and suffering, the participants found it difficult to trust anyone in an environment characterized by a lack of strong family ties and public ridicule. Homelessness remained an issue for those who had become wary of organizations that were unable to help participants obtain the assistance needed to combat their addictions and improve their general living situation. For most of the participants, abuse, neglect, and the absence of meaningful contact during their formative years led to a loss of trust that for some was irrecoverable. One participant spoke about his profound mistrust of the general non-Indigenous population while another believed that the researchers interviewing him were intent on assisting a local social organization to wrest away the control of his finances. Indeed, all participants were unwilling to be a part of the research until they were thoroughly convinced of our purpose and goals.

Addictions

Each participant was engaged in a desperate battle with alcohol addiction. For those living in the city core, alcohol is readily available at numerous bars, lounges, and liquor stores. Unlike living on the reserve, where not owning a vehicle can keep individuals from obtaining alcohol from a neighboring community, the same obstacles are not available in the city. The urban kinship networks can at times be an aggravating factor in that many individuals also experience similar substance abuse issues, leading to the development of a community of enablers. The participants appeared to use alcohol to help numb psychic and emotional pain resulting from past/present trauma, yet they were also aware that their addictions exacerbated an already dire situation. Many were in a self-admitted downward spiral and they still chose to participate in the study while encouraging others to pursue harmful activities. One participant blamed his homelessness on his alcoholism which he was helpless to control. Others suggested that addictions acted as barriers to obtaining adequate shelter. One suggested that most of his friends had good intentions and wanted to get off the street, "but when the time comes to pay [the] damage deposit, addictions get in the way and they've lost out." Mainstream society portrays urban Indigenous homeless as a group of endemic substance abusers, and the participants reluctantly admitted that this might be an accurate assessment. That being said, it is important to recognize that combined trauma and profound loss anchor these addictions. It was common when visiting the shelter to observe Indigenous guests under the influence. Alcohol was by far the most commonly abused substance, but we also witnessed prescription medication (ab)use.

Racism and Discrimination

Each of the participants identified racism and discrimination as an everyday aspect of city life, leading to substance use and abuse to numb both the pain being experienced and the feelings of resentment towards the dominant society. As noted above, it is not uncommon to hear insults while leaving and returning to the shelter. At the same time, the participants felt it was easier to manage this form of public ridicule than to face the subtle, personalized racism associated with trying to secure rental accommodations. Each participant concluded that any attempt to rent in the city is to actively court humiliation at the hands of landlords who will in most cases only rent to Indigenous peoples as a last resort. Citing poor past experiences and a fear of the unknown, many landlords judge renting to Indigenous people a "bad investment": property damage will result, squatting family members will arrive, and inevitably rent will remain unpaid (Belanger 2007). All Indigenous renters have thus been stigmatized as risks when all tenants pose similar risks. Addiction issues do, however, often compel individuals to spend beyond their meager means thereby compromising their ability to pay rent. Each of the participants acknowledged this while indicating that they must first address their substance abuse issues prior to being able to successfully rent a house or an apartment.

Furthermore, attempting to reconcile the need to conform to non-Indigenous social standards and the need to reconnect with Niitsitapi culture is an ever-present reality. What we found, in this case, was a sense of pride in Indigenous culture tempered by expectations about how to best integrate. Interestingly, the norms emphasizing social, political, and economic individuality conflicted with Niitsitapi values stressing reciprocity and collective community development. The implicit questions being posed to the project participants by non-Indigenous peoples, and also their Indigenous friends and neighbours, were as follows: (1) what type of Indigenous person do you want to be? (2) are you willing to remain homeless albeit guided by cultural norms that undermine individual efforts to exit the street? And, (3) are you willing to adopt mainstream norms that may mitigate homelessness in the short term but that may distance you from your identity, family, and history?

Estrangement from the Reserve

The research's most revealing facet was the participants' profound sense of alienation from their home reserve communities (see also Thurston et al. 2013). Most had lived in the city for years, if not the majority of their adult lives, and they felt that their home reserve communities set in the heart of the Niitsitapi homeland were inhospitable. Driving this resentment were band council decisions to offer resources to local citizens and not those who choose to live an urban lifestyle. First Nations are admittedly in a difficult position. Annual budgets are derived from per capita allocations, meaning that the bulk of revenue is intended for reserve populations, and those living off-reserve (even band members who are still acknowledged First Nations citizens) find themselves shut out from accessing these resources. Despite desires to remain on-reserve, the participants discovered that the lack of reserve jobs and poor housing conditions forced them off of the reserve and into racist and discriminatory urban environments. The various band councils' unwillingness to incorporate urban Indigenous citizens into the political decision-making process leads to feelings of alienation and growing resentment being directed at the reserve politicians.

The participants indicated that an invisible border was evident between the reserves and the city spaces that influenced their understanding of the other (urban Indigenous versus reserve resident). The resulting fragmentation of Niitsitapi territory into pockets of social inclusion and exclusion was disturbing. So were the individual feelings of disconnection from the lands the participants and their ancestors never physically abandoned but have nevertheless been made to feel unwelcome to reside within. Steady movement between the reserve and city occurs as people try to reconnect with family and elders and in search of education and employment opportunities. Where the city represents employment and education, the reserve symbolizes home and a place that buttresses First Nation identity. Separation between communities is a barrier to feeling welcomed in an urban environment that occupies traditional Niitsitapi territory. Feelings of alienation occur while living in the city, but the participants also feel as though they cannot return to the reserve. As such, they begin to feel trapped in their own homelands. The participants seek personal value as citizens, and to have their identity as Indigenous people and their Niitsitapi history acknowledged as significant and meaningful. They do not want to be seen as a relic or consequence of a colonial past.

Conceptualizing Modern Niistsitapi Homelessness, Home, and Land

Historically the Niitsitapi traditional homeland (Creation) was considered a key site of all relationships (i.e., of power, of the two- and four-leggeds, and of points of historical significance). Places of power, productive economic regions, and spiritual sites existed within Creation, and successfully navigating these spaces led to culturally specific understandings of home and the evolving land. Creation was above all home, within which groups of like-minded individuals united into larger communities. Many changes have accompanied the coming of permanent settlers in the 1870s, Indigenous homelessness—both reserve and urban—being one. It is now considered normative (Belanger 2011) and popularly traced to Niitsitapi mobility, poverty, addictions, and mental health issues. Niitsitapi homelessness in this context is reduced to an individual scale (Fiske, Belanger, and Gregory 2010; Kingfisher 2007). What this study confirmed was the existence of a more complex understanding of Niitsitapi homelessness that is grounded in historical and collective experiences that remain a part of colonialism's enduring effects (Christensen 2013). Creation, importantly, remains a central and comforting concept, where the stories, history, and identity reside. Yet, new ideas informed by the imposition of alien ways of comprehending land as private property have influenced individual and collective ways of conceiving Creation. All the same, the project participants refused to consider outright abandoning Creation despite some drastic changes. That being said, there are several issues confronting the Niitsitapi homeless that demand greater understanding for those seeking to develop effective intervention strategies.

Post-settlement changes emphasizing private property continue to inhibit how renewal is both conceptualized and practised. Likewise, the colonial model resulting in physical changes to Creation is a constant reminder that the once regionally dominant Niitsitapi are no longer as politically or economically influential. Colonial geographies (Peters and Robillard 2009) now inform the Niitsitapi encounter with Creation to a degree that the idea of home that was once grounded by historic land-use patterns and ideologies has become progressively more fractured in the post-settlement period. Individuals now emphasize the value of certain points of Creation over others, thus obscuring historic notions of community and cultural continuity. Beliefs in cultural inclusion and exclusion have thus emerged that can act as barriers to accessing financial and emotional resources. For the Niitsitapi homeless we spoke with this is a difficult issue: due to the limited options available they must frequently remain in the city in order to access limited resources that nonetheless outstrip those available on reserve. Consequently, the reserve is described as (1) less accepting of the urban Indigenous peoples' presence (especially the homeless); and (2) not willing to share the resources needed to help individuals to socially and economically flourish.

The physical and ideological fragmentation of land has from the Niitsitapi homeless point of view led to the fragmentation of Niitsitapi society, and distorted the nature of interpersonal relationships historically guided by the spirit of reciprocity. Guaranteeing personal survival now trumps the collective's needs, and this is troubling to individuals who in their mind are forced to reject Niitsitapi teachings in lieu of adopting the colonizer's method. Internalizing and acting on physical divisions imposed on Creation has led individuals to establish contemporary values emphasizing the importance of certain sites. The reserve materializes from this context as the last remaining symbol of a traditional homeland. Unfortunately, privileging one site over another encourages Creation's ongoing dissolution while advancing a process we identify as hierarchy of residence. Here, culturally contingent definitions of insider/outsider emerge that are based as much on cultural survival as they are reflective of an imposed colonial heritage. As a case in point, the Niitsitapi homeless we interviewed believe that their reserve communities willingly abandoned them, and that they are also increasingly hostile to those now deemed outsiders. The city is however also considered a hostile site, which makes it difficult to find a place to call home in Creation. Now trapped in a liminal space character- ized by the trauma associated with territorial dispossession and colonialism's psychological wounds, the participants helplessly watch as interpersonal relationships crumble based on choice of residential site (or a lack of choice thereof). Colonialism thus emerges as not an historic footnote but an active process that continues to influence Niitsitapi society's unraveling.

The larger discussion of land fragmentation that has led to interpersonal conflicts often consumes family members increasingly divided along geo- graphic lines (i.e., those living on- and off-reserve). Sadly, in such instances families are no longer considered symbols of inclusion and social stability but rather are obvious sites of discord and division. Individuals who likewise feel disconnected from Creation often are also dealing with family breakdowns. They consequently describe their existence as lonely, a word that each project participant used during the interviews to describe their current homeless state but also how they felt, at times, while permanently housed. The loss of relationships is reflected in the feelings of loneliness borne of being unwit- tingly jettisoned from their lands (even if one still "lives" on the land) and daily experiences with discrimination and racism. Loneliness is also analogous to being unable to successfully reconnect with Creation leading to spiritual homelessness, which is a "crisis of personal identity wherein one's understand- ing or knowledge of how one relates to country, family and Aboriginal identity systems is confused, or known but unable to be fulfilled" (Memmott, Birdsall- Jones, and Greenop 2012, 25). One could argue that intergenerational trauma also informs individual and collective experiences that are simultaneously historic and contemporary in scope, and sway what home means. This issue in particular demands greater investigation.

Despite regularly confronting similar pressures, none of the participants considered leaving Niitsitapi territory to seek work in the province's northern oil fields or in the forestry industry straddling the nearby Alberta/BC border. Everyone expressed a tremendous sense of pride in his or her traditional homeland. Interestingly, despite the substantial changes to the idea of home and land, the participants indicated that remaining nearby the reserve was rejuvenating. This small homeless community even tried to replicate cultural norms stressing the centrality of family and collective relationships to recreate a sense of belonging in the city. Unfortunately, these actions were informed by an impoverished sense of what constitutes an affirmative relationship. Also, substance abuse was endemic within a community that, while located in the heart of Niitsitapi territory, was nevertheless made to feel unwanted by the larger population whose heritage is rooted in the stories of brave settlers bringing life to an otherwise lifeless wasteland. Attempts were made to offset these impacts. For instance, the homeless shelter offers a handful of services that include cultural programming incorporating traditional practices such as smudging and sweat lodges, programming that the participants believed reinforced the traditional community. In lieu of a permanent home and failing kinship relations the shelter (itself a reserved and isolated space for the urban homeless) has come to represent "home" insofar as it has been the place where new family bonds are formed and meaningful existence is rediscovered within its walls.

Conclusion

The causes of Niitsitapi homelessness are complex and multi-layered, and we must begin to address these issues by focusing on rebuilding community connections, creating relationships, and acknowledging cultural histories. The participants' narratives indicate that a culturally unique definition of homelessness has emerged. That is, to be homeless is to subsist absent from family or community support networks, which the Keys Young (1998) report and Memmott and Chambers (2008) describe as spiritual homelessness. Being homeless does not necessarily mean not having a home, or shelter for that matter—the standard definitions of homelessness did not accurately reflect the participants' conceptualizations in this study. Lacking shelter is indeed problematic, but the participants also equated homelessness with being abandoned by their family and the traditional Niitsitapi community. Homelessness is a fluid condition that it is apt to alteration, providing new meanings for those who experience it. Even after obtaining shelter, many Indigenous individuals still felt homeless in the absence of family and the support of their peers. We should therefore endeavour to comprehend Niitsitapi homelessness not just as a lack of housing, but recognize that it is notably influenced by a lack of family and community ties. Perhaps, more importantly, we must begin to formally acknowledge how the trends identified in this research can be used to determine best practices for improving the situation for southern Alberta's Indigenous homeless community seeking to reconnect with Napi's Land.

Notes

1 The term "Indigenous peoples" indicates any one of the three legally defined culture groups that form what are known as Indigenous peoples in Canada (Metis, Inuit, and Indian) and who self-identify as such. The term "First Nation" is used here to denote a reserve community, or band. The term "Indian," as used in legislation or policy, will also appear in discussions concerning such legislation or policy.

2 This would be $142,318,107 in today's currency (April 2016), adjusted for inflation. Figures generated by using the online Bank of Canada *Inflation Calculator* (www.bankofcanada.ca/rates/related/inflation-calculator/).

3 There were just over 200,000 Aboriginal people occupying 2,241 reserves in Canada in 1964 (Tremblay, Vallee, and Ryan 1967, 23). It is estimated that only 6 percent of this population (n = 12,000) lived off reserve. The figures utilized can be found at LAC, RG10, Vol. 8190, File 1/29-2.

4 To date no book length manuscript has been produced exploring Lethbridge's historical evolution, and Crowson's and Johnston's titles are among the best, well-known local histories. In particular Crowson's (2011) work is unique in that it is aimed at a young audience. Pages 7–9 offer brief biographical snippets about some of the prairie region inhabitants: Red Crow, Joe Healy, Jim Shot Both Sides, and Canada's First Indigenous Senator Jim Gladstone. This is followed by the introduction of explorers and the gradual dispossession of Indigenous peoples from the land in the name of community building. In total Indigenous content amounts to roughly four pages out of ninety-two total.

References

Abbott, Carl. 2008. *How Cities Won the West: Four Centuries of Urban Change in Western North America*. Albuquerque: University of New Mexico Press.

Abele, Frances, Nick Falvo, and Arlene Haché. 2010. "Homeless in the Homeland: A Growing Problem for Indigenous People in Canada's North." *Parity* 23 (9): 21–24.

Andersen, Christian Trevor. 2002. *Courting Colonialism: Contemporary Métis Communities and the Canadian Judicial Imagination*. Paper presented at the Reconfiguring Aboriginal-State Relations: Canada State of the Federation 2003 Conference, 1–2 November, Kingston, ON, Queen's University.

Awad, Michael. 2004. "Aboriginal Affairs." *Canadian Architect* 49 (5): 53–54.

Basso, Keith H. 1996. *Wisdom Sits in Places: Landscape and Language among the Western Apache*. Albuquerque: University of New Mexico Press.

Bastien, Betty. 2004. *Blackfoot Ways of Knowing: The Worldview of the Siksikaitsitapi*. Calgary: University of Calgary Press.

Bear Robe, Andrew. 1996. "The Historical, Legal and Current Basis for Siksika Nation Governance, Including Its Future Possibilities Within Canada." In *For Seven Generations: An Information Legacy of the Royal Commission on Aboriginal Peoples* (CD-ROM). Ottawa: Canada Communications Group.

Beavis, Mary Ann, Nancy Klos, Thomas Carter, and Christian Douchant. 1997. *Literature Review: Aboriginal Peoples and Homelessness*. Ottawa: Canada Mortgage and Housing Corporation.

Begin, Patricia, Lyne Casavant, Nancy Miller Chenier, and Jean Dupis. 1999. "Definition of Homelessness." In *Homelessness*, PRB 99-1E. Ottawa: Parliamentary Research

Branch, http://www.parl.gc.ca/content/lop/researchpublications/prb991-e.htm#DEFINITIONtxt.

Belanger, Yale D. 2007. *Assessing Urban Aboriginal Housing Needs in Southern Alberta.* Public Policy Paper #51. Regina: Saskatchewan Institute on Public Policy.

———. 2011. *Lethbridge Sheltered Populations: An Overview of Current Trends, 2010–2011.* Lethbridge: Social Housing in Action Society.

———. 2013. "Breaching Reserve Boundaries: *Canada v. Misquadis* and the Legal Creation of the Urban Aboriginal Community." In *Indigenous in the City: Contemporary Identities and Cultural Innovation,* edited by Evelyn J. Peters, and Chris Anderson, 68–89. Vancouver: UBC Press.

Belanger, Yale D., Olu Awosoga, and Gabrielle Weasel Head. 2013. "Homelessness, Urban Aboriginal People, and the Need for a National Enumeration." *Aboriginal Policy Studies* 2 (2): 4–33.

Belanger, Yale D., Liz Barron, Melanie Mills, and Charlene Turnbull-McKay. 2003. *Urban Aboriginal Youth in Winnipeg: Culture and Identity Formation in Cities.* Winnipeg: Department of Culture and Heritage Canada.

Belanger, Yale D., and Ryan Walker. 2009. "Interest Convergence and Co-production of Plans: An Examination of Winnipeg's 'Aboriginal Pathways.'" *Canadian Journal of Urban Research* 18 (1): 118–39.

Belanger, Yale D., Gabrielle Weasel Head, and Olu Awosoga. 2012. "Housing and Urban Aboriginal People in Urban Centres: A Quantitative Evaluation." *Aboriginal Policy Studies* 2 (1): 4–25.

Binnema, Theodore (Ted). 2004. *Common and Contested Ground: A Human and Environmental History of the Northwestern Plains.* Toronto: University of Toronto Press.

Brasser, Ted J. 1982. "The Tipi as an Element of Historic Plains Indian Nomadism." *Plains Anthropologist* 27 (98): 309–21.

Bryman, Alan, and James J. Teevan. 2005. *Social Research Methods.* Toronto: Oxford University Press.

Bullchild, Percy. 1985. *The Sun Came Down: The History of the World as My Blackfeet Elders Told It.* San Francisco: Harper and Row.

Canada. 1966. *Opening Statement by the Honourable Arthur Laing to the House of Commons Committee on Indian Affairs, Human Rights and Citizenship and Immigration.* (91-558-IXE). Ottawa: Statistics Canada.

Canada. 1996. Royal Commission on Aboriginal Peoples (RCAP). *Report of the Royal Commission on Aboriginal Peoples.* Ottawa: Supply and Services Canada.

Christensen, Julia. 2012. "They Want a Different Life": Rural Northern Settlement Dynamics and Pathways to Homelessness in Yellowknife and Inuvik, Northwest Territories. *The Canadian Geographer / Le Géographe canadien* 56 (4): 419–38.

———. 2013. "'Our Home, Our Way of Life': Spritual Homelessness and the Sociocultural Dimensions of Indigenous Homelessness in the Northewest Territories (NWT), Canada." *Social and Cultural Geography* 14 (7): 804–28.

Crowson, Belinda. 2011. *So! You Think You Know Lethbridge? Lethbridge History for Kids.* Lethbridge: Lethbridge Historical Society.

Dempsey, Hugh Aylmer. 2002. *Firewater: The Impact of the Whiskey Trade on the Blackfoot Nation.* Calgary: Fifth House.

Dion Stout, Madeleine, and Gregory D. Kipling. 2003. *Aboriginal People, Resilience and the Residential School Legacy.* Ottawa: Aboriginal Healing Foundation.

Ewers, John C. 1955. *The Horse in Blackfoot Indian Culture: With Comparative Material from Other Western Tribes.* Washington, DC.: Smithsonian Press, U.S. Government Printing Office.

Fiske, Jo-Anne, Belanger, Yale D., and David Gregory. 2010. "Outsiders in Their Homeland: Discursive Construction of Aboriginal Women and Citizenship." *American Indian Culture and Research Journal* 34 (3): 71–92.

Furniss, Elizabeth. 1999. *The Burden of History: Colonialism and the Frontier Myth in a Rural Canadian Community.* Vancouver: UBC Press.

Gaetz, Stephen, Fiona Scott, and Tanya Gulliver. 2012. *Housing First in Canada: Supporting Communties to End Homelessness.* Toronto: Canadian Homelessness Research Network Press.

Gregory, David Michael. 1994. "Narratives of Suffering in the Cancer Experience." PhD diss., University of Arizona.

INAC (Indigenous and Northern Affairs Canada). 2011. *Evaluation of INAC's On-Reserve Housing Support.* Ottawa: Government of Canada.

Johnston, Alex. 1997. *Lethbridge: From Coal Town to Commercial Centre: A Business History.* Lethbridge: Lethbridge Historical Society.

Kaye, Frances W. 2011. *Goodlands: A Meditation and History on the Great Plains.* Edmonton: Athabasca University Press.

Keys Young Firm. 1998. *Homelessness in the Aboriginal and Torres Strait Islander Context and Its Possible Implications for the Supported Accommodation Assistance Program (SAAP).* Sydney, NSW: Department of Family and Community Services.

King, Thomas. 2003. *The Truth About Stories: A Native Narrative.* Toronto: House of Anansi Press.

Kingfisher, Catherine. 2007. "Discursive Constructions of Homelessness in a Small City in the Canadian Prairies: Notes on Destructuration, Individualization, and the Production of (Raced and Gendered) Unmarked Categories." *American Ethnologist* 34 (1): 91–107.

Knoblauch, Hubert. 2005. "Focused Ethnography." *Forum: Qualitative Social Research* 6 (3). Article 44.

Leach, Andrew. 2010. "The Roots of Aboriginal Homelessness in Canada." *Parity* 23 (9): 12–13.

Leslie, John. 1999. "Assimilation, Integration or Termination? The Development of Canadian Indian Policy, 1943–1963." PhD diss., Carleton University, Ottawa.

Letkemann, Paul G. 2004. "First Nations Urban Migration and the Importance of 'Urban Nomads' in Canadian Plains Cities: A Perspective from the Streets." *Canadian Journal of Urban Research* 13 (2): 241–56.

Little Bear, Leroy. 1996. "Relationship of Aboriginal People to the Land and the Aboriginal Perspective on Aboriginal Title." In *For Seven Generations: An Information Legacy of the Royal Commission on Aboriginal Peoples* (CD-ROM). Ottawa: Canada Communications Group.

McKenzie, B., and V. Morrisette. 2003. "Social Work Practice and Canadians of Aboriginal Background: Guidelines for Respectful Social Work." *Envision: The Manitoba Journal of Child Welfare* 2 (1): 13–39.

McManus, Sheila. 2005. *The Line which Separates: Race, Gender, and the Making of the Alberta-Montana Borderlands.* Edmonton: University of Alberta Press.

Memmott, Paul, Christina Birdsall-Jones, and Kelly Greenop. 2012. *Why are Special Services Needed to Address Indigenous Homelessness?* Brisbane: Institute for Social Science Research, The University of Queensland.

Memmott, Paul, and Catherine Chambers. 2008. "Homelessness amongst Aboriginal People in Inner Sydney." Paper presented at the 2nd Australasian Housing Researchers' Conference, The University of Queensland, Brisbane, Australia, 20-22 June.

Menzies, Peter. 2005. "Orphans within Our Family: Intergenerational Trauma and Homeless Aboriginal Men." PhD diss., University of Toronto.

_____. 2007. "Understanding Aboriginal Intergenerational Trauma from a Social Work Perspective." *Canadian Journal of Native Studies* 27 (2): 367–92.

Owram, Doug. 1992. *Promise of Eden: The Canadian Expansionist Movement and the Idea of the West, 1856–1900.* Toronto: University of Toronto Press.

Perry, Adele. 2003. "From 'the Hot-Bed of Vice' to the 'Good and Well-Ordered Christian Home': First Nations Housing and Reform in Nineteenth-Century British Columbia." *Ethnohistory* 50 (4): 587–610.

Peters, Evelyn J. 1996. "'Urban' and 'Aboriginal': An Impossible Contradiction?" In *City Lives and City Forms: Critical Research and Canadian Urbanism,* edited by Jon Caulfield, and Linda Peake, 47–62. Toronto: University of Toronto Press.

_____. 2004. "Three Myths About Aboriginals in Cities." Paper presented at the Breakfast in the Hill Seminar Series, Ottawa.

_____. 2005. "Indigeneity and Marginalisation: Planning for and with Urban Aboriginal Communities in Canada." *Progress in Planning* 63 (4) 327–404.

Peters, Evelyn J., and Vince Robillard. 2009. "'Everything you want is there': The Place of the Reserve In First Nations' Homeless Mobility." *Urban Geography* 3 (6): 652–80.

Prentice, Susan. 2007. "Childcare, Justice and the City: A Case Study of Planning Failure in Winnipeg." *Canadian Journal of Urban Research* 16 (1): 92–108.

Reeves, Brian. 1988. "The Oldman River Dam and Alberta's Heritage: Conservation or Desecration?" In *Economic, Environmental, and Social Aspects of the Oldman River Dam Project,* edited by S. B. Rood and F. J. Jankunis, 81–99. Lethbridge: Departments of Biological Sciences and Geography.

Regular, W. Keith. 2009. *Neighbours and Networks: The Blood Tribe and the Southern Alberta Economy 1889–1939.* Calgary: University of Calgary Press.

Richards, John. 2001. *Neighbours Matter: Poor Neighbourhoods and Urban Aboriginal Policy,* vol. 156. Ottawa: C.D. Howe Institute.

Ruttan, Lia., Patti LaBoucane-Benson, and Brenda Munro. 2008. "'A Story I Never Heard Before': Aboriginal Young Women, Homelessness and Restoring Connections." *Pimatisiwin: A Journal of Aboriginal and Indigenous Community Health* 6 (3): 31–54.

Savage, Candace. 2012. *A Geography of Blood: Unearthing Memory from a Prairie Landscape.* Vancouver: Greystone Books.

Sider, Debra. 2005. *A Sociological Analysis of Root Causes of Aboriginal Homelessness in Sioux Lookout, Ontario.* Toronto: The Canadian Race Relations Foundation.

Sommerville, Peter. 1992. "Homelessness and the Meaning of Home: Rooflessness or Rootlessness?" *International Journal of Urban and Regional Research* 16 (4): 529–39.

Sookraj, Dixon, Peter Hutchinson, Michael Evans, Mary Ann Murphy, and The Okanagan Urban Aboriginal Health Research Collective (TOUAHR) 2012. "Aboriginal Organizational Response to the Need for Culturally Appropriate Services in Three Small Canadian Cities." *Journal of Social Work* 12 (2): 136–57.

Stanger-Ross, Jordan. 2008. "Municipal Colonialism in Vancouver: City Planning and the Conflict over Indian Reserves, 1928–1950s." *Canadian Historical Review* 89 (4): 541–80.

Thurston, Wilfreda E., and Carol Mason. 2010. *Aboriginal Homelessness Research: The Context, What We're Doing, and the Future.* Calgary: Calgary Homeless Foundation.

Thurston, Wilfreda E., Katrina Milaney, David Turner, and Stephanie Coupal, S. 2013. *Final Report: No Moving Back: A Study of the Intersection of Rural and Urban Homelessness for Aboriginal People in Calgary, Alberta.* Calgary: Human Resources and Skills Development Canada, National Housing Secretariat.

Titley, E. Brian. 1986. *A Narrow Vision: Duncan Campbell Scott and the Administration of Indian Affairs.* Vancouver: UBC Press.

Treaty 7 Elders and Tribal Council, Walter Hildebrant, Sarah Carter, and Dorthy First Rider. 1996. *The True Spirit and Intent of Treaty 7.* Montreal and Kingston: McGill-Queen's University Press.

Tremblay, M.A., F.G. Vallee, and J. Ryan. 1967. *A Survey of the Contemporary Indians of Canada: Economic, Political, Educational Needs and Policies,* Part 2, edited by H. Hawthorn. Ottawa: Indian and Northern Affairs in Canada.

Vest, Jay Hansford C. 2005. "The Oldman River and the Sacred: The Meditation Upon Aputosi Pii'kani Tradition and Environmental Ethics." *Canadian Journal of Native Studies* 25 (2): 571–607.

Weasel Head, Gabrielle. 2011. "'All We Need Is Our Land': An Exploration of Urban Aboriginal Homelessness." MA diss., University of Lethbridge.

Whittles, Martin, and Tim Patterson. 2009. "Nápi and the City: Siksikaitsitapi Narratives Revisited." In *First Nations, First Thoughts: The Impact of Indigenous Thought in Canada,* edited by Annis May Timpson, 97–119. Vancouver: UBC Press.

Windsor, J. E., and J. Alistair Mcvey. 2005. "Annihilation of Both Place and Sense of Place: The Experience of the Cheslatta T'En Canadian First Nation within the Context of Large-Scale Environmental Projects." *The Geographical Journal* 171 (2): 146–65.

CHAPTER 9

Rural Indigenous Homelessness in Canada

REBECCA SCHIFF, ALINA TURNER, AND JEANNETTE
WAEGEMAKERS SCHIFF

The overwhelming body of literature on homelessness has concentrated on the people and problems of the urban environment. In both urban-focused studies, and in the small body of articles and reports that focus on small-town and rural settings, the challenges faced by homeless Indigenous people receive little notice. In Canada, several researchers have focused on migration between reserves and urban centres, but the experiences of those Indigenous people who do not live on reserves, but in small towns and outside of defined communities, is largely unexplored. While research strongly indicates that the overrepresentation of Indigenous people among the homeless is an issue across most major cities in Canada, there is little evidence about the extent to which Indigenous people represent those in rural areas who are homeless. In addition, not much is known about whether the rural homeless are primarily single, youth, women fleeing domestic violence, or those plagued by mental health and addiction problems. Resultantly, the specific challenges and struggles of these Indigenous people who are homeless and living off reserve and in the small towns and rural areas of the country are elusive. The problems of rural Indigenous people who are in a housing crisis are hidden in much the same way that rural homelessness is less visible outside of urban areas: it is not found on street corners and alley ways, but is experienced by those who live in squalid conditions and double up with friends and family.

The vastness of the Canadian rural landscape, and the complexity of its diverse Indigenous groups, makes it impossible to adequately describe homelessness in the rural context across all reaches of the country. The challenges of living in remote northern communities primarily inhabited by Innu and Inuit people are very different from those faced in coastal communities of British Columbia or Labrador or even from those faced on the Prairies and in Ontario forests. What this chapter does provide is a glimpse into what is known and what is unexplored about the problems encountered by Indigenous people who choose to live in rural areas.

The challenge of understanding Indigenous homelessness in rural areas is framed by the larger issue that there is little research examining Canadian rural homelessness in general. We explore the broader understanding of the dynamics of Canadian rural homelessness as an overreaching framework, and move to a more specific understanding of the ways in which Indigenous people in rural areas experience homelessness. Our discussion begins with an examination of the varied and debated definitions of rurality as reflected in the international literature on this subject. We then move to an analysis of the existing literature on rural homelessness in Canada, followed by an examination of the available research specific to rural homelessness and Indigenous people. While we make a brief mention of the challenges of homelessness in the remote Arctic communities of Nunavut, we acknowledge that northern Indigenous homelessness has unique characteristics not shared with most of the country and deserves its own separate discussion. In the course of this examination, we reflect on the analysis of several case study locations across Canada that suggest new insights into the nature and dynamics of this issue.

Rurality in the Canadian Context

As there are a number of ways in which rurality can be defined, the contested notions of "small town" and "rural" demand that any research or discussion of rural issues in Canada begin with a relevant definition to the ensuing analysis. While the term rural can have socio-political connotations that convey ideas of community, it is generally thought of in broad geographical terms. Even in this context, "rural" has multiple descriptors and meanings as indicated by the six different definitions used by Statistics Canada (Du Plessis et al. 2002). These definitions are based on the relative weighting of the parameters of population size, density, context, and consideration of the size of a territorial unit (local, communal, or regional). The research team headed by Du Plessis recommended that what encompasses the meaning of "rural" be classified according to the nature and needs of a specific study or project, with parameters that specify the following: zones which allow for commuting to urban areas; large or small communities; those outside of commuting zones but within proximity of towns of 1,000 or more; and those that are remote and located far from clustered habitation. Thus for the purposes of this research we use the term "rural" to identify those areas falling within codes 6 to 10 of the Modified Beale Codes for Canadian non-metropolitan analysis (Du Plesis et al. 2002). In this examination of rural Indigenous homelessness we focus predominantly on codes 7 to 10, which emphasize those communities that are situated within larger rural regions and are more distant from the services of large cities. Our definition includes many communities in the North, although we exclude larger, northern centres which fit within Modified Beale Codes for "small city zones" such as Whitehorse, Prince George, Fort McMurray, and Yellowknife.

Table 9.1. Rural populations by province/territory

Province/Territory	Rural Population (2011)	Rural as a percent of total population (%)
Newfoundland and Labrador	208,970	41
New Brunswick	356,692	48
Nova Scotia	400,389	43
Prince Edward Island	74,661	53
Quebec	1,534,731	19
Ontario	1,806,036	14
Manitoba	333,554	28
Saskatchewan	343,398	33
Alberta	614,855	17
British Columbia	609,363	14
Yukon	13,335	39
Northwest Territories, including Nunavut[1]	33,430	46

Source: Statistics Canada 2012.

1   The latest available figures list Nunavut along with Northwest Territories. Future demographic data will provide separate numbers for each.

Among the developed nations, Canada and Australia are the least populated with densities of four and three persons per square kilometre. The rural Canadian population in 2014 is about 19 percent of the total population and is thus one of the most sparsely inhabited countries in the world. There is considerable variation in the extent to which people in each province and territory live in a rural context. Table 9.1 provides a description of approximate percentage of population living in rural areas for individual provinces and territories. Most First Nations reserves, and most of the Indigenous population of Canada, are found in the vast, under-developed regions of the mid-lands of Ontario, the western provinces and northern territories.

Rural Homelessness in Canada

One of the first things of note in the literature on rural housing and home-lessness in Canada is that most articles and reports cite research conducted in other countries. There is a danger in extrapolating rural phenomenon in the UK or Australia into the Canadian context as rurality and climate are interconnected factors that influence the lived experiences of those in specific geographic locations. Cloke, Milbourne, and Widdowfield's (2000) work on rural homelessness in England noted a stereotype that homeless people migrate to rural areas for cheaper housing. As a result of this impression, homeless people are often blamed for bringing negative and anti-social behaviour to the community. In contrast, research suggests that the Canadian experience seems to be the opposite. In different parts of Canada, studies in urban contexts suggest that there is a pattern for homeless people, including youth, to migrate to urban centres where there are various housing options and more specialized services available (Christensen 2012; Forchuk et al. 2010; Gray et al. 2011; Karabanow, Aube, and Naylor 2014; Stewart and Ramage 2011).

The extent of homelessness in different parts of rural Canada is simply unknown. Several investigators have reflected on this paucity of information on rural homelessness, noting that methodological issues of data collection make this an almost impossible challenge (Waegemakers Schiff and Schiff 2016). In urban settings, most of those who are homeless seek some support services, ranging from food at a soup kitchen or food bank to overnight shelter and financial assistance. While some "sleep rough," most can be counted in regular counts by trained volunteers. Rural people, by virtue of their location, usually do not have a place to congregate unless they move to a town or a city that has identified services for those who lack housing. It has been postulated by researchers in the Unites States that housing insecurity may be as ubiqui-tous as it is in urban settings and, proportionately speaking, homeless rates may be even higher than in urban areas (Lawrence 1995). When those living in substandard or unfit housing are included, the number of people that are at risk of homelessness and facing housing insecurity in rural areas may be higher than in urban settings. In fact, it has been noted that houses routinely condemned in urban areas fall outside of the view of local officials in rural areas and remain inhabited despite their unsafe conditions (Robertson et al. 2007).

In a review of literature on the homeless in the Unites States, Robertson noted that those who are homeless in rural America are most often the hid-den homeless: doubled up or couch surfing with friends or family (Robertson et al. 2007). While these conclusions arise from localized reports rather than a strong national data gathering process, they have face validity, based on anecdotal reports and first-hand impressions that lead many to accept these conclusions. Thus the descriptor of rural homelessness as a largely invisible phenomenon has surfaced. Many rural homeless live with family and friends, moving from place to place as their welcome wears thin. They may live in dwellings considered substandard or not fit for human habitation (Hilton and DeJong 2010). Their home may be a travel trailer, a car, or an abandoned bus (Robertson et al. 2007). This "hiddenness" may for some also be seasonal, with visibility increasing during warmer months. For example, in many rural towns such as Kenora in northern Ontario, Peace River in northern Alberta, and Happy Valley-Goose Bay in Labrador, homeless people are visibly camped in or near town during milder weather (Falvo 2011; Waegemakers Schiff and Turner 2014b), a visible reminder of their lack of shelter or housing.

Indigenous Homelessness in Rural Canada

When we narrow our examination to the literature that focuses on Indigenous homelessness in Canada, peer-reviewed publications provide few answers to our questions. We located a handful of peer-reviewed articles that could be considered to encompass rural homeless issues. Five of these, (Belanger and Weasel Head 2013; Christensen 2012; Forchuk et al. 2010; Gray et al. 2011; Peters and Robillard 2009) focused on urban/rural migration patterns. Of these, two articles, by Belanger and Weasel Head and Peters and Robillard, examined Indigenous migratory patterns in western Canada, providing reasons why Indigenous people leave and return to their reserves. A detailed study by Christensen examined rural and migratory patterns in the Far North, encompassing both Indigenous Dene and Inuit people (Christensen 2012). The results of these investigations are reported by these researchers in other sections of this book. Other studies, such as those by Forchuck and co-authors and Gray and colleagues, were not specific to Indigenous people, despite the fact that the study areas were located close to Indigenous lands and reserves. In two instances, we encountered indications of rural studies that were misleading as the geographic areas under consideration did not meet the criteria of rurality (Gray et al. 2011; Skott-Myhre, Raby, and Nikolaou 2008). This led us to be vigilant about the criteria used for including studies that were based on a specific definition of rural.

Given the paucity of Canadian-based peer-reviewed articles, we expanded the search to include the grey literature of reports, commissioned by government and non-profit organizations, on rural homelessness. This included reports and research undertaken for Service Canada and Canada Housing and Mortgage Corporation, and research commissioned by local community advisory boards, established under the Homeless Partnering Strategy, and homeless consortiums, such as the one in northern Ontario that serves largely rural communities. Some reports included references to the overrepresentation of Indigenous people but none were specific to rural Indigenous issues. We also uncovered several reports from Quebec when we expanded the search into the francophone materials and websites. These focused on the Laurentian area north of Montreal (Laurentides) (Carle and Bélanger-Dion 2003) and the Montérégie area south of Montreal (Roy, Hurtubise, and Rozier 2003). As with the English language reports, these lacked inclusion of issues specific to Indigenous people despite that fact that both geographic areas include reserves. While these francophone sources provided valuable information on the views of homelessness in select rural areas of the country and many described specific rural areas and communities, in only a few instances did they provide information about rural homeless Indigenous people. In contrast, the pan-northern Ontario report by Stewart and Ramage (2011) and the work by Kauppi and co-authors (2009) explore Indigenous rural homelessness in terms of dynamics or implications.

Some of the best descriptors of rural homelessness, outside of a metropolitan commuting zone, come from the Kootenay region of southern British Columbia (Glass 2002), northern British Columbia (Halseth and Ryser 2010), Happy Valley-Goose Bay (HVGB), Newfoundland and Labrador (Lee, Budgell, and Skinner 2007; Schiff et al. 2012), rural Prince Edward Island (Smith and Fuller 2009), and rural Nova Scotia (Robertson and White 2007). Collectively they provide a fairly consistent picture of a lack of affordable housing, lack of subsidized housing, low income levels, and a lack of support services as main factors driving people into homelessness in these areas. Homeless and at high risk of homelessness people reported paying well over 30 percent and in many instances upwards of 50 percent of their income for housing (Glass 2002; Robertson and White 2007; Schiff et al. 2012). In some places, such as HVGB, a sheer lack of any available housing is driving prices both for market homes and rental housing up beyond affordability levels of most local residents (Schiff et al. 2012). As in other rural and remote areas, incomes are reportedly lower than in many urban communities, while food and utility costs are substantially higher. As most rural areas lack public transportation, the necessity of owning a vehicle and its attendant costs are not often factored into the higher cost of living. In addition to lack of housing, many rural buildings that are more than thirty years old are in need of substantial repairs, with a noticeable number failing to meet minimal health and safety standards. Glass (2002) provides some excellent descriptions of housing which has no electricity, no running water, is mould infested, and violates safety standards (CMHC 2012; Statistics Canada 2014).

In these communities mental health and addiction problems are recognized as propelling some people into homelessness. However, substance abuse, with the exception of alcohol, is generally not reported at as high rates as in urban settings. Thus, a significant pathway to homelessness in urban areas, the abuse of illegal substances and resultant loss of employment, income, and housing, is significant but not necessarily the principal cause of homelessness for most people in rural areas. However, for those who struggle with addictions or mental illness, treatment and support services are scarce and there is little (or none, depending on the location) supportive or rehabilitative housing (Glass 2002; Grodzinski et al. 2011; Stewart and Ramage 2011).

A significant precipitant of housing loss is experienced by women, with and without dependants, who are victims of domestic abuse. In contrast to urban areas, domestic violence and marital breakup are more frequently mentioned as precursors to homelessness in rural areas. People without a place to live most often double up. Youth will couch surf with friends and relatives during winter months and seek summer camps (as rustic cabins are named in many rural areas) or tent in warmer months. The report of homelessness in the Kootenays (Glass 2002) provided rich details about the unique challenges of rural life for those in marginal housing: "Another rural issue was the challenge faced when marriages or relationships break down. As a single adult, particularly with children, the challenges of rural living can be serious, especially in smaller communities. Gathering firewood, tending produce, repairing machinery, and feeding animals amongst other activities can be particularly arduous when only one adult is doing it. One woman commented (after separating from her husband) that she no longer had access to the tools (truck, chainsaw etc.) to collect firewood" (50).

The Stewart and Ramage (2011) report, covering extreme northern Ontario communities, itemized additional factors that collectively present the primary theme of poverty and lack of education/job skills as contributing but not necessarily the sole precipitating causes of housing insufficiency. Additional to poverty are psychosocial issues of poor mental health, addictions, and disabling physical conditions that restrict opportunities for earned income. Transportation, which is frequently mentioned, needs also to be viewed as a poverty-related issue, as those with financial means own their own vehicle: a factor that is usually necessary for access to services and employment in rural regions. It is the poor and disabled who most frequently rely on public transportation, which is rarely available in those areas.

A more recent survey of twenty rural communities throughout Alberta (Waegemakers Schiff and Turner 2014a) confirms that homelessness in rural areas may be more pervasive and dynamic than previously thought. This study indicates widespread economic issues of housing affordability, availability, and suitability, as well as interpersonal and personal issues, such as domestic violence, abusive homes (for youth), poor mental health, and addictions, as significant factors precipitating homelessness and severely marginalized housing situations. While much of the evidence in the reports points to hidden homelessness, there is also consistent discussion of absolute homelessness, indicating that there is a cohort of individuals and families who choose to remain in rural locations despite shortage of shelter.

None of the commissioned reports specifically focused on Indigenous homelessness in a rural context. The Alberta report did include a section on the plight of Indigenous people who did not live on a reserve but remained in a rural area. But the primary focus of this work was on rural homelessness and not on any specific subgroup in the homeless population. Reports from many small Alberta towns indicated shortage of resources and a lack of willingness of local town officials to take on the housing and services issues. They felt Indigenous people should be helped by the Department of Indian Affairs and not by small communities that lack the funding and infrastructure to deal with the issues that homeless people have. Hidden underneath these protests was a reluctance to give voice to perceived racism in these communities (Waegemakers Schiff and Turner 2014a).

Reports and academic articles nevertheless concur on the overrepresentation of Indigenous people among the homeless in Canada. Some also note that research on this topic is scarce. One detailed report, funded by the Homeless Partnering Strategy of the Canadian Government and the Social Sciences and Humanities Research Council, examined housing and homelessness in the remote Inuit community of Kinngait (Tester and The Harvest Society 2006). Shortage of adequate housing, both in quantity and quality, overcrowding, and lack of access to adequate food were cited as issues prompting people to consider leaving the community. It is difficult to put the struggles of Kinngait inhabitants alongside those of Indigenous people who have ready transportation away from and to their reserves and some options about whether to live in town or outside of town. Those possibilities do not realistically exist for people in the Far North.

A small body of literature contains some discussion of rural homelessness among Indigenous people, usually as anecdotal to the main focus of the report. What is missing in the literature is a fulsome examination of the needs, preferences, and lifestyles of Indigenous people who remain in rural areas and perhaps live close to but not on their home reserves. The assumption that there is no place to live except in the city or on the reserve, may be overlooking the reality that shortage of services, lack of a welcome, and discrimination in small towns may be driving Indigenous people to the city.

The assumption that Indigenous people prefer to move to the city is reflected in some of the literature that examines migration patterns between reserves and urban centres (Belanger and Weasel Head 2013; Christensen 2012; Peters and Robillard 2009). These works assume that the natural impetus for those leaving the reserve is to relocate to a major urban area, without considering the mitigating forces that may not allow for a move to a local town. The city may be the destination for some of those who seek services not found outside of an urban setting or those who do not want to remain on or near their home reserve, but it may not be the choice of all who leave. We do not know enough about the plight of Indigenous people who choose to remain close to, but not on, their home reserves in rural Canada. The existing reports overlook that there are alternatives to reserve and city life. Later in this chapter we reflect on reports from small towns that are adjacent to reserves and also have a significant Indigenous population.

There is also a body of literature that discusses housing issues on-reserve, much of it reflecting the inadequate amount and quality of available housing. Most Indigenous reserves are located away from major urban centres (the T'su Tina reserve adjacent to Calgary and the St. Mary's Reserve adjacent to Fredericton are notable exceptions). Because of their location, most reserves are considered to be rural and often remote as well. On-reserve housing and homelessness are significant issues requiring their own attention (Belanger and Weasel Head 2013; Hill 2010). On-reserve housing issues have been mentioned in the literature for a number of years and are frequently reported in the media, as in the extensive coverage in 2012 to 2013 of housing conditions on the Attawapiskat First Nation reserve in northern Ontario. Poor housing conditions are mentioned as a significant concern in a literature review by Beavis, Klos, Carter, and Douchant (1997), are featured in the work by Tester (2006), and are woven throughout the report on Indigenous housing by Hill (2010).

Hill's (2010) comprehensive review of past and current Indigenous housing policies and practices, noted vast inadequacies in the amount and quality of housing available on most of Canadian reserves. The supply of housing falls far short of what is needed to house those living on reservations. Included in Hill's report was the serious problem of substandard housing built by government contractors in the 1950s and 1960s—many homes did not meet building codes and were unfinished and poorly insulated. This has resulted in a widespread housing crisis on many reserves. Further lack of maintenance, repairs, and upgrading had made this housing stock dilapidated, substandard, and often hazardous to inhabit (4). Inadequate housing supply on reserves has also been exacerbated by the rapid increase in the Indigenous population, many of whom (54 percent) continue to live on reserves (Hill 2010). The current result is that many families are doubled up, with reports of ten to eighteen people living in a three-bedroom dwelling intended for a family of four or five. Several families live in one house and many are forced to live in units not considered acceptable by any housing standards (Hill 2010).

Another factor that has not often been taken into consideration in rural housing literature is the widespread use of mobile homes in trailer parks. Beginning in the 1970s these living arrangements found favour in and around many small communities and outlying areas throughout Canada. Many original units are now forty or more years old. Descriptions of this housing, its fragile nature and its near proximity to homelessness, has been documented in the United States (Salamon and MacTavish 2006), but not seriously considered as part of the continuum of homeless and near-homeless situations in rural Canada. Many of these units were not intended for long-term survival in the harsh Canadian winters. Coupled with lack of maintenance, mobile homes built over forty years ago are now falling into a dilapidated and unsafe state, but continue to be occupied by those who lack other affordable accommodations. These units are at high risk for becoming uninhabitable in the near future and there is no funding mechanism to help these owners and renters to rehabilitate or replace their homes (MacTavish and Salamon 2001; Salamon and MacTavish 2006). While used as permanent housing both on- and off-reserve, there is no data on the extent to which Indigenous people rely on mobile homes for their permanent housing or what proportion of the homes are not habitable.

Although we recognize the severity and complexity of on-reserve housing issues, our focus examines the context of these issues as they impact the complex relationships between rural towns and nearby reserves. As Distasio and colleagues indicate, there is a virtual non-existence (and need for) research and literature that examines Indigenous homelessness specifically in off-reserve rural areas (i.e., not within a larger context of urban homelessness) (Distasio, Sylvestre, and Mulligan 2005). We thus set out to begin a preliminary examination of Indigenous peoples' experiences of rural homelessness in Canada.

Case Study Analysis of Rural Indigenous Homelessness

To learn more about Indigenous peoples' rural homelessness, we used a multiple case examination across Canada. Case study research included review of relevant documents as well as semi-structured interviews with homelessness experts from rural communities across Canada's provinces and territories. Representatives were identified either through the researchers' professional networks, or by examining government reports and newspaper articles regarding rural homelessness to identify agencies or individuals who could speak knowledgeably about the subject. Most participants in the study worked in non-profit or government positions in the homelessness or broader social services sector. In communities lacking formal homelessness infrastructure, respondents were also volunteer leaders, often from the faith community.

Our research was included as part of a larger study on rural homelessness in Canada commissioned by the Human Resources and Skills Development Homelessness Partnering Secretariat. The original focus of the study was to examine the feasibility of a Housing First approach to homelessness in rural areas. Communities were selected based on their status according to the Modified Beale Codes (with an aim for diversity across codes) and to ensure representation across diverse Canadian rural geographies. This resulted in an example from every province or territory, with communities ranging in size and remoteness. We present a selection of this cohort and a diversity of rural areas (service-centre communities and their surrounding regions) that spoke explicitly to homelessness among Indigenous people in the region. We focus on case study results gathered at: Camrose, Alberta; Kenora, Ontario; Smithers, British Columbia; Pincher Creek, Alberta; Happy Valley-Goose Bay, Newfoundland and Labrador, and Old Crow, Yukon.

Camrose, Alberta

Camrose is a town of about 17,000 residents located in central Alberta. It is within 100 kilometres of Edmonton and 300 kilometres of Calgary, placing at 6 under the modified Beale Codes classification. As a result of macro-economic factors impacting the region, demand for housing grew in tandem with the 2005 and 2006 economic boom fueled by oil and gas industry growth in Alberta. Rents rose dramatically while vacancies shrank. In fact, the housing conditions in Camrose were as strained as those reported by Fort MacMurray at the height of the boom. The economic downturn in 2009 did result in some vacancies; however, rents remain too high for those in lower-paying jobs. Lack of new rental units being built and poor housing conditions of existing stock are cited as the main drivers of hidden homelessness in the community.

Homelessness in Camrose is generally hidden in comparison to larger urban centres where rough sleeping and a large emergency shelter population is common. Most homeless people are doubled up with friends and family or in unsafe housing conditions. A dramatic rise in homelessness was reported in the area starting in 2005. Our interviewee noted that although homelessness had been an issue before this period, the needs of Camrosians could be met with two to three rooms managed by existing non-profit providers in the area. As of 2005, more demand for shelter led to the opening of a new facility.

Camrose is an excellent example of the influence of neighbouring reserves on a town's homeless population. About 5 percent of the Camrose population is Indigenous; however, Indigenous people are reported to make up about 20 percent of the town's homeless. Proximity to several First Nations communities is reported to make an impact on homelessness locally. Additionally, on an average, 60 to 70 percent of the residents at the local women's shelter are Indigenous and come from one of the neighbouring reserves. Most want to remain in the local community, live near but not on their home reserve, as the "rez" is reported to be unsafe. For example, Hobbema, one nearby reserve, is identified as having difficult living conditions. In Camrose, poor on-reserve housing conditions and social issues are spurring migration, although these are only some of the factors impacting the local homelessness problem. Seasonality also seems to affect occupancy at the local homeless shelter with more demand reported in conjunction with worsening weather conditions. There is no specific action plan in place or under development to address homelessness at this time, though efforts to address youth homelessness have emerged. The interviewee stated that there is limited public understanding of homelessness as an issue outside of the social sector. In 2009, the town developed a social development strategy, but it did not identify homelessness as an issue. Affordable housing was noted, however.

Kenora, Ontario

Kenora is a town in northwestern Ontario with a population of 15,438. It lies well outside of the commuting zones of Thunder Bay and Winnipeg which are the two closest metropolitan areas. This places the town at 7 under the modified Beale Codes classification. It is the main municipality of the region and serves as a regional service centre. As a result, courts and comprehensive medical supports are located there. The Indigenous population of the town is pegged at 15.8 percent and there are eight First Nation reserves close by, some of which have experienced considerable hardship in recent years.

Kenora is experiencing homelessness, particularly visible street homelessness, characterized by an overrepresentation of Indigenous people sleeping rough and in shelter facilities. Kenora has a dry shelter where fourteen to twenty-three homeless people stay on nightly basis. Another nine to seventeen rough sleepers are reported as well on an annual basis. Homelessness, particularly among Indigenous people, is an issue for several of the northern communities in the Kenora district—in particular Pickle Lake (population 425), which is located next door to Mishkeegogamang First Nation. Red Lake (population 4,336) experiences homelessness issues as well and also serves as a gateway to the North for First Nations. Sioux Lookout (population approximately 5,000) is another community where homelessness is visible. It is a site where the Local Health Integration Network delivers service and where a new hospital was built, hence another gateway city serving twenty-nine northern First Nations. These three smaller centres are close to reserves and attract migration from northern communities. Once migrants arrive, they may not return to the reserve for a number of reasons: some miss appointments and therefore are ineligible for funds to return home, and others may face banishment from their home community. Although these communities may offer fewer services than larger urban centres, many choose to stay and migrate no further than Kenora in order to stay close to their home communities, relatives, friends, cultures, and support networks.

Smithers, British Columbia

Another community that is influenced by neighbouring reserves is Smithers, British Columbia. This small town has about 5,000 residents, of whom approximately 10 percent are Indigenous. Its service catchment area is estimated to be as high as 30,000, but the number of Indigenous people in the catchment area is unknown. It is located in northwestern British Columbia approximately halfway between the larger communities of Prince George and Prince Rupert, although well outside of their commuting zones. It is placed at 7 under the modified Beale Codes classification. Smithers is located in a region that attracts residents because of its natural beauty. As a result, housing prices are high and vacancies are low. This places significant pressure on low-income households, especially those with limited social assistance and those experiencing additional barriers, such as mental health issues and addictions.

Locally, social service organizations provide a range of housing and supports, including shelter, transitional and affordable housing, child and youth services, transportation, and a domestic violence shelter. However, in a small town, there is the added barrier of landlords spreading the word about tenants who damage units. This creates a blacklist of people who are denied housing consistently. The local emergency shelter offers nine beds per night and reports a 60 percent average occupancy. Interestingly, the interviewee reports the number of shelter users decreases in the winter despite concerns and expectations that the opposite would be the case. The hypothesis is that knowing the danger of the cold, individuals figure out doubling up or other strategies instead of sleeping rough through the winter period.

In terms of local needs, an estimated 250 people are believed to experience homelessness annually. Of these, about twelve to seventeen are considered to be chronic requiring very intensive housing and supports. Another fifty are believed to require some wraparound supports once rehoused. Another 150 are believed to be women escaping violence. Most of the clients served are reported to be Indigenous (95 percent) and informants attributed this to the proximity of the 1,200 person Wet'suwet'en First Nation near the town. Smithers is also reportedly absorbing some of the needs that spill over from migration and housing instability in the coastal community of Kitimat. The experience here clearly indicates a degree of migration between rural communities as well as between reserves and nearby rural towns.

Happy Valley/Goose Bay, Labrador

Happy Valley/Goose Bay (HVGB), Labrador, is a rural and remote northern community: rural because its size of approximately 7,500 inhabitants classifies it as a small town, remote because it is over 1,000 kilometres over mostly unpaved road and by ferry to the nearest urban area, Corner Brook, with a population of about 20,000. It is placed at 10 under the modified Beale Codes classification. Exhaustive reports on homelessness in the HVGB area in 2007 and 2012 provide more detail than is available on the other communities that we studied. Because it is uniquely remote, rural yet also a service centre of the area, we explore it in greater detail.

HVGB is a predominantly Indigenous community which also acts as a regional service centre with medical and social services for the extended rural and mostly Indigenous communities of central Labrador and the Labrador coast. It is the home of a Canadian Forces airbase and this has provided a long-time economic stabilizing force in the community. Recent mineral and energy explorations have resulted in an upsurge of development activities that are rapidly increasing the town population and creating a strain on local resources, especially housing and related services. The socio-economic profile and demographics of HVGB are similar to other service centres in the "provincial norths," such as La Ronge and Thompson, suggesting that comparable experiences and issues with homelessness and housing might also exist in those regions. While outside the scope of this study, it is suggested that further research is needed to determine the extent of such issues in small and remote service centre communities.

In 2007 the Happy Valley-Goose Bay Community Advisory Board on Housing and Homelessness developed a *Community Plan for Addressing Homelessness and Transitional Housing*. In 2012 the town completed a revised report on housing and homelessness. As a result there is a significant amount of community awareness and acknowledgement of housing and homeless problems in the area. The report notes the following:

> service providers and decision makers saw housing as an issue for many people in HVGB regardless of income level. There is a persistent concern surrounding the lack of affordable and available housing in general particularly in the rental market. Also articulated was the need for additional transitional and emergency housing as well as supportive housing for people with multiple and complex needs.

> Homelessness in HVGB is hidden, often characterized by overcrowding, couch-surfing, boarding houses, and violence...the housing situation in the town has worsened. This is largely attributed to permanent and temporary migration from the coast of Labrador as well as an escalation in rental rates and house prices due to anticipated industrial activity in the region. (Schiff et al. 2012, 3)

HVGB is experiencing an upsurge in absolute homelessness. Stakeholders report anywhere from fifteen to thirty people per night sleeping outdoors in the town centre during the spring, summer, and autumn seasons. During the coldest months many rough sleepers will couch surf, double up with friends or family, return to abusive households, and sleep in cars, other vehicles, and shelters not fit for habitation (e.g., garages and sheds). However, a few remain outdoors, camped in tents or other makeshift shelters outside of town. Reports indicate that most homeless people in HVGB (85 to 95 percent) are Indigenous.

Homelessness is exacerbated in HVGB by its location and function as a regional centre for central and coastal Labrador. Many people come to town from the nearby First Nation and coastal Inuit communities seeking medical and other services. They often remain in the area for various reasons but lack adequate accommodations. This is a similar dynamic to that reported by Stewart and Ramage in northern Ontario (2011). Stakeholders in HVGB also report that most people experiencing housing issues do not go to Corner Brook, St. John's, or other larger urban centres. They prefer to stay in Labrador, close to family, friends, familiar surroundings, and their culture. Those who do go to St. John's or other cities usually have a history of travel to the city for medical services. However, they often find the experience of living in a city quite different from "visiting" the city and many choose to relocate to smaller communities or return to Labrador. One exception exists to this reported trend: those who go to metropolitan areas for residential substance abuse treatment usually do not return.

Homelessness is recognized as a significant social problem by provincial and municipal government as well as the general public. Past homeless and housing reports from HVGB (Lee, Budgell, and Skinner 2007; Schiff et al. 2012; Schiff and Brunger 2015; Waegemakers Schiff and Schiff 2014) emphasize the need for affordable housing, with a mix of publicly funded and private market units. While mental health and addictions are acknowledged as important issues, they are not singled out as the primary causes of homelessness for many people. These reports note the dire condition of many rural housing units and that this situation continues to deteriorate. A few organizations in town provide supportive and affordable housing. There is a housing support worker, funded by the provincial government, who works with local service providers in providing support and locating housing for people who are homeless. Through fundraising conducted by the local housing and homelessness coalition, the housing support worker maintains an emergency fund to pay for emergency accommodations for homeless people.

Old Crow, Yukon

Old Crow is an isolated Indigenous community of approximately 240 people, located about 75 kilometres north of the Arctic Circle and about 100 kilometres from the Beaufort Sea. There are no roads to Old Crow and most travel, apart from local trips to traditional hunting camps, is by airplane. The community is placed at 10 under the modified Beale Codes classification. The community is an Indigenous community, but not a reserve, comprised almost entirely of Vuntut Gwitchin people who have inhabited this area for thousands of years. Contact with non-Indigenous people has existed for over 100 years and began with hunters and missionaries. Because of its remoteness, communication, including telephone and Internet, is by satellite service and is intermittent as weather conditions frequently interfere with reception. As the town has no high school, all secondary education is provided in Whitehorse and thus adolescents spend considerable parts of their teenage years in a more urban environment.

Most residents live in log homes built many years ago, or in more recently constructed government housing. However, the housing stock is in need of repair and upgrading, and is insufficient for the size of the community. As with many northern settlements, government housing is often poorly designed in relation to cultural aspects of shelter use and cannot respond to environments and the impacts of climate change. Lack of adequate housing is an ongoing problem and is exacerbated when domestic conflict or interpersonal problems necessitate that family living units split up. There is very limited alternative living space available.

Those who are homeless usually couch surf with friends or relatives during the cold weather months, and live off the land while the temperature is moderate. Those who are sent to Whitehorse for incarceration or psychiatric treatment often return to town with no appropriate accommodation arranged. The hardships this imposes on individuals and those who provide temporary shelter are compounded by limitations of availability and cost of food. Those who live off the land still require basic supplies that are costly and must be flown in. This creates a problem of food sufficiency for those who are dispossessed. Individuals and families who lack housing cannot, as in other regions, easily migrate to the nearest urban centre, as it requires a plane ride and thus the resources to fund this travel.

There is no formal acknowledgement of a problem with homelessness, and no official plan to address this issue at this time. Those who are without shelter are usually housed temporarily at the RCMP station, the nursing station, or in the local town hall. These arrangements generally last only for a couple of days until a community member or family offers shelter. Recently, several new dwellings have been erected, but they do not present an adequate response to a pressing issue of housing sufficiency, adequacy, and climatic and cultural appropriateness.

Case Study Discussion

The current body of literature related to rural Indigenous homelessness in Canada is predominantly derived either from reports on rural homelessness in general, or from academic literature that most often frames Indigenous issues in the context of urban homelessness. There is little in any of these reports and articles that documents the plight of Indigenous people who choose to live off-reserve in rural areas. Additionally, much of the existing research indicates that those who leave reserves find no stopping place in rural areas and that they largely seek big city life and its services. We suggest that this points to continued issues of discrimination in Canada's small communities. Our case study reveals that direct migration from reserve to urban areas may not always be the predominant trend and points to some additional factors not yet covered in the literature. We now turn to a discussion of these findings across communities and provide a basis for some preliminary recommendations on addressing rural Indigenous homelessness.

Absolute and Hidden Rural Homelessness among Indigenous People

Absolute and hidden homelessness are a reality for many rural communities. Not all of communities included in our larger study (on Canadian rural homelessness in general) reported overrepresentation of Indigenous people in the homeless population. However, the presence of Indigenous communities near a case study community was generally correlated with an overrepresentation in the homeless population (Waegemakers Schiff and Turner 2014b). This trend also indicated that, despite severe housing problems and racism among landlords or service providers, many Indigenous people remain in rural areas rather than migrate to larger urban centres.

Migration within and between Rural Communities

In many locations which are adjacent or relatively close to large urban centres (e.g., Camrose, Alberta), many people will choose to migrate directly from their home community to the city. In some other communities (e.g., Pincher Creek, Alberta) issues of racism discourage people from settling in the town, forcing migration to other rural communities or to the closest urban area. In instances of remote communities, people forced to seek specialized medical care in larger communities may not be able to leave urban areas because they need continued medical support. However, this is not the situation for all rural areas and migration does not just occur between Indigenous communities and urban centres. Some choose to stay close to reserve or land claims areas. This is especially the case in more isolated regions (e.g., Kenora, Happy Valley-Goose Bay, Smithers, Old Crow) where travel to the city might be preferably avoided due to more lengthy separation from land, family, friends, and culture.

Rural and remote service centre communities are especially impacted, acting as catchments from which people do not move on to large cities. In these towns, findings suggest that the rare occurrence of migration to cities is usually precipitated by a history of travel to those locations for medical, court, or other services. The challenges of city life may lead many to relocate to smaller communities or return to their home region. However, it appears that those who go to metropolitan areas for residential substance abuse treatment often do not return, as aftercare services are unavailable in rural areas, and the return home may precipitate a relapse, as substance using is associated with people and places.

Migration from Indigenous communities is motivated by a number of factors, including poor housing conditions on-reserve, lack of employment and education opportunities, as well as the need to access services (medical, judiciary, counselling, etc.). Often, smaller centres, regardless of their local economic growth, remain magnets for Indigenous populations who lack access to such services in their own communities. Others choose to leave their home community due to domestic violence and disputes. Notably, the movement between different reserves for these reasons are very common and some residents will migrate regularly.

Racism and Rural Indigenous Homelessness

Landlord discrimination against Indigenous tenants was consistently reported across the case study sites. This is particularly an issue in areas experiencing a strained housing market, and it further exacerbates the overrepresentation of Indigenous people in local homeless populations. In areas such as HVGB and Kenora, where a high number of Indigenous reserves exist near the town, this is even more visible given that the majority of homeless people in the area are reported to be Indigenous. However, in some areas, such as Pincher Creek, few homeless Indigenous people are reported and landlords do not face Indigenous housing demands, as First Nations people are discouraged from using town services and encouraged to "find their way down the highway" to Lethbridge or Calgary.

Rural Service System Responses

Rural communities face numerous challenges in addressing homelessness and marginal housing conditions. Not only are emergency shelter options limited, but most communities experience a significant lack of affordable and social housing infrastructure. Limited social services also precipitate and aggravate rural homelessness. Due to funding allocation based on population size, many communities are additionally limited in their access to federal and provincial funding for affordable housing and homelessness programs. For similar reasons, federal homelessness planning and systems level supports are usually focused on large urban centres, such that rural communities have limited access to such opportunities. All of this leads to challenges in implementing initiatives to address homelessness and shortage of affordable housing in rural communities, which in turn impact the capacity to address Indigenous homelessness in rural areas.

Recommendations and Conclusions

The overrepresentation of Indigenous people amongst homeless populations in many rural communities points to the need to recognize the factors engendering ongoing housing instability for this group on- and off-reserve. The capacity of small communities to absorb the needs of Indigenous migrants without additional funding is limited and further entrenches disparities. The findings of this study lead to the following four recommendations which are proposed to facilitate responses to homelessness among Indigenous people in rural communities.

Dismantling Racism

In most communities, homelessness and marginalized housing are aggravated by racism. In some areas, it is reported that strong racism pervades the region and this keeps Indigenous people away from town, except for access to basic needs such as groceries. For all other services, Indigenous people in these regions turn to larger urban centres where they can find Indigeneous-run organizations, and others that support cultural competence. Ultimately, there is an urgent need to address ongoing issues of racism that exacerbate rural Indigenous homelessness and unintended migration to urban areas. This calls for investment in education, awareness campaigns, and programs focused on dismantling racism.

Capacity Building and Support for Homeless System Planning in Rural Communities

This study has demonstrated the varied extent to which rural communities possess the capacity to systematically address housing and homelessness. While some sites have had the benefit of learning through participation in federal initiatives and networks that enhance understanding of homelessness responses, most are largely left on their own. Further, capacity building resources are usually intended for urban centres, where homelessness is most often visible.

In general, there is an urgent need for improvements to existing housing units and construction of new stock to meet the expansive need for affordable, social, and supportive housing. More support is also needed across rural Canada for systems planning to address homelessness in general, as well as rural Indigenous homelessness and the housing dynamics between reserves and rural towns. Resources and training in performance management and system planning, in managing emergency shelters and other care systems, and in adapting Housing First and other effective housing approaches should be tailored to the needs of smaller centres. Adaptations to meet the unique needs of Indigenous people should be developed in these specific contexts.

Developing and Supporting Housing First Rural Adaptations

Housing First, an orientation towards providing housing without prior requirements of treatment for mental health and addictions, has become ubiquitous in urban programs helping homeless people, despite strong evidence that it is also effective with people whose housing problems do not result from mental illness or substance abuse (Waegemakers Schiff and Schiff 2014). Furthermore, its efficacy and effectiveness have not been tested in rural settings. The findings of the study on rural homelessness reported above also included an examination of the viability of implementing a Housing First approach in rural communities. The rural scan found few rural services providers who had more than a passing awareness of this concept, fewer who were knowledgeable about this approach and the process of its implementation, and a very small number that were attempting a Housing First strategy. Even where rural programs used a Housing First approach, there was little to no uptake by Indigenous clients. This observation could spring from various sources such as service providers' lack of awareness or inability to make the program available. It could also signal that Indigenous people who are accustomed to living arrangements that include multiple and extended family members, or who may be fleeing domestic abuse and need a sheltered living environment, may not be interested in scatter-site housing, removed from supportive family and protective service providers.

Another finding, particular to Old Crow and communities of similar size, which advises against a Housing First program is that there are no social housing programs and no congregate living arrangements. Thus these communities echo a prevailing northern wisdom that Housing First is an Arctic survival theme—one must have adequate shelter for survival—and not a description of a specific housing program or approach. There are a number of barriers for rural communities in regards to Housing First programs in general: lack of funding for a relatively costly program, lack of access to market housing units, and challenges hiring trained mental health and addictions program staff. The lack of trained mental health and addictions clinicians rules out the viability of a program that focuses on housing with 24/7 treatment availability. Adapting Housing First also requires recognition that rural homelessness in general is not as pervasively characterized by the visible, chronic homelessness for which assertive community treatment and intensive case management teams are designed. The ability to develop separate intervention services to target different groups of people in need in urban areas may not be feasible or necessarily desirable in smaller communities. In rural areas, it will be more appropriate for any Housing First programs to have the capacity to manage diverse client needs at once, and use a regional approach to providing targeted services simply to achieve efficiencies of scale. This would also leverage the centres that operate in this fashion already, serving smaller communities throughout a particular region.

All housing approaches need the backup of support services. To overcome the lack of funding and shortage of mental health, medical, and addictions support, a viable alternative is for communities to develop Telehealth and internet-based options for delivering support to clients. This arrangement combines the use of case managers who provide in-house, wraparound supports with medical expertise using internet-based technology. Such an approach has been adopted in the state of Vermont, U.S. (Stefancic et al. 2013) and has demonstrated its effectiveness and its cost efficiency. Providing a computer and supporting the internet cost is more cost-effective than utilization of personnel for travel over long distances to connect with people. However, the vast remoteness of the Canadian rural landscape with attendant challenges of reliable access to the internet makes this a solution for some but not all areas; some communities in remote areas would be excluded due to lack of consistent internet access. Where this is a viable option, it should be explored further.

A final item concerns the importance of considering landlords in these arrangements. Engaging private sector landlords in solutions will require marketing to this group, particularly given the small numbers operating rental housing in these communities. Supporting advocates and providers with materials that educate small-scale landlords about working with home-less populations, and are aimed at dismantling racism, can assist further in the implementation of Housing First. Beyond information, housing specialists will have to establish relationships with landlords so that case managers can be viewed as supports for landlords as well as housing recipients, thereby providing intervention opportunities before eviction becomes a reality.

Comprehensive Research on Rural Homelessness

To date, attempts at capturing rural Indigenous homelessness trends have been largely localized in one community, or region, or framed in terms of ur-ban migration. While this study aimed to develop a comparative view of the issue across Canada, it was a preliminary effort rather than a comprehensive analysis. To this end, a final recommendation is the implementation of an ex-tensive research agenda on rural Indigenous homelessness to capture common emerging themes from a national, rather than a community-by-community, perspective. A number of local needs assessments and strategic plans were developed during the course of the study; future research should leverage this information to enhance analysis.

References

Beavis, Mary Ann, Nancy Klos, Thomas Carter, and Christian Douchant. 1997. *Literature Review: Aboriginal Peoples and Homelessness*. Ottawa: Canada Mortgage and Housing Corporation.

Belanger, Yale. D., and Gabrielle Weasel Head. 2013. *Urban Aboriginal Homelessness and Migration in Southern Alberta*. Edmonton, AB: Alberta Homeless Research Consortium.

Carle, Paul, and Lalie Bélanger-Dion. 2003. *Rapport de Recherche sur la Population Itinérante et sans Domicile Fixe des Laurentides*. Montreal: CLSC-CHSLD des Trois Vallées.

Christensen, Julia. 2012. "'They Want a Different Life': Rural Northern Settlement Dynamics and Pathways to Homelessness in Yellowknife and Inuvik, Northwest Territories." *The Canadian Geographer/Le Géographe canadien* 56 (4): 419–38.

Cloke, Paul, Paul Milbourne, and Rebekah C. Widdowfield. 2000. "The Hidden and Emerging Spaces of Rural Homelessness." *Environment and Planning A* 32 (1): 77–90.

CMHC (Canada Mortgage and Housing Corporation). 2012. "Housing in Canada Online: Housing Standards." http://cmhc.beyond2020.com/HiCODefinitions_EN.html#_Housing_Standards.

Distasio, Jino, Gina Sylvestre, and Susan Mulligan. 2005. *Home Is Where the Heart Is and Right Now That Is Nowhere—: An Examination of Hidden Homelessness among Aboriginal Peoples in Prairie Cities*. Winnipeg: University of Winnipeg, The Institute of Urban Studies.

du Plessis, Valerie, Roland Besheri, Ray D. Bollman, and Heather Clemenson. 2002. "Definitions of Rural." Agriculture and Rural Working Paper No. 61, Catalogue no. 21–601–MIE. Ottawa: Statistics Canada.

Falvo, Nick. 2011. *Homelessness in Yellowknife: An Emerging Social Challenge*. Toronto: The Canadian Homelessness Research Network Press.

Forchuk, Cheryl, Phyllis Montgomery, Helene Berman, Catherine Ward-Griffin, Rick Csiernik, Carolyne Gorlick, Elsabeth Jensen, and Patrick Riesterer. 2010. "Gaining Ground, Losing Ground: The Paradoxes of Rural Homelessness." *CJNR (Canadian Journal of Nursing Research)* 42 (2): 138–52.

Glass, Angus. 2002. *Faces of Homelessness in a Rural Area: Housing Issues and Homelessness in the West Kootenay Boundary Region*. Nelson, BC: The Advocacy Centre.

Graham, Katherine A., and Evelyn Peters. 2002. *Aboriginal Communities and Urban Sustainability*. Ottawa, ON: Canadian Policy Research Networks.

Gray, Diane, Shirley Chau, Tim Huerta, and Jim Frankish. 2011. "Urban-Rural Migration and Health and Quality of Life in Homeless People." *Journal of Social Distress and the Homeless* 20 (1–2): 75–93.

Grodzinski, Eden, Rebecca Sutherns, Jane Londerville, and Craig Bentham. 2011. *Rural Homelessness Study*. Prepared for the County of Wellington. Guelph, ON: Wellington County Ontario.

Halseth, Greg, and Laura Ryser. 2010. *A Primer for Understanding Issues around Rural Poverty*. Prince George, BC: Community Development Institute at UNBC.

Hill, Charles W. 2010. *Aboriginal Housing in Canada: An Informal Background Discussion Paper*. Vancouver, BC: Canadian Aboriginal AIDS Network.

Hilton, Timothy, and Cornell DeJong. 2010. "Homeless in God's Country: Coping Strategies and Felt Experiences of the Rural Homeless." *Journal of Ethnographic and Qualitative Research* 5 (1): 12–30.

Karabanow, Jeff, Calia Aube, and Ted Naylor. 2014. "From Place to Space: Exploring Youth Migration and Homelessness in Rural Nova Scotia." *Journal of Rural and Community Development* 9 (2): 112–27.

Kauppi, Carol, Janet Gasparini, Henri Pallard, Rashmi Garg, Phyllis Montgomery, Schuyler Webster, Wanda Eurich, Kayla Seyler, and Homelessness Partnering Secretariat. 2009. *Migratory and Transient Homelessness in Northern Ontario: A Study of the Pathways to Becoming Homeless in Sudbury and Its Related Impacts.* Sudbury, ON: Social Planning Council of Sudbury.

Lawrence, Mark. 1995. "Rural Homelessness: A Geography without a Geography." *Journal of Rural Studies* 11 (3): 297–307.

Lee, Dawna, Maxine Budgell, and Janet Skinner. 2007. *Happy Valley-Goose Bay Community Plan for Addressing Homelessness and Transitional Housing*. Happy Valley-Goose Bay NL: Happy Valley-Goose Bay Homelessness/Transitional Housing Working Group.

MacTavish, Katherine, and Sonya Salamon. 2001. "Mobile Home Park on the Prairie: A New Rural Community Form*." *Rural Sociology* 66 (4): 487–506.

Peters, Evelyn J., and Vince Robillard. 2009. "'Everything You Want Is There': The Place of the Reserve in First Nations' Homeless Mobility." *Urban Geography* 30 (6): 652–80.

Robertson, Karin, and Mair White. 2007. *Mapping Homelessness in Rural Nova Scotia: A Study of Community Resources*. Service Canada.

Robertson, Marjorie, Natalie Harris, Nancy Fritz, Rebecca Noftsinger, and Pamela Fischer. 2007. *Rural Homelessness*. Paper presented at the Toward Understanding Homelessness: The 2007 National Symposium on Homlessness Research, 1–2 March Washington, DC: US Department of Housing and Urban Development and US Department of Health and Human Services.

Roy, Shirley, Rich Hurtubise, and Marielle Rozier. 2003. *Itinérance en Montérégie: Comprendre le Phénomène et Identifier les Besoins*. Collectif de Recherche en Itinérance, Montréal. Montreal: Collectif de Recherche sur l'itinérance, la pauvreté et l'exclusion sociale, University of Montreal.

Salamon, Sonya, and Katherine MacTavish. 2006. "Quasi-Homelessness among Rural Trailer-Park Households in the United States." In *International Perspectives on Rural Homelessness*, edited by Paul Milbourne and Paul Cloke, 45–62. New York: Routledge.

Schiff, Rebecca and Fern Brunger. 2015. "Northern Housing Networks: Building Collaborative Efforts to Address Housing and Homelessness in Remote Canadian Aboriginal Communities in the Context of Rapid Economic Change." *Journal of Rural and Community Development* 10 (1), http://www.jrcd.ca/viewarticle.php?id=1217&layout=abstract.

Schiff, Rebecca, M. Connors, I. Allice, and V. O'Brien. 2012. *Housing and Homelessness in Happy Valley-Goose Bay*. Happy Valley-Goose Bay: Happy Valley-Goose Bay

Community Advisory Board on Housing and Homelessness and the Social Economy Research Network of Northern Canada.

Skott-Myhre, Hans A., Rebecca Raby, and Jamie Nikolaou. 2008. "Towards a Delivery System of Services for Rural Homeless Youth: A Literature Review and Case Study." *Child and Youth Care Forum* 37 (2): 87–102.

Smith, Nishka, and Shauna Fuller. 2009. *Homelessness in Rural PEI, "Research Report."* Charlottetown, PEI: John Howard Society of PEI.

Statistics Canada. 2012. "Population and Demography," http://www.statcan.gc.ca/pub/11-402-x/2012000/chap/pop/pop-eng.htm (accessed 19 July 2014).

_____. 2014. *2011 National Household Survey: Aboriginal Identity.* Ottawa: Government of Canada.

Stefancic, Ana, Benjamin F. Henwood, Hilary Melton, Soo-Min Shin, Rebeka Lawrence-Gomez, and Sam Tsemberis. 2013. "Implementing Housing First in Rural Areas: Pathways Vermont." *American Journal of Public Health* 103 (S2): S206–S209.

Stewart, Christopher J., and S. Ramage. 2011. *A Pan-Northern Ontario Inventory of Homelessness Problems and Practices.* Sudbury, ON: Northern Ontario Service Deliverer's Association (NOSDA).

Tester, Frank, and the Harvest Society Kinngait, Nunavut Territory. 2006. *IGLUTAQ (in my room), The Implications of Homelessness for Inuit.* Vancouver, BC: School of Social Work and Family Studies, University of British Columbia.

Tsemberis, Sam J. 2010. *Housing First: The Pathways Model to End Homelessness for People with Mental Illness and Addiction.* Center City, MI: Hazelden.

Waegemakers Schiff, Jeannette, and Rebecca Schiff. 2014. "Housing First: Paradigm or Program?" *Journal of Social Distress and the Homeless* 23 (2): 80–104.

_____. 2016. "Northern Housing Networks: Collaborative Efforts to Develop Innovative Housing Programs for High-Needs Indigenous Women in Northern, Remote Communities." In *Exploring Effective Systems Responses to Homelessness*, edited by Naomi Nichols and Carey Doberstein, 175–81. Toronto: The Homeless Hub.

Waegemakers Schiff, Jeannette, Rebecca Schiff, Alina Turner, and Karine Bernard. 2015. "Rural Homelessness In Canada: A Review Of The Literature." *Journal of Rural and Community Development.* 10 (4): 85–106.

Waegemakers Schiff, Jeannette, and Alina Turner. 2014a. *Rural Alberta Homelessness.* Calgary, AB: Alberta Centre for Child, Family and Community Research.

_____. 2014b. *Rural Homelessness in Canada & Alberta: A Review of the Literature.* Calgary, AB: Alberta Centre for Child, Family and Community Research.

Part 2

AUSTRALIA

CHAPTER 10

Indigenous Homelessness: Australian Context

PAUL MEMMOTT AND DAPHNE NASH

Indigenous homelessness in Australia is a multi-dimensional social issue recognizable from the shared histories between Indigenous peoples and non-Indigenous settlers, and from statistical overrepresentation in the national homeless population. There are also unrecognized cultural aspects of the issue. The dispossession of Indigenous people of their land and culture and their survival history have been significant contributors to Indigenous homelessness and mark it as qualitatively different from the experience of homelessness in non-Indigenous lifeworlds. The following chapters explore different dimensions of Indigenous homelessness in Australia. Figure 10.1 identifies the locations of the studies that follow.

The number of homeless Indigenous people in Australia is disproportionately high. Although not representative of all Indigenous groups across Australia, research suggests that Indigenous homelessness differs from other Australian groups across a range of socio-demographic characteristics. In particular, Indigenous public place dwelling or rough sleeping remains underrecognized and therefore misunderstood. Overall, it is clear that good practice in services for homeless Indigenous people hinges on the recognition that good policy can enable effective services.

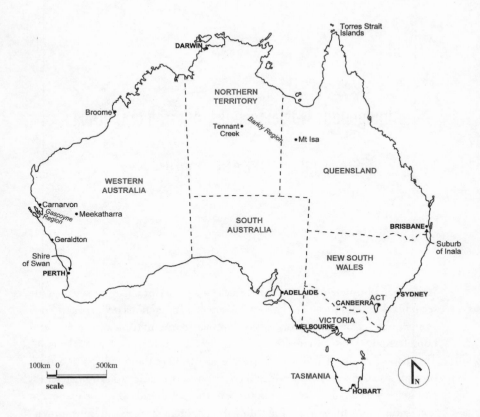

Figure 10.1. Map of Australia showing the sites of case studies. Map by Linda Thomson, Aboriginal Environments Research Centre.

Historical and Cultural Context to Indigenous Homelessness in Australia

Three-hundred-thousand Indigenous people occupied the entire Australian continent when the British colonization was imposed in 1788 (Harris 2003). The most common local Indigenous landholding group (also referred to as a "traditional owner group") was the patriclan, a group identified through male descent which held religious, hunting, and food-collecting rights in its estate. Such local groups were organized into larger regional groupings whose members intermarried according to strict rules, and shared some common aspects of social organization, beliefs, and customs (Stanner 1965). Altogether there were about 200 different languages spoken on the continent, but many of these had numerous dialects. People were conscious of their place within their own local territory, intimate with its geography, and spiritually attached to its sacred sites and histories, from which their totemic identities derived.

From the commencement of colonization in the late eighteenth century until the 1890s, the inward-moving frontier was largely characterized by the wholesale slaughter of Indigenous people, the spread of fatal diseases, and the taking of Indigenous land and water holes. Sporadic guerrilla warfare occurred in many regions. The frontier expanded slowly inland for 150 years with widespread impact on Indigenous cultures. Many of the unique ecologically adapted lifestyles of the Indigenous groups were lost.

By the beginning of the twentieth century, traditional styles of Indigenous camping and land use were no longer found in the eastern and southern regions of the continent. In the interior, displaced tribespeople camped in makeshift shelters near newly formed towns and pastoral stations. Here the social disruption by colonial settlement continued in the form of alcoholism, prostitution, disease, rape, economic exploitation, and general violence (Goodall 2008; Haebich 2000; Reynolds 1989). A demographic collapse of the Indigenous population occurred with the population falling by at least 80 percent, and they came to be represented as a "doomed race" which would inevitably become extinct.

This destruction culminated in a set of Indigenous protection legislations enacted between 1897 and 1915 in each Australian state. Government officials and police were empowered to control the movements of Indigenous individuals, families, and whole communities within and between settlements on newly established Aboriginal and Islander Reserves.[1] However, the directed movements of people were as often for punitive reasons as for their protection. Many people became disconnected from both their land and kin, resulting in the loss of social, psychological, and spiritual well-being. This was exacerbated by the implementation of an assimilation policy, which began in the 1930s, intensified in the 1950s, and was not abandoned until the mid-1970s. Only then were most Indigenous people able to travel of their own free will again.

By the 1980s, small groups of Indigenous people came to live in public places in the regional towns and metropolitan cities of Australia. In many cases these people resided in public places despite the existence of formal Indigenous town camps and an increasing range of other Indigenous housing options. Their numbers gradually increased in the 1990s and early 2000s. Although often categorized as homeless, some of these people saw themselves as being both placed and housed, and referred to themselves by regionally preferred names, such as parkies, goomies, ditchies, long grassers, or river campers (Memmott,

Birdsall-Jones, and Greenop 2011). Unfortunately, local government authori-ties, politicians, and members of the city business communities saw them as a public eyesore and nuisance. They were stereotyped as displaying anti-social be-haviour and causing a deterrent to general town business, particularly tourism.

Pathways to homelessness for contemporary Indigenous people involve social factors such as family violence that may have affected individuals from early childhood and also their families. Pathways into Indigenous homelessness also arise from colonial contact histories, such as displacement and loss of land and directed cultural change, such as loss of language and spiritual practices.

Demography of Indigenous Homelessness

As 2.5 percent of the total Australian population, Indigenous people are overrepresented in the homelessness statistics. In the 2011 census, 105,237 Australian people were identified as being homeless; this number included 26,744 Indigenous Australians or about 25 percent of the homeless popula-tion (ABS 2012, 5).

The high rate of homelessness for Indigenous Australians is currently exacerbated by a shortage of housing that is affordable (National Shelter 2011), as well as culturally and socially appropriate. In particular, Aboriginal and Torres Strait Islander families are large in comparison to mainstream Australian families. Cultural obligations to kin require Indigenous people to accommodate visiting members of their wider family group, often for extended periods. Visiting relatives are indicative of high rates of mobility by many Indigenous people as they travel for social and cultural reasons as well as to access services. These practices frequently result in crowding and associated tenancy problems. Violence associated with substance abuse also contributes to homelessness and Indigenous women experience an extraordinarily high rate of family violence (requiring hospitalization) compared to non-Indigenous women (AIHW 2006).

Considerable evidence now points to the problem of definitions used for categorizing Indigenous homelessness especially when viewed in terms of service needs. When the needs are not identified through robust measuring of the number of homeless people who are typically experiencing a range of vulnerabilities, policies and programs cannot be effectively developed and implemented.

Defining Indigenous Homelessness

The Australian Bureau of Statistics (ABS) currently estimates the number of homeless people on census night from data about the "adequacy," "security," and "control" that people have over the "home," where "adequacy" refers to the physical quality of the dwelling, "security" to having stable tenure arrangements, and "control" refers to control of and access to space for social relations (ABS 2012). This statistical approach, which the ABS continues to develop, allows valid comparison of data between censuses. For over a decade, Chamberlain and MacKenzie (2008) have advocated a "cultural definition" of homelessness so that changing attitudes to adequate housing can be taken into account. Neither the statistical nor the cultural definition accounts for those who are "at risk of homelessness." Also, for Indigenous Australians, neither approach fully recognizes the cultural and historical backgrounds that influence their housing preferences, or their ability to access adequate housing and feel "at home." In particular, the application of mainstream definitions of "homelessness" oversimplifies the composition of Indigenous groups dwelling in public spaces and leads to a failure to recognize the need for alternative pathways out of their different homelessness circumstances. Thus, their needs may be at best misunderstood and minimally serviced, and at worst overlooked and not addressed. This realization has prompted a process of refining the definitions of Indigenous homelessness in Australia.

Three useful broad categories of Indigenous homeless people can be identified from the limited empirical literature reviewed: (i) public place dwellers (comparable to the category of "absolute homelessness" as outlined in this book's introductory chapter), (ii) housed people who are nevertheless at risk of homelessness (in the "at risk" category in the introductory chapter), and (iii) spiritually homeless people. These can be further divided into subcategories and each will be briefly described in turn, but the reader is referred to Memmott, Birdsall-Jones, and Greenop (2012) for more detailed discussion.

Public Place Dwellers

Public place dwellers live in a mix of public or semi-public places, as well as some private places which are entered illegally at night to gain overnight shelter. These public places include parks, churches, verandahs, car parks, beaches, drains, riverbanks, vacant lots, and unoccupied derelict buildings. Public place dwellers can be further characterized as people who do not usually pay for accommodation, have a visible public profile (sheltering, drinking, rejoicing, arguing, partying, and fighting in public), have low incomes of which a substantial part is spent on alcohol, have few possessions (minimal clothing and bedding), and usually conform to a "beat" or a path of usual places visited where they camp and socialize in public or semi-public areas. Four subcategories of public place dwellers have been defined, although they are not mutually exclusive and one is often a pathway to another.

The first subcategory consists of voluntary, short-term, intermittent public place dwellers. These are often visitors who have come from rural or remote communities to have a good time socializing and drinking in town, but who intend to return home. Nevertheless, they have a potential to become medium-term public place dwellers (see next subcategory).

The second subcategory of public place dwellers consists of those who are voluntary and medium-term and who reside continually in public places (including overnight). They acknowledge they have another place of residence in a home community, but are uncertain whether and when they will return. They usually pursue this lifestyle for months or years.

The third subcategory of public place dwellers consists of those who are voluntary and long-term. They have typically cut off their ties with home communities, accept that their lifestyle will persist, and have a sense of belonging to the town and to their group. It is unclear whether it is possible for such individuals to reconcile with their original community and family, due to a range of emotional barriers. This subcategory fits with the definition of long-term or chronic homelessness, whereby homelessness has ceased to be a life crisis event and has become an accepted way of life.

The fourth subcategory of public place dwellers consists of those who do it by necessity. Despite continually residing in public places, they may wish to return to their home community where they have a house, but are obligated to remain in an urban area due to a service need or to support a hospitalized relative. Alternatively, they may wish to return home despite having no funds for or the capacity to organize travel. Finally, they may be on a waiting list for public rental housing elsewhere in the city but which is not eventuating in the short term.

Those at Risk of Homelessness

The second broad category of Indigenous homeless people are those at risk of homelessness. These people reside in some sort of physical housing but are at risk of losing it through a range of circumstances. Some are at risk due to a lack of tenure in the dwelling. Also those living in substandard housing which may be unsafe or unhealthy will eventually need to leave that housing. Crowded living conditions can compromise people's physical and social living space, often generating stress. Finally, people who are in a state of continual or intermittent residential mobility can become dysfunctionally mobile and unable to sustain their living pattern due to crisis events in their lives, such as family violence and substance abuse.

Spiritual Homelessness

A third broad category of Indigenous homelessness has been identified as spiritual homelessness, a state arising from separation from traditional land or family and kinship networks (often resulting from historical government policies). This state involves a crisis of personal identity wherein a person's understanding or knowledge of how they relate to country, family, and Indigenous identity systems is confused or lacking. Such feelings add to the already depressed emotional state in which Indigenous people, either public place dwellers or those at risk of homelessness, find themselves.

The above three broad categories of Indigenous homelessness are not mutually exclusive. For example, people categorized as at risk of homelessness may experience multiple periods of living on the streets, in rental housing, and in insecure accommodations (moving back and forth between insecure housing circumstances and public place-dwelling). In these circumstances, individuals may also suffer from spiritual homelessness.

Conclusion

It is not possible to effectively address the needs of Indigenous people who are homeless or at risk of homelessness without acknowledging the distinctive aspects of their homeless experiences in comparison to other social groups. Indigenous public place dwellers are a significant example of homelessness that is often ignored in the Australian community unless such people publicly perform anti-social behaviours. Furthermore, there is a relative lack of understanding amongst many policy-makers and service providers about the life circumstances and choices available to public place dwellers that limit their opportunities for assistance particularly in terms of shelter and other needs. The best responses to Indigenous homelessness will be based on recognition of past histories together with culturally aware research and broad community engagement.

Notes

1   From the late nineteenth century the state set aside areas of land for Indigenous and Torres Strait Islander people to live. Commonly known as Aboriginal reserves the system was to "protect" Indigenous people by separating them from other Australians.

References

ABS (Australian Bureau of Statistics). 2012. *Information Paper—A Statistical Definition of Homelessness, 2012*, cat. no. 4922.0. http://www.ausstats.abs.gov.au/ausstats/subscriber.nsf/0/B4B1A5BC17CEDBC9CA257A6E00186823/$File/49220_2012.pdf (accessed 27 June 2014).

AIHW (Australian Institute of Health and Welfare). 2006. *Family Violence among Aboriginal and Torres Strait Islander Peoples*, cat. no. IHW 17. Canberra: AIHW, http://www.aihw.gov.au/WorkArea/DownloadAsset.aspx?id=6442458606 (accessed 27 June 2014).

Chamberlain, Chris, and David MacKenzie. 2008. *Counting the Homeless 2006: Australia*, cat. no. 2050.0. Canberra: Australian Bureau of Statistics. http://www.ausstats.abs.gov.au/ausstats/subscriber.nsf/0/57393A13387C425DCA2574B900162DF0/$File/20500-2008Reissue.pdf (accessed 27 June 2014).

Goodall, Heather. 2008. *Invasion to Embassy: Land in Aboriginal Politics in New South Wales, 1770–1972*. Sydney: Sydney University Press.

Haebich, Anna. 2000. *Broken Circles: Fragmenting Indigenous Families, 1800–2000*. Fremantle, WA: Fremantle Arts Centre Press.

Harris, John. 2003. "Hiding the Bodies: The Myths of the Humane Colonisation of Aboriginal Australia." *Aboriginal History*, no. 27, 79–104.

Memmott, Paul, Christina Birdsall-Jones, and Kelly Greenop. 2011. *Why Are Special Services Needed to Address Indigenous Homelessness?* Brisbane: Institute for Social Science Research, University of Queensland, www.aerc.uq.edu.au/filething/get/2014/HL_special_services.pdf.

National Shelter. 2011. *Aboriginal and Torres Strait Islander Housing Round Table Report*, Brisbane: National Shelter, http://www.shelter.org.au/files/rpt11atsihousingroundtable.pdf (accessed 27 June 2014).

Reynolds, Henry. 1989. *Dispossession: Black Australians and White Invaders*. Sydney: Allen and Unwin.

Stanner, W.E.H. 1965. "Aboriginal Territorial Organization: Estate, Range, Domain and Regime." *Oceania* 36 (1): 1–26.

CHAPTER 11

Indigenous Fringe Dwelling in Geraldton, Western Australia: A Colonial Legacy

SARAH PROUT QUICKE AND CHARMAINE GREEN

The term "fringe dwelling" was popularized by celebrated Australian author Nene Gare when she published her novel *The Fringe Dwellers* in 1961. The book received critical acclaim and broke new ground as the first Australian literary work to explore Indigenous lived experience in urban Australia (Mattingley 2006). Fringe dwellers were Indigenous people who resided on designated reserves or in informal camps on the outskirts of established towns and cities. They were often characterized as spiritually, geographically, and culturally homeless: having abandoned, or been dislocated from, their customary moorings and attachment to country, but also simultaneously unable or unwilling to become immersed within the socio-spatial systems and norms of settler society (see Morgan 2006). Fringe dwelling was conceptualized as an equally psychosocial and geographical state of being.

At the time of Gare's publication, very little scholarly work had explored the experiences of Indigenous fringe dwellers. However, by the 1970s, several scholars had begun engaging in detailed ethnographies of fringe dwelling experiences (Collman 1979; Heppell and Wigley 1981; Memmott 1991; Sansom 1980). Much of this work focused on the cultural and economic practices of the residents of remaining town camps in northern and central Australia.[1] Perhaps the most nuanced sociological treatment of the constructions of Indigenous fringe dwelling in Australia was Elder's (1987) analysis of submissions to a 1982 federal government inquiry into the problems of Aboriginal town camps.

As Memmott (1996, 3) explains, four constructs emerged from Elder's analysis, each corresponding to a particular stakeholder group. First, local government representatives predominantly conceptualized fringe dwellers as "being between two cultures and embodying the worst aspects of both."[2] These local government characterizations were presented to the inquiry as justifications for excluding Indigenous people from the urban landscape. Second, state and Commonwealth government representatives saw the fringe as a transition space, and a place of cultural and socio-economic insecurity. Their submissions indicated a belief that with state intervention, Indigenous people occupying this urban fringe could find a meaningful place in mainstream society (Memmott 1996). Finally, there were, according to Elder (1987), two contrasting characterizations of fringe dwelling in Indigenous submissions to the inquiry. One view constructed fringe dwelling as a means of tempered (and in some cases highly strategic) engagement with the colonial frontier: they felt that being so located facilitated a form of engagement with non-Indigenous society while resisting assimilation (see also Jacobs 1996). However, for those who had been displaced from their homelands, or were forced to reside on fringe reserves despite aspirations of urban living, fringe dwelling was imbued with hopelessness and despair (Memmott 1996).

Though Elder's (1987) work concerned established town camps in the early 1980s, his findings bear uncanny similarities to the discourses and positions adopted by the same stakeholder groups decades earlier in relation to designated "native reserves" that had been established in many cities and towns in Australia during the 1940s and 1950s. Gare's *The Fringe Dwellers* explored the interplay between these multiple constructions. She was predominantly concerned with exploring the human implications, for Indigenous people, of living literally and figuratively, on the edges of urban Australian society. The novel was, in fact, a fictionalized account of her time living as the wife of the administrator of Native Affairs in the Western Australian port city of Geraldton during the early 1950s.

In this chapter, we return geographically and conceptually to the essence of Gare's notion of fringe dwelling and link it to the changing Indigenous housing policy landscape and contemporary notions of urban Indigenous homelessness. We argue that historical experiences of colonization and contested urban Indigenous presence are critical to understanding the drivers of contemporary urban Indigenous homelessness in all its forms, and to assessing the capacity of Australian towns and cities to accommodate Indigenous presence. The narrative relayed here gathers pace in the years preceding Gare's time in Geraldton. Although it outlines the evolution of Indigenous housing and homelessness from the time of British settlement until the present, it focuses in particular on the policy context and social climate of the 1930s and 1940s in Geraldton.

We demonstrate that contemporary challenges regarding Indigenous housing and homelessness in Geraldton are inextricably linked to this formative period of municipal colonialism.

Geraldton today is the largest regional city servicing Western Australia's vast north and is home to just over 36,000 people. Like many of Australia's regional cities (Taylor 2006), its Indigenous population is a much more visible minority (roughly 10 percent of the population) than is the case nationally (roughly 2 percent of the population). This visibility often fosters local socio-cultural tensions regarding Indigenous presence and belonging. And, like many other regional cities in Australia (Memmott, Long, and Thompson 2006; Prout 2011, 2014; Taylor 2002), Geraldton plays a particularly important role in the Indigenous settlement hierarchy in the immediate Murchison region. Geraldton has developed a sizable Indigenous population and is a key centre of service-related temporary population inflow from surrounding hinterland communities. These socio-demographic realities perpetuate a host of housing challenges.

In 2010, the Midwest Aboriginal Organisations Alliance (MAOA), deeply concerned about the ongoing struggle of many Geraldton Indigenous people in accessing and maintaining affordable and secure housing tenure, entered into a collaborative research partnership with the authors to examine the root causes of these chronic challenges. A high proportion of local Indigenous households in Geraldton found themselves in situations defined by Peters and Christensen (this volume) as at risk of homelessness, or as hidden homeless. That is, they were living in, or moving between, overcrowded homes and in or under precarious tenure arrangements. MAOA wanted to understand how this "silent social tsunami" had gathered force, and what could be done to positively transform the housing situations of hundreds of local Indigenous individuals and families, living daily with homelessness and experiencing its widespread ripple effects in their lives.

Our starting point was to look back through time. Through a process of archival research that drew on secondary documentary evidence, such as published biographies and memoirs of local residents, aerial photographs and maps, local newspaper articles (1900 to 1950), and published policy documents, we began to chronicle the evolution of Indigenous experiences of housing and homelessness in Geraldton. What emerged was a story of deeply entrenched, profoundly marginalizing, and actively contested fringe dwelling.

We acknowledge at the outset, that the narrative that follows is situated and partial. We are mindful of current debates and concerns amongst geographers and within the Indigenous studies arena about the positioning of Indigenous voice and agency within postcolonial scholarship (see Andersen

2009; Coombes, Johnson, and Howitt 2012). Our narrative indisputably emphasizes colonial conceptualizations of Indigenous presence in Geraldton. It does so, however, not because we seek to privilege these voices or caricature the historical experience of local Indigenous peoples as that of "billiard balls knocked around by powerful colonial powers and forces" (Champagne 2007, 360), but simply because the colonial narrative is more dominant, and therefore readily analyzed, within the (written) historical record.

We recognize, as Morgan (2006, 106) does eloquently, that such an approach will always be partial, as official records usually construct Indigenous people as "passive victims" who "dart in and out of the official/colonial field-of-vision, appearing only where they pose problems to authorities and disappearing when those problems subside." We argue, however, that these constructions are deeply instructive with regard to comprehending the structuring forces that shaped fringe dwelling in Geraldton—or the process to which Stanger-Ross (2008) referred to in the Vancouver context as "municipal colonialism." Furthermore, such analyses are fundamental to understanding the different kinds of homelessness that Indigenous people experience in urban settings today, and to developing culturally secure and better coordinated social housing responses for the future (Milligan et al. 2011). As Memmott and Chambers (2010), and other contributions in this volume have noted, including Christensen with Andrew, Belanger and Lindstrom, and Memmott and Nash, contemporary Indigenous homelessness is shaped by longitudinal and situational factors and circumstances, which are influenced by colonial history.

The Original Urban Dwellers

Few local historical accounts of Western Australia's Murchison region include anything more than a passing acknowledgement of an Indigenous presence in the place now known as Geraldton, during early colonial expansion (e.g., Bain 1996; Norris 1989). However, colonists' journal entries reportedly describe dense and semi-permanent Indigenous settlements in the region that were marked by well constructed huts, defined pathways, and intensive land and sea management practices (Museum of Western Australia 2011a, B). Large clan groups lived along the coast because the wealth of natural resources there could sustain a much larger and more permanent population than desert and hinterlands localities where water sources were sparse and seasonal. And, because natural resources were so readily available, seasonal hunting and gathering practices did not require the extensive migrations necessary in inland, desert country (Logan, Forrest, and Brock 1998). Local settlements were, therefore, more permanent in nature.

The northward push of the colonial frontier in the mid 1800s was marked by conflict. Logan, Forrest, and Brock (1998) describe how cultural groups, sometimes from considerably distant regions, would band together in efforts to raid or attack colonial outposts. Such attacks were a defensive response to the encroachment onto their country of foreigners staking claims of ownership and control over the region's resources. Settlers met these strikes with fierce retaliation. Frontier conflict, coupled with the ravages of disease (particularly smallpox and measles), saw the local Indigenous population decimated and profoundly affected the structure and fabric of socio-cultural moorings (Logan, Forrest, and Brock 1998; Toussaint 1995). Few of those who survived attacks and disease epidemics remained in the area. As colonial development spread, many were pushed east and/or took up work on emerging pastoral stations. Others were sent to Rottnest Island Prison or "native" missions further south.

An Upturned Urban Ordering

Increasing numbers of white settlers migrated to Murchison region in the early decades of the twentieth century due to its suitability for agriculture and mining along the area's two major river systems. In 1850, the town of Geraldton was officially established as a population centre that would support these industries. Some Indigenous people continued to camp in Geraldton's sandhills and along the river to the south of the town. In her memoir of the early 1900s, Geraldton resident Constance Norris (1989) recalls a large encampment of Indigenous people living on the site now occupied by the town's landmark cathedral, which was at the time, some distance from the expanding urban hub. There are also recorded references to camps, near and in town, that had always been used by Indigenous people, and references to other Indigenous families who rented houses and worked in the centre of town itself ("Geraldton Municipal Council" 1917, 2).

In the early part of the 1900s, the state seemed to largely ignore Indigenous people of mixed heritage who lived in or around developing towns and cities. The lack of colonial intervention was due in no small part to a widespread belief in social Darwinist doctrines that constructed Indigenous people as a dying race that would eventually die out entirely as contact with settler society increased.

Over time, however, the urban fringe dwelling group, some of whom were simply continuing the occupation of their territories of belonging, grew in size. state policy regarding Indigenous peoples also became centred on "protectionism" (Sanders 2000; Toussaint 1995). Under the Aborigines Act of 1905 the state could declare any place to be prohibited to any Indigenous person not in lawful employment (Biskup 1973). The state also retained the right to manage (including through sale or dispossession) any and all property an Indigenous person possessed. Through the policy apparatus of protectionism, the state sought to maintain a clear delineation, spatially and racially, between the "noble savage" of the wilderness, and the civilized, urban settler.

Urban-based Indigenous people became increasingly unfavourably characterized in colonial discourse, and more closely policed through the functions of the Aborigines Act. Popular opinion began to problematize the "half-caste" and those living in proximity to emerging urban centres, as somehow spoiled in comparison to the true Indigenous person. For example, in July of 1930, an article published in the local Geraldton newspaper asserted that "We can see the native at his best, if we care to go so far afield to look for him, in large portions of the Kimberley and Northern Australia where he is still given a natural life, unaffected by contact with a superior race" ("Australia's Aborigines" 1930, 2). Fringe dwellers were beginning to represent a threat to the clear colonial demarcations between the "civilized" settler population and the "noble savage" (Morgan 2006). Consequently, urban living was a precarious venture for Indigenous people. The policy of protectionism not only ignored the housing needs of urban Indigenous people, but actively worked to deter their presence entirely.

"You Weren't Meant to Be Seen": Reserve Negotiations

By the early 1930s, the Great Depression had impoverished a wide segment of the Western Australian population. In Geraldton, housing need had become acute for many residents and temporary camps with makeshift shelters had sprung up over time in various localities around the formal settlement. One of the most prominent camps was on a large sand dune behind the district hospital known as the "Edward Road" or "Hospital Hill" camp. It was close to the town's centre but generally away from the public eye, due to the difficulty of accessing the top of the sandy dune by vehicle. Residents of the camp, from wide ranging nationalities and ethnic backgrounds (including Indigenous people), were, as recalled later, locally referred to as the "League of Nations" ("Search for a Site: Council Objects to Mahomet's Flat" 1943, 4). In 1931, the Geraldton Municipal Council (GMC) received a strongly worded letter from residents near the camp asking that "the camp be removed and placed in an area where it could be under strict supervision." The complaints indicated that the camp was in a poor condition and a danger to women and children. Though the health inspector's reports did not support this view, the mayor indicated that a solution needed to be found for the campers.

The state government was also beginning to think through how it would respond to the growing presence of Indigenous people on the outskirts of urban centres throughout Western Australia (WA). In 1934, a state advisory committee recommended that special housing be provided for "detribalised Aborigines" in several country towns. Their report argued that "Aborigines 'capable of taking their place in the community' should be given houses of a standard comparable to the 'reasonable standard' laid down by the committee for European housing, with the government making a contribution towards the rent" (Biskup 1973, 205–206). The commissioner for Native Affairs responded that this was not a viable recommendation since fringe dwelling Aborigines still had nomadic tendencies and would abandon a house after a death. "Native Affairs" policy at the time instead chose to focus on the creation of reserves on the outskirts of towns to contain Indigenous people and place them under government control (Armitage 1995).

Indigenous people were often forced to move following threats to destroy their existing campsites (Department of Indigenous Affairs 2003). The living conditions on these reserves were poor. They lacked basic facilities and infrastructure, including water, bathroom, and laundry facilities. Ironically, the unsanitary conditions that the government forced Indigenous people to endure were used to justify further segregation, including the removal of Indigenous children from public schools (Department of Indigenous Affairs 2003).

In 1934, the Geraldton police sergeant reported to the GMC that they had begun searching for a reserve site to "deal with the native campers on Hospital Hill." Indigenous community member Alice Nannup noted in her memoir that when she moved to Geraldton that year, there were not many Indigenous families living in the town (Nannup, Marsh, and Kinnane 1992). Most that did—she estimated about five families—were camped on Hospital Hill. Building makeshift houses was one of the only options for Indigenous people at the time. They were unable to own land because they were not recognized as citizens. They could have land leased to them for personal use, but most experienced high levels of socio-economic disadvantage and suffered through discrimination in the private rental market. Of living on Hospital Hill, Nannup explains: "I wasn't living there because I wanted to—we had four kids, and steady work wasn't easy to get. Even if you had the money, you couldn't just go and find a place to rent—white people had first option there" (Nannup, Marsh, and Kinnane 1992, 167).

For the next four years, there were protracted, and at times acrimonious, negotiations between the GMC and the state government about containing and relocating the Indigenous campers in Geraldton. Cost and location were the two key points of tension. At no time during this process did Indigenous people appear to be consulted regarding their aspirations and preferences.

The primary site under consideration was at Mahomets Flat (Site 1 on Figure 11.1): an area close to the ocean (for sanitation purposes), with fertile soil (for growing vegetables). At a distance of approximately 2.5 kilometres from the town centre, and outside of the municipality, it was considered far enough away not to be a nuisance to the settlers, but not too far that residents would eventually just move back to town because the commuting distances were seen as an intolerable inconvenience. However, several municipal councillors were not in favour of this site since it was a popular resort location for local residents during the summer months. In November of that year, the state's Chief Protector of Aborigines, A.O. Neville, visited Geraldton and inspected both the Hospital Hill camp and the Mahomets Flat site. He advised that he would recommend the latter site to the government for the reserve.

Throughout 1935 the GMC repeatedly discussed their desire for a native reserve and lamented the lack of government action to this end, despite regular communication regarding the issue. In early 1936, the mayor met with Neville in Perth to discuss the reserve. Neville advised that he had spent considerable time gathering advice as to the suitability and cost of the Mahomets site. Though he had recommended the site to the Treasury department, they were reluctant to expend the necessary funds to purchase the land. A month later the GMC was advised that the government was exploring other government-owned sites for the reserve. The second favoured site was located roughly two kilometres to the east of the townsite and beyond the municipal boundary (Site 2 on Figure 11.1). The site was behind a large ridge of sand dunes and in bush land that had minimal road access.

The GMC was not in favour of this site because it was considered too close to town and not far enough away from the present campsite. They expressed dissatisfaction that though they agreed the Mahomets site was preferable, the government had been unwilling to "provide the small amount to purchase the site" ("Aborigines' Reserve: Questions of Site" 1936, 2). In July, Neville visited Geraldton again to discuss the reserve. Both parties were anxious for a resolution to what had been a testing set of negotiations. Neville explained that the Mahomets site was simply not viable from a government perspective and the 100-acre block behind Eastern Road (Site 2) should be selected. It was far enough away from the town, so as not to "cause annoyance." He indicated that the government could probably provide some galvanized iron for the shelters.

With the site now ostensibly settled on after a two-year process, the next round of negotiations, which consumed much of 1937 and 1938, concerned

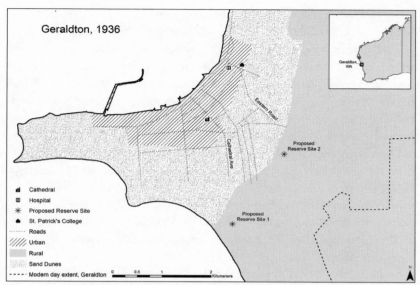

Figure 11.1. Proposed Reserve sites in relation to urban Geraldton, 1936.

site preparation. As these negotiations progressed, more public opinion articles were published in the local newspaper concerning the growing "half-caste problem" and the complexities of assimilation in Australia. These somewhat amorphous societal anxieties were reflected in local cross-cultural exchanges, as well as dialogues about dealing with the "native problem." Nannup recollected numerous personal accounts of being unwelcome at various public gatherings and sites during this period of the town's history. She described struggles in carving out spaces of legitimacy for her children at school and in the health care system, and keenly feeling the gaze of the law on herself and her family at every turn. She explained: "You see, if you were a blackfella in those days, you weren't meant to be seen" (Nannup, Marsh, and Kinnane 1992, 188).

The GMC continued to press the government about progress on the reserve while the government responded with concerns about the cost of clearing the site and laying a water pipe. The government indicated that perhaps they should consider alternative sites. At the 1938 March meeting of the GMC, one councillor expressed exacerbation, suggesting that the "sooner the present camp was disbanded, the better." He noted that the camp was near a school and "local residents would be delighted when it was moved" ("The Native Reserve" 1938, 4).

Later that year when the premier visited Geraldton, these sentiments were conveyed to him, along with an overview of the protracted process, and he agreed to expedite the process. By December, several "huts" had been erected on the reserve site. The road was not yet passable for vehicles and the water pipe still needed to be extended. The GMC was perturbed that the government had not completed the road and water works. Nevertheless, a police sergeant was dispatched to order Indigenous families to move to the reserve. Most local Indigenous people resisted. Alice Nannup recalls: "A lot of people were against the idea; when it was finished and the Sergeant came out and told us to move at a certain time, we didn't take any notice of him" (Nannup, Marsh, and Kinnane 1992, 167). The town clerk explained that "the natives wouldn't go to the reserve because they didn't think it was satisfactory: particularly with regard to sanitary conditions. They had scattered to various parts of the town" ("The New Reserve: Difficulties Encountered" 1938, 3). But as Nannup explains, there was another reason: "See, a lot of people didn't class themselves as Aborigines and they didn't want to get pushed onto a reserve" (Nannup, Marsh, Kinnane 1992, 167).

Indeed, the 1905 Aborigines Act had introduced a set of particularly challenging and discriminatory dynamics for Indigenous people seeking a legitimate place in urban Australia: "The object of the 1905 Act was protection. Most part-aborigines, however, felt no need to be protected: they were 'educated, and ratepayers, and not savages,' so they wanted to be treated 'like any other respectable man.' The effect of the Act on part-aborigines, as one parliamentarian remarked during the debate, 'was to make a very invidious and humiliating distinction'" (Biskup 1973, 143). Indigenous adults of mixed heritage could apply for an exemption from the stipulations of the Act, but only if they did not associate with any "full-blood" Indigenous people, or have children (Armitage 1995; Biskup 1973). Furthermore, exemptions were rarely granted and could be revoked at any time.

In 1939, the GMC authorized the condemnation and demolition of several shacks and camps around the town, including camps on Hospital Hill to force relocations to the reserve. However, in 1940, the GMC received further complaints from residents about "natives making camps and buildings in the vicinity of Eastern Road." The GMC noted that: "the trouble arose in connection with half-castes who did not regard themselves as natives. These people raised objections about going to the native encampment. If these people, however, regarded themselves on a plane with ordinary rate payers, they would have to live as such" ("Buildings for Natives" 1940, 3).

Eventually, reluctantly, Nannup moved her family to the reserve. She describes what met them there in particularly unfavourable terms. The "houses" she described as "a few sheets of corrugated iron knocked together into two rooms" (Nannup, Marsh, and Kinnane 1992, 171). The walls were not insulated and did not reach the ground so the wind would "tear through." There was no covering on the floor or fireplace for cooking and the only available water was a sand pipe some distance from the house. She concluded: "Our place [on Hospital Hill] might not have been great, but this was certainly no better. It was obvious from my days working as a housemaid that what meant houses for white people meant quite another thing for us" (Nannup, Marsh, and Kinnane 1992, 171).

"As If They Own the Place!"

By the late 1930s, the general Australian housing crisis had become extreme. The poor conditions generated during the Great Depression of the 1930s deepened during World War II (Hayward 1996). There were chronic housing shortages, many substandard houses that needed replacement, escalating building costs, and a lack of private investment. In 1943, the federal government established the Commonwealth Housing Commission to conduct an inquiry into the crisis. It concluded that the private market was unable to provide adequate housing for low-income earners, but that housing should be a right for all citizens (Hayward 1996). Consequently, a national public housing system was established in 1945.

Despite having filled crucial domestic labour shortages, as well as active service roles abroad during the war, Indigenous people were ineligible within this public housing scheme in the postwar years. They were not technically recognized as citizens until the 1948 Nationality and Citizenship Act. And even then, Indigenous people continued to be subject to the restrictions of prior legislation, much of which prevented them access to the rights of other citizens, such as entitlements to social welfare and public housing (Chesterman and Galligan 1997). This exclusion became particularly marginalizing in the Murchison region where Indigenous people were increasingly moving into towns to take advantage of the higher wages available as railway workers and miners, and to receive child endowments to which they were now entitled.

Alice Nannup recalls an increasing migration of Indigenous families into Geraldton during the war years and immediately afterward. Some set up camps near existing camps and in different locations between the reserve and the town. This whole area became known as "Blood Alley": a reference to the often violent, alcohol- and gambling-fuelled disputes that would bubble over there after dark.

Many residents of these camps were acutely aware of being alienated from the spaces created by the colonizers over their traditional homelands, and of

Figure 11.2. A Blood Alley Camp, 1960. Source: © *The West Australian*, reprinted with permission.

only being able to look in from the fringes. Indigenous artist Brian McKinnon grew up in this fringe camp. He recalls: "Blood Alley was built from recycled tin and timber from the rubbish tip over the sand dune. Our furniture was all makeshift old banana boxes for chairs, cable drums for tables and our cooking and heating came from an open fire" (Indigenart 2008). In 2008, he held an exhibition in Perth entitled "From Blood Alley to Anywhere." His work was explained as a portrait of growing up always feeling like he "existed on the fringes of society" (Indigenart 2008). Here, he found "pathos and beauty in the makeshift bricolage of life on the outskirts of white Australia" (Indigenart 2008).

As the war began to fade from memory, Indigenous presence in Geraldton once again returned to focus for local residents and governing authorities. At a 1945 meeting of the Murchison Road Board Association, a motion was carried to seek that all towns in the Murchison region be declared prohibited areas under 1936 Native Administration Act—a revision of the 1905 Act. Similar motions would follow in other regional towns throughout the state. The minister for Native Affairs responded forcefully, explaining that he did not support a policy of segregation and would not support a region-wide prohibition on urban living amongst Indigenous people. He argued that many Indigenous people in the Murchison region were not subject to the Act because of their ancestry, and that many of those who were, had jobs and contributed positively to the commercial life of their communities. Therefore, in response to local complaints received from town residents regarding Indigenous people in Geraldton, the GMC adopted a "tied-hands" approach. Indigenous people not subject to the Native Administration Act could not be forced from the town and onto the reserve, and those coming under the Act were the responsibility of the state government, which had in its view, to date, been negligent in the provision of services for Indigenous people.

Some GMC councillors agreed that many local Indigenous people had served in the war, and conducted themselves in the same manner as most other residents in the town. The GMC continued to press the administrator of Native Affairs to take action to accommodate the increasing Indigenous population in Geraldton. There was a growing recognition that the reserve conditions were unacceptable. The new commissioner for Native Affairs, Stanley Middleton, responded by suggesting that "every opportunity should be given to detribalised natives who wish to live under civilised conditions or are endeavouring to do so. These people are mostly employed at white rates of pay and since they receive social benefits and pay taxes and as many have served in the forces it is thought that every opportunity should be extended to them" ("Department's Concerns: Occupation of Houses" 1946, 1). This laissez-faire government position, packaged as a rights-based standpoint, conveniently aligned with the fiscal and political philosophy of Middleton's government. He also noted, for example, that the government simply lacked the resources to provide proper housing and facilities on all reserves and indicated that the "nomadic tendencies" of many "natives," who misused or underused existing housing, rendered such an undertaking a reckless waste of government revenue.

Meanwhile, conditions on the reserve continued to deteriorate, and there was growing discontent amongst many non-Indigenous residents regarding the Indigenous presence in Geraldton. Mirroring the trend in other parts of the country (see Morgan 2006); many complaints were framed in terms of issues of hygiene and perceived drunkenness. They were, however, deeply racialized. For example, in a letter to the editor of the *Geraldton Guardian* in early February 1949, one resident wrote:

> Sir, I am writing to ask why the native population of Geraldton is allowed to wander about the streets during the day, especially on Fridays. Some of them look simply revolting and are ill-mannered, bumping and pushing their way about on the streets as if they

owned the place. I would suggest that a store be set up somewhere out of the town for them so that they would have no need to enter the town at all. Geraldton would certainly be a more attractive place for the tourist if these people were kept off the streets and beaches close to the townsite. (T.M.S. 1949, 5)

Over the next few days, numerous responses—some in support, and some critical of this letter—made their way to the editor. Secondary sources suggest that at least some Indigenous people were upset and angered by this public debate and discussion. Eventually, the acting mayor weighed in. He insisted that Indigenous people had only recently been allowed any comforts or privileges in Australian society and it was everyone's responsibility to make sure they were not deprived of them. He expressed uncertainty at how to deal with the concerns raised within the community, but argued that no satisfactory resolution would be reached unless, and until, the government began to more systematically address the housing needs of the local Indigenous population. The editor of the newspaper agreed:

> The natives, with so many others in the community, are deleteriously affected and put at a very distinct disadvantage by the acute housing position. A first pre-requisite to raising the living standards of these people is to supply them with suitable homes. The old native reserve is totally inadequate and is an indictment of those who selected it.... The housing scheme for these people needs to be approached with a full appreciation of the debt the community owes them. It is doomed to failure if it is hemmed in by rigid economics and impenetrable red tape, so characteristic of everything undertaken by Governments. ("The Native Question" 1949, 2)

Late that year, the government began investigating the viability of a second reserve site in Geraldton: located to the north of the town on the Chapman River. This site was selected after vigorous local debate, primarily because the GMC wanted to ensure that the reserve was not too close to town, but also recognized that access to a water source was a critical condition that had been missing at the existing reserve. In 1951, the second reserve was formally established (Department of Indigenous Affairs 2003, 124), and in 1953, Frank Gare was stationed to Geraldton as the district officer of the Native Welfare department to attend to the basic needs of Indigenous reserves within the region. Alice Nannup explains that houses constructed under Gare's oversight were of better quality than the original reserve "houses" but still not of sufficient size and standard. Other assessments were not as gracious: "The reserve houses were a state-wide standard design of steel frames on a concrete slab with tin roofing, no ceiling, and single-sheet tin partition-like walls that did not touch the floor or reach the roof. Often there were no floor coverings, just the bare concrete particularly in the large living spaces in the middle" (Little 2000, 171).

This design became known as the "Geraldton House." It was used on numerous reserves and became a prototype described as popular amongst Indigenous people and approved by local authorities (Morgan 1972). Gare, however, regretted that the Geraldton House was rolled out across reserves in other parts of the state where weather and climatic conditions were not conducive to such a design. Indeed, Indigenous families would abandon these uninsulated and inflexible housing designs by constructing their own more culturally and climatically appropriate shelters (Grant and Memmott 2007).

Invisible, Homeless, Threatening

The colonial narrative of fringe dwelling in Geraldton prior to the 1960s can be divided into three overlapping phases. In the first phase, during the early 1900s, fringe dwellers were essentially invisible to the colonial gaze. Newspapers reported that Indigenous people were a "vanishing race," and in the settled parts of the Commonwealth, the "Aboriginal problem" had "largely solved itself." However with the passage of time it became increasingly clear that this first-phase narrative was based on a demographic fiction. Fringe dwellers gained increasing visibility within the colonial conscience and new narrative emerged.

Here, the urban "half-caste" was constructed as problematic and comparatively "spoiled." They were discursively positioned as spiritually, geographically, and culturally homeless. In his analysis of the postcolonial city, Blomley (2003) distinguishes between *dispossession*—the use of legal apparatuses to claim Indigenous land for the empire and justify the physical removal of Indigenous presence—and *displacement*, which he defines as the conceptual removal of Indigenous peoples from the urban landscape. Conceptual removal entailed the development of discourses of Indigenous urban nonbelonging and the simultaneous embedding of colonial settlement (Ibid. 2003). Paralleling Blomley's notion of displacement, we propose here that the second phase of the colonial narrative of fringe dwelling in Geraldton, as in Australia more generally, could be characterized as conceptual or projected homelessness. Indigenous people living on the edges of Geraldton were constructed as a people without a home: belonging neither to the settler society, nor to their natural, wilderness past. They were caught in a "homeless" middle ground.

As Indigenous presence in urban spaces grew, the narrative entered a third iteration: one more extreme in nature. Here, fringe dwellers became seen as a threat that needed to be contained. They disrupted the imagined colonial distinctions between wild and settled Australia. They unwelcomingly infiltrated white space. The system of urban reserves in Geraldton and beyond was the policy apparatus through which their containment could be secured.

By the 1960s, the reserves in Geraldton were officially closed. However, these evolving colonial narratives of fringe dwelling, and their resultant policies of attempted urban dispossession and displacement, left indelible marks on Indigenous housing policy from 1900s until the present. These narratives are inextricably linked to the persistent contemporary struggles of many Indigenous people to secure good quality, appropriate, and affordable homes in the city.

Fringe Dwelling Legacies

There are arguably many ways in which the corollaries of the colonial fringe dwelling narrative can be linked to contemporary housing struggles for Indigenous Australians. Here, we turn our attention to two struggles in particular: contemporary socio-spatial disadvantage associated with lack of access to market-based housing markets and contemporary policy framings of urban Indigenous housing as peripheral/tangential. While discussed separately, these legacies are entwined in their contemporary expression.

Limited Access to Real Housing Markets and Contemporary Socio-Spatial Disadvantage

From the 1960s onwards, the state government began purchasing and constructing basic housing in outer suburbs of Geraldton for Indigenous families (Department of Indigenous Affairs 2003). However, most of these new houses were located on the fringes of town and even on sites of the old reserves. In addition, the titles to these mini-reserves were held by the Crown, so there was no possibility for Indigenous people to own the land or the house in which they lived (Lovejoy 1972). While Indigenous people were not forced to live in state housing, discrimination within the private housing market left most Indigenous people dependent on it.

In allocating land for "native housing," in Geraldton and other towns across the state little consideration was given to the location, availability of resources, or the development and servicing of sites (Department of Indigenous Affairs 2003). Development was hindered by insufficient funds to meet the need and slow construction of housing (Grant and Memmott 2007). The demand for Indigenous housing considerably outstripped the supply. By 1963, for example, it was estimated that the state government required 2,000 houses for Indigenous people, but only 298 dwellings had been built by then (Lovejoy 1972).

By the early 1970s, there was still very little housing available to Indigenous people and much that existed was too small in configuration. Geraldton Indigenous resident Rod Little noted that at the time, the waiting period for a four-bedroom house—a minimum required size for many large Indigenous families—was four years (Little 2000). Five-bedroom houses did not appear to exist. Little (2000) describes the landscape of Indigenous housing in Geraldton, from the 1970s to 1990s, as being marked by three phenomena: poor living conditions—Indigenous families were repeatedly placed in houses that were not fit for occupancy; prejudice and discrimination; and alienation—many Indigenous families were locked out of the public housing system because they had accrued unpaid debts to the state from damage to properties during their tenancies. These unpaid debts sometimes led to evictions and the condition of debt repayment before another property could be leased to the applicant.

Nationwide, as in Geraldton, the major housing concerns for many Indigenous people related to inadequate supply of public housing, restricted access to private rentals, and limited opportunities for home ownership (Macintyre 1974). Although the housing market had ostensibly opened up in Geraldton, most Indigenous people still faced considerable barriers to moving beyond fringe dwelling.

Today, state housing continues to be concentrated in outer suburbs and in two- and three-bedroom configurations, as these are the most cost-effective construction and acquisition strategies for the state. This constrains low-income Indigenous families to residence in socio-economically disadvantaged, outlying suburbs. In his analysis of all major Australian urban centres, Biddle (2009) found that Geraldton ranked 7/61 on the Index of Dissimilarity with high concentrations of Indigenous people in low socio-economic areas.

Contemporary Urban Indigenous Housing Policy and Practice

In their incisive contribution to this volume, Christensen with Andrew demonstrate how the Canadian state has played a pivotal role in (re)producing Indigenous homeless geographies. They describe, for example, the role of welfare colonialism in creating a dependence on public housing amongst Indigenous peoples in the north, and the subsequent fracturing impact of certain public housing policies on Indigenous sense of home. The preceding section offers glimpses of the parallels shared by the Canadian and Australian experiences. In Western Australia, a lack of specific investment in urban

Indigenous housing programs, and continued disputes between various levels of government about whose responsibility such investment should be, have also perpetuated Indigenous peoples' ongoing struggles to access and maintain secure tenure in Geraldton.

In the 1960s, housing became a fundamental vehicle for driving assimilation policies, leading to the reform of Indigenous camps and the introduction of transitionary public housing programs (Grant and Memmott 2007). It was thought that "suitable" Indigenous candidates would adopt "mainstream" values when they were taught to live in European-style homes (Lydon 2009). Indigenous couples who were deemed to have reached a reasonable standard of living were selected to move into urban areas (Grant and Memmott 2007). Indigenous urban presence could now be tolerated, as long as it closely resembled non-Indigenous urban presence.

From the 1970s to 1990s, most federal funds allocated for Indigenous housing were directed to rural and remote programs, with limited resources allocated to maintenance or housing in urban centres (FaHCSIA 2010). In 2001, federal, state, and territory Housing ministers endorsed a statement recognising Aboriginal and Torres Strait Islander housing as a major national issue requiring immediate action. However, the resultant ten-year plan did not deliver support to improve urban Indigenous housing conditions. This reignited the debate about which level of government should be responsible for Indigenous housing in urban areas (Milligan et al. 2011).

A research study conducted in 2004 revealed little positive change for Geraldton's Indigenous residents (Flatau et al. 2005, 139). Appropriate and affordable housing remained a primary local concern. Study participants spoke consistently about unacceptably long waiting periods for public housing, the poor quality of existing dwellings, problems with repair and maintenance, and supply that was not maintaining pace with demand. The study also found that many houses were not deemed to be of sufficient size to properly accommodate Indigenous families and that the placement of feuding families next to each other in public housing was highly problematic within the Geraldton community (Flatau et al. 2005).

Concerns were also expressed about cultural safety within the DoH regional office. The study identified a general lack of trust of DoH amongst Indigenous people (Flatau et al. 2005). DoH's communication strategies were perceived as disempowering for many Indigenous people (Flatau et al. 2005). Many simply did not bother to approach DoH to get on the waiting list because they assumed they would be rejected. It was also difficult for tenants to remain tenancy-literate when the policies seemed to change with alarming regularity. Some interviewees explained that Indigenous people often asked non-government agencies to approach DoH on their behalf. Despite joint federal and state policy platforms of concentrated investment in improving housing outcomes for Indigenous people, positive changes seemed largely absent from the housing landscape in Geraldton.

In 2008, the National Affordable Housing Agreement was introduced, paving the way for a widespread "mainstreaming" of previously Indigenous-specific housing programs and structures. There was a marked political shift away from seeing Indigenous people as having unique housing needs and aspirations. There were also no secure and long-term funding arrangements made with regard to the provision of affordable housing for Indigenous people in urban areas like Geraldton (Milligan et al. 2011). Western Australia followed broader trends by transitioning to managing Indigenous clients within mainstream housing programs.

Despite these changes, the local housing situation for Indigenous people in Geraldton has remained remarkably consistent; concerns over supply, appropriateness, and tenancy management persist. In 2010, an investigation commissioned by the state government revealed little change from the situation described in the 1930s. The report identified a lack of housing for Indigenous people, particularly large families and young people, as a pressing concern in the Murchison region (Cant et al. 2010). The investigation further indicated that these housing shortages had produced overcrowded homes, in turn leading to a series of social problems.

Home ownership and private rental accommodation were also described as options financially beyond the reach of many Indigenous people in the region (Cant et al. 2010). In relation to public housing, the report indicated that there continues to be a tenuous relationship between many Indigenous communities in the region and DoH, particularly with regard to transparency and the provision of clear and accurate information to Indigenous clients. Long waiting times for basic repairs and maintenance, and inadequate mechanisms for assessing housing need place further strain on the relationship.

While homeownership and private rental have become a reality for a proportion of the Geraldton Indigenous community in the last decade, urban presence has been characterized by considerable turmoil and uncertainty for many local Indigenous people. Shifting housing policy "goal posts" and the exchanges of funding and responsibility for affordable housing programs at all levels of government, have generated considerable confusion about housing availability and tenancy expectations for Geraldton's Indigenous residents who are unable to access other housing options due to financial constraints and discrimination. The legitimacy of Indigenous urban presence in Geraldton remains contested.

Conclusion

Although the long-range history of Indigenous residence in and around the area now known as Geraldton was marked by refined practices of environmentally adapted "urban living," the last 150 years have been characterized by a series of evolving challenges to the legitimacy of Indigenous presence in the town. From the time of earliest contact, the colonial frontier has sought to push Indigenous people, literally and figuratively, to the fringes of Geraldton. The establishment of colonial Geraldton engendered forms of homelessness for Indigenous Traditional Owners by dislocating many of them from their customary grounds and living spaces, and for future generations that were forced to contend with, and at times subvert, forces of municipal colonialism that would seek to keep them at arm's length.

Indigenous presence in the town has historically been viewed as a problem that needed to be solved, but never with regard to the aspirations or perspectives of Indigenous people themselves. Municipal colonialism has played out powerfully as a structuring force increasing experiences and risks of homelessness amongst local Indigenous people. Indigenous presence in Geraldton, as mediated by housing policy, has been a political football repeatedly tossed between local and state governments, with varying degrees of impact on the lived experience of local Indigenous people. Governments made decisions on behalf of Indigenous people without concerning themselves with their aspirations, perspectives, and life projects. This invariably led to further alienation and poor housing outcomes for Indigenous people.

Indigenous people were largely excluded from the real housing market until very recently. It was not until the 1970s that home ownership and access to affordable public rental housing became available for most Indigenous people. From our present-day vantage point, this is a short, thirty- to forty-year history when compared with the 130 to 140 years over which non-Indigenous people have enjoyed such access. The intensely discriminating private rental market continues to remain a contested and largely inaccessible or undesirable domain for many Indigenous people in Geraldton. The dominant historical narrative, then, is of exclusion and projected un-belonging for local Indigenous people, which has led to persistent struggles to secure good quality, appropriate, and affordable homes.

The minor narrative of persisting strength and progressive reform is also, however, instructive and important. Indigenous people in Geraldton have remained and returned: not as a passive presence, but with agency and voice. When attempts were made to move the "Aboriginal problem" to the fringes of town, Geraldton's Indigenous residents resisted through evasion and some-times confrontation, asserting their rights to decent and self-determined living conditions. Over time, housing policy has responded slowly through reform. Segregated and oppressive reserves were abolished, a public housing system was established, and Indigenous people eventually gained access to it as citizens with equal rights.

The Geraldton narrative illuminates the links between the historical colonial narratives of fringe dwelling and the drivers of contemporary Indigenous homelessness. It ties current struggles, to access and maintain secure tenure, to decades of exclusion from the real housing market as a result of powerful colonial narratives that constructed fringe dwellers as invisible, homeless, and threatening. It also highlights the intersecting political, geographical, and social scales at which local colonial visions of identity and coexistence have been constructed, enacted, and contested. And finally perhaps most instructively, the Geraldton narrative demonstrates the significance of the unique histories and cultures that characterize the specific localities where Indigenous people have lived, moved, and worked to carve out places of belonging for generations.

Acknowledgements

Funding for the research project was provided by Australian Government Department of Families, Housing, Community Services and Indigenous Affairs (FaHCSIA), and the City of Greater Geraldton. The authors are indebted to the Midwest Aboriginal Organisations Alliance (MAOA) and particularly the MAOA Housing Project Reference group for their invaluable guidance, input, and partnership in this project. We are also grateful to Mary Murphy for her support with map production, and to Steve Vigilante for his assistance in identifying archival materials during the research process.

Notes

1   Most designated "Native Reserves" were closed down in the 1960s.
2   In some places, this view was shared by Indigenous people who lived in rural and remote localities, largely under the colonial radar (see Fink 1960).

References

"Aborigines' Reserve: Question of Site." 1936. *Geraldton Guardian and Express*, Saturday 30 May, Council's Recommendation.

Andersen, Chris. 2009. "Critical Indigenous Studies: From Difference to Density." *Cultural Studies Review* 15 (2): 80–100.

Armitage, Andrew. 1995. *Comparing the Policy of Aboriginal Assimilation: Australia, Canada, and New Zealand.* Vancouver: UBC Press.

"Australia's Aborigines." 1930. *Geraldton Guardian and Express*, Thursday 24 July.

Bain, Mary Albertus. 1996. *A Life of Its Own: A Social and Economic History of the City of Geraldton and the Shire of Greenough, 1846–1988.* Geraldton: City of Geraldton.

Biddle, Nicholas. 2009. *Location and Segregation: The Distribution of the Indigenous Population across Australia's Urban Centres.* Canberra: CAEPR (Centre for Aboriginal Economic Policy Research), ANU (Australian National University).

Biskup, Peter. 1973. *Not Slaves, Not Citizens; The Aboriginal Problem in Western Australia, 1989–1954.* St Lucia: University of Queensland Press.

Blomley, Nicholas. 2003. *Unsettling the City: Urban Land and the Politics of Property.* London: Routledge.

"Buildings for Natives." 1940. *Geraldton Guardian and Express*, Thursday 31 October, Local and General edition.

Cant, R., C. Penter, D. Henry, and J. Archibald. 2010. Mapping and Gap Analysis of Human Services for Indigenous People in the Murchison-Gascoyne Region. Perth: Department of Indigenous Affairs, Government of Western Australia.

Champagne, Duane. 2007. "In Search of Theory and Method in American Indian Studies." *American Indian Quarterly* 31 (3): 353–72.

Chesterman, John, and Brian Galligan. 1997. *Citizens without Rights: Aborigines and Australian Citizenship.* Cambridge: Cambridge University Press.

Collmann, Jeff. 1979. "Fringe-Camps and the Development of Aboriginal Administration in Central Australia." *Social Analysis*, no.2, 38–57.

Coombes, Brad, Jay T. Johnson, and Richard Howitt. 2012. "Indigenous Geographies II: The Aspirational Spaces in Postcolonial Politics—Reconciliation, Belonging and Social Provision." *Progress in Human Geography* 37 (5): 691–700.

Department of Indigenous Affairs. 2003. *Lost Lands Report.* Perth: Government of Western Australia.

"Department's Concerns: Occupation of Houses." 1946. *Geraldton Guardian and Express*, Thursday 11 April, Natives in Geraldton.

Elder, D. R. 1987. "The social construction of Aboriginal Fringe Dwellers." MA diss., Australian National University.

FaHCSIA (Department of Families, Housing, Community Services and Indigenous Affairs). 2010. *Housing Assitance Act 1996.* Annual Report 2007–08 and 2008–09. Canberra: Commonwealth Department of Families, Housing, Community Services and Indigenous Affairs.

Fink, R. 1960. "The Changing Status and Cultural Identity of Western Australian Aborigines: A Field Study of Aborigines in the Murchison District, Western Australia, 1955–1957." PhD diss., Columbia University.

Flatau, Paul, Lesley Cooper, Natalie McGrath, Donna Edwards, Amanda Hart, Mary Morris, Carol Lacroix, Marc Adam, Dora Marinova, Andrew Beer, Selina Tually, and Catherine Traee. 2005. *Indigenous Access to Mainstream Public and Community*

Housing, AHURI Final Report no. 85. Melbourne: Australian Housing and Urban Research Institute.

"Geraldton Municipal Council." 1917. *Geraldton Guardian*, Thursday 24 May.

Grant, Elizabeth, and Paul Memmott. 2007. "Forty Years of Aboriginal Housing, Public and Community Housing in South Australia from 1967 to 2007." In *Reflecions: 40 Years on from the 1967 Referendum*, edited by Neil Gillespie, 79–95. Adelaide: Aboriginal Legal Rights Movement.

Hayward, David. 1996. "The Reluctant Landlords? A History of Public Housing in Australia." *Urban Policy and Research* 14 (1): 5–35.

Heppell, Michael, and Julian J. Wigley. 1981. *Black Out in Alice: A History of the Establishment and Development of Town Camps in Alice Springs*. Development Studies Centre, Monograph no. 26. Canberra: Australian National University.

Indigenart. 2008. "From Blood Alley to Anywhere: Brian McKinnon." Subiaco, Western Australia: Mossenson Galleries, http://www.indigenart.com.au/Dynamic/display_ex.asp?id=290 (accessed 7 January 2012).

Jacobs, Jane M. 1996. *Edge of Empire: Postcolonialism and the City*. London: Routledge.

Little, Rod. 2000. "Two Generations of Housing in the South and Mid-West, Western Australia, 1960–95." In *Settlement: A History of Australian Indigenous Housing*, edited by Peter Read, 167–76. Canberra: Aboriginal Studies Press.

Logan, R., S. Forrest, and P. Brock. 1998. "Greenough Hamlet: An Aboriginal History of the Region." Unpublished report for the Geraldton Aboriginal Community, Geraldton.

Lovejoy, F. 1972. "Housing for Aborigines." MA diss., University of New England.

Lydon, Jane. 2009. *Fantastic Dreaming: The Archaeology of an Aboriginal Mission*. Lanham: AltaMira.

Macintyre, K. 1974. "Report on Aboriginal Housing and Accomodation in the Towns of Kalgorlie and Boulder." Unpublished Report.

Mattingley, Christobel. 2006. "An Unassuming Radical." *National Library of Australia News* XVI (7): 19–21.

Memmott, Paul. 1991. *Humpy, House and Tin Shed: Aboriginal Settlement History on the Darling River*. Sydney: Department of Architecture, University of Sydney.

_____. 1996. "From the 'curry to the weal': Aboriginal Town Camps and Compounds of the Western Back-Blocks." *Fabrications* 7 (1): 1–50.

Memmott, Paul, and Catherine Chambers. 2010. "Indigenous Homelessness in Australia: An Introduction." *Parity* 23 (9): 8–11.

Memmott, Paul, Stephen Long, and Linda Thompson. 2006. *Indigenous Mobility in Rural and Remote Australia: Final Report*. Australian Housing and Urban Research Institute.

Milligan, Vivienne, Rhonda Phillips, Hazel Easthope, Edgar Liu, and Paul Memmott. 2011. *Urban Social Housing for Aboriginal People and Torres Strait Islanders: Respecting Culture and Adapting Services*. AHURI Final Report no. 172. Queensland: Australian Housing and Urban Research Institute.

Morgan, George. 2006. *Unsettled Places: Aboriginal People and Ubranisation in New South Wales*. Kent Town: Wakefield Press.

Morgan, K. 1972. "Aboriginal Housing: Western Australia 1946–1971." In *A Report of a Seminar on Aboriginal Housing*. Canberra: The Royal Australian Institute of Architects.

Museum of Western Australia. 2011a. *Home Sweet Home: The Geraldton Reserve*. Geraldton: Exhibition panel at the Museum of Western Australia.

_____.2011b. *Yamatji: Early Views*. Geraldton: Exhibition panel at the Mueusm of Western Australia.

Nannup, Alice, Lauren Marsh, and Stephen Kinnane. 1992. *When the Pelican Laughed*. Fremantle, WA: Fremantle Arts Centre Press.

"The Native Question." 1949. *Geraldton Guardian*, Thursday 10 February.

"The Native Reserve." 1938. *Geraldton Guardian and Express*, Tuesday 1 March, Municipal Council.

"The New Reserve: Difficulties Encountered." 1938. *Geraldton Guardian and Express*, Tuesday 20 December, Native Problem.

Norris, Constance. 1989. *Memories of Champion Bay or Old Geraldton*. Geraldton: Soroptimist International of Geraldton.

Prout, Sarah. 2011. "Urban Myths: Exploring the Unsettling Nature of Aboriginal Presence in and through a Regional Australian Town." *Urban Policy and Research* 29 (3): 275–91.

_____.2014. "Interrogating the Image of the 'Wondering Nomad': Indigenous Temporary Mobility Practices in Australia." In *Aboriginal Populations: Social. Demographic, and Epidemiological Perspectives*, edited by Frank Trovato, and Anatole Romanuik. Toronto: University of Toronto Press.

Sanders, Will. 2000. "Understanding the Past, Looking to the Future: The Unfinished History of Australian Indigenous Housing." In *Settlement: A History of Australian Indigenous Housing*, edited by Peter Read, 237–48. Canberra: Aboriginal Studies Press.

Sansom, Basil. 1980. *The Camp at Wallaby Cross: Aboriginal Fringe Dwellers in Darwin*. Canberra: Australian Institute of Aboriginal Studies.

"Search for a Site: Council Objects to Mahomet's Flat." 1943. *Geraldton Guardian and Express*, Natives Reserve.

Stanger-Ross, Jordan. 2008. "Municipal Colonialism in Vancouver: City Planning and the Conflict over Indian Reserves, 1928–1950s." *The Canadian Historical Review* 89 (4): 541–80.

T.M.S. 1949. "Natives in Geraldton: Segregation Proposed." *Geraldton Guardian*, Tuesday 1 February, Letters to the Editor.

Taylor, John. 2002. *The Spatial Context of Indigenous Service Delivery*. Canberra: CAEPR, ANU.

_____.2006. *Population and Diversity: Policy Implications of Emerging Indigenous Demographic Trends*. Canberra: CAEPR, ANU.

Toussaint, Sandy. 1995. "Western Australia." In *Contested Ground: Australian Aborigines under the British Crown*, edited by Ann McGrath, 240–68. St Leonards, NSW: Allen and Unwin.

CHAPTER 12

Looking through the Service Lens: Case Studies in Indigenous Homelessness in Two Australian Towns

PAUL MEMMOTT AND DAPHNE NASH
(WITH ROB WILLETTS AND PATRICIA FRANKS)

Although empirical research studies on Indigenous homelessness in Australia are relatively sparse, recent work has investigated the effects of available accommodation and other socio-cultural pressures on Indigenous people that may destabilize their rental housing. The main purpose of this research has been to understand how crisis responses can be more appropriate and how the pathways in and out of homelessness can be most effectively serviced. This chapter aims to define "good practice" in regional Indigenous homelessness service delivery in Australia from our profiles of the Jimaylya Topsy Harry Centre (JTHC) and the Tennant Creek Women's Refuge (TCWR) (see Memmott and Nash 2012; Memmott et al. 2013), and to explore the social networks of the Centres at both individual and community levels, particularly in terms of potential impacts of services on client groups (Figure 12.1). The chapter begins with an overview of Indigenous homelessness. We offer further cultural context through an introduction of the distinctive features of alcohol consumption, in the study regions of Mount Isa in Queensland and Tennant Creek in the Northern Territory. The concept of social capital provides an analytical framework for the chapter and foregrounds the later discussion of social networks in the towns.

Following this we present our findings on good practice at the Centres by exploring the relationships between the institutions, the roles of managers, and the impact on client pathways into and out of homelessness. These networks contain locally defined social and cultural aspects of Indigenous homelessness, which tend to be overlooked. Our analysis draws on the concept of social capital as it applies to our preliminary qualitative and ethnographic investigations. More specifically, the concept of linking capital effectively highlights some aspects of good practice and so can lead to better and more informed policy for Indigenous people. The relevance of social capital to an understanding of the dynamics of Indigenous social exclusion is a matter for general debate (Hunter 2008; Mignone 2009), but nevertheless our research focuses on the potential for established local networks to effect pathways out of homelessness for Indigenous people who are appropriately linked to institutions responsible for service delivery.

Indigenous Homelessness in Regional Australia: An Overview

Homeless Indigenous Australians can be accurately described as overrepresented and under enumerated in official records. As 2.5 percent of the total Australian population, Aboriginal and Torres Strait Islander peoples comprise 25 percent of the homeless with a rate nearly fourteen times that of non-Indigenous Australians (adapted from Table 1.1, ABS 2012). Much of the debate on Indigenous homelessness in Australia has centred on definitions and estimates of homelessness on the one hand, and effective delivery of services on the other.

While there are differing views on "what works," clearly the solutions remain elusive. Overall, the provision of more affordable and accessible housing to Aboriginal and Torres Strait Islander people is most important; however, it also needs to be stated that housing is seldom the full answer for Indigenous people. Homelessness can involve a wide range of problems and service needs, which may be specific to cultural groups and their geographic location.

Although limited in number, empirical qualitative studies of Indigenous homeless people over the last twenty-five years highlight some of the specific multiple causes, conditions, and implications of Indigenous homelessness. In previous research, Memmott and colleagues (2003; 2012b) developed and later refined a set of homeless categories to fit the specific conditions of Indigenous homelessness. We argue that these categories are more relevant and useful for policy makers and service practitioners than other definitions, for example, those suggested by the ABS (2012b). These categories aid the understanding of people's movements along complex pathways into homelessness and so include those at risk of homelessness (Memmott, Birdsall-Jones, and Greenop 2012b, 24–25). In particular, these definitions differentiate between (i) public place dwelling persons; (ii) housed people but who are at risk of homelessness; and

(iii) spiritually homeless persons. Within this categorization, homeless people may be either voluntary or involuntary, and short-term or long-term homeless. The categories have been described in detail earlier (Chapter 10 in this book) and elsewhere by the authors (Memmott, Birdsall-Jones, and Greenop 2012b). These categorizations were expanded to account for the influence of cultural motivations on mobility that results in various forms of homelessness and/or public place dwelling.

Indigenous patterns of mobility are central to understanding the nature of Indigenous homelessness. People maintain active social relations with extended family and kin at locations within their cultural region as well as other places further afield, and can call on them for accommodation and other resources. These and related behaviour patterns can increase the risk of homelessness for those who are requesting resources and for the wider household (for more on cultural perspectives see Memmott, Birdsall-Jones, and Greenop 2012b, 37–46 and Birdsall-Jones [in this book]). As for mobility, understanding Indigenous drinking behaviours is an important aspect of Indigenous homelessness.

The well-established link between alcoholism and homelessness is compounded for a proportion of Indigenous people by particular drinking patterns. Since white settlement in Australia, the availability of alcohol in rural, remote, and urban communities has led to an identifiable, well-documented, and culturally distinct style of drinking by some Indigenous people that has been well documented (see, e.g., Brady 2010). Over recent decades, the practices of Indigenous drinkers have been characterized by the propensity to binge drink, the preference for drinking with kin, the inclination toward demand sharing (Peterson 1993) and reciprocal shouting, and the expectation that they would not be held accountable for their actions while they are drunk (Memmott 1991).

Social Capital

Social capital can be defined as the "networks of relationships among people who live and work in a particular society, enabling that society to function effectively" (Oxford Dictionaries 2016). In the social science literature, social capital is an "essentially contested concept" (Szreter and Woolcock 2004, 654) and has been used in many different contexts. In his well-known research about the demise of positive social networks in late-modern suburban U.S., Putnam (2000) argued that the lack of social capital led to identifiable negative social effects in many communities. Recent studies of Indigenous social issues in Australia have drawn on social capital and other related concepts to explain the social inequalities experienced by Indigenous people. To take an urban example, the health and well-being of Indigenous people in urban Adelaide appears to be both negatively and positively impacted by engagement in bonding and bridging networks (Browne-Yung et al. 2013). Some positive aspects of social capital included accessing information (e.g., about employment) from others in a social network, but there may also be negative associations through pressure on members to engage in anti-social behaviour. In other words, not all social capital based on people's networks of relationships can build better citizens.

For the context of homelessness in our study region, however, the idea of linking capital is particularly significant, as well as bonding and bridging capital. Whereas the importance of family/friends is encompassed by the term bonding capital which holds people of generally like-minds together, and bridging capital includes the networks between people from different social groups, such as different classes/races who recognize their differences yet interact within a certain domain, linking capital moves "vertically" in the sense of social hierarchy. Both bridging and bonding capital have limited application for relationships with structural inequalities because perceptions and trust particularly are not necessarily shared between different social groups (Mignone 2009). As a conceptual device, linking capital can explain how especially for poorer communities "respectful and trusting ties to representatives in formal institutions" can have "a major bearing on their welfare" (Szreter and Woolcock 2004, 655).

All three types of social capital listed above are products of the relationships between people but linking capital is "qualitatively different" as individuals within a network recognize that they do not share aspects of bridging capital or share access to power and resources (Szreter and Woolcock 2004, 655–56). For people with low socio-economic status it is improbable that they can directly connect with people or institutions in ways that can improve their situation. Linking capital provides the opportunity or leverage to obtain access to power and resources.

In 2002, one of the authors assisted a team of sociologists in adapting the social capital construct to Indigenous communities in Australia (Memmott and Meltzer 2005). In terms of network modelling, the study differentiated between Indigenous cultural networks (extended family, skin relations, ceremony partners, etc.) and whitefella-type organizations (Indigenous-run corporations). The cultural networks exist in varying ways and extent in many Indigenous communities and societies, but are often unrecognized or at least unfamiliar to government and non-governmental organization (NGO) service delivery agents. The latter allow Indigenous people to have a legal identity and to engage with the government and NGOs to receive grants for particular service programs. We shall return to these aspects of social capital in our concluding analysis. In the section below, we provide brief descriptions of the regions of Northwest Queensland and the Barkly as well as profiles of homeless service providers, the Jimaylya Centre and the Refuge in their regional contexts.

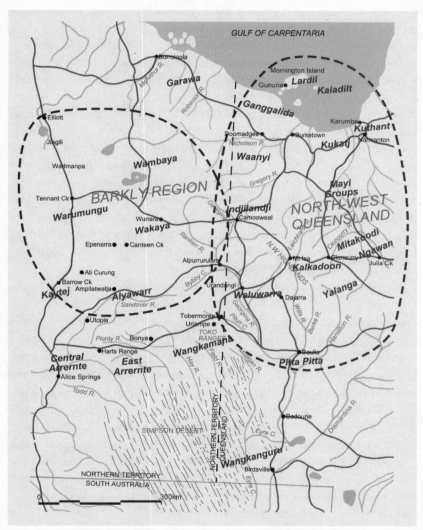

Figure 12.1. Map of Northwest Queensland Region and Barkly Region showing their regional centres, Mount Isa and Tennant Creek respectively, and other Indigenous population centres and Indigenous language groups. Map by Linda Thomson, Aboriginal Environments Research Centre.

Study Regions and Centre Descriptions

Our study area includes the Northwest Queensland region, centred on the city of Mount Isa, and the Barkly region of the Northern Territory, with Tennant Creek as the service centre town. The two regions are contiguous at the Northern Territory and Queensland border and they have two separate state bureaucracies and regionally based agencies that manage homelessness services (see Figure 12.1).

The social history of the regions has influenced the residential patterns of Indigenous people today. In Queensland, Indigenous movement in the region was strongly constrained by the Aboriginals Protection and Restriction of the Sale of Opium Act 1897 for the first three-quarters of the twentieth century. Along with various successive revised Acts, the 1897 Act gave the state control over all aspects of people's lives, particularly their labour—often people had to move away from their traditional homelands and places of residence to work (see Kidd 1997). When cattle stations stopped employing many Indigenous people and legislative change introduced government (welfare) support, some people moved to Mount Isa and to the smaller towns. Others remained in Indigenous communities in the region, visiting Mount Isa for a range of services and to see family and friends. According to the 2011 census, Indigenous people comprise 3,204 people or about 15 percent of Mount Isa's 21,237 population (ABS 2013a).

Tennant Creek is also a regional service town. It began as a station on the Overland Telegraph Line in 1872, which facilitated the spread of the pastoral (mainly cattle grazing) industry through this remote area. Although Indigenous people provided the labour pool, they did not experience the same oppressive controls of the Queensland Aboriginal Acts and so were able to maintain much of their traditional culture—this was a strong motivation for staying in the region. As measured by the 2011 census, the population of Tennant Creek was 3,061 with a relatively high proportion of 1,591 (52 percent) of Indigenous people (ABS 2013b). Roughly an equivalent total number of people most of whom are Indigenous live in the small towns and bush communities across the region. Despite its vast size, over 283,000 square kilometres, the semi-arid Barkly Region has a relatively small population. Constraints to service delivery are typical of remote Australian regions and reflect the significant levels of socio-economic disadvantage across the Barkly Region.

Aspects of the Indigenous style of drinking have been observed for our study regions. During the colonial period, Indigenous drinkers developed this style through their experiences of state-imposed living conditions for

Indigenous people, such as on missions run by Christian churches. On missions in Queensland (up to the 1970s), alcohol was generally not available, so when Indigenous people travelled to places where they could drink, such as the centres of Cairns and Mount Isa, they would typically drink heavily for an extended period. In the 1970s and 1980s in Mount Isa, Memmott (1991) observed that a number of bars as well as the riverbed near Town Bridge were popular places for Indigenous visitors to drink—all were characterized by excessive drinking. In recent times, the binge-drinking pattern has persisted in the riverbed. The drinkers have moved further up and down but old "spots" are still used; the practice is further complicated by additional risky behaviours, such as the taking of other drugs. Reports on Indigenous drinking in Tennant Creek document similar behaviours and also the effects of alcoholism in terms of homelessness (Wright 1997).

The Jimaylya Topsy Harry Centre in Mount Isa[1]

The Jimaylya Topsy Harry Centre (JTHC) in Mount Isa integrates the front-line treatment of Indigenous alcoholism into its responses to homelessness. The Centre is unusual in that it not only provides crisis accommodation with the long-term goal of facilitating clients through various stages towards stable urban public housing, but the JTHC also incorporates a managed drinking program for alcoholic clients. In some ways, the Centre aligns with programs in mainstream and other Indigenous centres. However, it also departs from usual practices in significant ways, most particularly in the managed consumption of alcohol and an Indigenous-oriented approach. Through its experience of service delivery in Mount Isa, the then Queensland Government Department of Community Services (DoC) recognized a gap in services for homeless Indigenous people with long-term substance abuse problems and established the Centre.

Located on the southern end of town in Mount Isa, the Centre consists of administration and service buildings and several different accommodation facilities (see Figure 12.2). Apart from the main office and the caseworker's office, there is a kitchen, laundry, large multi-functional room used as a dining room, and television lounge for common use. Accommodations include: a number of outdoor individual semi-enclosed sleeping shelters; the "yudu" or single men's quarters (single rooms); single women's quarters (dormitory-style sleeping); a three-bedroom house for couples in crisis; and six two-bedroom houses used by clients transitioning to rental housing.

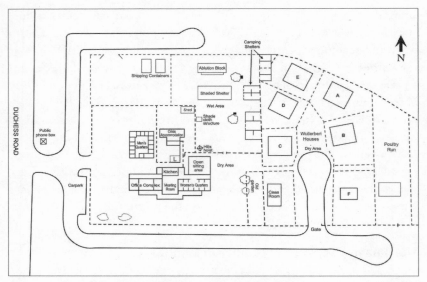

Figure 12.2. Plan layout of Jimaylya Topsy Harry Centre, Mount Isa. Figure by Linda Thomson, Aboriginal Environments Research Centre.

The Centre operates with six to eight staff on duty, including an administration leader, team leaders, support staff, and a full-time counsellor. Mount Isa Technical and Further Education (TAFE) offers a program at the Centre, and numeracy and literacy sessions are compulsory for those on the housing waiting list. Other courses include creative skill-building activities, such as furniture making, sewing, leather-craft, and small-motor repair. Over the years, the Indigenous manager in conjunction with relevant government departmental contacts has developed the policies and procedures which he regularly updates in consultation with other Indigenous staff. Managing the clients' behaviour particularly around the limits on alcohol consumption can be very demanding. In this context the understanding and rapport between clients, management, and staff are paramount.

Client Pathways in and out of Jimaylya

As a homeless centre in Mount Isa, the JTHC does not exist in isolation. At the level of the institution, there are active social networks in town (and beyond) connecting the Centre to other organizations that contribute significantly to its operations.

Typically, support from many agencies is required to help the homeless and those people "at risk" of homelessness, but this is especially the case for remote Indigenous clients. Local service agencies are well aware that some Indigenous people in the Mount Isa region are highly mobile, especially at particular times of the year such as mid-August when the annual rodeo is held. Many also visit Mount Isa regularly for a range of reasons, such as health appointments, court appearances, recreation, and family visits. Whether visiting for short or extended periods, Indigenous people coming to Mount Isa often choose to sleep rough although some do so involuntarily. As argued elsewhere (e.g., Memmott, Birdsall-Jones, and Greenop 2012b), many Indigenous public place dwellers are not homeless although they may be at risk of homelessness. The fact that their return to their home communities may be delayed by lack of transport and/or lack of financial support, adds further to the risk. To minimize the risk, local agencies step in.

The Jimaylya Topsy Harry Centre is one of three key centres for homeless Indigenous people in Mount Isa, the others being the Arthur Peterson Special Care Centre (APSCC) known as "AP," an overnight shelter mainly for intoxicated people, and the Kalkadoon Aboriginal Sobriety House (KASH), which runs an alcohol treatment program. The strong association between public place dwelling and public drunkenness in Mount Isa is well recognized by these agencies and their support services and so their programs primarily target both these areas. For various historical and policy-related reasons, each centre has developed a different approach and mode of operation. AP and KASH offer short-term crisis accommodation and other support but no tenancy, and no alcohol is allowed in either.

While clients are categorized as homeless, they also have a range of complex health issues and other needs. It is significant therefore that JTHC relies on inter-agency collaboration as part of its case management for individual clients. The supporting local agencies include the Homeless Help Outreach Team (HHOT), Riverbed Action Group Outreach and Support Services (RAGOSS), Alcohol, Tobacco and Other Drugs Services (ATODS), Mount Isa Community Mental Health Services, and Mount Isa Sexual Health Services; clients have access to professional counsellors (such as social workers and psychologists) and also to employment agencies, such as Centrelink and Job Services Australia. The Queensland Department of Housing, the Queensland Police Service, Queensland Legal Aid, Queensland Transport, and the Queensland Ambulance Service are also support agencies.

Both non-Indigenous and Indigenous organizations in Mount Isa reportedly work well together, and in terms of social capital, the clients access the Centre's bonding, bridging, and linking capital through its agency networks. The manager of JTHC commented favourably on the Centre's connections, particularly with the frontline help teams, such as HHOT and RAGOSS. From the preliminary investigations done for this case study, we have learnt that with the support from a range of services, individual clients can make certain progress towards rehabilitation and the Centre has a strong track record of providing appropriate assistance. For the short-, medium-, and long-term clients, there is quite a range of expectations and need. To succeed, in the short and medium terms, the support staff focuses on the practical aspects of shelter and reduced risks in terms of drinking behaviour and therefore general safety. For some, this is also achieved by facilitated return to their home communities. In the medium and long term, clients' take-up of training opportunities is significant for setting themselves on a path to successful housing (with a prioritized position on the public rental waiting list). This path, however, is made at times more difficult due to the short supply of housing, exacerbated by the "two-speed" mining economy that operates in Mount Isa. Mining companies are the biggest employers in the region and most of their employees are non-Indigenous people who can access the limited rental market comparatively easily because they have a relatively high and reliable source of income as well as good rental histories.

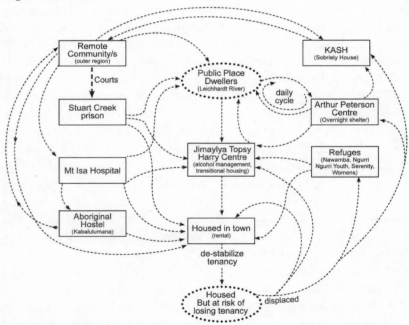

Figure 12.3. Typical movements of Indigenous people through Mount Isa housing and institutionalized residences, including pathways in and out of the Jimaylya Centre. Figure by Linda Thomson, Aboriginal Environments Research Centre.

The Tennant Creek Women's Refuge and the Refuge Report[2]

Founded in 1989, the Tennant Creek Women's Refuge aims to provide "support, accommodation and protection for women and children who are effected by violence or are in crisis and [to] network with other organisations to provide education and advocacy on the effects of violence on families and individuals. All services are designed to encourage the empowerment of women and children in the Barkly region" (Memmott et al. 2013, 24).

The Refuge is rented from Territory Housing and includes a crisis accommodation house of eight beds, offices, a children's activity room, an outdoor recreation area, a separate counsellor's office, and a storeroom (see Figure 12.4). The Refuge primarily services women who are victims of domestic violence (DV) or family violence (FV), or at risk of violence. Other needs include: transport assistance to return home (i.e., for dysfunctionally mobile women); respite from crowded households and very stressful domestic environments; and survival help within non-functional houses (e.g., for women living with disabilities).

Clients typically have many coexisting problems including poverty, multiple and complex health issues, social and personal conflicts, dysfunctional children and other family members, as well as substance abuse problems. The referral service thus links female clients to a range of networks and agencies.

Overall, the Refuge struggles weekly to meet demand. Despite the Refuge having many service functions and goals, there is a practical limit to the services that can be delivered at any one time, dependent on the staff capacity and other limitations of space and funding. As reported to us by local Indigenous people in Tennant Creek, there was strong evidence that people's housing needs were not being met and that the Indigenous community was experiencing considerable stress which impacted negatively on their health and well-being. Furthermore, our findings suggested a clear link between the Indigenous women's use of the Women's Refuge and the interconnected and complex set of social problems in the town.

Our parallel crowding study of Indigenous rental tenancies (Memmott et al. 2013, 50–58) revealed that there was an average of around ten Indigenous people per house with a range of three to twenty-five occupants. Furthermore, the level of crowding may have been relatively low at the time of our survey which was undertaken when there were no major events (e.g., football) in Tennant Creek to attract visitors from the bush communities in the region. The study also found that there were high stress levels amongst many households and relatively high frequencies of family violence. Altogether it became

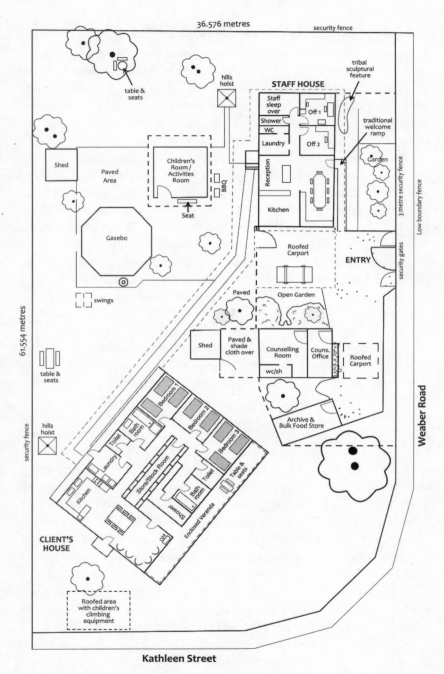

Figure 12.4. *Plan layout of Tennant Creek Women's Refuge, July 2012. Figure by Linda Thomson, Aboriginal Environments Research Centre.*

clearer why between thirteen and thirty-nine adult women arrive at the refuge seeking help each month.

The study raised the issue of whether there is room for improvement in how the national census records visitors in general (by usual residence), and in particular for Indigenous households. By masking or discounting the number and presence of visitors in regions of high regional (or circular) mobility, the census fails to capture the relevant data. Such information is salient to understanding the underlying reasons why social problems (including FV and DV) and personal psychological health problems (including stress) are prevalent and increasing in particular regional cities of Australia. Most critically for Tennant Creek the services in the town have not expanded commensurately with the increased population.

The population of Tennant Creek has grown only slightly over the ten inter-census years from 2001 to 2011 but the Indigenous population has increased by about 50 percent in this time. Throughout that period however the institutions which provide supported accommodation apart from the Refuge, including Pulkapulka Kari (residential Aged Care), The Barkly Region Alcohol and Drug Abuse Advisory Group or BRADAAG (primarily alcohol rehabilitation), Julalikari Council, Christian Outback Fellowship, Wangkana Kari Hostel, and the Tennant Creek Hospital have not substantially increased their accommodation supply (Memmott et al. 2013, 38–43). It is not surprising therefore, that the waiting lists are long (and getting longer). Also, (as illustrated in Figure 12.5), these services are pressured for accommodation by mobility (bush visitors), recycling clients (between services within the town), as well as pre- and post-release clients from the relatively new Barkly Work Camp. These pressures resound throughout the entire services network with each agency constantly aware of how other agencies are operating and when possible moving clients to better meet their needs.

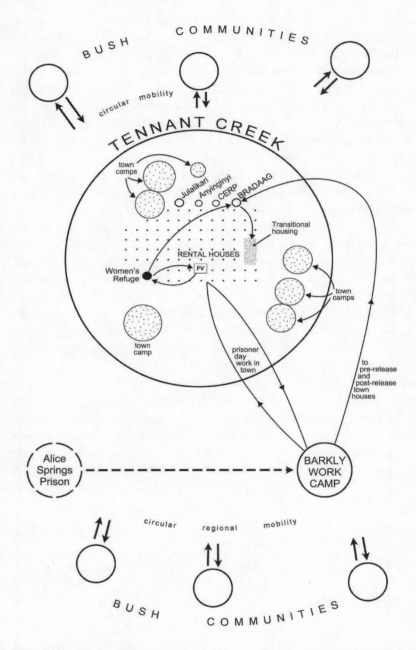

Figure 12.5. Movements of Indigenous people from the Barkly region into Tennant Creek, showing flows between rental housing and traditional housing. Figure by Linda Thomson, Aboriginal Environments Research Centre.

Good Practice and Social Capital

The preliminary analysis of service delivery at the Jimaylya Topsy Harry Centre informs our profiling of good practice at both the Centre and at the Tennant Creek Women's Refuge. Within the focus study, discussion centred on core principles of harm minimization, accommodation leading to housing, and cultural maintenance and building of social capital. After closer examination, the principle of cultural maintenance and building of social capital and resilience can be further refined. In addition we have identified the role of Indigenous staff and management as a core principle.

Harm minimization at Jimaylya is achieved by maintaining a balance between (a) reduction in the supply of alcohol, and (b) reduction in the client's demand for alcohol, within the field of alcohol rehabilitation.[3] JTHC is significant because it offers the opportunity to work on both aspects listed above, voluntary personal supply reduction and demand reduction, which are not offered in other centres. The JTHC has had many successes in terms of harm minimization through provision of *emergency accommodation and transitional accommodation* as well as through providing significant numbers with access to services and training. The transitional accommodation can move people from the "tin shed" style camping with external hearths, to personalized single rooms, and eventually into conventional two-bedroom houses. However success can be temporarily impeded particularly by the lack of surplus rental housing in Mount Isa and the long waiting times for available social housing. Informal and formal *cultural maintenance* and capacity building programs contributed to client resilience both within the Centre and outside. TAFE programs were conducted for those on the waiting list for housing, and counselling support and referrals were available through case management for social, psychological, and health problems. The high percentage of *Indigenous management and staff* at Jimaylya has also established a comfortable social environment for the clients. Most notably the current manager, a local Indigenous man has been in the position since the Centre began and is also anecdotally well-liked and professionally respected by clients and the community.

As well as the significant strengths in its approach, the Jimaylya Centre has a physical capacity to accommodate the majority of those in need (although constrained at times of recurring peak demand, for instance during football finals and annual rodeo). Nevertheless, some clients are a part of Indigenous networks which keep them in a cycle of homelessness, including riverbed drinking and other risky behaviours. There is evidence to suggest that a minority of clients are able to use the Centre in ways not necessarily consistent with its goals. By recycling though the Centre and other facilities (as illustrated in

Figure 12.3), they demonstrate that progression through the JTHC to tenancy is not readily achievable for this minority group. For such residents, the Centre can also become a place of stability through which they enjoy the balance of drinking and safety after several unsuccessful attempts at passing through.

In comparison to the JTHC, the Tennant Creek Women's Refuge also presents a range of good practice principles and possesses different strengths but is limited by reduced resources. The Refuge primarily provides *crisis accommodation* to women (and children) who are victims of domestic and family violence, as well as counselling, outreach support for families, and education. Services are available to Indigenous women from all over the very large Barkly Region, which is characterized by regular circular mobility patterns in and out of its regional centre of Tennant Creek. Although Indigenous women access the Refuge services primarily when they are victims (or at risk) of violence, the facility also helps with other needs as already discussed above. Unfortunately, due to the relatively small population of the Barkly Region and the social dynamics of Indigenous peoples, it is not always possible for women who are victims of violence to simply avoid or evade their families and husbands. Therefore, the clients often return to their problematic circumstances and eventually develop a cyclic pattern of return visits to the Refuge.

On the other hand, a primary strength of the Refuge is its *Indigenous management and staff*, who are committed, long-term employees. Recruiting and retaining Indigenous staff is critical for clients to feel safe and comfortable and also for promoting *cultural maintenance*. This need encompasses social and cultural sensitivity as well as physical comfort, and the Centre focuses on known concerns for local Indigenous women and families. Where possible, the Refuge also attempts to build family connections for clients, helping them to travel and visit home communities.

A primary challenge for the Refuge is its accommodation capacity. Very simply, demand exceeds supply and the Refuge has had to manage this by limiting the lengths of stay and by referring clients appropriately (e.g., to BRADAAG if intoxicated). It was this information that motivated our original research question: how can an eight-bed facility provide good service in a town with a reported widespread Indigenous crowding problem?

Table 12.1 sets out the principles of "good practice" with some comment on their success as well as the challenges for each centre. When comparing the centres, we conclude that there are significant contrasts in the potential for effecting change.

Table 12.1. Social capital perspective on good practice at JTHC and TCWR.

	Jimaylya Topsy Harry Centre	Tennant Creek Women's Refuge
Harm minimization	Working well–safe place, managed alcohol consumption	Working well within constraints–only eight beds, safe, no alcohol
Accommodation	Working well accommodating about thirty to fifty people, flexible shelters "out the back", demand exceeds supply for crisis accommodation several weeks each year	Working well but very limited (only eight women and max. seven days stay due to new admissions)
Capacity building	Strong results for transitioning clients, weaker for "cycling" clients	Counselling during short stay and also referrals, counsellor runs DV workshops at "Stronger Families" to women who cycle through Refuge
Cultural maintenance	Embodied in Centre ethos and practice, Developing programs	Centre operations responsive to Indigenous client needs,
Indigenous management/staff	Strong Indigenous input through Centre management and daily operations	Part Indigenous membership on Centre's Board, majority of workers are local Indigenous women, strong links with other Indigenous agencies

The above profile of good practice at the JTHC and TCWR sets the context to explore each organization's impact on Indigenous homelessness from a social capital perspective. As discussed above, Memmott and Meltzer's (2005) analysis of Indigenous cultural networks and "whitefella-type" organizations provides a way of understanding Indigenous community strengths in relation to community networks and social capital. Building on this analysis, this chapter focuses on the institutional level, involving regional service delivery of two centres, as opposed to the connections between individuals. Our contention is that JTHC's and TCWR's Indigenous networks are built through the connections of the management and staff, and that it is these networks which facilitate the movement of some clients into pathways out of homelessness. Further, we add that strong Indigenous social or cultural networks alone cannot achieve any significant reduction in homelessness. Other conditions need to be met.

If we consider public place dwellers in Mount Isa or Tennant Creek, they usually maintain strong Indigenous cultural networks, but their engagement with "whitefella-type" of organizations is minimal, if not zero, except insofar as being picked up by an outreach group and then being taken to a shelter for a night's sleep and a meal. The modus operandi of the Jimaylya Centre starts with the capacity of the senior Indigenous staff to connect into the Indigenous cultural networks of the river campers and demonstrate to them that these networks can be activated and maintained from within the Centre, for example, in the supervised drinking area. Their second task then is to provide their newly arrived clients with introductions into both Indigenous-run and government/ NGO-run "whitefella-type organizations" in Mount Isa that can fulfill their particular set of needs. This linking represents a type of vertical social capital in many cases (as illustrated in Figure 12.6). Jimaylya's networking capacities with other government and non-government agencies have been strengthened in recent years by an Australian, government-funded homelessness strategy called "Sheltering the Isa" which regularly brings together agency staff.

Jimaylya's active role in the reduction of homelessness is in large part due to the Centre's accumulation and maintenance of its linking capital. The relationships between the Department of Housing and Public Works (DHPW) and the Centre is illustrative of the way a small institution can assist its clients by trading on its closely networked position within the services industry in Mount Isa, and enabling former public place dwellers to go on an expedited waiting list for public rental housing. DHPW and other housing service agencies liaise regularly about clients in terms of the waiting list and appropriate available housing.

One of the Jimaylya Centre's strengths is that it is professionally recognized for effective services by many other agencies, which refer clients there. Over the years the Centre's reputation has built up so that its place in the services networks is acknowledged; this reputation extends beyond crisis accommodation for public place dwellers and responds to changing needs of the community and the service providers. For example, for the first time, the hospital recently referred four pregnant Indigenous women without a home to stay temporarily at Jimaylya. Referrals of this kind are made because of the strong reputation of the Centre and the trust in the Indigenous management/staff. The referring agencies are confident that the Indigenous clients will accept the Centre as an Indigenous-friendly place and benefit from the admission. The Centre is keen to help the clients and at the same time demonstrate its effectiveness and maintain its social capital in the services network.

Most clients at Jimaylya have had multiple experiences of recycling through the pathways into and out of homelessness (as depicted in Figure 12.2). In some ways the drinking clients are the most intransigent in the system of homelessness and service delivery; there are attractions for some of them in re-cycling through rather than committing to progressing to permanent housing.

For that proportion of clients who have successfully transitioned through supported tenancies to mainstream housing, the Centre maintains connections through regular visits by its counsellor. Furthermore the Jimaylya manage-ment activates connections to other agencies in its networks (as in Figure 12.5). Jimaylya's management has built up good rapport with Centacare, the largest service agency in Mount Isa and their case managers work with the ex-Jimaylya clients to support them in their tenancies. In this way the clients are able to step out of the cycle of homelessness where previously they might have had to return to Jimaylya. When there is no suitable housing available for long periods, as is often the case in Mount Isa, Jimaylya is unable to readily convert its good practice into housing outcomes—a frustrating situation for the management staff and clients.

In Tennant Creek, social networks between agencies also appear strong and highly significant for clients. The Refuge (TCWR) and most service organizations seem to be following a collaborative or network model rather than a "silo" approach to servicing homeless and "at risk" people in the Barkly Region. In general, two sorts of clients use the Refuge: women seeking respite from difficult living conditions, such as severe crowding, and women who are victims of DV or FV. Many clients have a drug and/or alcohol problem (but clients must be sober to enter the Refuge). Their needs cannot be fully met by the Refuge alone and so integration with other services is critical.

Refuge management and staff maintain constructive relationships with other agencies and with funding bodies in Tennant Creek. For some clients, the Refuge can expedite a move to supported tenancy or mainstream hous-ing but this is highly contingent and not a common occurrence. If there is housing available, clients can be placed in BRADAAG accommodation but they must be compliant tenants and able to obey the rules there (particularly with regard to no alcohol consumption). As the Refuge manager attests, the possibility of housing through BRADAAG exists only because of the close working relationships between the two agencies' management and staff. The senior staff of the Refuge (both Indigenous and non-Indigenous) also have a network of peers in other women's refuge centres in Central and Northern Australia with whom they share practice knowledge, and to whom they refer clients so that their particular needs can be met.

Within the Tennant Creek Indigenous community, kinship relationships are the foundation of social life and people draw on their family "rights" and re-sponsibilities in almost all interactions (Christen 2009). The Refuge also works in this way. The manager is non-Indigenous but strongly connected to the local Indigenous community through her partner and also through her long-term affiliations with the service agencies and with local women (Indigenous and non-Indigenous) engaged with social issues. A major finding regarding the Refuge is that good practice effectively taps into the Indigenous social connectedness and associated social problems. As a long-standing service (since 1989), the Refuge has become an organization that has a good reputation in the Barkly Region communities; Indigenous women have demonstrated their trust by coming to the Refuge with all kinds of problems. An understanding of the trust relationship reveals how the social problems in Tennant Creek and the Barkly Region are in many ways interconnected and moreover that the effectiveness of the Refuge stems from its esteemed place in the region's networks.

The social capital of the Refuge is embedded amongst all its past clients; this is a real strength that can be called upon to provide a wide network of support, including advice or direct action to address community problems as they arise (Memmott et al. 2013, 9). Distinctive forces in the social lives of female clients in Tennant Creek (mobility, crowding, DV/FV, binge drinking) can work against good practice at the Refuge, as can aspects of service delivery in the town (very limited housing stock, other agencies struggling against demand, lack of funding). Accommodation is limited to about seven days for women coming to the Refuge, and in this time frame the Refuge's focus is on respite from the client's crisis situation. The manager can write support letters about a client's housing needs which can be helpful but in general there is "no exit" because the waiting lists for housing in Tennant Creek are notoriously long—recently the manager spoke about a client who has been recycling through the centre for ten years because she has not been able to achieve appropriate rental accommodation (Bracken 2014).

The significance of considering the Refuge from a social capital perspective is a capacity to focus on its values and strengths and the effective role it plays in reducing the impact for women and families at risk of homelessness. If the organization's achievements were viewed solely in terms of movement of clients from crisis into sustainable tenancy then the true positive impact of the Refuge would appear very limited. Yet with strong community links which generate linking capital there is much scope for better outcomes. What is needed is increased funding as well as other resources at the Refuge and also more housing in Tennant Creek in which people can be placed.

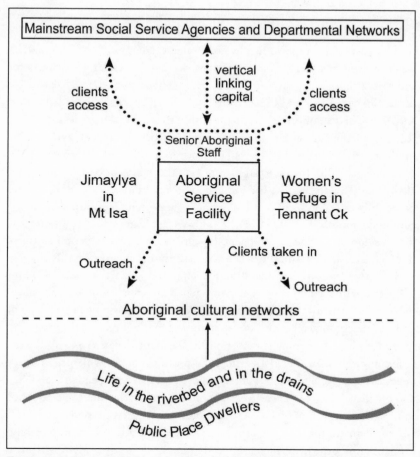

Figure 12.6. Diagram illustrating vertical capital attainment for rough sleepers via Indigenous service facility. Figure by Linda Thomson, Aboriginal Environments Research Centre.

Implications for Policy and Practice

Our chapter findings support the recommendations of our previous research in the regions, and further highlight the value of fine-grained local research (in this case of social networks) to inform policy and practice for Indigenous people. In a recent report on Indigenous homelessness in regional Australia (Memmott, Nash, and Birdsall-Jones 2013), we outlined how policy and service delivery could be improved for the centres under discussion here. In broad terms, we followed the cultural argument for special services and a better understanding of Indigenous homelessness categories but also argued that partnerships between government and service agencies need refinement and strengthening.

In another recent report for the government (Memmott and Nash 2012), we have also explained the policy frameworks that govern service delivery for Indigenous homeless people in the Mount Isa region to contextualize the role of the Jimaylya Centre (JTHC). With its unusual approach to homelessness and managed drinking, the Centre fits within the regional homelessness plan, "Sheltering the Isa," as a front-line service, a tenancy support, and a training institution. Under the Australian Government's umbrella policy of *The Road Home* (2008), the regional plan targets the causes of homelessness and alcoholism. "Sheltering the Isa" indicates a policy framework that values and necessarily relies on local and community-supported solutions, such as the combined approach of JTHC. Relevant policy changes could focus on early intervention and support of Indigenous people who are at risk of homelessness in Mount Isa and also on the necessary institutional support. In this chapter, we have argued for the consideration and support of social networks in Mount Isa to strengthen connections between agencies for the benefit of Indigenous tenants. In particular, the contribution of effective Indigenous management and staff can be increased with targeted support for their roles in the programs.

In a further government report on the Tennant Creek Women's Refuge (Memmott et al. 2013) we identified the pressures under which the Refuge operates (as listed in Chapter 4 of that report) and so recommended that policy and practice changes occur with respect to funding cycles and the amount of funding and other support. We also noted that as the Refuge is unable to meet current demand for women's crisis accommodation adequately, it is seeking infrastructure growth to increase the number of beds. In tandem with this, provision is required for more support staff, particularly younger Indigenous women. This current chapter reinforces the view that the Refuge is operating well despite its funding and accommodation constraints but we also have focused on the capacity derived from its connections to local networks of service delivery. With their professional networks, the majority Indigenous management and staff, as well as women who were past clients together with members of their extended families, provide the basis for an effective local crisis support centre. Some women are eventually able to use the social capital of the Refuge to move out of their cyclical crisis situations.

Conclusion

In profiling good practice in Jimaylya and the Refuge we found that the two centres represented the social issues of their regions in microcosm. The client pathways in and out of Jimaylya pointed to the extent of associated problems in the Mount Isa region and similarly the women (and families) in crisis in Tennant Creek indexed the largely unexplored Indigenous homelessness there. Our research brought forward some significant findings regarding the Indigenous homelessness and service delivery in both regions. In terms of "good practice" we were able to expand on the core service principles of harm minimization, transitional accommodation, and capacity building to include Indigenous staffing and social capital. Our research also clearly demonstrated how each centre has adapted these principles in locally defined ways relying on the efficacy of social networks particularly at the institutional level and within specific parameters of available funding and political opportunity.

The populations that the regional cities of Mount Isa and Tennant Creek service are of contrasting size; Mount Isa region has about 27,000 people and Tennant Creek about 6,000 people, and the cities possess parallel but contrasting services for homeless people. Nevertheless, the cultural lifestyles and circumstances that create pathways into homelessness (regional mobility, visiting kin, and alcohol consumption style) are clearly shared attributes of the two centres. Also shared are the necessary understandings of Indigenous social capital, values and networks, and the "vertical" linking capital from collaborative networks of government and non-government agencies that are leveraged by the staff in the two centres to effectively move clients out of their circumstances. Critical professional values in the two centres highlighted in our analysis are their trust and integrity, values shared with both their clients and other agencies. There are also some structural impediments in both cities for many clients trying to exit homelessness, the most striking of which is the severe shortage of social housing for public rental. Both centres, as a result, deal with recycling clients, providing dedicated attempts over long periods of time in the face of adversity. A hidden danger for a minority of these clients is becoming institutionalized in the centre. With greater understandings of how the social networks are built and maintained, it should be easier for policy makers and funding bodies to recognize the strengths in service delivery and develop ways to reinforce and enhance positive outcomes for the Indigenous regional homeless population.

Notes

1   This case study is summarized from Memmott and Nash 2012.
2   This case study is summarized from Memmott et al. 2013.
3   As summarised in Memmott, Nash, and Birdsall-Jones 2013.

References

ABS (Australian Bureau of Statistics). 2012. *Census of Population and Housing: Estimating Homelessness, 2011,* cat. no. 2049.0, http://www.ausstats.abs.gov.au/Ausstats/subscriber.nsf/0/EB59F237159F7102CA257AB100170B61/$File/20490_2011.pdf (accessed 5 March 2014).

_____. 2013a. "2011 Census QuickStats Mount Isa," http://www.censusdata.abs.gov.au/census_services/getproduct/census/2011/quickstat/LGA35300?opendocument&navpos=220 (accessed 5 March 2014).

_____. 2013b. "2011 Census QuickStats Tennant Creek," http://www.censusdata.abs.gov.au/census_services/getproduct/census/2011/quickstat/702021056 (accessed 5 March 2014).

Australian Government. Department of Families, Housing, Community Services and Indigenous Affairs. 2008. *The Road Home: A National Approach to Reducing Homelessness.* Canberra: Commonwealth of Australia.

Bracken, G. 2014. Personal Communication. 28 February.

Brady, Maggie. 2010. "On- and Off-Premise Drinking Choices among Indigenous Australians: The Influence of Socio-Spatial Factors." *Drug and Alcohol Review* 29 (4): 446–51.

Browne-Yung, Kathryn, Anna Ziersch, Fran Baum, and Gilbert Gallaher. 2013. "Aboriginal Australians' Experience of Social Capital and Its Relevance to Health and Wellbeing in Urban Settings." *Social Science and Medicine,* no. 97, 20–28.

Christen, Kimberly. 2009. *Aboriginal Business: Alliances in a Remote Aboriginal Town,* Canberra: Aboriginal Studies Press.

Hunter, Boyd. 2008. "Indigenous Social Exclusion: Insights and Challenges for the Concept of Social Exclusion." In Proceedings of Social Inclusion Down Under Symposium, 26 June 2008, Brotherhood of St Lawrence, University of Melbourne, Parkville, http://www.bsl.org.au/pdfs/Hunter_symposium_paper_26Jun08.pdf (accessed 1 February 2014).

Kidd, Rosalind. 1997. *The Way We Civilise: Aboriginal Affairs—the Untold Story.* St Lucia, Queensland: University of Queensland Press.

Memmott, Paul. 1991. "Queensland Aboriginal Cultures and the Deaths in Custody Victims." In *Appendix 2: Regional Report of Inquiry in Queensland, Royal Commission into Deaths in Custody,* L. Wyvell, Commissioner, 171–289. Canberra: AGPS (Australian Government Publishing Service).

Memmott, Paul, Christina Birdsall-Jones, and Kelly Greenop. 2012a. "Australian Indigenous House crowding," AHURI Final Report no.194. Melbourne: Australian Housing and Urban Research Institute.

_____. 2012b. *Why Are Special Services Needed to Address Indigenous Homelessness?* St Lucia: Institute for Social Science Research, University of Queensland, http://

www.aerc.uq.edu.au/filething/get/2014/HL_special_services.pdf (accessed 30 March 2016).

Memmott, Paul, Stephen Long, Catherine Chambers, and Frederick Spring. 2003. *Categories of Indigenous "Homeless" People and Good Practice Responses to Their Needs*, AHURI Final Report no. 49. St Lucia: Australian Housing and Urban Research Institute, Queensland Research Centre.

Memmott, Paul, and Anna Meltzer. 2005. "Modelling Social Capital in a Remote Australian Indigenous Community." In *Social Capital and Sustainable Community Development: A Dynamic Balance*, edited by Ann Dale and Jenny Onyx, 105–26. Vancouver: UBC Press.

Memmott, Paul, and Daphne Nash, 2012. *No Wrong Door? Managing Indigenous Homelessness in Mount Isa*, St Lucia: Institute for Social Science Research, University of Queensland, http://www.aerc.uq.edu.au/filething/get/2011/HL_No-Wrong-Door.pdf (accessed 30 March 2016).

Memmott, Paul, Daphne Nash, Bernard Baffour, and Kelly Greenop. 2013. *The Women's Refuge and the Crowded House: Aboriginal Homelessness Hidden in Tennant Creek*. St Lucia: Institute for Social Science Research, University of Queensland, http://www.aerc.uq.edu.au/filething/get/2017/HL_Womens_Refuge.pdf (accessed 30 March 2016).

Memmott, Paul, Daphne Nash, and Christina Birdsall-Jones. 2013. *Indigenous Homelessness in Regional Australia*, St Lucia: Institute for Social Science Research, University of Queensland. http://www.aerc.uq.edu.au/filething/get/2019/HL-Indigenous-Homelessness-in-Regional-Australia.pdf (accessed 30 March 2016).

Mignone, Javier. 2009. "Social Capital and Aboriginal Communities: A Critical Assessment—Synthesis and Assessment of the Body of Knowledge on Social Capital with Emphasis on Aboriginal Communities." *Journal of Aboriginal Health* 5 (3): 100–47.

Oxford Dictionaries Online. Oxford University Press. http://www.oxforddictionaries.com/definition/english/social-capital (Accessed 30 March 2016).

Peterson, Nicolas. 1993. "Demand Sharing: Reciprocity and the Pressure for Generosity among Foragers." *American Anthropologist* 95 (4): 860–74.

Putnam, Robert. D. 2000. *Bowling Alone: The Collapse and Revival of American Community*. New York, Simon and Schuster.

Szreter, Simon, and Michael Woolcock. "Health by Association? Social Capital, Social Theory and the Political Economy of Public Health." *International Journal of Epidemiology* 33 (4): 650–67.

Wright, Alexis. 1997. *Grog War*. Broome, WA: Magabala Books.

CHAPTER 13

"We Are Good-Hearted People, We Like to Share": Definitional Dilemmas of Crowding and Homelessness in Urban Indigenous Australia

KELLY GREENOP AND PAUL MEMMOTT

This chapter is centred on findings from fieldwork undertaken in 2011 in two cities in Queensland Australia: Mount Isa in the far northwest of the state, remote from major metropolitan cities but an important regional centre of industry; and the suburb of Inala in the state capital of Brisbane, in the far southeast of the state (see Figure 13.1). These locations have significant Indigenous populations, both as a percentage of the total population and in terms of overall numbers of Indigenous people, who occupy an important part of the housing stock in both these places. This tenure type was chosen because of the controls and metrics involved in counting, recording, benchmarking, and evaluating Indigenous people in relation to homelessness and crowding in these types of accommodation. The extensive findings of this field research, and of two additional sites in Western Australia, were reported by Memmott, Birdsall-Jones, and Greenop (2012). In that report, and here, we discuss the complex and significant relationship between crowding and homelessness, including individuals living with kin or family and people at risk of losing their housing. We use environmental psychologist Robert Gifford's (2007) model of crowding, characterized by residents experiencing stress, to contrast with the statistical definitions of crowding used in Australia and elsewhere.

In this chapter we interrogate the underlying assumptions behind mainstream statistical, bureaucratic, and governmental notions of home and homelessness which incorporate ideas of how one should live "properly," and

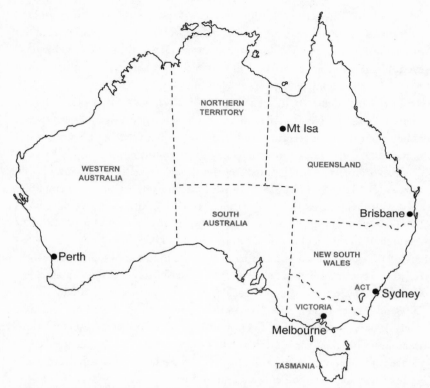

Figure 13.1. Map of Australia showing major cities and the field sites of Mount Isa and Inala (a suburb of Brisbane). Map by Linda Thompson, Aboriginal Environments Research Centre.

the use of "levers" in housing policy to attempt to promote behavioural and other changes. We contrast these government definitions with residents' notions of living "properly," grounded in cultural norms, and the kinds of factors that they believe induce crowding and ameliorate it. Ultimately our discussion aims to examine the cultural assumptions embodied in housing, homelessness, and housing statistics, and to investigate the importance of culturally appropriate definitions in housing analysis.

Defining and Counting Homelessness and Crowding in Indigenous Australia

Definitions of homelessness seek to enumerate, and locate geographically, those people for whom housing is lacking. This in turn enables governments and policy makers to compare changes in homelessness rates over time and hopefully to record improvements in conditions for those who are homeless.

In this volume the terms "absolute homelessness," "at risk of homelessness," and "inadequately housed" are used to define scales of housing need from the most severe, to the least. We approach all three states as forms of homelessness, even though some are more difficult to detect. In other literature this is often termed "hidden homelessness" (see Memmott et al. 2003).

In Australia, the Australian Bureau of Statistics (ABS) conducts and then analyses the Census of Population and Housing every five years, and policy makers and governments adopt its subsequent data and definitions of homelessness and house crowding. This same counting method for housing occupancy is used in the National Aboriginal and Torres Strait Islander Social Survey (NATSISS). NATSISS is a separate and important complementary survey also conducted by the Australian Bureau of Statistics; we have written a commentary on its measure of crowding (Memmott et al. 2012). Key researchers in this field, Chris Chamberlain and David MacKenzie, have discussed the definitions and meaning of the data in numerous landmark works (Chamberlain and MacKenzie 1992, 1998; MacKenzie and Chamberlain 2003; Chamberlain, Johnston, and Theobald 2007; Chamberlain and MacKenzie 2008, amongst others). The ABS and these texts have centred on statistical analyses of homelessness and an overview of populations as snapshots in time. In contrast, our fieldwork and this analysis seeks to understand the lived experiences of housing in order to shed light onto the factors that affect crowding and homelessness in Indigenous communities.

While both the ABS and Chamberlain and MacKenzie acknowledge the importance of social and cultural settings in affecting homelessness and crowding (ABS 2012a, 2012b; Chamberlain and MacKenzie 2008), especially in Indigenous and other non Anglo-Australian communities, it is beyond the scope of their analyses to examine these factors in detail. However, their definitions of crowding and homelessness do imply "correct" ways to live, by identifying norms of numbers and arrangements of people in a house, which of course are culturally derived. The crowding definition utilized by the ABS is based on an international crowding model from Canada, the Canadian National Occupancy Standard (CNOS) (CMHC 1991), rather than one specifically designed for use in Indigenous Australia. ABS definitions of homelessness are based, in part, on circumstances including crowding, but also of course on the cultural notions of home, the implications of a certain permanence of residence, and the exclusivity of household membership.

Chamberlain and MacKenzie have advocated for a culturally specific definition of homelessness (2008), but ABS has not adopted this because it seeks a single robust conceptual model for all Australian homelessness, one that will not change as cultures change over time (ABS 2012c, 15). Yet the ABS definition of homelessness incorporates crowding, which in this case is culturally defined, based on the norms of behaviour and privacy from Anglo-Canadian culture, and deemed a best fit for Australia twenty years ago. This culturally specific definition of crowding depicts a correct way to occupy a house, and these values are presumed to be universal and so are made invisible within the metric. The use of an Anglophone norm is ironic given that large households and crowding are much more prevalent and in need of monitoring in Indigenous communities than non-Indigenous ones. While we agree that definitions should be based on principles rather than shifting benchmarks, the principles adopted should acknowledge the influence of personal, cultural, social, and neighbourhood settings on people's experiences of home, crowding, and homelessness. A truly robust model will include concepts of what constitutes homelessness and its relationship to crowding, and will allow for consideration of social and cultural factors, and personal circumstances that may affect the situation.

In 2012 the ABS did update its definitions of homelessness to reflect the varied experiences of people with housing need, ranging from "rooflessness" or rough sleeping, through "houselessness" which includes people living in sheltered accommodation, to "insecure" housing which includes people living in "extreme overcrowding" (ABS 2012d, 17). Even so, the CNOS still makes up part of this definition, and determines levels of crowding in a house. This volume mirrors the homelessness terms ranging from absolute homelessness, through hidden homelessness, to being inadequately housed. More broadly, there is a recognition of the negative effects of living in crowded houses, and of the effects of poor housing on people's health and other quality of life indicators (Baker et al. 2013), particularly in Indigenous households in Australia (Bailie, Stevens, and McDonald 2012) and in Māori households in New Zealand (Maani et al. 2006).

Coupled with data on the negative effects of crowding on health, there is a fear amongst some Australian government and policy sectors that large households (whether crowded or not) can lead to child abuse and dysfunction, and this has influenced decisions on housing types in recent government housing programs, which specifically aim to reduce Indigenous house crowding (Bardon 2011). It is important, then, to be clear about what constitutes crowding and homelessness and examine the housing factors that may cause illness, stress, and social dysfunction. This has not been well explored in the statistical analyses to date.

If the aim of counting people who are not housed or inadequately housed is to improve their circumstances, then an examination of those circumstances, which are affected by the social setting, is an important task. The definition of crowding, based on Anglophone ideals of a small nuclear family, has seldom been challenged in Australia. This is so despite well-known practices of extended family living, demand sharing, household mobility, and kinship obligations in Indigenous Australia and despite Indigenous Australians being subject to the most crowded housing conditions. Living amongst many other cultural groups, including Anglo-Australians, does not necessarily mean conforming to assumed norms. Crowding is based on a static and a culturally defined measure, rather than a set of principles as to what constitutes the experience.

Funding, Undercounts, and Problems with Data

Definitions of crowding are utilized in allocating federal government funding to state housing providers in Australia and in evaluating their success or failure in providing housing for their populations (AIHW 2011). Meeting targets that reduce crowding presumes that residents will benefit from the consequential improved health, child safety, and household functionality. This is problematic because of ongoing, acknowledged, issues with the serious undercount of both homeless and Indigenous and Torres Strait Islander people in the census data, and therefore in the statistics on crowding and homelessness. The undercount has been presumed to be caused by poor engagement of census staff with Indigenous communities and in recent counts the ABS has put in place measures to reach out more effectively to Indigenous families and households during the census collection. These measures have focused mainly on remote and regional areas rather than metropolitan centres, but in 2006 the census undercount of Indigenous and Torres Strait Islander people was estimated to be 11.5 percent, while in 2011 it grew to an estimated 17.2 percent (ABS 2012a). Establishing reliable baseline data for these counts is therefore difficult, as is estimating any change over time. The undercounts diminish the validity of the data and the basis of it as a decision making tool.

Health statistics for Indigenous Australia are more reliable but they indicate that illnesses typically associated with dense households, such as chronic ear problems and asthma, are among Indigenous people still well above those rates in the rest of the Australian population, despite some small improvements in some areas (ABS 2013b). Health improvements based on hygiene, separation of different genders of adolescents, and other moral concerns have motivated definitions of household adequacy for decades in Australia, and yet we see only small improvements in Indigenous and Torres Strait Islander health statistics.

This persists as typical Indigenous households continue to clash with norms of living and size requirements. The prescribed "proper," healthy mode of occupation in Australia, a typical three-bedroom house, does not fit many Indigenous and Torres Strait Islander families. We argue that it conflicts with the ongoing, dominant cultural obligations of Indigenous people. The origin and evolution of government housing standards that resulted in such a prescription is discussed below, followed by our examination of how housing is used by Indigenous people in two contemporary cities of Australia.

A Brief Overview of Housing Standards in Australia

In 1944 the Commonwealth Housing Commission of the Ministry of Post-War Reconstruction prepared to ameliorate the housing shortage that had built up during the years of World War II. The Commission's report established the occupancy standard for a house, that is the maximum number of people per household based on its size, but this calculation did not sit alone in determining its adequacy. Also included were factors such as size of rooms and land allotment, adequacy of ventilation, and construction standards. These standards of decent housing construction and size were to be met when determining the number of occupants for a house. The 1944 Australian Commonwealth Housing Commission report states:

> It was agreed that the accommodation to be provided in any dwelling must be directly related to the number of intended occupants. This basis, adopted for calculating the number of occupants, is that all adults and children eight years and older shall count as one person, children between eight years and one year of age count as half, children under one year of age do not count. No two persons of the opposite sex eight years of age and over, [who are] not husband and wife, should occupy the same bedroom; the age for sex separation of children, which is less than common overseas practice, has been determined after considering the opinions of various medical and health authorities. (88)

Subsequent to this standard being adopted, a review of housing in the 1970s by Neutze stated that the average household size had declined from 3.8 to 3.3 people per dwelling between 1954 and 1971 (Neutze 1977, 150). In other words, postwar crowding was diminishing and thus the pressure to accept larger numbers of people into a house was reduced. The so-called "over-crowding standard," established in Neutze, importantly acknowledged the need for both bedrooms and living spaces in defining housing suitability. It stated: "Households with up to and including 4 persons need one room per person and thereafter 1 bedroom for each 2 persons with 2 additional living rooms" (Neutze 1977, 151).

We should be mindful however, that at this time while crowding pressures and housing conditions for the general Australian population were improving, the housing standards for Indigenous people in Australia were very poor. The size, quality, and amenity of dwellings for Indigenous people did not have to meet the standards for Anglo-Australians (see Memmott 1988), based on the assumption that Indigenous people must first become assimilated, through a transitional stage of "basic" housing, to learn to utilize Anglo-Australian style housing. The infamous Kingstrand Houses of the 1970s (see Keys 2000) were a case in point and were abandoned by the intended Indigenous occupants, being poorly constructed and totally unsuitable for habitation.

In 1995 the Australian Institute of Health and Welfare (AIHW) began to use the 1991 Canadian National Occupancy Standard (CNOS) as part of its efforts to establish basic conditions that should be met for all Australian housing, on the recommendation of Foard and colleagues (1994). They had evaluated other crowding measures including Neutze's analysis and the British Bedroom Standard, and aimed for a more generous allowance of space entitled to residents from a younger age, as advocated by the Canadian Standard, and in line with the work of King (1994) earlier that same year.

The CNOS is best summarized in table form. As shown in Table 13.1, the main criterion of housing adequacy in CNOS is bedroom density within the dwelling.

Table 13.1. The Canadian National Occupancy Standard for residents.

Canadian National Occupancy Standard Criteria	Bedroom Requirements
General	No more than two people per bedroom
Gender and Age	Children aged under 5, of the **same** or **different** genders can share a bedroom. Children aged over 5 and under 18, of the **same** gender, can share a bedroom. Children aged over 5, of **different** genders should not share a bedroom.
Relationship Status and Age	**Couples** and their **children** should not share a bedroom. A household of one **unattached** individual may occupy a bed-sit. **Single** household members, aged over 18, should have their own bedroom.

Table by Greenop.

King and the AIHW acknowledge that metrics require context and that the CNOS has limitations for reporting on homelessness and crowding. King states: "while lack of agreement about the definition of homelessness would create problems for data collection, the crucial problem is the lack of coverage of many homeless people in major social surveys" (King 1994, 45). Similarly he comments that, while crowding measured using the CNOS was the best match for the Australian norms at the time, "any further work on the physical occupancy of dwellings should look beyond bedroom requirements to consider, for example, matters such as floor area" (1994, 57).

The implementation of CNOS was seen to be an improvement to the minimum housing standards, because the lowered age of "sex separation," to five years old, presumably granted more space to individuals from an earlier age. The need for additional living spaces, advocated by Neutze in 1977, was dropped during the 1995 implementation of CNOS, and the orthodoxy of the three-bedroom, single-living area house continued to dominate the public housing model in Australia.

The postwar reconstruction report (Commonwealth Housing Commission 1944), which acknowledged the intended number of occupants as imperative to the design, seems to have been long forgotten when planning for new housing, especially for large households. Australia still uses the CNOS today to define both housing adequacy and crowding, ironically though crowded housing is not considered inadequate enough to result in granting residents new houses, unless it is "severe." Continued focus on bedroom occupancy to define crowding and its use as a proxy for housing adequacy ignores the non-bedroom-related uses of housing. The size and utility of other parts of the house are not considered: the number of toilets or bathrooms, the number or location of living spaces, the ability for a resident to have a quiet space or room to study, or the relationships of the house's occupants that are not part of housing adequacy or crowding calculations. Avoiding crowding is seen as a tenant's responsibility once a lease agreement is signed, and tenants living in public housing can at times be in breach of their tenancy agreement if their living arrangements deviate from these standards.

The calculability of the CNOS has become an orthodoxy; it is bolstered by its international status as a benchmark but blind to the cultural differences between and within countries in which it is applied. It is so embedded in Australian calculations of crowding and homelessness that it is difficult to replace, and the predominance of statistical comparisons over qualitative analysis prevails.

Gifford's Model of Crowding Including Stress

While we agree that crowding is a problem, we argue that the understanding of what actually constitutes as crowding in Indigenous Australia is more complex than the current definitions of crowding and homelessness allow. We advocate for a resident-centred model of crowding that includes the cultural context within which housing is used. We draw on the broader social psychology definition of crowding, and argue that it is needed to supplement the density-focused measures that have persisted in Australia, in order that we may better assess and improve housing adequacy.

Gifford's model of crowding is based on the concept that crowding is the *experience* of a resident, rather than a measure of the density of people within a house, or the number of people per square meter. He defines crowding as referring to a person's perception of the number of other people around: "Rather than a physical ratio, crowding is a personally defined, subjective feeling that too many others are around. Crowding may correspond to high density, but often the connection is not as strong as one might think...crowding is a function of many personal, situational, and cultural factors" (2007, 192).

Gifford's model incorporates antecedent factors that can include cultural preferences, and affect the experience of crowding. These factors need to be accounted for in contemporary definitions (see Figure 13.2), and we discuss them at length in our other work (Memmott et al. 2011). Similarly situational social factors such as alcoholism, unemployment, and poor health, can also affect people's experiences of crowding. It is important to recognize that housing cannot solve these problems simply by providing every person with the correct bedroom arrangement, as defined by CNOS.

Gifford offers precisely what the ABS is looking for—a model that is based on principles, rather than changing views on homelessness. Existing antecedent factors for both crowding and homelessness which are discussed in the overview of this section include a severe shortage of housing in many Indigenous communities, poor education and subsequent poverty, and ongoing effects of racist policies of economic and social marginalization that affect many Indigenous communities. However, other antecedent factors based on cultural strengths are also present such as cultural value of immersive sociality and strong kinship ties obligating the sharing of food, housing, and company.

It must be said that if stress if a major factor in crowding, then its opposite, lack of people in a house, is an important factor that can cause stress for Indigenous people (Musharbash 2008). Some research indicates that self-reported health status is not strongly linked to large households (Booth and Carroll 2005), and in other cases that protective psychological effects are felt

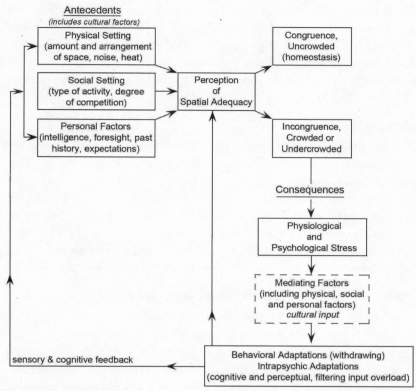

Figure 13.2. An integrated model of crowding including antecedent and mediating factors. Adapted from Gifford (2007, 195, 214, Fig. 7.12).

by Indigenous people in large households (whether they were crowded or not) (Zubrick et al. 2004, 102). Thus a "proper" way of living according to cultural protocols, which affects resident's stress and self-reported health, can be related to higher levels of household occupancy than allowed for by the CNOS.

Reconciling the positive with the damaging effects of living in a crowded house comes from an understanding of the causes of crowding-related disease, which include poor hygiene and poor health infrastructure in the house (Bailie 2008, 59–60; Baker et al. 2013). The importance of the connection between Indigenous housing and health has been well reported by Pholeros, Rainow, and Tarzillow (1993). The landmark Housing for Health program (Pholeros 2002) reports and addresses the effects of the chronic poor construction and lack of maintenance of Indigenous housing, and its strategies were incorporated into design guidelines for remote Indigenous Communities (NIHG 2007). Pholeros wisely recommends that housing be designed to reduce the impact of crowding and involve strategies to reduce stress through culturally appropriate design and provision of sufficient space for all desired residents, rather than reduction of people in the household (2002, 35–37). A key to good housing design for Indigenous people is a better understanding of the expected number of people in households, and the facilities these family members require, including living, bathroom, and kitchen spaces.

Methods

Our field method sought to understand the factors that determine crowding as an experience of stress in Indigenous communities, examining the numbers of people in a house, their behaviours, and the social and cultural drivers that are missing from statistical analysis. Using local Indigenous research assistants, we sought out large households and conducted interviews with the household heads on their own house rules, the interaction with government regulation, and their desires for housing family and kin. We interviewed approximately twenty people at each site, most of whom resided in government housing.

Homelessness among Australian Indigenous People

In his work over a decade ago, Memmott describes the range of people and situations that are included on the Indigenous homelessness spectrum in Australia: "People who move frequently from one form of temporary shelter to another...people using emergency accommodation (such as hostels for the homeless or night shelters), teenagers staying in youth refuges, women and children escaping domestic violence (staying in women's refuges), people residing temporarily with other families (because they have no accommodation of their own) and those using boarding houses on an occasional or intermittent basis" (Memmott et al. 2003, 16).

In the 2012 ABS definitions of homelessness, people in some of the same situations described above by Memmott are termed as being in "insecure" housing, that is, living temporarily with family and friends, having no legal sub-tenancy, having legal tenancy orders enforced, and living at the highest national norm of overcrowding (ABS 2012d, 40). These circumstances existed for very many of the people who we interviewed in both Mount Isa and Inala. While the number of interviews is not statistically significant, the insights the residents offered explain why insecure housing or invisible types of homelessness are a particular problem in Indigenous communities and households.

In the Mount Isa interviews we found that sixteen out of twenty-one households, and in Inala fourteen out of seventeen households, contained "hidden homelessness" or were "at risk of homelessness." The instances of hidden homelessness indicate the importance of family and cultural obligations, and the importance of demand sharing as a continuing contemporary practice (Table 13.2).

Table 13.2. Table of households, resident type, total number of residents, and any tenure problems, for Inala and Mount Isa, 2011.

Mount Isa					
House no.	Extended family?	Large family (4+kids)	Visitors	Total incl. visitors	Hidden homelessness? If so, type of homelessness
1	yes	no	yes	10	no/unsure about tenancy agreement
2	yes	no	no	3	yes - house not in a state of repair fit for habitation
3	yes	yes	yes	14	yes – some adults with no legal sub-tenancy
4	yes	yes	yes	13	yes - some adults with no legal sub-tenancy
5	yes	no	yes	7	yes - some adults with no legal sub-tenancy
6	yes	no	yes	9	yes - some adults with no legal sub-tenancy
7	yes	yes	yes	12	yes - some adults living temporarily with no alternative accommodation
8	no	yes	no	6	no/unsure about tenancy agreement
9	yes	yes	yes	8	yes - house not in a state of repair fit for habitation
10	yes	yes	yes	16	yes - house not in a state of repair fit for habitation; some adults living temporarily with no alternative accommodation
11	no	no	no	1	no
12	yes	yes	yes	11	yes - some adults living temporarily with no alternative accommodation
13	yes	yes	yes	15	yes - some adults with no legal sub-tenancy
14	yes	yes	yes	10	yes - some adults living temporarily with no alternative accommodation
15	yes	yes	no	8	no
16	yes	yes	yes	13	no
17	yes	yes	yes	10	no
18	yes	no	yes	5	yes - some adults with no legal sub-tenancy
19	yes	yes	no	8	yes - some adults with no legal sub-tenancy
20	yes	yes	yes	19	yes - some adults with no legal sub-tenancy
21	yes	yes	yes	12	yes - some adults living temporarily with no alternative accommodation

Inala House no.	Extended family?	Large family (4+kids)	Visitors	Total incl. visitors	Hidden homelessness? If so, type of homelessness
1	yes	no	no	3	no
2	yes	no	no	6	yes - some adults with no legal sub-tenancy
3	yes	no	yes	7	yes - house is in state of unsuitable disrepair: persistent mold and damp problems
4	see no. 15 for repeat survey at time of max household occupancy				
5	yes	no	no	6	yes - some adults living temporarily with no alternative accommodation
6	yes	yes	yes	12	yes - some adults with no legal sub-tenancy
7	no	yes	no	9	yes - legal orders being enforced, eviction was imminent due to domestic violence problems
8	yes	no	yes	9	no
9	yes	yes	yes	12	yes - some children living temporarily with no alternative accommodation
10	yes	yes	yes	9	yes - some adults with no legal sub-tenancy
11	yes	no	no	5	yes - insecure tenancy, threat of legal order being enforced
12	yes	no	yes	9	yes - some adults living temporarily with no alternative accommodation
13	yes	no	no	7	no
14	yes	yes	yes	10	yes - some adults with no legal sub-tenancy; some adults living temporarily with no alternative accommodation
15	yes	yes	yes	17	yes - some adults with no legal sub-tenancy
16	no	yes	no	6	yes - some adults with no legal sub-tenancy
17	yes	no	yes	7	yes - insecure tenancy, threat of legal order being enforced
18	yes	no	yes	7	yes - some adults living temporarily with no alternative accommodation

Table by Greenop based on interviews by Greenop and Memmott.

* Note that "living temporarily with no alternative accommodation" is a situation which can persist for month or years. The situation is considered temporary because there is a desire or a waiting list placement for alternative accommodation, but this may not be a short stay.

Tenants without a Legal Sub-Tenancy

The most common type of homelessness is among adult residents who have no legal sub-tenancy. These can be divided into two categories. The first category comprises of those who hide the presence of a spouse in order to qualify for housing as a single parent. Most commonly, mothers who were the leaseholders did not tell the housing organization that their partners were living in the house. Both adults therefore had to be vigilant to not let housing know about the additional adult, as not only the viability of the tenancy, but the rental rate, which is based on the income of all adults in the household, can be affected. In places where there is an extreme housing shortage, some mothers resorted to moving into a women's hostel to prove their desperation prior to being allocated a house, while their partner stayed with relatives. They did not see this as deceptive, but merely as the step required to getting a house that was clearly much needed. One interviewee stated: "I had to stay in the shelter for two months with the kids to get this house otherwise it would take two years. [My partner] stayed with his sister while we were waiting" (Interviewee MI19). This strategy of moving into a women's shelter, re-categorizes this female householder into a more serious kind of homelessness, that of being absolutely homeless (in ABS terms "houseless") rather than "inadequately" housed as in the case of "extreme overcrowding" (ABS 2012d). The difference between these two states is recognized by housing authorities who prioritize those who are roofless, over those who are insecurely housed.

A second reason for the lack of legal sub-tenancy is the presence of relatives who are "visiting" for an extended period of time, possibly for years, as they wait for a house to become available. Given the willingness of their hosts to accommodate them despite large household numbers, they are somewhat down on the priority lists to receive a house. One Inala resident stated: "Everyone is moving between family all the time. [Tenant's sister] is just moving between family—people move out and go to other family to avoid the place [if it becomes too full of people]" (Interviewee IN18). This sister was moving in a constant pattern between regional centres in Queensland, over a distance of several hundred kilometres between towns, to stay with family as she did not have a safe house to live in because of domestic violence. She also stayed with friends in Inala who were "like family" to her, trying to spread her stays between households to ease the burden on family members.

Legal Orders Enforced or Threatened

Further types of homelessness we encountered included those with legal orders for eviction already enforced or about to be enforced. This occurred in three cases across our two case study areas. These householders had breached tenancy agreements in some way. In one case, a family of two adults and seven children were imminently to be evicted at the time of interview. The parents needed to prove that they had suitable accommodation for the children or they would be taken into state care. The children were subsequently housed in two groups, split between an aunt and a cousin both of whom already had large households. Their parents, who had serious problems with alcohol and violence, were refused accommodation with their siblings and niece and went to a hostel in the Central Business District (CBD). Nevertheless, the aunt, who housed five of the children, stated "I decided to take them on because they are family" (IN9), stressing that this was a choice linked to her family obligations. She also stated, "No one will take [my brother and his wife], they are at the... Hostel in West End—they are drinking and about to get kicked out!" (IN9).

In a contrasting example in Inala, legal orders for eviction were threatened because the combined incomes of the householders had risen beyond housing agency limits. In this case the house had been in the family for over fifty years and the tenancy had been taken over by an adult daughter of the original tenant after his death. She and her own adult daughter maintained the tenancy but their modest incomes rose beyond the maximum threshold, as the main tenant in her fifties reached the peak of her public service career. She was certainly too old to apply for a mortgage, and was unlikely to be able to rent in the area with its limited and increasingly expensive private rental housing. Furthermore this family was highly attached to the house that had been a haven for the extended family for many years. The householder stated, "[My daughter and her husband] will [have to] move out so we can keep the house. It's important to the family to keep the house" (IN11).

This brings the issue of social capital to the fore. A stable and connected household such as this is an important part of the social capital of the area, for not only kin but neighbours and the wider Indigenous community as well. Evicting such people on the basis of income diminishes the surrounding social networks. Notwithstanding the severe shortage of housing for those on very low incomes, the threat of loss of this house and of the family's heritage is a major life stressor for the tenants, and extended kin who could rely on this household in the past as a refuge.

The third case, from Mount Isa, was a tenant threatened with eviction because of the ongoing presence of homeless people camping out in tents in his yard. We discuss this further in the section on neighbourhood crowding.

Homes Unfit for Habitation

A few of the houses we visited had large numbers of residents but also seemed to us, as architects and academics accustomed to examining housing, to be unfit for habitation. This was due to a long-standing lack of repairs and maintenance, the age of the properties, and the large numbers of people who had used the houses over decades, which had accelerated their degradation. One Inala householder alerted us to the damp and mould problem in her house, the structure clearly had major issues with water ingress (Figure 13.3). The mould caused her to have to throw out clothes that became contaminated, and she also claimed that it affected her asthma and other aspects of her health. She stated that her electricity supply was unreliable and frequently shorted out, requiring a lengthy wait for the housing authority to carry out repairs. She saw a likely link between this and the water problems in the house, including a lack of downpipes, and considered the house unfit for living in, but had no alternative accommodation (IN3). Similarly, in Mount Isa there were several houses that lacked proper security such as a closable front door (MI5), and in one dwelling the kitchen tap was unable to be turned off at all and the kitchen was not usable (MI9). Another house also lacked basic amenities such as a working kitchen and beds or mattresses (MI10).

Figure 13.3. Mould in the bathroom of an Inala house, caused by poor initial construction and ventilation. The resident requested to have this documented by researchers. Photo by Kelly Greenop.

These issues are not limited to metropolitan areas and they have plagued the Indigenous housing sector for decades. The Housing for Health movement identified a major problem with the initial build quality, maintenance, and durability of houses in remote Indigenous communities, and continues to advocate strongly for improvements in housing quality (Pholeros, Rainow, and Tarzillow 1993). While the ABS definition of houses unfit for habitation emphasizes structural problems with the housing, the Housing for Health Program, and the subsequent National Indigenous Housing Design Guide (2007) have identified in detail the elements that are required for a house to be safe and habitable. These include functioning places to wash people, clothes, and bedding and spaces to prepare, store, and cook food. We found these elements lacking in some of the houses. Pholeros and Phibbs also identified that, according to ABS data, in non-remote communities Indigenous housing required major repair or replacement in 28 percent of cases (2012, 15). This certainly contributes to a circumstance of crowding, where house fittings and fixtures are so poor that they contribute to general stress caused by the inadequacy of the house.

Sharing and Large Households

The Inala and Mount Isa households demonstrate that they vary greatly from typical households in Australia and that Indigenous cultural values persist in city areas. We deliberately sought out larger or "crowded" houses in these locations, so it is unsurprising that we found large numbers of people in them. However, we could identify the recurring cultural drivers of these visitors and long-term residents to be very consistent across both communities despite the relatively small number of people interviewed in each location. These factors also help to explain why crowding in Indigenous households occurs, why homelessness can be easily overlooked, and why current counting methods do not capture the situations adequately.

Extended Family Life

At both sites we asked people to identify the regular household members, the visitors (as defined by the householder), and the kin relationships between them. While we did identify five houses out of twenty-one in Mount Isa, and seven out of seventeen in Inala that did not have visitors, as Table 13.2 illustrates, there are other factors that we argue typify the sharing and kin obligations in housing. We found that living with extended kin networks was extremely common; we would argue it is the norm, even if only while visitors are staying over, as this occurs often for extended periods or on a very frequent basis. Of the total of thirty-eight households, only four did not have extended kin living permanently or staying at the time of the interview within the house. Amongst these four households, one had recently had extended kin staying (MI8), one was possibly concealing the presence of extended kin due to stress about breaching a pensioner's flat tenancy rule (the bedroom appeared to be made up for two girls, while the tenant had evidently been sleeping in the lounge room) (MI11), one was a large family about to be evicted and not in a position to host family (IN7), and one frequently hosted extended family, but not at the time of the interview (IN16).

It should also be noted that extended family can include very distant biological relationships that are nevertheless socially and by kinship category very strong. Terms such as "brother," "cousin," "aunty," "granny," and "nanna" apply to numerous people beyond blood relatives, who are classified as kin and who have earned respect through investing in hosting others. Closer relationships within a nuclear family are more intense, as an adult daughter and her children frequently live at her mother's house, or a pair of adult sisters may share a house bringing up all their children as siblings. One householder, one of the few homeowners we interviewed, stated that she hoped her son and his pregnant partner would move in with her when the baby was born, so she could help out the young couple and bond strongly with her grandchild (IN8). The grandmother-grandchild relationship is one of the most important and generous in Indigenous families.

Some households accommodated people during the day and for meals instead of at night for sleeping. This can be a stress on some householders, but most feel it is their obligation to feed and provide showers, hospitality, and company to extended kin. One interviewee stated, "My house is pretty much a halfway house! They come over for tucker, pretend it's to visit, but I know what they want, a feed!" (MI20). Visitors may not always forewarn of this kind of visiting, and a frequent comment by householders was explained thus: "People just show up when they come and stay, they don't let you know first!" (IN4).

In the Inala community there were a number of senior women who considered themselves community elders and their identification with the suburb extended to a generosity to its youth and those in trouble. One woman described how "street kids" were welcome at her house and they knew they could come for a shower or a sleep or some food; or that those who did have homes but did not want to return because of family problems, would also sometimes visit or stay. She said: "When people come here they learn respect. If I can help anybody I will. I love this community. Especially travellers who don't know the community" (IN5). Many residents in both places stated that they "would never" and "could not" turn away kin needing either accommodation, food, or company. This was not seen as a weakness but as a cultural strength and a point of pride for most people, despite occasions of stress when houses were inadequate for the numbers, or visitors stayed longer than the house-holder would have liked. People are proud to be known as generous, and for many people this was a key to their identity as an Indigenous person, and they distinguished these from what they inferred were the selfish and materialistic ways of non-Indigenous people who may have larger houses that they did not fill with relatives and friends. One resident stated that when she moved away from family and friends in Inala, to the nearby city of Ipswich: "We got no visitors, but now [that we're back in Inala] we get them all the time" (IN10).

Large Households with More Children

The average number of children per household in Australia is 1.9 (ABS 2013a) and across the national Indigenous population there is an average of 3.3 people per household compared to 2.6 people per household across the nation as a whole, according to census data (ABS 2013a). In our sample we had twenty-two out of thirty-eight households that we identified as having more than four children in the house at the time of interview. It should be noted that some of these children were a part of the extended kin networks and were staying as long-term or frequent visitors to households. This is part of ongoing tradi-tions of strong relationships across one's kin group that are important to both children and adults, so that aunties and uncles, and also cousin-sisters and cousin-brothers want to spend time with their kin and ensure that they have lived with them during their childhood or young adulthood. This bonding also occurs through children being babysat and having playtime with family while their parents work or are busy with other activities. As one Mount Isa resident described: "On a busy day we have twenty-three kids here. They go home at night" (MI13).

Some of the homes that did not have visitors contained families with babies and primary school-aged children, so visitors tried not to burden them with ex-tra people in the house. Some of these householders also had strict rules about no drinking and partying, which may also have discouraged some visitors from coming. Although one householder with strict rules on not drinking and party-ing around the children, calculated that she had had forty-two extra people staying at her house for an extended period over the past five years (MI20). She was proud of her ability to run a tidy and well-organized house with her six children, be able to host visitors, and be a hub of extended family life.

In a reciprocation for the looking after that extended families do for young children, one grandmother noted about her grandchildren who no longer lived with her: "I reared them up...[and now] they just come and sit with me for the day" (MI18). To be alone or worse, lonely, is avoided by most people, and kin are keen to ensure that the elderly are not left on their own, if they do not desire it.

Visitors: Frequent, Long-Staying and Always Welcome

We are good-hearted people, we like to share. Some people don't do that, they don't let anyone stay, they are private and protective of their space...you might need people later on. (MI5)

This resident typifies ideas about what we term "living properly." For her, the sharing of housing (amongst other material possessions) was important as part of her Indigeneity, and she saw this as a key difference between the generosity of her and her people, and the privacy and protectiveness of non-Indigenous people. Importantly though, this generosity is also an investment in the network of social relations that allow people to call on others to reciprocate such generosity at some future time. In this way people frequently visit others, can stay for lengthy periods even if that was not their original intention, and are made to feel as welcome as possible by their kin and social groups. Again, this is not seen as a weakness but as strength, and such practice facilitates important social obligations of connecting with extended family members and visiting places where one may have connections.

Caring for "country," one's inherited homeland, is central to many Indigenous peoples' identity, and constitutes part of their obligations to kin and the wider Indigenous community. The location of one's country may help to determine where a person lives, or induces people to travel long distances to fulfil obligations to both country and family, and to activate their rights to these homelands. Without a physical presence in country at some stage, rights remain as potential, and can fade or be overshadowed by others who are more active at that place (Sutton 2003). Mobility is therefore still a key element in Indigenous cultures, and forms part of the sharing and sociality when people are travelling (see Memmott et al. 2004; Habibis et al. 2011).

Householders we interviewed in Mount Isa and Inala indicated that funerals, family parties, sporting events, and medical treatment also motivated travel, especially when specialist services are only available in cities. Both Mount Isa and Inala people had visitors who were making use of local services not available outside the city, and many also brought travelling companions with them. Having company on a journey is usually desirable and can result in people bringing their children or grandchildren. Medical treatments and similar causes of mobility are often situations of high stress in themselves, thus a swelling of household numbers coupled with a high-stress situation can produce crowding at these times.

While visitors are welcomed, some householders do nevertheless feel the strain of added people in the house. The increased people can stress the available resources including food, electricity (and subsequent bills), hot water, and access to bathrooms. And lack of privacy can be stressful, despite the desire to embrace and oblige visitors. One householder stated: "I do get worried and stressed with too many people in the house, you can't get the house clean, it makes you wild. I just have to wait till people go away. You can't growl at them because they're family. They might think you're rubbishing them or their kids, you can't send them away. You don't want to upset them. You get worried but you've got to put up with it" (MI15).

Social and Cultural Aspects of Homelessness and Crowding

This brings us to the social and cultural aspects of homelessness and crowding that we reported from our fieldwork and findings in Mount Isa and Inala. We found that the commitment to maintaining a house was a strong one, but not stronger than the social and cultural obligations of kin and extended networks. As householders described above, they will often sacrifice the utility of their home to fulfill the stronger and more important values and obligations of their culture, and are proud to do so.

Mobility, both forced and desired is common and affects both crowding and homelessness. Some people will give up a job and a house to fulfill their obligations, which can leave them without secure accommodation, despite often having employable skills and being experienced in the workforce. Conversely, mobility is also caused at times by the desire to find work, and people will also move away from secure housing to take employment, staying with relatives or extended networks if this is convenient for work. The concept of the house as a family "home base" is often not as strong as the concept of social networks providing the security function of home, that is availability of food, rest, and company, and the correct forms of sociality that allow one to relax and be "at home." This means Indigenous people are more likely to move, temporarily or for an extended period, yet, like all people, they still require functioning accommodation wherever they might be.

The well-known concept of Indigenous demand sharing (Peterson 1993), voiced by so many of our interviewees, includes obligations to share housing and the associated comforts of home. Those who give accommodation to others also often provide food, clothing, bedding, and transport. The reciprocity of demand sharing means that people providing hospitality hope to enjoy it in return from others in the future, while not keeping a formal tally of favours given and received. The relationships between particular family members are also framed by sets of mutual obligations, and help to form a fundamental aspect of people's identity through connections. These values persist in Australian cities today, and for many people remain just as strong as in previous generations.

Many interviewees stated that connectedness to family networks and what we have termed elsewhere an "immersive sociality" (Memmott, Birdsall-Jones, and Greenop 2012) is the norm in metropolitan Indigenous households. While actual numbers of household companions vary, there is an emphasis on family members, extended family, and social networks being the dominant contacts for many people, such that their households are very social and can include babysitting, meals with daytime visitors, keeping old people company, and ensuring no one is lonely. This characteristic of sociality means that those who are staying either temporarily or long-term in this way would be unlikely to record their status on census or other documents, as being "without a usual address" (Morphy 2007), and thus they are part of the undercount of homeless people in statistical analysis.

Neighbourhood Crowding

Neighbourhood crowding is caused by people in a neighbourhood behaving in a disruptive manner, often in the public realm or yards in close proximity to others. This phenomenon was noted in both Mount Isa and Inala, at times caused by large numbers of people, and other times, by specific people who affected many others. Feuds between families, public drunkenness, and other problematic behaviour caused neighbourhood crowding at various times in both locations, and we argue that it is both a cause, and a consequence, of homelessness. Some residents reported that people squatting in vacant, derelict housing, and drinking caused neighbourhood crowding, which they described as stress about feeling unsafe or troubled on their streets or in their yards. Some householders seek to accommodate extended family or kin, who have been camping in squats or other public places, so that they are not accosted or jailed. This situation reflects both the lack of housing for Indigenous people, and the cultural value of accommodating people rather than turning them away. One interviewee was threatened with eviction because of the additional people camping in his back garden, who had previously been sleeping in the riverbed. He explained: "I don't want them old people to go anywhere. They got a story to tell about country" (MI10). When a housing department official arrived with a police officer, she explained the housing regulations to the householder: "This house is for you, [your wife] and children only. We are coming back in two or three days time and this yard better be spotless" (MI10). Meanwhile neighbours stated that they had trouble with the noise, fighting, and drunken people from this house invading their yards, despite guard dogs and high fences. They feared for the safety of their children at times, while acknowledging the rights of those people to be in the suburb and being empathetic to their plight.

Neighbourhood crowding reflects larger societal problems of housing shortage, concentrations of poverty, unemployment, and the consequences of damaging past social policies. These past policies include segregation and marginalization from employment and education in remote locations and subsequent welfare dependency.

Strengths Alleviating Homelessness and Crowding

While problems with housing in Indigenous communities include crowding, being without tenure, being at risk of homelessness, and being inadequately housed, many people discussed the strengths they draw upon to overcome housing-induced stress or to ameliorate the situation. In Gifford's model of crowding (see Figure 13.2), this response comes after the initial perception of being "crowded" or "not crowded," but affects the outcome for each person in the situation. In our 2012 report we noted several factors that alleviate feelings of crowding: householders who are able to enforce strict household rules and thus control the house more effectively; careful management of people within households to ensure that culturally prescribed avoidance and companionship protocols are recognized to avoid shaming people or putting them at risk; management of neighbourhood crowding through neighbour-hood diplomacy and the judicious calling of the police to quieten or disperse drunken people or large, loud gatherings or fighting; and withdrawing from crowded households or diverting visitors to other houses nearby (Memmott, Birdsall-Jones and Greenop 2012).

Some of these techniques rely on the very socio-spatial arrangements that can at first induce stress, showing that as in most cultures there are strengths as well as stresses involved in meeting social and cultural norms. A key example is where householders, often women, are assisted to manage the people within a house by their adult children. These women often reported that they found visitors and large numbers of people in their house stressful when they had small children, but as the children became adults and maintained their presence, permanently or regularly within the home, they could "backup" the household rules and advocate for standards of behaviour and cleanliness within the house. Most women over forty (who often had several young adult children by this time) reported that they had become skilled at managing people staying in their house through years of practice. They also found their authority bolstered by the presence of their grown children and other family members in the house. Thus, in some cases, high numbers of the right kind of householders can actually alleviate feelings of stress and thus crowding by maintaining a (culturally) "proper way of living."

Conclusion: Moving Beyond Assimilation Models in Housing Adequacy

Returning to the definitions of crowding and homelessness that have been used and continue to dominate the reporting of these issues in Australia, we argue that these definitions do not currently capture the reality of what constitutes adequate housing for Indigenous people, and do not reflect the cultural and social values that will inevitably affect their housing situation. This mismatch is the result of a dominant view that housing will trump culture, that Indigenous people will, eventually, assimilate into anglophone norms and that the housing will eventually mould the users. This architectural determinism was debunked decades ago in mainstream architecture and environmental psychology, but somehow remains dominant in public housing policy and results in housing that clashes with the cultural requirements of Indigenous residents.

Until the 1970s, assimilationist views held that Indigenous people living in cities and towns were already assimilated, or on their way to being so (Reay and Sitlington 1948; Brereton 1961; Berndt 1962). This is despite reports that large households of extended families were the norm, and that other non-anglophone traditions were observed (for example Brown, Hirschfield, and Smith 1974). And as Morgan (2000) noted in his history of this era, values and traditions were prized and resistance to assimilationist housing policies was strong. Further research by Keys (1999), Fantin (2003), Musharbash (2008) and Fantin and Greenop (2009) indicate that specific, Indigenous ways of occupying housing continue to persist and show few signs of aligning to a CNOS type norm, even in major metropolitan areas such as those within southeast Queensland.

When assessing new measures of housing adequacy in the 1990s, ultimately resulting in the CNOS becoming the standard of housing measure in Australian statistics, King noted a word of warning: "The quality of occupancy concerns further aspects of the relationship between characteristics of the dwelling and characteristics of the occupants...the quality of physical characteristics, such as dwelling type and the presence of certain amenities, can in some cases only be fully assessed with reference to characteristics and preferences of the occupants" (King, 1994, 54).

Gifford's model of crowding as a stress response, and Memmott's approach recognizing the cultural factors affecting homelessness, better reflect the lived experiences of Indigenous people than the ABS metrics, which are problematically inadequate as statistics, let alone as holistic indicators of housing adequacy. Based on our research, the CNOS as a stand-alone measure of crowding does not apply well to the Indigenous context, and it does not account for factors that reduce stress when large numbers are desired, or that increase stress through a general housing shortage or the application of anglophone norms by housing authorities.

We argue that the CNOS has become part of the orthodoxy of measuring crowding in Australia in such a way that homelessness is difficult to measure and does not reveal some of the key problems with housing and urban planning (Memmott et al. 2012). If we do not use the CNOS, we are left with a gap in measurable, comparable data drawn from surveys; however, we would argue that a self-reported housing adequacy response in the National Aboriginal and Torres Strait Islander Social Survey, designed to complement the CNOS Census data, could shed more light on the housing issue than metrics alone. A more holistic approach, in which qualitative data are used in conjunction with quantative data, aligns with decades-old approaches to housing adequacy that stressed the house as a whole, not merely focusing on the bedroom occupation density.

We are not arguing that crowding is a natural state for Indigenous people, rather that housing measures can both hide homelessness as crowding, and measure crowding in ways that imply that the occupants, instead of the housing, are at fault. Housing measures become assimilationist when they continue to prescribe housing need according to Anglo-Australian nuclear family norms, and that such a family will need only three bedrooms, one living space, and will behave in particular ways in their house.

The 1944 report on housing advocating flexible design and the inclusion of sleep-out and verandah spaces, adequate storage, and climatically responsive design principles for the region (1944, 89) seems more enlightened than most of the housing designs we encountered in Inala and Mount Isa some six decades later. Standardized, state-wide models of housing that bring with them assumptions of a small nuclear Anglo-Australian family are patently inadequate for the occupancy levels and cultural values of many Indigenous households. In this sense the definitions that are brought to bear on housing, such as definitions of what constitutes crowding, and who in a community is homeless, are vitally important, and until we can more reliably and sensitively account for these it is difficult to imagine significant improvements in the housing adequacy experienced by Indigenous Australians.

Acknowledgements

We acknowledge first and foremost the contribution of our research participants in Mount Isa and Inala and thank them for taking part in the research project. We also acknowledge the funding provided by the Australian Housing and Urban Research Institute, AHURI, which funded the original project from which we draw our fieldwork material, as well as our co-researchers on that project: Christina Birdsall-Jones, Carroll Go-Sam, and Vanessa Corunna. We also acknowledge the assistance provided by our local Indigenous fieldworkers in Mount Isa and Inala, Mr Keith Marshall and Ms Patricia Conlon. Finally, we acknowledge the support of the School of Architecture at the University of Queensland.

References

ABS (Australian Bureau of Statistics). 2012a. *Census of Population and Housing—Details of Undercount, 2011*, cat. no. 2940.0. Canberra: Australian Bureau of Statistics.

_____.2012b. *Census of Population and Housing: Estimating Homelessness 2011 Factsheet: Aboriginal and Torres Strait Islander Homelessness*, cat. no. 2049.0. Canberra: Australian Bureau of Statistics.

_____.2012c. *Information Paper—Methodology for Estimating Homelessness from the Census of Population and Housing, cat. no. 2049.0.55.001*. Canberra: Australian Bureau of Statistics.

_____.2012d. *Information Paper—A Statistical Definition of Homelessness*. Canberra: Australian Bureau of Statistics.

_____.2013a. *2011 Census QuickStats All People—Usual Residents*. Canberra: Australian Bureau of Statistics. www.censusdata.abs.gov.au.

_____.2013b. *Australian Aboriginal and Torres Strait Islander Health Survey: First Results, Australia, 2012–13*, 4727.0.55.001. Canberra: Australian Bureau of Statistics.

AIHW (Australian Institute of Health and Welfare). 2011. *Government-Funded Specialist Homelessness Services: SAAP National Data Collection Annual Report 2010–11: Queensland*, Technical report, cat. no. hou254. Canberra: Australian Institute of Health and Welfare.

Bailie, Ross S. 2008. "Better Health through Better Housing—This is No Clockwork Universe." In *Which Way?: Directions in Indigenous Housing: A National Conference Shaping the Future of Housing for Indigenous Communities*, National Indigenous Housing Conference, 26–27 October, Alice Springs. Melbourne: RAIA Knowledge Services.

Bailie, Ross S., Matthew Stevens, and Elizabeth L. McDonald. 2012. "The Impact of Housing Improvement and Socio-Environmental Factors on Common Childhood Illnesses: A Cohort Study in Indigenous Australian Communities." *Journal of Epidemiology and Community Health* 66 (9): 821–31.

Baker, Emma, Laurence Lester, Andrew Beer, Kate Mason and Rebecca Bentley. 2013. "Acknowledging The Health Effects Of Poor Quality Housing: Australia's Hidden Fraction." In *State of Australian Cities Conference 2013: Refereed Proceedings*, edited by Kristian Ruming, Bill Randolph, and Nicole Gurran, n.p. Sydney: State of Australian Cities Research Network.

Bardon, Jane. 2011. "Indigenous Housing Staff on $450k: Senator," *ABC News online*, 25 February. http://www.abc.net.au/news/2011-02-25/indigenous-housing-staff-on-450k-senator/1957228.

Berndt, Catherine H. 1962. "Mateship or Success: An Assimilation Dilemma." *Oceania* 33 (2): 71–89.

Booth, Alison, and Nick Carroll 2005. "The Health Status of Indigenous and Non-Indigenous Australians," CEPR Discussion Paper 486. Canberra: Centre for Economic Policy Research School of Social Sciences, Australian National University.

Brereton, J.Le Gay. 1961. "An Estimate of Assimilation Rate of Mixed Blood Aborigines in New South Wales." *Oceania* 32 (3): 187–90.

Brown, J.W., R. Hirschfield, and D. Smith. 1974. *Aboriginals and Islanders in Brisbane*. St Lucia, Queensland: Department of Social Work, University of Queensland.

Chamberlain, Chris, Guy Johnston, and Jacqui Theobald. 2007. "Homelessness in Melbourne: Confronting the Challenge." Melbourne: RMIT Publishing.

Chamberlain, Chris, and David MacKenzie. 1992. "Understanding Contemporary Homelessness: Issues of Definition and Meaning." *Australian Journal of Social Issues* 27 (4): 274–97.

_____. 1998. *Youth Homelessness: Early Intervention and Prevention.* Erskineville, NSW: Australian Centre for Equity through Education.

_____. 2008. *Counting the Homeless 2006: Australia.* Canberra: Australian Bureau of Statistics.

CMHC (Canada Mortgage and Housing Corporation). 1991. *Core Housing Need in Canada.* Ottawa: Canadian Mortgage and Housing Corporation.

Commonwealth Housing Commission (Australia). 1944. *Final Report, 25th August 1944.* Canberra: Ministry of Post-War Reconstruction.

Department of Families, Community Services and Indigenous Affairs. 2007. *National Indigenous Housing Guide: Improving the Living Environment for Safety, Health and Sustainability,* 3rd edition. Canberra: Department of Families, Community Services and Indigenous Affairs.

Fantin, Shaneen. 2003. "Yolngu Cultural Imperatives and Housing Design: *Ramaru, Mirriri* and *Galka.*" In *Take 2: Housing Design in Indigenous Australia,* edited by Paul Memmott and Catherine Chambers. Canberra: Royal Australian Institute of Architects.

Fantin, Shaneen, and Kelly Greenop. 2009. "Sorcery and Spirits: Intercultural Housing and Place in Aboriginal Australia." In *Cultural Crosswords: The 26th Society of Architectural Historians, Australia and New Zealand (SAHANZ) Annual Conference,* edited by Julia Gatley, 1–13. Auckland: Society of Architectural Historians Australia and New Zealand.

Foard, G., R. Karmel, S. Collett, E. Bosworth, and D. Hulmes. 1994. *Public Housing in Australia, cat. no. AIHW 296.* Canberra: Australian Institute of Health and Welfare.

Gifford, Robert. 2007. *Environmental Psychology: Principles and Practice.* Colville, WA: Optimal Books.

Habibis, Daphne, Christina Birdsall-Jones, Terry Dunbar, Margaret Scrimgeour, Elizabeth Taylor, and Megan Nethercote. 2011. "Improving Housing Responses to Indigenous Patterns of Temporary Mobility," AHURI Final Report no. 162. Melbourne: Australian Housing and Urban Research Institute

Keys, Catherine Ann (Cathy). 1999. "The Architectural Implications of Warlpiri *Jilimi.*" PhD diss., School of Geography, Planning and Architecture, University of Queensland.

_____. 2000. "The House and the *Yupukarra,* Yuendumu, 1946–96." In *Settlement: A History of Australian Indigenous Housing,* edited by Peter Read, 118–29. Canberra: Aboriginal Studies Press.

King, Anthony. 1994. *Towards Indicators of Housing Stress.* Canberra: Department of Housing and Regional Development Housing and Social Policy Group, Australian Government Publishing Service.

Maani, Sholeh A., Rhema Vaithianathan, and Barbara L. Wolfe. 2006. *Inequality and Health: Is Housing Crowding the Link?*. Motu Working Paper no. 06-09. Wellington: Motu Economic and Public Policy Research.

MacKenzie, David, and Chris Chamberlain. 2003. *Homeless Careers: Pathways in and out of Homelessness*. Counting the Homeless 2001 Project. Melbourne: Swinburne and RMIT Universities.

Memmott, Paul. 1988. "Aboriginal Housing: The State of the Art (or Non-State of the Art)," *Architecture Australia* June, 34–47.

Memmott, Paul, Christina Birdsall-Jones, Carroll Go-Sam, Kelly Greenop, and Vanessa Corunna. 2011. *Modelling Crowding in Aboriginal Australia*, AHURI Position Paper no. 141. Melbourne: Australian Housing and Urban Research Institute.

Memmott, Paul, Christina Birdsall-Jones, and Kelly Greenop. 2012. *Australian Indigenous House Crowding*, AHURI Final Report no. 194. Melbourne: Australian Housing and Urban Research Institute.

Memmott, Paul, Kelly Greenop, Andrew Clarke, Carroll Go-Sam, Christina Birdsall-Jones, William Harvey-Jones, Vanessa Corunna, and Mark Western. 2012. "NATSISS Crowding Data: What Does It Assume and How Can We Challenge the Orthodoxy?" In *Survey Analysis for Indigenous Policy in Australia: Social Sciences Perspectives*, CAEPR Research Monograph no. 32, edited B. Hunter and Nicholas Biddle, 241–79. Canberra: Australian National University, ANU E Press.

Memmott, Paul, Stephen Long, Martin Bell, John Taylor, and Dominic Brown. 2004. *Between Places: Indigenous Mobility in Remote and Rural Australia*, AHURI Positioning Paper no. 81. Melbourne: Australian Housing and Urban Research Institute.

Memmott, Paul, Stephen Long, Catherine Chambers, and Frederick Spring. 2003. *Categories of Indigenous "Homeless" People and Good Practice Responses to Their Needs*, AHURI Final Report no. 49. Melbourne: Australian Housing Research Institute.

Morgan, George. 2000. "Assimilation and Resistance: Housing Indigenous Australians in the 1970s." *Journal of Sociology* 36 (2): 187–204.

Morphy, Frances. 2007. "Mobility and Its Consequences: The 2006 Enumeration in the North East Arnhem Land Region." In *Agency, Contingency and Census Process: Observations of the 2006 Indigenous Enumeration Strategy in Remote Aboriginal Australia*, CAEPR Research Monograph no. 28, edited by Frances Morphy, 33–54. Canberra: ANU E Press.

Musharbash, Yasmine. 2008. *Yuendumu Everyday: Contemporary Life in Remote Aboriginal Australia*. Canberra: Aboriginal Studies Press.

Neutze, Max. 1977. *Urban Development in Australia: A Descriptive Analysis*. Sydney: George Allen and Unwin.

Peterson, Nicolas. 1993. "Demand Sharing: Reciprocity and the Pressure for Generosity among Foragers." *American Anthropologist* 95 (4): 860–74.

Pholeros, Paul. 2002. "Housing for Health and Fixing Houses for Better Health." *Environmental Health* 2 (4): 34–38.

Pholeros, Paul, and Peter Phibbs. 2012. "Constructing and Maintaining Houses," Resource sheet no. 13, Closing the Gap Clearinghouse. Melbourne: Australian Institute of Health and Welfare and Australian Institute of Family Studies.

Pholeros, Paul, Stephen Rainow, and Paul Tarzillow. 1993. *Housing for Health: Towards a Healthy Living Environment for Aboriginal Australia*. Newport Beach, NSW: Healthabitat.

Reay, Marie, and Grace Sitlington. 1948. "Class and Status in a Mixed-Blood Community (Moree, N.S.W.)." *Oceania* 28 (3): 179–207.

Sutton, Peter. 2003. *Native Title in Australia An Ethnographic Perspective*. Cambridge, UK: Cambridge University Press.

Zubrick, Stephen, David Lawrence, Sven Silburn, E. Blair, Helen Milroy, Edward Wilkes, S. Eades, Heather D'Antoine, A. Read, P. Ishiguchi, and S. Doyle. 2004. *The Western Australian Aboriginal Child Health Survey: The Health of Aboriginal Children and Young People*, vol. 1. Perth: Telethon Institute for Child Health Research.

CHAPTER 14

Enforcing "Normality": A Case Study of the Role of the "Three-Strikes" Housing Policy Model in Australian Indigenous Homelessness

CHRISTINA BIRDSALL-JONES

The present welfare policy climate in Australia tends to follow a punitive theme, and housing policies using the "three-strikes" model are potent examples of this. This punitive theme in welfare policy has been noted internationally in the United States (Karch and Cravens 2014), the United Kingdom (Slater 2012), South Africa (Daya and Wilkins 2013), and Canada (Tonry 2013). In terms of international trends, this appears to be a natural development of neo-liberalism (Hall 2011; Wacquant 2013). According to the relatively liberal outlook of the mid-twentieth century, poverty resulted from the deleterious impacts of the social, economic, and political forces of the wider society, and the global economy acting upon particular groups within society. This outlook resulted in welfare provisioning following a protective theme; wealth should be redistributed, and access to good quality education, housing, and health care should be seen as a right rather than a privilege (Jacobs and Flanagan 2013).

In contrast, the neo-liberal framework views the situation of economic insecurity and diminished life chances which besets the poor (in Australia, Indigenous people in particular) is not understood as the result of the hegemonic forces of a dominant society upon a subculture. Rather, the root cause of poverty is understood as ensuing from the behaviour of the poor, and therefore poverty becomes the responsibility of the poor. Accordingly, current welfare policy in Australia is aimed at enforcing personal responsibility through welfare processes that are both disciplinary (Wacquant 2013) and punitive.

The measures that have been introduced into the welfare policy setting are intended to change behaviour by punishing "wrong" behaviour. Hence, the three-strikes policies.

The three-strikes policy model has been applied to public housing in the Australian states of Western Australia (ABC 2011), which is the concern of this chapter, and Queensland (Queensland Government 2016). In Western Australia (WA), the three-strikes model has been incorporated into the Department of Housing's (WADOH) Disruptive Behaviour Management policy (DBM) (WADOH 2014, 79). The policy (which is explained in more detail further on) sets out three levels of disturbance: dangerous behaviour, serious disruptive behaviour, and minor disruptive behaviour. Dangerous behaviour results in immediate proceedings to evict. Serious disruptive behaviour results in eviction after one verified report. Minor disruptive behaviour that is verified by the WADOH results in one strike, and where three strikes are accrued within a twelve-month period, eviction will occur. The DBM policy has become a significant driver of Indigenous homelessness in WA.

While acknowledging that neo-conservatism is an international development, we should interrogate the local development of this ideology as it applies to homelessness. In doing so, we find that in Australia there is a long-standing stigma attached to public housing tenure. There is a combination of forces and ideologies that lie behind the formulation of housing policy that functions to impose a certain discipline upon Indigenous household behaviour and punishes deviance from a particular understanding of "normalcy."

The three-strikes policy model in housing involves a process of quasi criminalization of some forms of household behaviour. This process of quasi criminalization depends initially on the neighbours. In order for the policy to come into play, members of the public must first come to view the behaviour of their public housing neighbours as so unwanted that it is worthy of the quasi criminalization that flows from the processes of the policy. This portion of the policy model bears some resemblance to community policing, which recruits neighbourhood individuals to report and thereby combat crime. The three-strikes policy in public housing management likewise recruits individuals in reporting and combatting any behaviour that is unliked, and that can be locally attributed to public housing tenants. This recruitment of individuals to police transgressions is an international development that has come into being in the context of the neo-conservative development of "zero tolerance" public policy. This "call to action" from government to citizens can look like vigilantism, if not to the non-Indiginous people, certainly to the Indigenous community (Memmott, Birdsall-Jones, and Greenop 2012).

When the WADOH announced its Disruptive Behaviour Management (DBM) policy, there was an initial wave of reports to the department of sanctionable behaviour (WAEOC 2013). Although this has tapered off to some extent, it is significant that the department reports that in the first two years of its application of the DBM policy, the department received 26,212 reports of sanctionable behaviour (Western Australian Government, Hansard 2013). Of these, 2,609 (9 percent) were verified by the department, and fifty-eight tenants were evicted. There are (not surprisingly) no figures available from the WADOH on the number of Indigenous tenants implicated in these reports, however, one source claims that almost 60 percent of those tenants evicted under the DBM policy between May 2011 and December 2013 were Indigenous (Secretariat of National Aboriginal and Islander Child Care 2014). In addition, anecdotal evidence indicates that Indigenous tenants bear the main brunt of the complaints to the department (WAEOC 2013; O'Connor 2013). If we consider this with the fact that only 9 percent of these complaints were verified, then there is a substantial portion of the non-Indigenous population of Perth who may be using the DBM policy in an effort to remove their Indigenous neighbours.

The DBM policy was not introduced in response to the specific behaviour of Indigenous public housing tenants;[1] however, it has put power in the hands of some individuals over their Indigenous neighbours. Gurney points out Foucault's understanding that power can be productive rather than simply negative, or repressive (Gurney 1999). In the case of the three-strikes policy model in housing, this is certainly true, to the extent that when this model is applied to public housing, it produces homelessness. Gurney's argument is in regard to private home ownership, but what he has to say about the function of tenure to impose "normality" on homeowners is also true of the ways in which public rental tenure enforces "normality" on public housing tenants. He states that: "tenure is imbued with a disciplinary power which normalizes home owners in the same way that Foucault's inmates, orphans and soldiers are normalized. The mechanisms, processes and outcomes of power are, of course, different in this analogy but home owners nevertheless are simultaneously undergoing and exercising this normalizing power" (Gurney 1999, 166).

The same can be said about the power of non-Indigenous homeowners to exercise a normalizing power over their Indigenous public housing tenants. Under the DBM policy, home-owning neighbors can construct a coordinated complaint process aimed at normalizing their neighbourhood by ridding it of Indigenous neighbours. Their complaints apparently are not often upheld by the WADOH, but their normalizing power is still being exerted because in consequence of those complaints, their Indigenous neighbours are subjected to the department's investigation. The Indigenous public housing tenants will experience the force of the normalizing power of their non-Indigenous neighbours whether or not the complaints are upheld.

The next section draws upon research that was carried out as part of a series of projects funded by the Australian Housing and Research Institute (Birdsall-Jones and Corunna 2008; Birdsall-Jones et al. 2010; Memmott, Birdsall-Jones, and Greenop 2012) and took place in the Western Australian towns of Carnarvon and Broome, and in the state capital of Perth. These projects concerned Indigenous housing careers, homelessness, and household crowding. The methods of data gathering included ethnographic interviews, interview schedules, and survey questionnaires. Data analysis was carried out primarily through thematic analysis enhanced by quantitative data gathered in the course of the research.

Mobility and Kinship

The link between Australian Indigenous mobility patterns, homelessness, and household crowding is recognized among Australian researchers and has been examined in some studies (Altman 1978; Birdsall-Jones and Corunna 2008, Birdsall-Jones et al. 2010; Habibis et al. 2011; Memmott et al. 2006; Memmott, Birdsall-Jones, and Greenop 2012). The link between mobility, crowding, and homelessness arises from the cultural imperative to aid and support kinfolk in need. This extends to the housing of kinfolk who would otherwise be homeless.

Studies of Indigenous household crowding are important because one of the primary drivers of crowding in the Indigenous context is homelessness among kinfolk. Not all crowding results from homelessness. For example, funerals bring together hundreds of kinfolk, many of whom must be offered housing by the close kinfolk of the deceased. Generally speaking, however, crowding arising from funerals and other cultural matters (such as ceremonies) is short-term. In contrast, crowding resulting from homelessness lasts for years.

Public housing waiting lists in Western Australia vary from region to region, but in the state capital (Perth) applicants for two- and three-bedroom public housing homes have waited seven to eleven years (WADOH 2013a). While they are waiting, many Indigenous people will live with their housed kinfolk. Because of this, it may appear that the membership of some Indigenous households is quite high, in both Indigenous and non-Indigenous terms, when in fact a significant portion of the members are long-term homeless relatives of the householder.

Indigenous household crowding is a rule driven phenomenon in that it generally occurs according to patterns determined by kin relationships. The access to the homes of relations is founded in what many Indigenous people refer to as "rearing up" kin relationships or the child rearing process, which is multidimensional. Rearing up consists of the experiences of raising the child, growing up as the child, and growing up with the child. These represent different roles and statuses, but what they all have in common is that in order to access the rights accruing to these rearing up relationships, individuals must enact them, the geographical distance notwithstanding. Rearing up relationships are therefore performative relationships (Sansom 1991) and maintaining them requires regular and frequent travel.

Patterns of mobility are the result of long-standing relationships between large kin groups and places. The relationship between Indigenous people and place represents considerable time depth in the multi-generational lifespan of the kin group, and to a lesser extent this reflects the life experience of the individual. The relationship with place depends on a group's history more than on an individual's history because individuals acquire relationships with place through their association with the kin group.

In this section, I will explain in detail how Indigenous household crowding and mobility patterns influence the distribution of homeless Indigenous people over ranges of places specific to individual kin groups. Indigenous people travel regularly and often. Their pattern of movement is defined by the location of kinfolk within a region including, but not limited to their ancestral land which in Australia is referred to as "traditional country." There are two other factors shaping Indigenous mobility patterns. One of these is marriage across kin groups, which provides access to towns within the traditional country of affinal connections. The second is the fallout from 200 to 250 years of government policies specifically aimed at severing the link between Indigenous people and land. These policies consisted of transporting whole communities to places distant from their traditional country and of removing Indigenous children from their families to be raised in isolation from Indigenous culture (Biskup 1973; Haebich 1992; Ward 1987; Hodson 1987).

The work and intermarriage patterns that resulted from the removal policies and processes have opened a much wider and more varied basis for regional association than traditional country. These policies were seriously damaging to Indigenous culture, but were ultimately unsuccessful either in suppressing ties to country or wholly eliminating Indigenous culture. This was, in part, because of the deep structure of Indigenous culture (Sutton 1998). I use the term "deep structure" to refer to the principles of social organization underlying current

Indigenous culture.[2] The particular principle I call upon here is the identification of lateral kin with lineal kin. For example, mother's sisters are equated
with mother, and the mother's sister's children are equated with siblings. As
I will show, this principle has far reaching effects on Indigenous social life.

Particular configurations of kin relationships may vary between language
groups, but the overall form of the operative collectivity of kinfolk may be
characterized as a family community (Birdsall 1988). This is a tightly knit set of
kinfolk who cooperate socially, economically, and politically. In most Western
Australian town and city dwelling groups, this family community is recruited
ambilineally but with a matri-bias from a large group of cognatic kinfolk all
claiming descent from a named apical ancestor.

The set of towns and cities among which the family community is distributed and between which kinfolk travel is termed "mobility range" by
anthropologists (Memmott et al. 2006). The places within a mobility range
can be hundreds of kilometres from each other and this presents a problem
for maintaining social organization and unity of a kin group. The only way
to resolve this problem is regular and frequent travel among the towns of the
claimed region.

Aboriginal social life is bounded by an institution of reciprocal obligation.
Rules of common practice define the rights and obligations pertaining to specific role relationships, for example, mother and dependent child, dependent
child and mother, and in the adult years, mother and son, mother and daughter,
daughter and mother, son and mother, and so on (Birdsall 1988). Among the
town and city groups of my acquaintance, women and girls in particular refer
to their female matri-cousins as sisters. In one inland group, the Wajarri of
the Burrungurrah community, this identification of cousins with siblings is
more clearly bilateral. Here, cousins are referred to as "cousin-brothers" and
"cousin-sisters" (Habibis et al. 2011). In any case, these are strong relationships
maintained by regular visits. In consequence, these relationships tend to shape
the overall pattern of visiting, and create the avenues of support that are available to people in times of need (Birdsall-Jones and Corunna 2008; Habibis et
al. 2011; Memmott, Birdsall-Jones, and Greenop 2012).

People visit one another for a variety of reasons. Generally the reason is
reflective of gender and time of life. Women visit their adult daughters to
maintain a strong role in the upbringing of their grandchildren. If the daughter
lives in a place dominated by her in-laws, her mother will visit to ensure that
her daughter's rights are protected. These include a woman's right to respect,
personal safety, the economic integrity of her household, and her right as a
mother to hold the primary authority in regard to her children. Women also

visit their mothers and sisters to ensure their children's ongoing relationship with their extended family. Older adolescent boys and young men spend a number of years travelling widely, usually around the broad region known to their own extended family, but some may travel more widely still. Usually there comes a point at which young men judge that this time of life is over, and they return to their home communities to settle down. Some men become involved in Indigenous law matters[3] and may continue to travel extensively around their region. The most general reason for visiting is for funerals, which concern all age groups of both genders. All of these reasons for travelling are expressive of Indigenous culture (Birdsall-Jones and Christensen 2007; Habibis et al. 2011; Memmott, Birdsall-Jones, and Greenop 2012).

People also travel for a variety of reasons that arise from social interactions with the wider society. For example, they may need to visit kinfolk in a hospital or in a prison, or for reasons connected with their own or their children's health, education, and recreation, such as sporting events. The agency driving the mobility in such circumstances arises outside of Indigenous culture; however, the activities themselves are a part of Indigenous social life and are carried out in a way that involves kin lines. As such, they provide reasons for travel that are socially rather than culturally legitimated. Another socially legitimated form of mobility occurs when people are forced to find shelter in the homes of kinfolk. Most Indigenous people live in poverty and have few or no savings to draw upon in the event of an unexpected expense, which happens from time to time over the career of any household. When this happens in Indigenous households, it may lead to the loss of housing directly through nonpayment of rent, or indirectly through nonpayment of water, gas, or electricity bills rendering a house uninhabitable. On such occasions, Indigenous people ordinarily will call on their housed kinfolk to provide them with housing. They use the rules governing kin-based relationships in Indigenous society in this process. However, the need itself does not arise out of Indigenous social structures but out of the relationship between Indigenous society and the wider Australian society. The visiting they do on the basis of Indigenous culture and society serves to strengthen the relationships that Indigenous people call upon in times of need. This is regarded as a legitimate use of kin relationships (Birdsall-Jones and Christensen 2007; Birdsall-Jones et al. 2010; Memmott, Birdsall-Jones and Greenop 2012).

Circumstances in which women in particular will be forced to call upon their housed kinfolk are those that involve deserting their own houses suddenly, with haste and in a state involving high emotion. Women in mourning and women escaping domestic violence may respond to their situations by leaving their homes having made no plan for their absence. This is because the nature of death and domestic violence do not lend themselves to planning. In these circumstances, a woman will precipitately leave the home, and leave it unoccupied. An empty house invites vandalism and when the WADOH finally learns that the house is unoccupied and more or less severely damaged, the woman's tenancy will be cancelled and she will be charged for the cost of repairs to the house. Until she has repaid her debt, in the thousands of dollars, she is ineligible to apply for another WADOH home. Women and children can be made homeless for years in this way.

Grey Areas

The distinction between homelessness and visiting is sometimes difficult to see. For example an extended period of travel and a certain amount of irresponsible behaviour is expected from older adolescent boys and young men (who are collectively referred to as "the boys"). Not unusually, they drink to excess and can be noisy and unruly in consequence. This is within the expected range of normal behaviour for the boys. However, their behaviour quite often goes outside the limits tolerated by households and then the boys must move on. For the period of their grand tour, they appear to be homeless; however, they can go back home any time they wish (Birdsall-Jones et al. 2010; Memmott, Birdsall-Jones, and Greenop 2012). This situation displays characteristics of homelessness as well as visiting. It also exemplifies a culturally legitimated range of normal behaviour, and a culturally non-legitimated imposition on the domestic resources of the family community. There is one other cultural driver of Indigenous homelessness.

Deserting the home is a well-known response to a death in the family in some north Australian Indigenous communities. The practice of deserting the home on account of a death within the household varies among groups. In the south, it is not usual, whereas it is more common in the north and in the eastern desert areas of the state. The appearance of traditionality is not a useful indicator of the commonality of the practice. Indigenous people in the large mining towns of the Northwest may choose to withdraw from the house when a member of the household dies. In the more tradition-oriented communities of the Fitzroy River Valley, east of Broome, some people do it, but others choose not to. It is best to regard deserting the house in response to the death of very close kin as being within the lexicon of expressing grief among Indigenous people.

In the course of a research project investigating homelessness in the north-west coastal town of Broome (Birdsall-Jones et al. 2010), one of the participants was a man from a Fitzroy River Valley community who had been brought up from a very young child by his older sister who was therefore like a mother to him. When she died, he said that he simply could not go on living in the home that he and his female partner and children had shared with her. This man and his female partner decided to leave their jobs in their community and make their home in Broome.

Some of "the boys," the man's cousin-brothers, came along so that the man would not be "too sad" while he was getting over the death of his sister. Together, they went first to the female partner's aunt's house. Because they were in Broome, the boys wanted to get drunk and have parties. When this started, the aunt requested that the man and his female partner make the boys leave. Because the boys had come with them especially to be with their cousin-brother, the man and his wife felt obliged to leave the house with them. They had nowhere else to go and so they arranged with the aunt that the children remain with her, and then took the boys with them to make a camp together in the sand hills across the road from the big hotels along Roebuck Bay.

You Can't Say No to Your Family

The couple were obligated to the six young male cousins of the man because they came to "keep him company." Although the boys were enjoying themselves, they also had a duty, which was a matter of sincere feeling. They had to watch their cousin-brother to make sure he did not become "too sad." Part of the mourning response to the death of very close family in their Indigenous society is that the principal mourner may not eat properly. One of the women informed us that for some period of time a person who is this sad will not feel able to eat meat and will choose to eat only fish. If this goes on too long, someone has to do something about it, and the way this happens is that someone must push some meat into his face so that he'll get the smell of it and he'll want to eat meat again. The person who would do this would most likely be one the man's cousin-brothers.

In any case, the couple were bound culturally to accept responsibility for these young men as long as they reasonably could. Even though they were camped in the sand hills instead of living with their children in the aunt's house, they accepted this. Smiling, the woman said, "You can't say no to your family," and the man nodded, and repeated after her, "You can't say no to your family."

However, there are circumstances which will make it more likely that people will say no to their family. One such circumstance occurred, at the woman's aunt's house, when a group of the boys exceeded the limits of the householder's tolerance for drinking and related behaviour. In addition to this, research has revealed differences according to tenure among Indigenous people regarding the practice of housing kinfolk on demand. Some Indigenous people who own their own homes appear to be more likely to deny housing to their homeless kinfolk than are those who rent from the public housing provider. This extends to kinfolk who are casual visitors and have housing elsewhere (Szava and Moran 2008). Indigenous people who are employed and have private rental housing also report controlling access to their homes in this way (Birdsall-Jones and Christensen 2007). This is not a complete denial but rather controlled access. It is not surprising, given the way that kin obligation is embedded within Indigenous culture, that both employed Indigenous people in private rental housing and Indigenous homeowners have difficulty in explaining their reasoning to their kinfolk who expect to be housed upon request, as in this statement from an Indigenous homeowner: "Sometimes it is hard to own a place: it goes against trying to help your family and people; I can starve to pay the loan but how do you explain that to other people [i.e., family]?" (Szava and Moran 2008).

Kinship obligation is thus one of the strongest agents that shape the structure of Indigenous household membership, the density of household occupancy, and patterns of mobility. Alcohol, similarly, acts as an agent here. The next section examines how alcohol and drug abuse produce generational cohorts of homeless Indigenous people.

Alcohol and Drug Abuse within the Home

On account of alcohol abuse, the home may become a venue for gatherings resulting in intoxication and sometimes violent behaviour, which may include the physical and sexual abuse of women and/or children in the household. Children are particularly vulnerable when their parents are not in a condition to be sufficiently aware of what is happening in their home. In response to these circumstances, children may leave home.

If this behaviour is temporary and if the circumstances improve, the children return. However, if the home continues to operate as a venue for alcohol and/or drug abuse, these circumstances may drive the children away permanently. Some children in this situation find shelter with various kinfolk around town. In the process they may learn to protect themselves through fighting, and support themselves by engaging in "humbugging"[4] and breaking and entering. As a consequence of fending for themselves by these means, they become involved with the judicial system. Hardened by their life on the street, jail is not necessarily a fearful prospect for these children. Indeed, prison can represent a semblance of stability for them. Some say they look forward to it because of the provision of regular meals and good accommodation in the juvenile justice system. When this occurs, it can set future behavioural patterns leading to a cycle of arrest, conviction, and imprisonment over an individual's life. This cycle makes it very difficult for such an individual to maintain rental tenure, either public or private. Therefore, in turn, the cycle of arrest, conviction and imprisonment sets up a lifestyle of homelessness. On account of this, nighttime street roaming and home abandonment in childhood creates a population of long-term, if not permanent, homeless adults.

People may take up a lifestyle in which substance abuse becomes the dominant theme. As a result, they abuse their kin-based relationships as well as their substance of choice. Children whose parents are devoted to this lifestyle may leave home because of the violence and disorder that occurs in the wake of drinking parties and drug taking. While these children may begin by moving among the homes of their kinfolk within the town, some will travel far more widely around the region of their extended family as they grow older.

Meanwhile, the substance-abusing adults may lose their homes through nonpayment of rent or by falling afoul of the DBM policy. They will have to call on their housed kinfolk to obtain shelter. Given their compromised lifestyle, their presence in a household is too disruptive to be tolerated in the long-term, and, after a time, they will be asked to move on. Because they have no homes of their own, they travel widely around the region of their extended families staying with various kinfolk, progressively wearing out their welcome and moving on as they go. Rarely, they may refuse to move on and back this up with violence or the threat of violence. In these circumstances, the habitability of the home declines and individuals may desert the home to find safer shelter elsewhere.

The substance abusers utilize the same network of kin relationships as do those who have fallen on hard times. However, this way of using kin relationships is not regarded as legitimate, and despite the fact that kin relationships structure the pattern of mobility among substance abusers, this behaviour is not regarded as an expression of Indigenous culture by Indigenous people (Birdsall-Jones and Corunna 2008).

A Typology of Legitimation in Mobility and Housing

In general terms, we see here three types of mobility: culturally legitimated, socially legitimated, and that which is not legitimated. Visiting of the kind listed in the table above has the effect of strengthening the bonds of kinship and Indigenous culture. The practice of providing shelter to kinfolk in need of housing is one of the reasons that the bonds of kinship and culture must remain strong and the process of strengthening them must be ongoing.

Table 14.1. Drivers of mobility and associated housing requests

Culturally legitimated visiting	Socially legitimated housing requests	Non-legitimated
To maintain strength of relationship among kinfolk	Loss of housing through unexpected expense, unable to manage household economy, failure to pay rent/bills	Loss of housing through failure of household economy, domestic disorder owing to substance abuse lifestyle
Law business	Loss of housing amenity	Inability to secure ongoing membership in a household because of effects of substance abuse
Funerals	Abandonment of home to escape violence or abuse	
Deserting the home of an important deceased family member	School or sporting events, health and medical needs, etc.	

The non-legitimated pattern of mobility is connected with the substance abuse lifestyle and utilizes the same Indigenous social structures as the culturally and socially legitimated patterns of mobility. However, it puts great strain on the network of kin relationships and expends the resources of households to no good purpose. Kin networks which experience this kind of strain may be unable to perform some of the most important functions of Indigenous extended family groups—principally to support family members who need help for legitimate reasons, particularly women and children escaping from violence or who have suffered the loss of their own housing through other causes.

All of these patterns of mobility can lead to household crowding, which can be short- or long-term. For example, there are many instances in which people who intended to make a limited-term visit for a legitimate purpose get "stuck": their car breaks down and they can't afford to have it repaired; the people they got a lift with become unavailable for the return journey; or due to unforseen circumstances they haven't the money for the return bus fare. While people are stuck, they are homeless and must either rely on their kinfolk's continued willingness to house them or live out of doors.

The reason for distinguishing social causes from cultural causes is to properly understand Indigenous mobility and homelessness. Mobility arising from cultural motivations generally serves to strengthen the fabric of Indigenous society by permitting people to perform their obligations to their kinfolk in a positive way. Mobility arising from agents of mainstream Australian society, that is, from the Indigenous response to the ways in which the wider society deleteriously impacts the Indigenous world, may not serve such a constructive purpose. Indigenous people must depend on their networks of kin in times of need, but they must spend their own social capital to do so. As well, the kinfolk on whom they rely are placed at a disadvantage with regard to housing amenity and household economic organization when this happens.

There are two cultural drivers of Indigenous homelessness and these are: home abandonment in response to the death of a beloved member of the household and the "grand tour" undertaken by the boys. All other drivers of Indigenous homelessness come from the interaction of Indigenous people with wider society. The management of homelessness within Indigenous society depends on strong, viable kin relations. In order to produce and maintain these relations, Indigenous people engage in patterns of visiting. The destinations and the frequency of these visits are carefully calculated with the objective of achieving the sufficiency of contact among kinfolk necessary to maintaining key kin relations over the long-term life of the family community. In the next section, I add the element of the WADOH's DBM policy to the matrix of factors that induce homelessness in Indigenous communities.

Policy-Driven Homelessness

The three levels of disturbance and penalties set out in the WADOH's DBM policy are described in the WADOH Rental Policy Manual (2014, 79–70):

- Dangerous behaviour is defined as activities that pose a demonstrable risk to the safety or security of residents or property; or have resulted in injury to a person in the immediate vicinity with subsequent police charges or conviction.

- Serious disruptive behaviour is defined as activities that intentionally or recklessly cause serious disturbance to persons in the immediate vicinity, or which could reasonably be expected to cause concern for the safety or security of a person or their property.

- Disruptive behaviour is defined as activities that cause a nuisance, or unreasonably interfere with the peace, privacy or comfort, of persons in the immediate vicinity.

Dangerous behaviour and serious disruptive behaviour both result in immediate eviction proceedings. Each substantiated instance of disruptive behaviour results in a "strike" being placed against the tenant. If three strikes are accumulated in one twelve-month period, eviction proceedings will commence.

The WADOH Rental Policy Manual includes a clause stating that "where strong mitigating circumstances exist, the matter may be referred to the Executive Director Client Services for approval to manage the situation through alternative action" (WADOH 2014, 80). To date, however, there are no reported instances of any matters that have been so referred (WAEOC 2013; Shelter WA n.d.). There have been, though, a number of evictions that have involved tenants with serious health issues, and two in which the tenant died resulting in the withdrawal of the complaints (WAEOC 2013, 57).

The policy in its present form was introduced in 2011 and since then, there have been a steadily rising number of evictions, primarily of Indigenous tenants by the public housing provider (ABC 2011; Harris 1995). Research interviews undertaken in 2011 suggest that the majority of evictions occur as a result of minor disruptive behaviour such as noisy children, loud parties requiring police attendance, and domestic disputes (Memmott, Birdsall-Jones, and Greenop 2012).

Triggering the Disruptive Behaviour Management Policy

Within the everyday life of the family community there are several agents that can trigger the complaints that lead to the application of the DBM policy, but the events leading up to the moment of that trigger involve long social processes. The children who leave home to escape abuse from alcohol- and drug-addicted adults grow up. In the course of growing up, some of them will become alcohol and drug addicts and adopt a lifestyle that prevents them from finding homes of their own and so they will be homeless. They will demand shelter from their housed kinfolk, and some of those kinfolk will allow them to stay. As adults, they will engage in the kind of behaviour that drove them from home when they were children. This behaviour will trigger complaints from the neighbours, visits from the police, and the summary eviction of the tenant in response to the dangerous and serious misbehaviour classifications in the DMB policy. This is essentially what happened to a participant in the household crowding study: "This woman, partner and family are currently homeless on account of the way the '3 strikes' policy works. An incident that is classed as serious results in immediate eviction. Some of her extended family carried out a home invasion ransacking the house and punching the woman and her sisters when they tried to stop them. The family now shifts between the houses of 3 relations, her 2 sisters and one of his brothers. When that's not possible they sleep in the car in sheltered locations such as under bridges or 'out in the bush somewhere'"(Notes of Interview 1, 14 November 2012).

The incident to which these notes refer to was determined to be dangerous behaviour as defined in the WADOH Rental Policy Manual. The activities posed a "demonstrable risk" to the safety of residents, in particular the tenant and her family, and did result in "injury to a person in the immediate vicinity," again, the tenant and her family. "Subsequent Police charges or conviction"were carried out against the perpetrators of the home invasion, and since this was the case, the tenant and her family was evicted. This participant's experience is not an isolated instance of punishing the victim in such situations. Elderly and ill Indigenous tenants are particularly vulnerable to home invasion and other less severe activities which fall into the category of humbugging. On account that these actions upset their non-Indigenous neighbours, these tenants tend to be evicted (O'Connor 2013).

Interviewees spoke about the way in which Indigenous culture is contravened by the DBM policy. Indigenous people are obligated as a matter of culture to house their homeless kinfolk, but the application of the DBM policy in response to this threatens them with eviction. For example, in answer to my question "how do you cope with this situation?" one woman responded: "One big happy family! Well, that's the way I see it. You know, we help each other out, and that's it. But I had Homeswest [WADOH][5] come and everyone condemn you, about [a group of kinfolk that] was there" (Interview 2, 11 November 2012). This woman was providing housing in her WADOH home for four other adults and eleven children, nine were her nieces and nephews, and two her own children. They ranged in age from two to seventeen. The children were noisy and so she accumulated three strikes. At the time of her interview she was in court proceedings to appeal her eviction notice from the WADOH. She is one of those Indigenous public housing tenants that white neighbors do not want on their street:

> They [neighbours] just said they don't want an Aboriginal family
> next to them, that's what it is. The neighbours, when we first moved
> in, they didn't want two Aboriginal families [can't make this word
> out], and I told them [WADOH] from the start not to put me in a

place like that. Where there was going to be that kind of trouble...
we had to put up with these neighbours complaining about every
little thing. They were swearing me and all it was, me looking at
their Labrador, that was running out the front. And Gemma and
Girelle was sitting out with front, waiting for Malika to bring the
other kids to come home from school. And the man across the road
started swearing at her. So I got one more. You know? It's ridiculous
(Interview 2, 4 November 2012).

Many tenants accumulate strikes when kinfolk come to stay for funerals.
On one occasion Indigenous householder's white neighbours became alarmed
when a number of her relatives came to visit for a funeral, apparently assuming
they were there to take up residence: "She's got 1 strike from DOH essentially
for accommodating her family. She had herself, her partner and their kids, her
brother and sister in-law, her niece with her de facto and their daughter, her
niece and her son. This kind of thing happens only for funerals mainly and
once for the old man's birthday" (Notes of Interview 3, 7 November 2014). It
remains to be seen whether or not practices that are deep-seated in Indigenous
culture will change in response to the DBM policy. There is some evidence to
suggest this. Interviewee 7, above, said, at one point, that until that one strike
was removed from her record with WADOH, she would not let any of her
family stay in her home. This is a question of whether one should or should not
have to contravene the dictates of Indigenous culture. Could one adhere to the
dictates of respect for family that constitutes one of the strongest themes in
Indigenous culture, without provoking the DBM policy, thereby putting one's
own housing in danger? These effects of the policy were predictable, and the
misgivings the policy's introduction excited, appear to be playing out.

What is happening here is place-defending, a phenomenon described by
Nelson (2014) in the context of community action against racism. However, she
notes that place-defending may also be motivated by "the desire to maintain a
cultural status quo, or a desire to protect a place from outsiders" (Nelson 2014,
75). Her case in point is the Cronulla riots, which took place in South Sydney
in 2005, involving young white Australian men in open conflict with young
men who were the children of migrants from Middle Eastern countries. In the
Perth suburbs, white Australian homeowners are responding to the presence
of Indigenous public housing tenants whom they view as belonging "outside"
the boundaries of their neighbourhoods, physically, behaviourally, and culturally. This place-defending arises out of the long-standing prejudice of a certain
proportion of white Australians against Indigenous people, which bears some

resemblance to moral panic. A moral panic occurs when a course of events becomes demonized in the public consciousness. This particular moral panic might be said to underlie non-Indigenous Western Australia's relationship with Indigenous people. In response to acts interpreted as a threat to the terms of that relationship—which involves the ongoing hegemony of the ruling non-Indigenous class—white prejudice and moral panic is brought to the surface with surprising facility (Jones 1997; Shaphan et al. n.d.).

In addition to place-defending, and ongoing but subsurface moral panic, we are also dealing here with a stigmatized housing tenure, public housing, and a stigmatized people who live primarily in the stigmatized public housing. People are, or tend to be, concerned that their neighbours are public housing tenants (Palmer et al. 2004; Troy 2011; Arthurson 2002, 2004; Arthurson and Jacobs 2004). They become all the more concerned when their public housing neighbours are Indigenous (Dufty 2009; WAEOC 2013).

Notes

1   The DBM policy was intended to be the state government's response to the moral panic that ensued when a methamphetamine lab blew up in a WADOH flat. It turned out that there had been a long series of complaints from neighbours about the activities of the tenants in that flat, but the WADOH had made no response. The Minister for Housing brought in a bill that made changes to the public tenancy law empowering, and requiring, the WADOH to evict tenants according to the formula outlined in this discussion (Emerson 2011; Rickard 2011).

2   This usage has a somewhat more direct relationship with Chomsky's original usage of the term than is generally the case in some social science literature (Myers 1987). While he eventually abandoned the notion of "deep structure" (Zwart 1998), Chomsky's usage indicated a linguistic formulation of "deep structure" as defining the core semantic relations of a sentence which are reflected in the surface structure (Harris 1995; Chomsky 1995; Chomsky, Hauser, and Fitch 2005). My usage indicates that the principles underlying social organization are reflected in the arrangements of social relationships.

3   These principally concern manhood ceremonies and the activities surrounding them.

4   Humbugging means to engage in increasingly menacing demands in order to obtain money or goods from another person.

5   Homeswest was the name used by the WADOH for its public housing management directorate between 1985 and 1999. Since then the public housing directorate has been called the Ministry of Housing (1999-2001), and the Department of Housing and Works (2001-2009). Since 2009 it has been called the Department of Housing (WADOH 2014).

References

Altman, J. 1978. "Crowding: Historical and Contemporary Trends in Crowding Research." In *Human Responses to Crowding*, edited by Andrew Baum and Yakov M. Epstein, 141–50. Hillsdale, NJ: Lawrence Erlbaum.

Arthurson, Kathy. 2002. "Creating Inclusive Communities through Balancing Social Mix: A Critical Relationship or Tenuous Link?" *Urban Policy and Research* 20 (3): 245–61.

＿＿＿. 2004. "From Stigma to Demolition: Australian Debates about Housing and Social Exclusion." *Journal of Housing and the Built Environment* 19 (3): 255–70.

Arthurson, Kathy, and Keith Jacobs. 2004. "A Critique of the Concept of Social Exclusion and Its Utility for Australian Social Housing Policy." *Australian Journal of Social Issues* 39 (1): 25–40.

ABC (Australian Broadcasting Corporation). 2011. "Concerns Evictions Could Increase Homelessness." Australian Broadcasting Corporation, 22 March, http://www.abc.net.au/news/2011-03-22/concerns-evictions-could-increase-homelessness/2647338.

Australian Human Rights Commission. 1996. *Indigenous Deaths in Custody 1989 to1996: A Report Prepared by the Office of the Aboriginal and Torres Strait Islander Social Justice Commission for the Aboriginal and Torres Strait Islander Comission*, https://www.humanrights.gov.au/publications/indigenous-deaths-custody.

Birdsall, Chris. 1988. "All One Family." In *Being Black: Aboriginal Cultures in "Settled" Australia*, edited by Ian Keen, 137–58. Canberra: Aboriginal Studies Press.

Birdsall-Jones, Christina, and William Christensen. 2007. *Aboriginal Housing Careers in Western Australian Towns and Cities*, AHURI Positioning Paper no. 95. Melbourne: Australian Housing and Urban Research Institute.

Birdsall-Jones, Christina, and Vanessa Corunna. 2008. *The Housing Careers of Indigenous Urban Households*, AHURI Final Report no. 112. Melbourne: Australian Housing and Urban Research Institute.

Birdsall-Jones, Christina, Vanessa Corunna, Nalita Turner, Gemma Smart, and Wendy Shaw. 2010. *Indigenous Homelessness*, AHURI Final Report No. 143. Melbourne: Australian Housing and Urban Research Institute, Western Australia Research Centre.

Biskup, Peter. 1973. *Not Slaves, Not Citizens: The Aboriginal Problem in Western Australia, 1898–1954*. St. Lucia, Queensland: University of Queensland Press.

Chomsky, Noam. 1995. *The Minimalist Program*. Cambridge, UK: Cambridge University Press.

Chomsky, Noam, Marc D. Hauser, and W. Tecumseh Fitch. 2005. "Appendix. The Minimalist Program." Unpublished. Available at www. wjh. harvard. edu/~ mnkylab.

Daya, Shari., and Nicola Wilkins. 2013. "The Body, the Shelter, and the Shebeen: An Affective Geography of Homelessness in South Africa." *Cultural Geographies* 20 (3): 357–78.

Dufty, Rae. 2009. "'At Least I Don't Live in Vegemite Valley': Racism and Rural Public Housing Spaces." *Australian Geographer* 40 (4): 429–49.

Emerson, Daniel. 2011. "Welfare Fear as Tenants Face State Axe." *The West Australian Newspaper*, Wednesday, 6 April.

Gurney, Craig M. 1999. "Pride and Prejudice: Discourses of Normalisation in Public and Private Accounts of Home Ownership." *Housing Studies* 14 (2): 163–83.

Habibis, Daphne, Christina Birdsall-Jones, Terry Dunbar, Margaret Scrimgeour, Elizabeth Taylor, and Megan Nethercote. 2011. *Improving Housing Responses to Indigenous Patterns of Temporary Mobility*, AHURI Final Report no. 162. Melbourne: Australian Housing and Urban Research Institute.

Haebich, Anna. 1992. *For Their Own Good: Aborigines and Government in the South West of Western Australia, 1900–1940*, 2nd ed. Nedlands, Western Australia: University of Western Australia Press.

Hall, Stuart. 2011. "The Neo-Liberal Revolution." *Cultural Studies* 25 (6): 705–28.

Harris, Randy Allen. 1995. *The Linguistics Wars*. Oxford: Oxford University Press.

Hodson, Sally. 1987. "Nyungars and Work: Aboriginal Labour in the Great Southern Region, Western Australia 1936–1972." Honours diss., Department of Anthropology, University of Western Australia.

Jacobs, Keith, and Kathleen Flanagan. 2013. "Public Housing and the Politics of Stigma." *Australian Journal of Social Issues* 48 (3): 319–37.

Jones, Ray. 1997. "Sacred Sites or Profane Buildings? Reflections on the Old Swan Brewery Conflict in Perth, Western Australia." In *Contested Urban Heritage: Voices from the Periphery*, edited by Brian J. Shaw and Roy Jones, 132–55. Aldershot, UK: Ashgate.

Karch, Andrew and Matthew Cravens. 2014. "Rapid Diffusion and Policy Reform: the Adoption and Modification of Three Strikes Laws". *State Politics and Policy Quarterly*: 14 (4): 451–91.

Memmott, Paul, Christina Birdsall-Jones, and Kelly Greenop. 2012. *Australian Indigenous House Crowding*, AHURI Final Report no. 194. Melbourne: Australian Institute of Housing and Urban Research.

Memmott, Paul, Stephen Long, Martin Bell, John Taylor, Dominic Brown, and Linda Thomson. 2006. *Indigenous Mobility in Rural and Remote Australia*, AHURI Final Report no. 90. Melbourne: Australian Housing and Urban Research Institute.

Myers, Linda James. 1987. "The Deep Structure of Culture: Relevance of Traditional African Culture in Contemporary Life." *Journal of Black Studies* 18 (1): 72–85.

Nelson, Jacqueline. 2014. "Place-Defending and the Denial of Racism." *Australian Journal of Social Issues* 49 (1): 67–85.

O'Connor, Andrew. 2013. "Public Housing Evictions Are on the Rise and Families Face Homelessness with Three Strikes Policy." *ABC News*, 26 December, http://www.abc.net.au/news/2013-12-26/wa-evictions-feature/5170316 (accessed 7 September 2014).

Palmer, Catherine, Anna Ziersch, Kathy Arthurson, and Fran Baum. 2004. "Challenging the Stigma of Public Housing: Preliminary Findings from a Qualitative Study in South Australia." *Urban Policy and Research* 22 (4): 411–26.

Queensland Government. 2016. "Tenant Behaviour: Information for Queensland Public Housing Tenants." http://www.qld.gov.au/housing/public-community-housing/tenant-behaviour/(accessed 7 September 2016).

Rickard, Lucy. 2011. "Housing Policy Changed after 'Drug Lab' Blast." WAtoday. com.au. 5 April.

Sansom, Basil. 1991. "A Grammar of Exchange." In *Being Black: Aboriginal Cultures in "Settled" Australia*, edited by Ian Keen, 159–78. Canberra: Aboriginal Studies Press.

Secretariat of National Aboriginal and Islander Child Care. 2014. "Policy Failures and Disadvantage Leading to High Number of Aboriginal and Torres Strait Islander Child Removals in WA," Media Release, 30 June 2014.

Slater, Tom. 2012. "The Myth of "Broken Britain": Welfare Reform and the Production of Ignorance." *Antipode* 46 (4): 948–69.

Shaphan, Cox, Thor Kerr, Roy Jones, and Christina Birdsall-Jones. Forthcoming. "Generations of Resistance: The Aboriginal Occupation of Sites of Contested Heritage in Perth, Western Australia." Forthcoming issue of the *Journal of Historical Geography*.

Shelter WA. n.d.. *Report on Disruptive Behaviour Management Strategy*. Perth: Shelter WA, http://www.shelterwa.org.au/wp-content/uploads/2013/05/SWA-Final-DBMS-Report-May2013.pdf.

Sutton, Peter. 1998. *Native Title and the Descent of Rights: Kinship, Descent and Aboriginal Land Tenure and Families of Polity: Post-Classical Aboriginal Society and Native Title*. Perth: National Native Title Tribunal.

Szava, Anna, and Mark Moran. 2008. *Perceptions of Home Ownership among IBA Home Loan Clients*. Alice Springs: Centre for Appropriate Technology and Indigenous Business Australia.

Tonry, Michael. 2013. " 'Nothing' Works: Sentencing 'Reform' in Canada and the United States." *Canadian Journal of Criminology and Criminal Justice* 55 (4): 465–80.

Troy, Patrick. 2011. "The Rise and Fall of Public Housing in Australia." In *Proceedings of the State of Australian Cities Conference* 29 November–2 December 2011. Melbourne: University of Melbourne.

Ward, Glenyse. 1987. *Wandering Girl*. Broome, WA: Magabala Books.

Wacquant, Loïc. 2009. *Punishing the Poor: The Neoliberal Government of Social Insecurity*. Durham: Duke University Press.

____. 2013. "Constructing neoliberalism: opening salvo." *NEXUS: Newsletter of the Australian Sociological Association* 25, no. 1.: 1, 8–9.

WADOH (Western Australia Department of Housing). 2013a. "Applicants Waiting for Housing," edited by Department of Housing. Perth: Government of Western Australia.

____. 2013b. "The Department of Housing Rental Policy Manual," edited by Department of Housing. Perth, Western Australia: Government of Western Australia and the Department of Housing.

____. 2014. "Our History," in About Us Section. http://www.housing.wa.gov.au/abou-tus/thehousingauthority/history/Pages/default.aspx.

WAEOC (Western Australia Equal Opportunity Commission). 2013. *A Better Way: A Report into the Department of Housing's Disruptive Behaviour Strategy and More Effective Methods for Dealing with Tenants*. Perth: Equal Opportunity Commission, http://vivid.blob.core.windows.net/eoc-sitefinity/publications/a-better-way-report.pdf?sfvrsn=2.

Western Australia Police. n.d. "Indigenous Communities," http://www.police.wa.gov.au/ourservices/indigenouscommunities/tabid/995/default.aspx .

Western Australian Government. 2013. Public Housing-Tenant Behaviour, extract from *Hansard,* Assembly. Thursday, 13 June 2013: 1490b–1491a.

Zwart, Jan-Wouter. 1998. "The Minimalist Program." *Journal of Linguistics* 34 (1): 213–26.

Part 3

NEW ZEALAND

CHAPTER 15

Indigenous Homelessness: New Zealand Context

SHILOH GROOT AND EVELYN J. PETERS

In New Zealand many Māori live in impoverished and overcrowded conditions and, as such, are overrepresented in the homeless population (Groot et al.
2011a). In this chapter, we argue that homelessness is endemic to experiences
of colonialism, not only at the personal, but also at the *hapu* (subtribe), *iwi*
(tribe), and national level where many Māori have experienced over 150 years
of being rendered out of place in their *hau kainga* (ancestral homelands). We
consider colonialism and societal developments that have impacted *whānau*
(extended family) economically, culturally, and socially, contributing to high
rates of homelessness among Māori today.

This chapter begins with a brief historical overview, followed by a discussion of the definitions of homelessness unique to the socio-political context
of New Zealand, and is supplemented by lived understandings. Particular attention is given to the contributing health, policy, and relational consequences
of rapid urbanization for Māori. Homelessness as a human rights issue and
treaty obligations are also considered. Contributing chapters in this section
will extend the arguments placed here through a consideration of how Māori
cultural practices shape people's efforts to retain a positive sense of self and
place, and to engage in homemaking while dwelling on the streets.

The Experiences of *Tangata Whenua* (People of the Land)

New Zealand or Aotearoa (as it is often referred to by many *iwi*/tribal groups)
is a relatively remote island country in the southwestern Pacific Ocean.
Geographically, New Zealand encompasses two main landmasses—that of
the North Island, or Te Ika-a-Māui (the fish of Maui), and the South Island,

or Te Waipounamu (the water[s] of greenstone)—as well as a number of smaller surrounding islands. Throughout history, the Māori population has been concentrated on the North Island. In 1996, 87.5 percent of the Māori people lived on the North Island, and over half of this population resided in either Auckland, Waikato, or the Bay of Plenty regional council areas. Māori comprise 14.6 percent of the population of New Zealand, and the largest Māori *iwi* (tribe) is Ngapuhi with 24 percent of the Māori population (Statistics New Zealand 2013). The collective name Māori, for Indigenous New Zealanders, began with the arrival of the first colonialist ships and by 1850 the term was in common usage in order to differentiate them from Pākehā (European) settlers (Williams 1973). *Mā* denotes brightness, freshness, and purity. It accompanies specific word groupings to convey illumination, whereas *ori* is vibration. If we are vibrating the *Mā*, we are being in truth with what is (Hāweatea Bryson 2015). Māori then is the essence of our human possibility. Although dialectal and cultural differences most certainly exist(ed) between Māori, a common language allowed them to mount a quicker response to European contact. Further, the relatively small size of New Zealand compared to Australia or Canada meant that Māori could more easily coordinate plans and share information.

In the 1790s, when Europeans began to settle in New Zealand, they were highly dependent on Māori goodwill and economic and social support. The 1840 Treaty of Waitangi signed between the British and many tribal leaders "had the potential to deliver benefits to all parties" (Durie 2005, 15). This was unique; even at the height of British imperialism fuelled by greed and pseudo-scientific racism, the colonial government was unable to dismiss the Indigenous right to political recognition. The 1840 Treaty of Waitangi recognized distinctive rights that stemmed from notions of the doctrine of Indigenous title, and went beyond a simple acknowledgement to prescribing a relationship between Māori and the Crown (Durie 2002). While it would appear that the development of New Zealand was firmly grounded in egalitarian values, we know this was not always so in practice (see Brown for a comprehensive historical overview, in this book). The settler government quickly imposed British concepts of title and ownership, and the resulting alienation from and the confiscation of land from Māori, who resisted, meant that by the mid-1800s the Crown and the New Zealand Company had purchased nearly 99 percent of the South Island and 20 percent of the North Island (Durie 2005, Ministry for Culture and Heritage 2015). The settler government failed to recognize Māori fishing, subsurface, and water rights. Māori dispossession, impoverishment, and illness due to the introduced diseases led to massive population decline. Expectations of extinction were popularly expressed through ostentatious memorials and commissioned art fare-welling the "noble savage."

The emptying of rural tribal homelands through the flooding of Māori people to towns and cities, which began in the 1930s, has been described as rapid (Durie 1998; King 2003; Metge 1964). Metge (1964) records that, in 1936, about 13 percent of the Māori population lived in urban areas. In 1951 the percentage rose to 23 percent. By 1981, 80 percent of Māori were living in urban regions (Metge 1995). Along with the socio-economic marginalization brought upon Māori by continued colonization, such migrations have contributed to the overrepresentation of Māori among homeless populations in urban centres. Although structural intrusions have clearly posed challenges to Māori wellness, it is crucial to note that Māori are not passive in the face of socio-political upheavals. Maori are resilient and adaptive (Nikora, Rua, and Te Awekōtuku 2007). Claims to, and the affirmations of, cultural identities and practices by Indigenous peoples are common responses to histories of oppression, and offer authenticity, a sense of belonging, and the basis for gaining human rights (Dudgeon and Fielder 2006; Smith 1999).

Problem Definition: Homelessness in New Zealand

Homelessness has been a feature of urban life in New Zealand for over a century, inciting public deliberation as government officials and service providers contend with sourcing an adequate definition to respond effectively to the needs of those affected. No existing definition is fully adequate due to the complexities of homelessness and differing views on causes and solutions (Moore 2007; Roche 2004). Most agree that a continuum of housing situations, ranging from street life (the absence of a dwelling) to inadequate and insecure housing is useful (Laurenson 2005; O'Brien and de Haan 2002). Kearns, Smith, and Abbott (1992) argue that although New Zealand may experience low proportions of primary or street homelessness in comparison to what is experienced internationally, there is striking evidence of a large proportion of people in insecure living situations, inadequate housing, and approaching the agencies with serious housing needs. In light of this, they argued: "Absolute [primary] homelessness represents only the tip of the iceberg ... there are many thousands more who represent the incipient homeless ... the plight of the currently homeless is desperate, but just around the corner is a potentially vast population of ill-housed people, many of whom are little more than one additional domestic crisis away from being on the streets" (369). In 2009 Statistics New Zealand formulated a report with the aim of producing an official definition of homelessness. This national development reflected an acknowledgement of a gap in official statistics that needed to be addressed so that the government and the community groups could better respond to homelessness. The concepts and definitions utilized were adapted from the European Typology of Homelessness and Housing Exclusion (ETHOS), while also attempting to recognize the societal, cultural, and environmental contexts particular to New Zealand. The Statistics New Zealand definition constitutes an *attempt* to capture some of the complexity of homelessness. It also constitutes an acknowledgement of movement between the different forms of homelessness including living rough, staying in temporary shelter, and depending on the generosity of others.

The intersections of the social, physical, and legal domains within the housing sector are used as the basis for the Statistics New Zealand framework. The social domain encompasses people being able to enact "normal social relations," maintain privacy and a personal space, and have safe accommodation. The physical domain refers to the structural aspect of housing and involves people residing in habitable housing. The legal domain extends to having exclusive possession or security of occupation or tenure. It is with reference to the intersections between these domains that a more complex conceptualization of homelessness emerges. The resulting conceptual categories are: "without shelter" (living on the streets and inhabiting improvised shelters, including shacks and cars); "temporary accommodation" (hostels for homeless people, transitional supported housing, women's refuges, and long-term motor camps and boarding houses); "sharing accommodation" (temporary accommodation for people sharing someone else's private dwelling); and "uninhabitable housing" (people residing in dilapidated dwellings).

Such official definitions are produced for administrative and governance purposes (Roche 2004; Whiteford 2010). If complemented by lived understandings and everyday cultural practices we can develop a more contextualized understanding that supports the needs of Māori homeless people (Groot et al. 2011b). The situations in which many Māori find themselves require us to extend such official definitions of homelessness (Groot et al. 2011b). Memmott and colleagues (2003) refer to "spiritual homelessness" in an effort to explain situations in which Indigenous people are displaced from ancestral lands, knowledge, rituals, and kinship relationships. Māori often experience homelessness as a loss of physical connection with *whanau* (family), *hapu* (subtribe), and *iwi* (tribe) which results in cultural and spiritual disconnection to varying degrees (see King, Hodgetts, Rua, and Te Whetu, in this book). In reaching an agreed definition of homelessness, it is necessary to seek Māori input and acknowledge its cultural, spiritual, and experiential dimensions.

Such complexities surrounding homelessness, home, and place are particularly apparent in research on Māori homelessness. For example, Groot and colleagues (2011b) have demonstrated through the accounts of Māori who are homeless that there are tensions between the profound sense of *whakamā* (shame and humiliation) at being dislocated from *whanau* (family) and *hau kāinga* (ancestral homeland), wanting to reconnect back with such places and relationships, and affiliating with life somewhere new.

Responding to Homelessness

Interest in homelessness and housing affordability from academics, researchers, and government leaders has been sporadic (Groot et al., 2011b). With the exception of a few, even Māori and Iwi authorities appear to hesitate when responding to inquiries about homelessness. Perhaps this situation reflects the increasing social and economic stratification of Māori society, or the position that homelessness is a government responsibility. Such a stance ignores the critical importance of differential access to economic and political power within and across Māori society. Whatever the argument, there is undeniably a "Māori underclass" that comprises a large proportion of the homeless population in New Zealand. It emerges from economic and social deprivation and encompasses substance misusers, mental health clients, and long-term recipients of welfare, also known as the permanent poor (Auletta 1999; Kelso 1994; Zelley, 1995).

Despite this situation there is no coordinated response to homelessness or nationally funded program of research and action in New Zealand. Further, in housing initiatives, Walker and Barcham (2010) have argued that New Zealand has lagged behind Canada and Australia in supporting initiatives that recognize Indigenous self-determination in the design and delivery of social housing. No single government department has a statutory responsibility for homeless people or for coordinating services. As a result, service provision has developed in a fragmentary manner in New Zealand. Alongside private charities and faith-based social services, government agencies such as Ministry of Social Development, Housing New Zealand Corporation, The Department of Corrections, Child, Youth and Family Services, and District Health Boards are involved in addressing the complex needs of homeless people.

In the framework of the Treaty of Waitangi, relating to *kawanatanga* or governance, Article 1 requires the Crown to provide services that meet the needs of Māori people. Māori service users and providers need to be included in the research, definition, planning, implementation, and evaluation of homelessness prevention services to ensure that they are informed by Māori values.

Government agencies and many non-Māori service providers are frequently not well equipped to offer a culturally sensitive service due to an undersupply of speakers in *te reo* Māori, staff trained in bicultural protocols, and referral processes that allow for working constructively with Māori service providers. This often leads to short-term solutions that result in many Māori homeless people re-entering the cycle of homelessness on multiple occasions.

Article 3 of the Treaty refers to *oritetanga* or equity of health outcomes for Māori. Māori are overrepresented in the areas that compound the risk of becoming homeless. It is important that people have access to Māori specific services to reduce the negative impact of homelessness on health and to assist in their reintegration long term. For example, marae-based programs are doing preventative work to address problems that create and put people at increased risk of homelessness (see King, Hodgetts, Rua. and Te Whetu in this book). This typifies the type of partnerships that need to be formed with service providers as a means of integrating Indigenous homeless supports and organizations into a broader service mix.

Conclusion

Despite a lack of official statistics or national recognition, homelessness is a serious issue in New Zealand. Like many Indigenous peoples, Māori people are overrepresented among New Zealand's homeless populations. Māori homelessness also exhibits some unique features including the role of cultural frameworks in supporting kin and family, which often results in crowding and hidden homelessness. The colonial legacy of dispossession and exclusion also plays a role in exacerbating and maintaining Māori homelessness. These particular aspects emphasize the need for culturally appropriate initiatives with respect to Māori homelessness and the involvement of Māori organizations in designing and delivering responses.

References

Auletta, Ken. 1999. *The Underclass,* updated and revised edition. Woodstock, NY: Overlook Press.

Durie, Mason. 1998. *Whaiora: Māori Health Development,* 2nd ed. Auckland, New Zealand: Oxford University Press.

_____.2002. "Universal Provision, Indigeneity and the Treaty of Waitangi." *Victoria University of Wellington Law Review* 33 (3-4): 591–601.

_____.2005. *Ngā Tai Matatū: Tide of Māori Endurance.* South Melbourne, AU: Oxford University Press.

Dudgeon, Pat, and John Fielder. 2006. "Third Spaces within Tertiary Places: Indigenous Australian Studies." *Journal of Community and Applied Social Psychology* 16 (5): 396–409.

Groot, Shiloh, Darrin Hodgetts, Linda Waimarie Nikora, and Chez Leggat-Cook. 2011a. "A Māori Homeless Woman." *Ethnography* 12 (3): 375–97.

Groot, Shiloh, Darrin Hodgetts, Linda Waimarie Nikora, and Mohi Rua. 2011b. "Māori and Homelessness." In *Māori and Social Issues,* edited by Tracey McIntosh and Malcolm Mulholland, 235–62. Wellington, New Zealand: Huia Publishers.

Hāweatea Bryson, Bahadur. 2015. *8 Māori Words to Have You Celebrating Exactly Who You Are,* 2 August, http://www.elephantjournal.com/2015/08/8-maori-words-to-have-you-celebrating-exactly-who-you-are/ (accessed 18 August 2015).

Hond, Mereana. 2002. "Resort to Mediation in Māori-to-Māori Dispute Resolution: Is It the Elixir to Cure All Ills?" *Victoria University of Wellington Law Review* 33 (3-4): 579–90.

Kearns, Robin A., Christopher J. Smith, and Max W. Abbott. 1992. "The Stress of Incipient Homelessness." *Housing Studies* 7 (4): 280–98.

Kelso, William A. 1994. *Poverty and the Underclass: Changing Perceptions of the Poor in America.* New York: NYU Press.

King, Michael. 2003. *The Penguin History of New Zealand.* Auckland, New Zealand: Penguin.

Laurenson, Penelope J. M. 2005. "Public Space and Anti-Homeless Regulation: Local Government Responses to Homelessness in Three New Zealand Cities." MA diss., Otago University, Dunedin, New Zealand.

Memmott, Paul, Stephen Long, Catherine Chambers, and Frederick Spring. 2003. *Categories of Indigenous 'Homeless' People and Good Practice Responses to Their Needs,* AHURI Final Report no. 49. St Lucia: Australian Housing and Urban Research Institute: Queensland Research Centre.

Metge, Joan. 1964. *A New Māori Migration: Rural and Urban Relations in Northern New Zealand.* London, University of London: Athlone Press.

_____.1976. *The Māoris of New Zealand,* rev. ed. London: Routledge and Kegan Paul.

_____.1995. *New Growth From Old.* Wellington: Victoria University Press.

Ministry for Culture and Heritage. 2015. *Māori Land Loss, 1860-2000,* http://www.nzhistory.net.nz/media/interactive/maori-land-1860-2000 (accessed 18 August 2015).

Moore, Jeanne. 2007. "Polarity for Integration? Towards a Fuller Understanding of Home and Homelessness." *Journal of Architectural and Planning Research* 24 (2): 143–59.

Nikora, Linda Waimarie, Mohi Rua, and Ngatuia Te Awekōtuku. 2007. "Renewal and Resistance: Moko in Contemporary New Zealand." *Journal of Community and Applied Social Psychology* 17 (1): 477–89.

O'Brien, M., and I. de Hann. 2002. "Empowerment Research with a Vulnerable Group— Homelessness and the Social Services: The Story of a Research Project." *Social Work Review* 14 (1): 29–34.

Roche, Martin. 2004. "Complicated Problems, Complicated Solutions? Homelessness and Joined-Up Policy Responses." *Social Policy and Administration* 38 (7): 758–74.

Smith, Linda Tuhiwai 1999. *Decolonizing Methodologies: Research and Indigenous Peoples.* Dunedin, New Zealand: University of Otago Press.

Statistics New Zealand. 2014. *2013 Census QuickStats about Culture and Identity,* http://www.stats.govt.nz.

Walker, Ryan, and Manuhuia Barcham. 2010. Indigenous-Inclusive Citizenship: The City and Social Housing in Canada, New Zealand, and Australia. *Environment and Planning A* 42 (2): 314–33.

Whiteford, Martin. 2010. "Hot Tea, Dry Toast and the Responsibilisation of Homeless People." *Social Policy and Society* 9 (2): 193–205.

Williams, Raymond. 1973. *The Country and the City.* New York: Oxford University Press.

Zelley, E. Walton. 1995. "Is the Underclass Really a Class?" *Journal of Sociology and Social Welfare* 22 (1): 75–85.

CHAPTER 16

Tūrangawaewae Kore: Nowhere to Stand

DEIDRE BROWN

We didn't cede our sovereignty, and if we did, we didn't do it to
become paupers in our own land.
— Haami Piripi, Chairman of Te Rūnanga
o Te Rarawa (quoted in Field 2010)

Tūrangawaewae, or having an ancestral "place to stand," is central to individual
and collective New Zealand Māori identities, and is strongly associated with
contemporary notions of "home." While colonization is often cited in New
Zealand literature on homelessness as the mechanism for estranging Māori
from their tūrangawaewae,[1] the processes by which this has happened are
not often described in detail. Understanding the past is central to developing
strategies for the future in Māori custom. This chapter defines tūrangawaewae,
landlessness, homelessness, and houselessness within Māori history. It then
identifies the key historical moments at which Māori have experienced
tūrangawaewae, and the loss of land, and the effect that this has had on housing
the Māori community in general and for housing specific families.

The journey to homelessness for Māori began with landlessness. Severe
housing need and houselessness have, at times, also been an inherited outcome of the colonial acquisition of Indigenous resources to support Pākehā
(European) settlement. By the end of the nineteenth century, Māori were
dispossessed of most of their land and appeared to be a "dying race" due to sus-
ceptibility to Pākehā diseases that was in no doubt heightened by the poor living
conditions some of the most vulnerable endured. Māori responded with active
and passive resistance, utilizing alternative governance and religious systems.
Instead of simply disappearing or assimilating, the Māori population grew from
the beginning of the twentieth century onward, but as a predominantly rural
people, their material suffering was largely invisible to the Pākehā majority.

Their plight became increasingly difficult for the government to ignore after World War I, with the spread of serious infectious diseases and an accelerated migration into urban centres. Inheriting an Indigenous homelessness problem that began with the first permanent settlement of Pākehā, successive twentieth-century governments have since failed to reduce the number of Māori who are houseless and in severe housing need. Although my purpose in this chapter is not to propose specific policy initiatives or interventions, I suggest that for the journey to homelessness to be reversed any long-term strategies must address current Māori landlessness and its historical consequences.

Tūrangawaewae

Tūrangawaewae shares many similarities with the concept of "home," but as this chapter demonstrates it does not correspond in the same way to the notion of being housed. Tūrangawaewae (*tūranga*/standing place; *waewae*/feet) describes one's sense of belonging or attachment to a particular place and the ability to locate oneself there physically and spiritually. Personal *whaka-papa* (sequences of descent or ancestry) are an expression of tūrangawaewae as they always begin with one's *waka* (migratory vessel from Hawaiiki, the homeland), and include *iwi* (tribe; also the word for bones), *hapū* (subtribe; also the word for pregnancy), *whare tīpuna* (meeting house), *marae* (forum on which the meeting house stands), *maunga* (mountain associated with marae or ancestry), *awa* (river associated with marae or ancestry), *wāhi tapu/urupā* (burial grounds), *moana* (harbour or sea), and *tīpuna* (founding ancestor of tribe). For example, my *whakapapa* is recited as follows (where "*ko*" is a noun particle and "*te*" means "the"):

Ko Mataatua **te Waka**

Ko Ngapuhi **te Iwi**

Ko Ngāti Rehia **te Hapū**

Ko Tau Te Rangimarie **te Whare Tīpuna**

Ko Mangaiati **te Marae**

Ko Emi Emi **te Maunga**

Ko Mangaiti **te Awa**

Ko Pahuhu **te Wāhi Tapu**

Ko Whangaroa **te Moana**

Ko Puhimoanaariki **te Tangata**

Ko Puhimoanaariki

Ko Puhitamiwharau

[and twenty-six more succeeding generations to ...]

Ko Deidre Brown *tāku ingoa* ["is my name"]

Thus, I and everyone preceding me in my descent line are connected to a cultural landscape and my entitlement to claim Mangaiati Marae, and the surrounding environment, as my tūrangawaewae is indisputable. I am also entitled to claim other landscapes as my tūrangawaewae if I can demonstrate a *whakapapa* connection. All animate and inanimate entities have a *whakapapa*.

The severance from landscapes and family that occurred through colonization has left some Māori with an incomplete, or no, knowledge of their *whakapapa*, although they are still regarded as possessing one that is not *yet* known. Their association with a tūrangawaewae depends very much on individual circumstances and whether they have been able to maintain *ahi kā* (literally home fires) by visiting in body or *wairua* (spirit) a place they might generally, if not actually, know to be their tūrangawaewae. People with *whakapapa* connections to their tūrangawaewae may feel distressingly dislocated from lands that were taken away from them (either by conflict with other Māori or through colonization). Many Māori who are houseless or in severe housing need still have strong place attachments which, as the geographer Robin Kearns notes can be "stronger than their status as being adequately housed" (Kearns 2006). They maintain their ancestral tūrangawaewae through recalling family connections or create additional or alternative tūrangawaewae with a new network of place associations (Groot et al. 2011b). In the latter instance, removal from the street by agencies or authorities can be more inhibiting than helpful. There are others who feel completely estranged from their tūrangawaewae through an intentional or unintentional loss of culture or relationships.

Houselessness and Homelessness

The current definitions of homelessness in New Zealand are under debate (see introduction to this section), and for the purposes of this chapter a more inclusive definition will be used that comprises severe housing need (including inadequate and emergency housing) and street dwelling. "Crowding," another measure of Western homelessness, is a more problematic term. Historically it has been applied as a form of criticism, particularly aimed at Indigenous peoples, of households that include three or more generations or accommodate the short- and long-term needs of relatives who are not in parent/child relationships with the principal householders. There are many households in New Zealand that would be defined as "crowded" under the nationally accepted crowding indicators,[2] yet are functioning well due to respected Indigenous leadership and householders' patterns of behaviour or "house rules."[3] In this chapter, I contend that extended family living is important to Māori well-being, and when family stress results from having too many people under one roof (or roofs, if auxiliary buildings are included) it is architecture that has failed family need not the reverse scenario.

Recent Australasian research on Indigenous homelessness has highlighted that being "housed" does not necessarily correlate to having a "home" (See Kelly Greenop's and Paul Memmott's chapter in this volume; Groot et. al. 2011a; Groot et. al. 2011b). As discussed above, Māori can have one home, many different homes, or no home, within the tūrangawaewae concept. As the Māori architectural practitioner Rau Hoskins and colleagues have argued, a house is a single architectural entity, whereas a home could be equated to the Māori concept of *kāinga*, usually translated as a "village" (Hoskins et al. 2002). In a contemporary setting, *kāinga* includes outdoor spaces such as garages, sheds, yards, streets, public amenities, and neighbours' houses. "Home" can still be a permeable environment in rural and urban Indigenous communities where the responsibility for dependents is spread across many households, and dwelling can occur outside of buildings (see Greenop's and Memmott's chapter in this volume).

Indigenous researchers have also questioned the relevance of Western definitions of homelessness when applied to Indigenous societies. Retelling life histories of Māori street dwellers, the social psychologist Shiloh Groot and colleagues have demonstrated that it is possible, at least in some instances, to maintain a sense of tūrangawaewae while not being "housed" (Groot et al. 2011a; Groot et al. 2011b). Critical to the maintenance of this sense of belonging is the identification with a tūrangawaewae that can be performed, for example, through culturally defined relationships with others (such as street dwellers assuming an elder role by mentoring younger street dwellers) and maintained through the retention of family *taonga* (treasured objects, such as photograph albums). Groot and co-researchers also observed that for some people life on the street offered more security than living in a Western-style house, demonstrating their preference of tūrangawaewae over shelter.

There is currently no quantitative measure of tūrangawaewae or *tūrangawaewae kore* (where "*kore*" is a qualifier meaning "without"). Some work has already been undertaken on quantifying another cultural concept, *mauri* (life force), using a "*mauri*-o-meter" matrix that provides a spectrum of effect across different categories, such as the ecological, cultural, community, and economic impact of interventions and disasters.[4] The meter's purpose is to provide advice for *mauri* management and enhancement within a resource management paradigm. Whether such a measure could be applied on a spectrum of tūrangawaewae to tūrangawaewae kore, and for what purpose, are questions that deserve further investigation.

Qualitative measures of Māori houselessness or severe housing need in a tūrangawaewae context have usually been based on empirical evidence such as interviews and statistics in which participants are subjects of academic discourse.[5] As a Māori architectural historian I am interested in how the complexity of tūrangawaewae is revealed through experience and history, taking into account that Māori time is relational rather than linear (Brown, Ellis, and Mane-Wheoki 2013). Historical sections in this chapter are complemented by *kōrero tuku iho* (stories passed down) about tūrangawaewae, severe housing need, and houselessness from my own family. This approach captures a multigenerational experience of Indigenous homelessness that spans the colonial era in New Zealand. It reveals a cyclical experience of events, people, and tūrangawaewae place associations that have meaning within a *whakapapa* but are difficult to record using the Western linear systems of history.

Given the extensive nature of colonial land alienation, there is unlikely to be a Māori family anywhere in New Zealand or overseas that has not had to face these issues. My *kōrero tuku iho* also dissolves the "fifth wall" that normally sits between researchers and participants. As an Indigenous researcher, I cannot position myself outside of a discourse that sometimes deals with poverty without being seen as *whakahīhī* (elevating oneself culturally; or being arrogant) (Smith 1999, 139). Therefore I give my *kōrero tuku iho* as a *koha* (reciprocal exchange to maintain cultural balance) and also a demonstration of the *mana* (status) that my family has maintained despite some trying circumstances.

Landlessness: A Case Study at Wairoa and Rangihoua Bays

The first permanent removal of Māori from their tūrangawaewae through eviction or land alienation by Pākehā occurs early in the historical record, in 1810, at Wairoa Bay on the northern side of the Bay of Islands, Northland. It sets the scene for all subsequent land loss. Through retelling the story I demonstrate that imperialist colonial attitudes to Māori and land were present from the very beginning of Pākehā settlement and I establish a set of signifiers that recur in *kōrero tuku iho* associated with this tūrangawaewae.

During the early years of the nineteenth century and under the leadership of Te Pahi, the paramount chief of the Bay of Islands, a thriving cross-cultural

trading enterprise had developed at Wairoa Bay in which Māori-grown po-
tatoes, felled timber, and fresh water were traded with Pākehā whaling and
sealing vessels for iron and possibly muskets. Iron, made into Māori-style
tools, liberated Northland Māori from the end of a long supply change for the
hardstone *pounamu* (also known today as greenstone or New Zealand jade),
which could only be sourced from the South Island. A deep anchorage off one
of the four small islands in Wairoa Bay was the stopping point for the ships, the
mainland reserved for potato cultivation. So successful was the enterprise that
in 1806 the governor of New South Wales (then the principal Pākehā colonial
outpost in Australia) made two gifts to Te Pahi, one a specially made silver
medal commemorating their meeting, and the other a prefabricated house for
the purpose of "appropriately" accommodating Australian trade agents. It was
erected on the principal of the four islands and was the first European-style
house in New Zealand, although it would only ever be used by Māori since
the trade agents never arrived. Wairoa Bay became the most economically
successful and perhaps the most densely populated Māori settlement of the
time with hundreds of people living and working on site.

Not all early-nineteenth-century Pākehā were as appreciative as the
governor of New South Wales when it came to the recognition of Indigenous
human rights and their rights to property. Blackbirding (a form of enslave-
ment), kidnapping, and the abuse of Māori and other Pacific Island crew
members and passengers were not uncommon on ships working the southern
oceans. In 1809 matters came to a head when the Ngāti Pou subtribe of the
Whangaroa Harbour, just north of the Bay of Islands, attacked and killed most
of the seventy crew and passengers of the brigantine *Boyd,* as *utu* (reciprocal action) for the physical abuse of one of its chiefs by another ship (Nicholas 1817,
144–53; Marsden 1932, 87). Te Pahi was blamed for the incident, although
historians now largely agree that he attempted to prevent it from occurring.
Pākehā mounted at least two revenge attacks on Wairoa Bay and its islands.
The last, on 10 April 1810, resulted in the mortal injury of Te Pahi, the looting of his European-style house of its Pākehā and Māori contents, and the
killing and clearing of the islands of their inhabitants (Finucane 1998, 100).
Te Pahi's people and their descendants have never gone back to the islands
since they were declared *tapu* (restricted) because of the deaths that occurred
on them. The islands remain as lasting memorials to the unrealized promise
of an equitable Māori-Pākehā relationship.

Another four years passed before Pākehā were again invited to live in
the region. Te Pahi's successor, Ruatara, continued intercultural commercial
operations on shore, even marking out a proposed township for Pākehā in the

foothills above Wairoa Bay, but he succumbed to tuberculosis before this dream could be realized. His final months coincided with the arrival of the missionaries to neighbouring Rangihoua Bay in December 1814, where they built the first permanent Pākehā settlement on the shore. The missionaries and other settlers progressively divested Māori of their lands beginning with the purchase of 200 acres for twelve axes on 22 February 1815 (Middleton 2008, 55). This was the first Māori land transaction with Pākehā in New Zealand. Local *korero tuku iho* has always maintained that Māori were only offering exclusive rights of land occupancy through the exchange, believing that it would remain their tūrangawaewae. By the time the mission closed to relocate elsewhere in 1832, not one Māori conversion had been achieved but large parts of Wairoa and Rangihoua Bay were in Pākehā possession.

The story of Wairoa and Rangihoua Bays, between 1806 and 1832, illustrates how quickly Māori, within a generation, were alienated from large areas of their land. The assault on the Te Pahi's islands and their inhabitants was a demonstration of Pākehā armed force outside of any legal system. Pākehā asserted, through the practice of looting, that Māori had no property rights even within a recognizably "housed" environment. Although the intent of the missionaries who followed was to civilize and convert, these objectives were regarded as achievable only if Māori were brought into a Pākehā property system that divested them of their tūrangawaewae and placed their land in individual and perpetual ownership. Māori were made homeless as a result, and had no choice but to move away from their tūrangawaewae and live elsewhere. The lack of recognition of tūrangawaewae's cultural importance in land transactions and the dismissal of Māori rights to equal or equitable treatment would be running themes throughout nineteenth-century history and leading factors in homelessness, houselessness, and serious housing need:

> My mother raised me with many stories passed down about my ancestors, and they were always articulated to make a "point" about something that may have an impact on my own life. I've since sought out more of these stories to pass on to my sons and my students. Some of these stories are about houses and land, and they are presented throughout this chapter to demonstrate the relationship between lived and historical experiences of "home" and being "housed." The earliest ones I have are about my ancestor Te Pahi, who was my maternal grandmother's great great grandfather, and Wairoa and Rangihoua Bays my tūrangawaewae. There is a story in my family that Te Pahi, wounded in one of the attacks,

was supported by his wife as they swam for their lives from their island home to the safety of the mainland. This was not the last of the conflict on this land. In 1814 the missionaries threatened to set the canons of their ship, the *Active,* on Rangihoua Pā (our fortified hill in the Bay), if Ruatara did not get up from his deathbed and welcome them. Just before they arrived he'd been having second thoughts about letting them settle here. After the attack, and possibly once the missionaries had acquired our land, my surviving Wairoa Bay ancestors appear to have moved to Taupō Bay and then Kāeo, both in the Whangaroa Harbour to live with another branch of our family. My *whakapapa* (above) principally connects me to the local *marae,* and my brother still lives in Whangaroa. Today, Wairoa Bay and one of the Te Pahi islands, thought to be his European house site, are part of a luxury gated community, with the largest mansion occupying the site of Ruatara's proposed town. When I visit Rangihoua and Wairoa, my sense of sadness about the attacks and land losses is nothing compared to the joy I experience when standing on my tūrangawaewae. That moment and feeling of belonging can never be taken away from me or my family. (DB)

The 1840 Treaty Of Waitangi and Land Pre-Emption

Pākehā misunderstanding of Māori land as a commodity rather than as tūrangawaewae at Wairoa and Rangihoua Bay was perpetuated by the Crown's right to pre-emption in the 1840 Treaty of Waitangi. Pre-emption would inexorably lead to significant Māori land losses, houselessness, and severe housing need. It was signed by the British Queen's representative in New Zealand, William Hobson (who also drafted the document), and around forty Māori chiefs at Waitangi in southern Bay of Islands on 6 February 1840. Afterwards the Treaty was circulated around the country and a further 500 Māori signatures were collected. Episodes of intercultural conflict such as the *Boyd* massacre and the attack on Te Pahi's people, the fear of illegality of land transactions outside of the British legal system, as well as the threat of French or American colonization prompted the British to reluctantly annex New Zealand through the Treaty. A three-clause document, it recognizes Māori property rights (although sovereignty and governance are confused in translation) and extends British law to the country's inhabitants as a means to address pre-existing concerns. It also asserts the Crown's right of pre-emption, in other words, to be the exclusive purchaser of Māori land. The intention of pre-emption was to ensure that there was an adequate supply of land, that could be sold to settlers, and to provide the new colonial government with an income derived from the profits of their monopoly (Hooper and Kearins 2003, 104–5). Māori would, in effect, finance the Pākehā settlement of their country and the Pākehā instruments of colonial rule. The value they placed on their land was immaterial in a colonial process where they could never be partners on equal terms with the Crown.

The pre-emption clause appears in Article 2 of the treaty, and in the English version reads: "the Chiefs of the United Tribes and the individual Chiefs yield to Her Majesty the exclusive right of Preemption [*sic*] over such lands as the proprietors thereof may be disposed to alienate at such prices as may be agreed upon between the respective Proprietors and persons appointed by Her Majesty to treat with them in that behalf." However, the Māori translation of the clause was ambiguously worded and led many of the signatories to believe that they were at most offering the Queen first right of refusal. Sir Hugh Kawharu's translation of this into English demonstrates the difference in meaning: "the Chiefs of the Confederation and all the chiefs will sell land to the Queen at a price agreed to by the person owning it and by the person buying it (the latter being) appointed by the Queen as her purchase agent" (Kawharu n.d.).

Through pre-emption large profits were made by the government, and large losses attained by the Māori. In 1841, the acquired Māori land was sold to settlers at seventeen times its original price, and this difference comprised 75 percent of the government's total income for that year (Great Britain Parliamentary Papers in 1846, vol. 5, no 37, 44 quoted in Hooper and Kearins, 2003, 106–7). The next most important source of revenue was customs duty on alcohol, tobacco, sugar, flour, wheat, and tea purchased by Māori using funds that were partly, if not largely, raised through land sales. Thus began a vicious cycle of sale, consumption, and dependence that continued throughout the nineteenth century. After being for the most part left landless, Māori continue to be dependent, with type-two diabetes and substance abuse being two of the most critical issues facing the population today.

Land sales to the government considerably accelerated from 1847 onward, with the arrival of a new governor of New Zealand, George Grey, in 1845. He focused his attention on the South Island, which had a much lower Māori population than the North, purchasing almost thirty million acres for £15,000. By 1860, almost the entire island had been transferred into Pākehā ownership, the North Island mostly remaining in Māori possession (McKinnon, Bradley, and Kirkpatrick 1997, pl. 31). That year also marked a turning point in the country's colonial history, with Māori and Pākehā populations becoming equal in number, and the outbreak of war between Māori and the government over a disputed land purchase at Waitara, in the Taranaki region of the western North Island. The conflict spread to the Waikato region, in the central North Island three years later, amidst propaganda that the newly elected Māori "King" of the Waikato tribes had formed a "land league" and was planning to attack Auckland (then the country's capital city) (Belich 1986, 76, 119). Grey built a road from Auckland to the border of the King's territory, invading it when the King and his people refused to take an oath of allegiance to the Queen. War raged for the next nine years in Waikato region, in Taranaki, and in parts of the eastern region of the North Island. The New Zealand Wars caused the deaths of 2,000 Māori fighting against the British and colonial forces, and displaced a significant, but yet to be estimated, number of people (Belich 1986).

In the midst of the conflict the government passed three acts of legislation that would effectively ensure the alienation of Māori from most of their land in the North Island. The 1863 New Zealand Settlements Act enabled the confiscation of three million acres of land as a punishment for the rebellion against the government. Although half of the land was later returned or purchased by the government, the remaining lands paid for the £3 million loan that funded the government's participation in the conflict. The effects of the confiscation were dispossession and a loss of trust in the government. Under the 1864 Public Works Land Act, Māori land was taken, sometimes without compensation and sometimes in preference to neighbouring Pākehā-owned land. On occasion, to disrupt Māori occupation, the land was not used for the purpose it was taken yet still remained in government ownership, or roads were purposefully built through the middle of Māori land (Ministry of Culture and Heritage 2012a). The 1865 Native Land Act removed the Crown's right to pre-emption and established a system to individualize Māori title under a new Native Land Court, to make the land available for direct sale to Pākehā. Any person could apply to have the title of any piece of ground investigated. Regardless of its size, title would be given to no more than ten individuals. The system was ripe for exploitation. Courts did not necessarily sit in or were located close to the land under investigation. Those Māori living on land under investigation were forced to cede their rights and become landless, become tenants, or relocate to where the Courts were sitting to apply for title (Ministry of Culture and Heritage 2012a).

A predatory industry developed around the latter, indebting Māori so that if title was successfully awarded, they would have to sell the land to settle their accounts (Binney 1990, 144–46). Māori were occasionally unaware that their

Figure 16.1. Māori waiting for a Native Land Court hearing, Whanganui district, late 1860s. Photograph by William James Harding. Alexander Turnbull Library, 1/1-000013-G.

lands were under investigation, or refused to attend court in protest, and had their title awarded to others. The individualization of title divided communities and demonstrated that the government did not recognize tūrangawaewae. By the 1910s, one century after the first permanent Pākehā settlement was established at Rangihoua Bay, only 25 percent of the North Island and 1 percent of the South Island was in Māori "ownership" (Ministry of Culture and Heritage 2012a). Māori who had lost or sold too much of their land were unable to sustain customary modes of living or initiate sustainable and profitable farming initiatives on remaining landholdings. Many had no option but to leave their tūrangawaewae. They were forced to live on reserves that were generally inadequate in size, or share land with relatives, or engage in itinerant lifestyles within the Pākehā waged economy.

Dispossession and Resistance

It is not clear how many nineteenth-century Māori were moved from their tūrangawaewae due to land transferral into Pākehā ownership. However, the lifestyles that they were forced into had a significant effect on their mental, often referred to in documents of the time as "demoralization," and physical

Figure 16.2. Parihaka on 5 November 1881. Residents congregated centre right, waiting for the invasion by the Armed Constabulary. Photograph by William Andrews Collis. Alexander Turnbull Library, PA1-q-183-6.

well-being. The Māori population reached its lowest level in 1896 with 42,000 (Pool 2012). Men engaged in the waged economy as labourers in gum fields, on farms, and in public works were often forced to look for work away from their tūrangawaewae. Sometimes their immediate families followed them, or new families started, wherever they could find employment and housing (Sorrenson 1956, 364). How being estranged from tūrangawaewae affected nineteenth-century Māori women remains to be investigated. Increasing numbers married Pākehā, there being anecdotal evidence that this was regarded as a survival strategy for them and their future children (see Wanhalla 2013). The disconnection from extended families caused by this mobility led to lower self-sufficiency and a loss of customary practices, such as the knowledge of how to build and maintain watertight buildings.

Māori were not passive victims in this process of land alienation. They not only resisted encroachment on their lands during the New Zealand Wars, but they have also fought against it through political, spiritual, and social action and continue to do so to the present day. Four Māori parliamentary movements, the Kotahitanga 1 (1879) and 2 (1881), Te Kauhanganui (1890), and the Paremata Māori (1892), were established as systems of self-governance (Keane 2012). The Māori prophet leaders Te Whiti-o-Rongomai and Tohu Kakahi reoccupied confiscated Taranaki lands, and established a thriving

Māori urban centre at Parihaka in 1866 which grew to a population over 2,000 Māori, many of whom had been dispossessed through land confiscations. The government troops invaded Parihaka in 1881, arrested and imprisoned the two leaders, evicted 1,600 Māori, and pillaged and burned parts of the settlement still occupied by the remaining 600 residents.

Te Whiti and Tohu returned to Parihaka on their release in 1883, further developing it with street lighting, macadam roads, and many colonial-style residential and communal buildings (Brown 2009, 71–9). The Parihaka story remains, for Māori, an affirming narrative about counter-colonization and the power of passive resistance. Another Māori prophet leader, Tahupotiki Wiremu Ratana, emerged in the early twentieth century "with a Bible in one hand and the Treaty of Waitangi in the other" (Henderson 1972, 76–7). At its peak of popularity his eponymous church attracted 40,000 Māori followers (about 1/3 of the Māori population), and by 1943 an alliance with the Labour Party had won his Ratana political party all four Māori seats in the New Zealand parliament (Brown 2009, 111). The restitution of Māori land was central to all of these religio-political missions:

> After Te Pahi, my family found other means by which to make their way in an increasingly Pākehā world that seemed to have no place for them. My great great grandmother, Hana Riwhi (nee Rogers), was half Pākehā. Her father William Rogers was an early Pākehā settler in Whangaroa and his marriage to her mother, Peti Ngapapa, was probably more a land deal than a love match. It was likely a personal protection policy too as Peti was Te Pahi's granddaughter and the might of the Pākehā had already been felt by the family. The marriage of Hana and Te Pahi Riwhi (also a great great grandchild of Te Pahi) brought the *whakapapa* and no doubt the existing landholdings in Whangaroa back together again to consolidate our tūrangawaewae. Hana's daughter (my great grandmother) Harata Riwhi married Hapeta Renata, who became a Methodist Home Minister and later in life a Ratana Āpotoro (Apostle). Ratana's rise had been prophesied by the northern Māori leader Aperahama Taonui in 1863, so everyone had been expecting him when he started his mission in 1918 after the influenza epidemic. His message about holding onto the land resonated with Hapeta. I read that Hapeta had even tried to set-up a Māori university through the Ratana movement. Unfortunately the local Native School at Whangaroa didn't provide his children with the

education they needed. It was really just about farming, trades, and housewife training, not about going to university, not much better than the mission school back in Rangihoua 100 years before. (DB)

The Abandonment of *Whare*

Between the late nineteenth and early twentieth century, Māori moved away from constructing *whare* (customary thatched houses) for domestic residences as the government branded them unsanitary and dangerous. James Pope's 1884 book *Health for the Māori*, a guide to Western sanitation and hygiene practices, advocating the abandonment of *whare* was a compulsory text in Native Schools and an influential book in Ratana's mission (Wanhalla 2006, 115; Henderson 1972, 35). Western-style buildings presented their own sets of problems. They were very insular in design. They divided and compartmentalized aspects of life that were usually shared, such as family sleeping, and incorporated activities always kept separate, putting living areas close to *noa* (common) activities, like cooking and dining, and later washing and toileting. Buildings were also too small to accommodate large multigenerational families and their plans were not adaptable enough to suit the changing numbers of occupants associated with *whānaungatanga* (hosting long- and short-term family visitors). Not all Māori builders had the skills or means to construct with Western materials using the types of Western detailing that would prevent building failure through ground or airborne moisture damage. That knowledge had to be contracted from outside of the communities if it could be afforded, creating further dependence on Pākehā. Furthermore, Western planning methods tended to isolate family units on sections of land, rather than encourage conglomerations of family homes with shared external spaces for living, working, and play.

Government attention was drawn to the state of Māori housing by the impact of disease on the community. The 1918 to 1919 influenza epidemic claimed seven times as many Māori lives as Pākehā, tuberculosis ten times as many in the 1930s and 1940s, and typhoid forty times as many in the late 1930s (Lange 2012). Government reports suggested a causal link between poor health and poor housing conditions, identified as crowding (often just extended family living), polluted water supplies, and below Western standard sanitation. The inference was that customary modes of living, rather than a lack of access to adequate housing and health care, were perpetuating disease and death. In response, the 1935 Native Housing Act was passed to provide loans for Māori to build new homes and fund the replacement of "dilapidated" residences. New houses constructed under the scheme were of a similar style but typically (and unhelpfully) smaller than those offered non-Māori through the state housing program (Ministry of Culture and Heritage 2012b). The buildings' shortcomings did little to alleviate the perceived problems of crowding and poor sanitation that they were intended to solve (Wanhalla 2006, 116–17). Uptake was also hampered by difficulties in finding sites due to land alienation and problems with communal and individual titles. Māori also had difficulty raising security and finding affordable building materials

Many highly influential Māori leaders, such as Apirana Ngata, Maui Pomare, Peter Buck, and Te Puea Herangi, were in favour of the adoption of Western living standards as a means to reduce the impact of Western diseases (Wanhalla 2006, 103). They also attempted to address the relationship between land alienation and poor housing. On becoming minister of the Native Department in 1928, Ngata began a far-reaching land development scheme that, in the 1930s, had employed 5,000 Māori men to develop 200,000 acres of Māori land as farms (Harris and Tipene 2006, 74). The perpetual issue of land in communal title was overcome by consolidating Māori land through incorporations. Central to his programs was the redevelopment of the *whare whakairo* (decorated nineteenth-century Māori meeting house), led by the School of Māori Arts and Crafts that Ngata established through a 1926 Act of Parliament. These large elaborately decorated buildings became the community centres and forums for Māori farming incorporations on tribal and subtribal marae (Brown 2009, 85).

Ngata persuaded Te Puea, a leader of the Kīngitanga (Māori King Movement), to overcome seventy years of government distrust and join him in these schemes. Te Puea had been instrumental in the re-establishment of the Kīngitanga at Ngaruawāhia. She bought back a ten-acre block of confiscated land in 1920, and mobilized the labour of those among her people who were "orphaned" by the New Zealand Wars to build a capital town, known as Tūrangawaewae, for the Māori King (Brown 2009, 101). Her work fulfilled a prophecy by a former Māori King, Tawhiao:

> *Ko* Arekahānara *tōku haona kaha*
>
> *Ko* Kemureti *tōku oko horoi*
>
> *Ko* Ngāruawāhia *tōku tūrangawaewae.*
>
> Alexandra [Pirongia township] will ever be a symbol of my strength of character
>
> Cambridge a symbol of my wash bowl of sorrow
>
> And Ngāruawāhia my footstool. (Royal 2012)

In the earlier years of Tūrangawaewae, these workers lived in sugar-sack covered tents. A government inspection of living conditions at Tūrangawaewae, prompted by local Pākehā intervention, found that these dwellings were on a par, if not better, than those of their Pākehā neighbours due to Te Puea's determined approach to sanitation, hygiene, and tidiness. She extended her influence to domestic house design, developing residences for some Kīngitanga land development schemes that were a quarter of the cost of Western houses due to their combination of Māori and Pākehā building materials and technologies (Brown 2009, 104). The approach of Te Puea and Ngata demonstrated that the most responsive solutions for Māori without tūrangawaewae, land, and adequate housing were those developed by Māori. Indeed, even after Ngata's resignation from Parliament in 1934, the government's housing program assumed the objective of his Land Development Schemes of keeping Māori on their remaining lands as farmers. Land development loans could be used to construct houses and farm buildings and this program remained the most successful of all pre–Second World War Māori housing initiatives. By 1940, 1,224 houses had been built under the Land Development Scheme and only 368 with funds from the 1935 Act and its 1938 amendment (Wanhalla 2006, 106–8).

In the years before the Second World War the government promoted the idea that to be without a home, in the Western sense of that term, was to live in cultural, social, and economic regression. Home ownership could only be achieved through the acceptance of individual title to land and house, while a sanitary home and healthy family were considered by government officials and ministers to indicate successful integration and progression within the Western economic system (Wanhalla 2006, 105). Much emphasis was placed on the role of Māori men as property owners, wage earners, and farmers, which subordinated the role of Māori women within families and assisted in their repression within the New Zealand society. Women were instead judged, in government surveys of Māori housing, on the cleanliness and tidiness of their homes. Some communities were wary of the government housing schemes and loan packages, fearing these were yet another attempt to indebt them and alienate their lands should they default on the loans (Wanhalla 2006, 115). It might be concluded that since Māori had lost most of their land, government housing policy became the final instrument used to complete the colonization of New Zealand, controlling Māori access to, and lives within, their place of last resort, their houses:

> There are only remnants of our best "European" houses. My great grandparents, Hapeta and Harata Renata, had eighteen children

and at least five of them died at birth and in infancy, one in 1918, the year of the "Spanish Lady" influenza epidemic. Their first grandchild was also a victim of the flu. No one wanted to handle the dead in Kāeo, so my grandfather as Minister buried them. When he ran out of coffins, Hapeta built boxes out of weatherboards from his house, which made it *tapu*. It had been a beautiful weatherboard house. My great grandmother grew her own tobacco out the back and refused to speak English; being a Pākehā-style housewife wasn't for her. After Hapeta died, the house was left to fall to the ground, like Te Pahi's pre-fabricated house was left to decay on his island. There's nothing remaining of either of them, except for a door from Hapeta's house which sits alongside exhibits about the *Boyd* in the Kāeo Museum. (DB)

Urbanization and Poverty

Like other Indigenous urban migrants, Māori relocated to the cities for a variety of reasons, and had to find a place to dwell, a new type of tūrangawaewae. Discrimination in the job and housing (rental and sale) markets limited their choices. In 1936 around 13 percent (10,000) of the Māori population lived in urban centres, but that soon changed when Māori men decided or were directed to move by the Department of Labour and tribal committees to work in essential industries as part of the war effort. A number of Māori servicemen, who had been exposed to European and North African urban environments while on duty or on leave, also chose to settle in cities upon their return (Nikora et al. 2004, 94–5). As more Māori relocated, more family members came to join them. They came for various reasons, attracted by the possibility of better employment and educational opportunities, or seeking refuge from emotional stress and family conflict back on their tūrangawaewae. Some were made homeless by the 1953 Town and Country Planning Act, which only granted permission for the construction of new rural homes if the owner was a rural worker or had enough land to be self-sufficient (between five and ten acres) ("Town and Country Planning" 1962, 23). These conditions were difficult to meet when landholdings were either communally owned or had been severely fragmented through the individualization of land title. The 1953 Act was a tipping point in legislative attempts to deny Māori their tūrangawaewae by making many of those who had managed to hold onto their lands effectively homeless. With nowhere to live, they had no choice but to move away from their tūrangawaewae and start again with limited or no capital. By 1951, 23 percent (27,000) of the Māori population were living in cities, and by 1961 the total Māori population was double (201,159) of what it had been thirty years before, as adult and infant mortality rates declined (Nikora et al. 2004, 94). The Māori urban population grew rapidly from this point with 80 percent of Māori living in cities by 1981, and just under 85 percent in 2006.

Discrimination in the private rental sector had forced the first wave of Māori urban migrants to rent decrepit mid-nineteenth-century workers cottages in the industrial zones of Auckland, such as Freeman's Bay.[6] Crowding was a serious issue with up to ten people sleeping in a single room, and in one instance sixty people living in one house (Schrader 2005, 61). It was not until 1948 that Māori were brought into the state housing system when, prompted by the rural to urban migration, the Department of Māori Affairs partnered with the State Advanced Corporation to build them homes. Individual Māori families were resettled among Pākehā through the "pepper-potting" policy in order to break ancestral links, suppress customary behaviours, and hasten assimilation into Western culture (McKay and Stevens 2014, 95–6). Racism effectively isolated these families, and a dislocated and sometimes disaffected generation of urban-born and urban-raised Māori emerged from this resettlement. By the 1950s it became clear that the policy was unsustainable due to the sheer volume of Māori moving to cities, and the growing numbers of migrants joining from nearby Pacific island groups. Mainstream state housing neighbourhoods that accommodated predominantly Māori and Pacific peoples were developed on the city fringes, like Ōtara and Māngere in Auckland and Linwood and Avonside in Christchurch. Commuter towns also opened up through major roading projects, such as Wainuiomata and Porirua in the Wellington region (Brown 2009, 126). Mortgages in the form of state advances attempted to overcome the discrimination that Māori (including people of mixed heritage) and interracial couples faced from lending institutions when attempting to buy their own homes or build on communally owned land.

The state houses and state-assisted housing plans available to Māori families were indistinguishable from those offered to Pākehā and were a clear continuation of a government policy designed to break down Māori extended families and living patterns.[7] This was not a case of designers being unaware of Māori needs. Prominent New Zealand architects Gerhart Rosenberg, Don McRae, Max Rosenfeld, John Scott (who was Māori), and Bill Wilson (who was married to Scott's sister) designed and promoted housing concepts that would accommodate extended families, outdoor living, and, in some cases, differentiated living activities that responded to *noa* activities (McKay 2011). Their schemes were largely ignored by the state, and only in a few instances were single prototypes built. There is also some evidence that Māori families

Figure 16.3. State houses in Champion Street, in the Wellington satellite suburb of Porirua East, c. 1950s. Alexander Turnbull Library, 1/2-051884-F.

who requested housing that observed the separation of *noa* activities from living and sleeping were not provided with state housing (Schrader 2005, 128). The rest had to compromise or abandon their belief systems.

Surprisingly there has been little change in the government's approach to the supply of loans to house Māori since 1935. The Land Development Scheme and loans program established under the 1935 Native Housing Act, persisted until the 1980s. These were replaced by the Papakāinga Lending Scheme and the Low Deposit Rural Lending Scheme in 1994, which were better adapted to funding construction on communally owned land (New Zealand Productivity Commission 2012, 252).

A more dramatic government policy that has had a devastating effect on Māori housing needs was the 1992 Housing Restructuring Act, which marked a shift from income-related rents to market rentals in the state housing sector. Even with targeted subsidies for low-income families, the change in some cases doubled tenants' rent, leaving them with little money for food and medical care (Waldergrave, Love, and Stuart 2000, n.p.). Less income has also meant less housing choices. The changes have also increased household crowding, which has had consequential effects on health, particularly that of children, as diseases long-dormant have resurfaced. New Zealand's rheumatic fever rate is on a par with that of developing countries, while Māori and Pacific children make up more than 90 percent of acute hospital admissions (Janie, Baker, and Vanugopal 2008). Cases of tuberculosis and meningitis within the Māori community have also risen significantly.

In spite of difficulties, some families have managed to maintain their *ahi kā* over a number of generations by frequently visiting their tūrangawaewae. Others have had their connections severed due to poverty and intentional or unintentional loss of familial relationships, leaving them and their succeeding generations struggling to maintain their Māori identity due to tūrangawaewae kore. It should be noted that the Māori urban migration has not been contained by national boundaries. In 2011, 128,000 people of Māori descent, one-sixth of the total Māori population, were living in Australia (Kukutai and Pawar 2013). In Sydney this community has its own *urupā* (burial ground) in the Rookwood Necropolis, where the first Māori to die in Australia was reinterred (Te Pahi's daughter Atahoe, a.k.a. Mary Bruce, c. 1891–1909). Other historical *wāhi tapu* (sacred places) in Sydney include the 1819 Māori seminary in Parramatta, known today as Rangihoua, due to its association with the 1814 mission (Kamira 2010, 25–6). There is also a growing trans-Tasmanian commuter community, predominantly male, that takes advantage of the high wages offered in the Queensland mining industry, the low cost of living in rural New Zealand, and budget airfares between both countries. Their movement between countries is fundamentally economic and not significantly different from working in a New Zealand urban centre to support a family on one's rural tūrangawaewae. The imprinting of a landscape with sacred memories has always been the process by which Māori have acculturated landscapes to become their tūrangawaewae, and its extension to urban areas and international locations can be seen as a continuation of the practice:

> City life has been a mixed blessing for my family. When my grandmother Puti Renata married my grandfather, Ivan Slater, and moved to the town of Gisborne (in the eastern North Island) in the 1920s, they could only afford to live in a former shop. Three of their five children had been born by 1930, including my mother. Despite tribal differences, my grandmother managed to make connections with the local Māori by joining their *kapa haka* (Māori performance) group led by Lieut. Col. Peter Awatere, a World War II Māori Battalion hero. She was a fluent speaker of *te reo* (the Māori language) but whatever she taught her children at home was defeated by the "no Māori talk" policy at their school. As a child my mother was embarrassed by where they lived and used to pretend that a sprawling bungalow on Gladstone Road was her home by sitting on its fence and claiming it to be hers to anyone who would listen. My grandmother persuaded my grandfather to get her a mortgage from the bank, as Māori women were not allowed to borrow, and with it she purchased the Gladstone Road home. She ran it as a boarding house to repay the loan. Although the purchase of this house was my mother's dream come true, she had to share it with about a dozen otherwise homeless men who

my grandmother took in, fed, and cared for in return for their state benefit. At the age of fifteen, my mother decided to leave home and she took off with her suitcase in search of brighter city lights, which she found in the South Island, in Dunedin. (DB)

Nowhere Left to Stand in the City

Additional housing pressures have been brought to bear on urban *mana whenua*, the customary landholders of places that became cities in the nineteenth century, and they have more recently been affected by urban sprawl. Many have vigorously defended their tūrangawaewae and *kaitiakitanga* (guardianship; stewardship) of local resources while becoming a minority in their own lands. The employment and housing stresses on Māori who have migrated to the city have been so great that some have elected or been forced to return to their ancestral tūrangawaewae, only to encounter the same issues of long-term unemployment and inadequate housing there.

The resilience of the Ngāti Whātua tribe of Tāmaki-Makarau (Auckland) is the most well-known example of *mana whenua* resistance. The tribe had lost most of their lands through pre-emption within ten years of inviting the Governor of New Zealand, William Hobson, to live in their region in 1840. A little over a century later, Ngāti Whātua were evicted from their remaining city landholding in Ōkahu Bay when the government compulsorily acquired the land and destroyed their homes on the pretense that, ahead of a Royal Tour, they were unsanitary and unsightly (McKay 2014, 95).

They were moved to nearby state housing. In 1976, the conservative National Government announced that it was going to sell adjacent land at Takaparawhau, or Bastion Point, to the highest bidder for a high-cost residential development. Under the leadership of Joe Hawke, the Orakei Māori Action Committee occupied Takaparawhau in protest, building a village centred on a new marae as an affirmation of their tūrangawaewae. Their occupation ended on 25 May 1978, after 507 days, when 800 police officers invaded the settlement removing 222 protestors and destroying the village (Taonui 2012). The eviction was broadcast on television news and generated significant public sympathy for the plight of Ngāti Whātua. In 1987, Takaparawhau was among 700 acres of land restored to Ngāti Whātua by the government, after the Waitangi Tribunal (see below) recommended its return. Only a fraction of this land can be built on, and Ngāti Whātua have had to consider densification through proposed multi-storey developments as the only means to accommodate members on their tūrangawaewae. Ngarimu Blair from Ngāti Whātua

Maori Shacks Go Up in Smoke

One of the ramshackle homes at Orakei set on fire after demolition yesterday.

Figure 16.4. Ngāti Whātua homes at Ōkahu Bay burned on the instructions of the Commissioner for Crown Lands, 1951. Photograph by New Zealand Herald. Auckland Library, 995.1103 O63 O63p.

comments "this city [Auckland] has been pretty good at teaching us to forget about out past, to forget our traditions, forget the stories and so on," continuing "we see urban design as a way for people to access tribal knowledge as they move about this urban landscape, which quite frankly we've been ethnically cleansed of" (Blair 2010, 50).

As cities such as Auckland and Tauranga grow, these problems are spreading to *mana whenua,* who until recently would have regarded themselves as living in a rural context. Māori landholders on the city fringes have found their land rezoned, restricting building opportunities, while the provision of reticulated water and sewage lines has reduced self-sufficiency and therefore social and cultural autonomy.

The emotional pull of tūrangawaewae is evident in a small-scale but nevertheless steady urban to rural Māori migration that began in the mid-1980s. Māori urban unemployment increased dramatically as a consequence of the neo-liberal economic policies of the 1984 to 1990 Labour Government. Significant job losses in sectors where Māori had found blue- and white-collar employment ensued as the public service was downsized, state-owned companies corporatized, and subsidies and trade protections removed from local manufacturing industries. Facing the prospect of long-term unemployment, individuals and families began to return to their tūrangawaewae. The prohibitive 1953 Town and Country Act was repealed and replaced by a new act in 1977, and then again replaced by the 1991 Resource Management Act, both of which allowed for more intensive building on communal lands and for smaller rural "lifestyle" blocks. Here the returned re-established their customary occupation rights on inherited landholdings, often inhabiting older buildings suffering from deferred maintenance. Some Māori purchased lifestyle blocks in the vicinity of marae, building on this land small, low-cost, and portable or prefabricated houses that have not survived well in exposed environments. The return of Māori to their tūrangawaewae in the wake of economic reforms and urban housing unaffordability has put additional pressure on the rural housing resources in terms of the availability of livable housing and extended families growing in numbers to embrace the returned. Yet, in Māori terms, many rural Indigenous families are "home" on their tūrangawaewae rather than inadequately housed or houseless (Kearns 2006, 251).

Inspired by the social and political gains of the African American civil rights movement, rural and urban Māori adopted political activism as a means to raise awareness of the legacies of land alienation, including poor housing, health, and educational outcomes, as well as the loss of *te reo* and Māori cultural practices. A principal demand was that the government uphold the guarantees of Māori sovereignty over land in the Māori version of the Treaty of Waitangi. The 1975 *hīkoi* or Māori land march from Te Hapua, a small Māori settlement in the north of the North Island, down to the country's capital in Wellington captured the essence of Māori grievances with the protest slogan "Not One Acre More." Such direct action initiatives prompted a sequence of government responses that included the 1975 establishment of the Waitangi Tribunal to hear Māori Treaty claims, and the bicultural transformation of local and central government organizations and systems in the 1980s and 1990s. However, biculturalism has not adequately addressed landlessness, homelessness, poor housing, and other inequalities. Māori leaders are now lobbying the government for a binational approach to Māori issues, in which Māori are decision makers and service deliverers, through constitutional transformation.

Street Dwelling, Houselessness, and Extreme Housing Need

The drivers behind Māori street dwelling and extreme housing need are complex and include mental and physical well-being issues, financial pressures, and relationship stresses among other factors. Urbanization and poverty caused by landlessness certainly influence the context that leads to the emergence of these drivers. But they are also significant impediments to *whānau* (extended family)-based initiatives to reduce street dwelling and extreme housing need.

The most accurate figures of street dwelling are derived through City Mission records. In Auckland, New Zealand's largest city with a current population of 1.4 million people, seventy-nine people were recorded as sleeping in doorways, on benches, and outside within a three-kilometre radius of the Sky Tower during the 2013 annual City Mission street count census (Statistics New Zealand 2013a; Auckland City Mission 2013, 18). Most of these rough sleepers were men and around half of them were Māori. The situation of Māori women without housing is somewhat masked by their ability to use social networks and "couch surf" in the homes of friends and relatives. The situation is more complicated in Christchurch, New Zealand's next most populous city of about 350,000 inhabitants, due to the February 2010 earthquake and aftershock sequence which left 11,500 homes, a little over 6 percent of the total housing stock, uninhabitable (Statistics New Zealand 2013b). Māori are disproportionately reflected in these figures as most of the houses damaged were in the city's eastern suburbs where more of the Māori population lived. Houseless families have generally either found alternative rental accommodation, purchased other homes, or are couch surfing. However, the number of Christchurch houseless seeking government assistance through the Housing New Zealand Corporation,[8] over a six-month period, has increased from its lowest number in August 2012 to its highest (64) in February 2013 (Ministry of Business, Innovation and Employment 2013, 21). Similar increases have occurred for families living in cars, garages, and caravans (102), as well as camping grounds (13), and emergency housing (58). Christchurch street dwellers seeking accommodation in the City Mission night shelter in 2012 also increased 20 percent above the pre-earthquake figure with users staying longer and presenting more complex physical and mental well-being issues (Ministry of Business, Innovation and Employment 2013, 20). Although publically available data does not record ethnicity, we might assume that a significant number of these families and individuals were Māori. Reflecting on Māori street dwelling, Groot and colleagues note that "With the exception of a few, even Māori and iwi [tribal] authorities appear to hesitate when responding to [Māori homelessness], perhaps reflecting the increasing social and economic stratification of

Māori society or the position that homelessness is more a government issue than a Māori one" (2011b, 237).

Māori and Pacific peoples living in cities are more likely to be poorly housed and suffer "psychological distress" (the modern "demoralization") as a consequence (Kearns and Smith 1993, 275). Māori already living with mental illness are further disadvantaged as they compete in an open rental and ownership market for housing appropriate for their well-being and within their income. The true extent of Māori in serious housing need is apparent in the disproportionate number of Indigenous individuals and families living in crowded accommodation, emergency housing, and unhealthy homes.

Since the majority of Māori live in cities, and predominantly Auckland, the issue of Indigenous rural housing need is a hidden phenomenon that has proved difficult to address. It is estimated that up to 10,000 rural Māori homes require repair or replacement, and 75 percent of these buildings are in the Northland (i.e., north of Auckland) region (New Zealand Productivity Commission 2012, 243). Given the long history of Māori land alienation, and its economic and social consequences, it is not surprising that rural Māori have high rates of unemployment and draw lower median incomes than most other ethnic groups. Families under financial stress put a lower priority on home maintenance, and over generations this has led to the growing pool of old houses in poor condition that the rural Māori occupy. The relocation of the working-age (twenty to fifty years old) population away from rural areas since the mid-1980s, has left a noticeable generational gap in some rural Māori communities that has likely contributed to the deferred maintenance of buildings (Nikora et. al. 2008). Māori with both skills and finances to attend to dampness and cold caused by building failure are absent:

> Dispersed from the top to the bottom of the country, my grandparents' family had to make-do with housing built by their own hands, or rented with whatever money they could spare. My mother was still living in Dunedin when her two youngest siblings, her sisters, came to stay. My grandparents had decided to return to Whangaroa and left Gisborne in 1952, but country life had not suited the girls. My grandmother loved being "home" with her family, even when they swapped Gladstone Road for a small dwelling built by my grandfather. After one sister got married in Dunedin, mum and her other sister moved to Auckland. They lived in a caravan park in Avondale before getting a flat in New Lynn. In the mid-1960s, despite her excellent work, Mum's boss had threatened to fire

her from her job on the production line of a box factory when he realized she was Māori. Her boss recanted when the union representative threatened to bring the factory out on strike in protest. Then her sister got married and moved out. Mum told the newly married couple that she was ready to settle down in a proper house and lead a more settled life. She said that she would marry the next man she met. That man was my father. (DB)

Conclusion

Only 6 percent of land in New Zealand remains in Māori freehold title. In a little more than two centuries Māori have lost their tūrangawaewae, and with it, their ways and means of living. From the outset, the colonial process has been one of stripping Māori of their assets to support the needs of Pākehā with almost no regard to how this would affect the well-being of the Indigenous population. This process had been supported through the articles and acts of annexation and law. Māori have always resisted the more obvious attempts to destabilize their society with armed resistance, protest, and religio-political mobilization, yet it was the subtle effects of Westernization, the suggestion that Māori living was somehow unsanitary and substandard, that led to the abandonment of customary housing. With it went much of the control that Māori had over the construction and maintenance of their buildings.

It was not until the early twentieth century that the plight of Māori in severe housing need became so dire, through serious contagious illnesses and inadequate housing, that the government was forced to act. But it was too little too late for many Māori. The loss of community title made it difficult to finance better housing and a lack of understanding about Māori lifeways provided inappropriate architectural solutions. Unable to make their way on their tūrangawaewae, the majority of Māori moved to cities (in New Zealand and later in Australia) in the mid-twentieth century to start again, usually with little capital. Confronted with discrimination and inequities in housing, employment, and education, "getting by" and "getting on" has been a challenge, and Māori are disproportionately represented in every measure of poverty. "Talking back" to neo-liberalism, the Māori scholar Mike Walker argues the socio-economic development of New Zealand rests on the progress of Māori and Pacific peoples, as theirs are the only growing populations.

Street dwelling, severe housing need, and inadequate housing are Western-defined physical measures of dispossession and have been discussed here within a historical context. It has been suggested that if Māori landlessness is the root cause of Māori homelessness, then any long-term solution to housing the Māori must address the loss of land title and involve Māori as decision makers if not also service deliverers. Houselessness, for Māori, is one outcome of the loss of tūrangawaewae that has occurred with land alienation. *Tūrangawaewae kore* is not an exact fit with homelessness, but perhaps a better indicator of Māori well-being.

As my *korero tuku iho* have demonstrated, Māori stories about tūrangawaewae, land loss, and housing do not unfold in a linear fashion, but are cross-referenced to other events, places, and people, collapsing space and time. Recurrences which might seem serendipitous, in the Western sense (for instance, references to Te Pahi, strong women, the *Boyd*, the Mission, and axes), are signs in the Māori world. These stories are comforting when times are hard. They reinforce the bravery, resistance, and resilience of one's ancestors: a woman supporting her wounded husband while they are swimming for their lives as their tūrangawaewae is desecrated; another woman who refuses to speak the language and adopt the habits of the colonizer; her husband ensuring that his kin have a dignified entry into the next world at the cost of his own home; their daughter who opens her family home to the homeless; and my mother who lived her life by her own set of rules and housing choices:

> My mother always said that life was a repeating cycle and that the ancestral stories she told would help me when things "swung around" again. I'd just finished writing this chapter on homelessness for Evelyn and Julia, and had the research on Te Pahi fresh in my mind, when I received an email from Hugh Rihari, an elder of the Ngāti Torehina *hapū*, the descendants of the people who had stayed behind after the 1810 attack on Wairoa Bay. "I was given a very small clipping from a news article titled 'Medal Auction,'" Hugh wrote, "The medal to be auctioned next month was presented to Te Pahi in 1806 by Philip Gidley King. It was thought to have been lost to the world until it was brought into Sotheby's in Australia by a family who had had it for 100 years.... It would also be interesting to know, whether or not anything can be done to recover this '*taonga*' before it's lost for another 100 years. Fruit for thought." Armed with the primary documents accumulated for the chapter as evidence, Hugh and I, and others from our respective *hapū* began a campaign of public awareness, museum lobbying, legal action, and protests ahead of the auction in Sydney. After all else had proved fruitless, the Museum of New Zealand Te Papa Tongarewa and

Figure 16.5. Repatriation of the Te Pahi medal, Papuke (above Wairoa Bay), 29 November 2014. Photograph by Grant Bulley.

Auckland War Memorial Museum purchased the medal for $AUS 300,000 with our full support.

The museums consented to the medal's formal Māori welcome back at Wairoa Bay immediately on its return from Australia in late November 2014, 204 years after we believe it was stolen from Te Pahi's house and we had been forced to leave. That same week, the Waitangi Tribunal found that Ngāpuhi never intended to cede its sovereignty by signing the Treaty of Waitangi. Many commentators saw the medal as evidence of Governor King's recognition of our sovereignty. As my people brought the medal back to Wairoa Bay, a cousin called out to Motuapo Island from the shore "We didn't die! We're alive!" momentarily causing us to pause and reflect before we ascended Pāpuke hill where Hugh's *hapū* were waiting to receive us. Finally, we had returned to our tūrangawaewae. (DB)

Notes

1 See for example the outstanding work by Robin Kearns and Shiloh Groot on Māori, homelessness, and tūrangawaewae.

2 Statistics New Zealand uses the Equivalised Crowding Index, Canadian National Occupancy Standard, and American Crowding Index, http://www.stats.govt.nz/tools_and_services/nzdotstat/housing-quality-tables/crowding-occupancy-rate.aspx.

3 House rules have been observed to be effective in Australian Indigenous urban communities as identified by Paul Memmott, Christina Birdsall-Jones, and Kelly Greenop in *Australian Indigenous House Crowding*, Australian Housing and Urban Research Unit, 2012: 152–3.

4 The Mauri-o-Meter project is led by Dr. Kepa Morgan, University of Auckland. More information about the project can be found at http://mauriometer.com/DataEntry/index.

5 See for example the excellent work by Shiloh Groot, Robin Kearns, and Linda Waimarie Nikora and their collaborators.

6 In the 1970s, after industry had relocated to the city fringes, these buildings and areas became popular again among Pākehā wishing to live and work closer to town and wanting to renovate the Victorian building stock. Māori and Pacific families who had remained now found that rents increased beyond what they could afford and they were forced to move to cheaper suburbs or into state housing.

7 See for example the plans in *Nga Whare Ataahua mo te Iwi Maori: Homes for the People*, Department of Maori Affairs, 1963.

8 Housing New Zealand Corporation is a Crown agent with delegated responsibility to provide housing service to people in need, http://www.hnzc.co.nz/about-us.

References

Auckland City Mission. 2013. *Annual Report for the Year Ending 30 June 2013*. Auckland: Auckland City Mission.

Belich, James. 1986. *The New Zealand Wars and the Victorian Interpretation of Racial Conflict*. Auckland, New Zealand: Auckland University Press.

Binney, Judith. 1990. "The Native Land Courts and the Māori Communities, 1865–1890." In *The People and the Land: Te Tangata Me Te Whenua*, edited by Judith Binney, Judith Bassett, and Erik Olssen, 143–63. Wellington: Bridget Williams Books.

Blair, Ngarimu. 2010. "Orakei Papakāinga Ki Mua: Towards 2030 and Beyond." In *Tāone Tupu Ora: Indigenous Knowledge and Sustainable Urban Design*, edited by Keriata Stuart and Michelle Thompson-Fawcett, 50–59. Wellington: New Zealand Centre for Sustainable Cities, University of Otago.

Brown, Deidre. 2009. *Māori Architecture: From Fale to Wharenui and Beyond*. Auckland: Raupo Publishing.

Brown, Deidre, Ngarino Ellis, and Jonathan Mane-Wheoki. 2013. "Does Māori Art History Matter?" Address presented at the 12th Annual Gordon H. Brown Lecture, Victoria University, Wellington, 14 November.

Department of Māori Affairs. 1963 *Nga Whare Ataahua mo te Iwi Māori: Homes for the People*. Wellington: Department of Māori Affairs.

Field, Michael. 2010. "Hearing Starts into Ngapuhi's Claims." *Stuff*, 5 May, http://www. stuff.co.nz/national/politics/3674280/Hearing-starts-into-Ngapuhis-claims (accessed 5 January 2014).

Finucane, James. 1998. *Distracted Settlement: New South Wales after Bligh from the Journal of Lieutenant James Finucane 1808–1810*. Edited by Anne Maree Whitaker. Melbourne: Melbourne University Press.

Groot, Shiloh, Darrin Hodgetts, Linda Waimarie Nikora, and Chez Leggat-Cook. 2011a. "A Māori Homeless Woman." *Ethnography* 12 (3): 375–97.

Groot, Shiloh, Darrin Hodgetts, Linda Waimarie Nikora, and Mohi Rua. 2011b. "Māori and Homeless." In *Māori and Social Issues*, edited by Tracey McIntosh and Malcolm Mulholland, 235–47. Wellington: Huia Publishers.

Hargreaves, R. P. 1960. "Māori Agriculture after the Wars (1871–1886)." *Journal of the Polynesian Society* 69 (4): 354–67.

Harris, Graham, and Percy Tipene. 2006. "Māori Land Development." In *State of the Māori Nation: Twenty-First-Century Issues in Aotearoa*, edited by Malcolm Mulholland, 67–79. Auckland: Reed, Auckland.

Henderson, James. 1972. *Ratana: The Man, the Church, the Political Movement*. Wellington: A.H. and A.N. Reed and the Polynesian Society.

Hooper, Keith C., and Kate Kearins. 2003. "Substance but Not Form: Capital Taxation and Public Finance in New Zealand, 1840–1859." *Accounting History* 8 (2): 101–19.

Hoskins, Rau, Rihi Te Nara, Peter Rhodes, Philip Guy, and Chris Sage. 2002. *Ki te Hau Kainga: New Perspectives on Māori Housing Solutions*. Auckland: Housing New Zealand Corporation.

Jaine, Richard, Baker, Michael, and Kamalesh Venugopal. 2008. "Epidemiology of Acute Rheumatic Fever in New Zealand 1996–2005." *Journal of Paediatrics and Child Health* 44 (10): 564–71.

Kamira, Jo. 2010. "Māori." *Sydney Journal* 3 (1): 23–34.

Kawharu, Hugh. n.d. "The Kawharu Translation." Waitangi Tribunal, http://www. justice.govt.nz/tribunals/waitangi-tribunal/treaty-of-waitangi/the-kawharu-translation (accessed 5 January 2014).

Keane, Basil. 2012. "Kotahitanga—Unity Movements—Parliamentary Unity Movements, 1870 to 1900." *Te Ara: The Encyclopedia of New Zealand*, http://www. TeAra.govt.nz/en/kotahitanga-unity-movements/page-3.

Kearns, Robin. 2006. "Places to Stand but not Necessarily to Dwell: The Paradox of Rural Homelessness in New Zealand." In *International Perspectives on Rural Homelessness*, edited by Paul Milbourne and Paul Cloke, 247–60. London and New York: Routledge.

Kearns, Robin, and Christopher Smith. 1993. "Housing Stressors and Mental Health among Marginalised Urban Populations." *Area* 25 (3): 267–78.

Kukutai, Tahu, and Shefali Pawar. 2013. *A Socio-Femographic Profile of Māori Living in Australia*, Nidea Working Papers 3. Hamilton: University of Waikato, National Institute of Demographic and Economic Analysis.

Lange, Raeburn. 2012. "Te Hauora Māori i Mua: History of Māori Health—Slow Progress, 1920 to 1945." *Te Ara: The Encyclopedia of New Zealand*, http://www. TeAra.govt.nz/en/te-hauora-maori-i-mua-history-of-maori-health/page-4.

McKay, Bill. 2011. "Modernists and Māori Housing 1960." In *Audience: 28th Annual Conference of the Society of Architectural Historians, Australia and New Zealand*, edited by Antony Moulis and Deborah van der Plaat. Brisbane: University of Queensland.

McKay, Bill and Andrea Stevens. 2014. "Māori and State Houses." In *Beyond the State: New Zealand State Houses From Modest to Mondern*, edited by Bill McKay and Andrea Stevens, 95–98. Auckland: Penguin.

McKinnon, Malcolm, Barry Bradley, and Russell Kirkpatrick. 1997. *New Zealand Historical Atlas: Ko Papatuanuku E Takoto Nei*. Wellington: Bateman and the Department of Internal Affairs Historical Branch.

Marsden, Samuel. 1932. *The Letters and Journals of Samuel Marsden, 1765–1838*. Edited by John Rawson Elder. Dunedin: Coulls, Somerville and Wilkie.

Middleton, Angela. 2008. *Te Puna: A New Zealand Mission Station*. New York and London: Springer.

Ministry of Business, Innovation and Employment. 2013. *Housing Pressures in Christchurch: A Summary of the Evidence 2013*. Wellington: Ministry of Business, Innovation and Employment.

Ministry of Culture and Heritage. 2012a. "The Treaty in Practice: Obtaining Land," http://www.nzhistory.net.nz/politics/treaty/the-treaty-in-practice/obtaining-land (accessed 2 April 2016).

_____. 2012b. "State Housing: Outside the Mainstream." http://www.nzhistory.net.nz/culture/we-call-it-home/outside-the-mainstream.

Newman, Keith. 2009. *Ratana: The Prophet*. Auckland: Raupo Penguin.

New Zealand Productivity Commission. 2012. *Housing Affordability Inquiry*. Wellington: New Zealand Productivity Commission.

Nicholas, John Liddiard. 1817. *Narrative of a Voyage to New Zealand. Performed in the Years 1814 and 1815, in Company with Rev. Samuel Marsden*, vol 1. London: James Black and Son.

Nikora, Linda Waimarie, Bernard Guerin, Mohi Rua, and Ngahuia Te Awekotuku. 2004. "Moving Away from Home: Some Social Consequences for Tūhoe Migrating to the Waikato." *New Zealand Population Review* 30 (1 and 2): 93–109.

Nikora, Linda Waimarie, Mohi Rua, Ngahuia Te Awekotuku, Bernard Guerin, and Jane McCaughey. 2008. "Social Consequences of Tūhoe Migration: Voices from Home in Te Urewera." *Mai Review* 2. Article 1. http://www.review.mai.ac.nz/index.php/MR/issue/view/10.

Pool. Ian. 2012. "Population Change—Māori Population Change." *Te Ara: The Encyclopedia of New Zealand*, http://www.TeAra.govt.nz/en/population-change/page-6 (accessed 2 April 2016).

Royal Te Ahukaramū Charles, "Papatūānuku the land, Tūrangawaewae a place to stand," *Te Ara: The Encyclopedia of New Zealand*. , http://www.TeAra.govt.nz/en/papatuanuku-the-land/page-5 (accessed 2 April 2016).

Schrader, Ben. 2005. *We Call It Home: A History of State Housing in New Zealand*. Auckland: Reed Publishing.

Sorrenson, M. P. K. 1956. "Land Purchase Methods and Their Effect on Maori Population 1865–1901." *Journal of the Polynesian Society* 65 (3): 183–99.

Smith, Linda Tuhiwai. 1999. *Decolonizing Methodologies: Research and Indigenous Peoples.* Dunedin: University of Otago Press.

Statistics New Zealand. 2013a. "2013 Census Population Tables: Auckland." http://www.stats.govt.nz/Census/2013-census/data-tables/population-dwelling-tables/auckland.aspx.

———. 2013b. "2013 Census Population Tables: Canterbury." http://www.stats.govt.nz/Census/2013-census/data-tables/population-dwelling-tables/canterbury.aspx.

Taonui, Rāwiri. 2012. "Ngāti Whātua: Ngāti Whātua and the Treaty of Waitangi." *Te Ara: The Encyclopedia of New Zealand.* Accessed 2 April 2016. http://www.TeAra.govt.nz/en/ngati-whatua/page-4.

"Town and Country Planning." 1962. *Te Ao Hou: The New World* 38 (March): 23.

Waldegrave, Charles, Catherine Love, and Shane Stuart. 2000. "Urban Māori Responses to Changes in State Housing Provision." *Social Policy Journal of New Zealand* 14 (July). http://www.msd.govt.nz/about-msd-and-our-work/publications-resources/journals-and-magazines/social-policy-journal/spj14/urban-maori-responses-to-changes-in-state-housing-provision.html.

Wanhalla, Angela. 2006. "Housing Un/Healthy Bodies: Native Housing Surveys and Maori Health in New Zealand 1930–45." *Health and History* 8 (1): 100–120.

———. 2013. *Matters of the Heart: A History of Interracial Marriage in New Zealand.* Auckland: Auckland University Press.

CHAPTER 17

Emplaced Cultural Practices through which Homeless Men Can Be Māori

PITA KING, DARRIN HODGETTS, MOHI RUA,
AND TINIWAI TE WHETU

As noted in the introduction to this section of the book, colonization in New Zealand led to massive land confiscations, economic exclusion, large-scale ruptures to communal life and identities, and mass movement of Māori from homelands to urban centres (Groot et al. 2011b; Jackson 1992). These events are an ongoing legacy and they contribute to the well-being of Māori and our participation in contemporary society (Durie 1998). Given our history of disruption and displacement, it should be no surprise that Māori remain disproportionately affected by homelessness when compared to the population of the settler society (Groot et al. 2011b). The research documented in this chapter was located at one key site of Māori resistance to colonialism and depicts Māori efforts to renew a key place to stand. Ōrākei marae (communal complex used for everyday Māori life) is at the heart of Takaparawhau (Bastion Point, central Auckland) and became a national focal point for Māori protests over land confiscations by the Crown. This culminated in a mass occupation of the site for 504 days between 1977 and 1978 and ended with 222 arrests, prior to the land being returned to its rightful owners, the Ngāti Whātua (a local tribal group in the Auckland area). Figure 17.1 shows the Ōrākei marae garden overlooking the Auckland harbour.

Figure 17.1. A researcher and a participant working in the marae gardens. All photographs courtesy of the authors.

Below, a representative from Ngāti Whātua reflects on the establishment of a gardening project involving homeless Māori as part of the *iwi*'s (tribe) reconciliation of Takaparawhau, encompassing Ōrākei marae:

> They [homeless Māori men] are Māori and this is a marae and they have the *reo* [the Māori language]...They just felt at home. And they had a place to come to for their *wairua* [spirit] and to just be themselves.... As a people we could identify with them because we were homeless in our own land. We had nothing left. We could identify with them and how they were feeling. We almost got wiped out. So that was our *aroha* [love/compassion] to them. We couldn't have it that we owned all of this and we left them over there.... We are giving respect to our ancestors by helping other people. The *manaakitanga* [caring/nurturing] that we got from our ancestors, we have to carry that on.... They're in town, but up here they've got the peacefulness. They're Māori so they know this. They're part of our reconciliation of our land. (Matipo)

This quote reflects the value many Māori groups place on the care, support, and inclusion of others. It invokes an understanding of the importance of maintaining cultural spaces, such as marae, for preserving associated Māori *ways of being*. Further, by helping and caring for others, members of Ngāti Whātua are able to rebuild their connections with the land by reproducing cultural values and activities that reaffirm their traditions, honour their ancestors, and assert their guardianship over Takaparawhau. The above quotation invokes broader considerations of the issue beyond conventional Eurocentric understandings that often reduce homelessness to a matter of housing, without addressing broader societal, historical, and political influences that continue to shape Māori homelessness today (Groot et al. 2011b; Johnson, Hodgetts, and Nikora 2013).

Central to Ngāti Whātua's response to homelessness is the marae: a culturally patterned space of belonging, connection, and being. Marae are traditional communal spaces for mundane and everyday activities, such as eating and socializing, and also spaces for highly ritualized cultural events, such as *tangihanga* (Māori death ritual), *hui* (meetings), and weddings (Salmond 2004; Walker 1990). By and large, marae are run by the *whānau* (families) and *hapū* (subtribe) members of the marae, volunteering time where and when they can, and in doing so, they reaffirm their membership to that marae (Mead 2003; Walker 1992). Such marae remain at the heart of many Māori communities as sites of respite for local people and visitors, and have served as beachheads in revitalising Māori culture and language during the twentieth century (Walker 1990). Marae also comprise much more than "activity settings" or backdrops for social interaction (Hodgetts et al. 2010a). Within the Māori world, a marae cannot be reduced to a container for social actions (see Tilley 1994). Rather, marae provide the "focal point of Māori culture" (Walker 1992, 15); their continued presence in Aotearoa (New Zealand) provides an overt statement of Indigenous identity and rights. Marae stands as symbols of resistance to colonial oppression (Mead 2003). The production and reproduction of culture through everyday material practices is directly facilitated by the marae space, which serves social, financial, logistical, and spiritual functions. Marae remain central to the reproduction of cultural relationships and ways of being Māori.

This chapter explores the involvement of a group of older Māori men who are homeless, and who work in the gardens at Ōrākei marae on Tuesdays and Thursdays. This is not the ancestral marae of the homeless participants themselves, but it is a culturally familiar space to them (Mead 2003; Salmond 2004). We (the authors) consider the navigating of the culturally patterned spaces as a necessary and appropriate aspect of our research. Community involvement guided our actions and allowed us to demonstrate our respect to the people and to the land. After outlining our engagements with the participants on this marae, we consider the interrelated issues of place, homelessness, and Māori ways of being. These preliminary sections establish the conceptual and cultural context for our analysis of our homeless participants' culturally anchored social practices in the marae. The chapter is completed with general reflections that emerge from this research, including some comments relating to service provisions for Māori homeless people.

Conceptualizing Our Research into Māori Homelessness from within a Marae Garden

This project was formally initiated with a *pōwhiri* (welcoming ceremony) at Saint Matthew's church in August 2012. Members of Ngāti Whātua, the Auckland City Mission (a partner in the gardening project), and a group of homeless Māori men ("Streeties") engaged the research team in *whaikōrero* (formal oration), *waiata* (song), and *hongi* (pressing of noses to symbolize the breath of life). Following the formalities of the *pōwhiri*, a conversation about this research was facilitated by the authors and colleagues. This continued the fostering of connections through dialogue, reciting of *whakapapa* (genealogy) and tribal links, and general rapport building, after which we shared a meal to symbolically close the event and acknowledge our ongoing relationships.

As a result of the initial *pōwhiri*, we were invited to spend time with tribal members of Ngāti Whātua and the Streeties at the Ngāti Whātua-based Ōrākei marae garden. Our fieldwork involved weekly visits between October 2012 and April 2013, which enabled us to get to know the participants and to contribute to the garden by getting our own hands dirty digging holes, clearing weeds, and planting vegetables. These activities allowed us to continually connect and reconnect with the Streeties and people of the marae, and for them to get to know us as people first and researchers second. After each visit, we individually completed field notes on our observations and conversations, and then shared these notes with the wider research team. We engaged in a range of informal conversations with participants (identified using pseudonyms) and conducted audio-recorded interviews with five homeless Māori men (aged fifty-four to sixty-nine), three representatives from Ngāti Whātua, and one representative of the Auckland City Mission. Three of the homeless men (Miro, Tōtara, and Rātā) were considered to be *kaumātua* (male elder status) by Ngāti Whātua representatives. Recorded interviews were conducted using a mix of Māori and English languages, were conversational in style, and were conducted after we had been involved with the garden for four months and had built up meaningful relationships with the participants. Additionally, photography provided a means of documenting spaces, practices, relationships, and events at the garden.

Figure 17.2. Our research in action.

During all our engagements with the participants, a priority for us was to observe and take part in Māori practices that were enacted by Ngāti Whātua representatives and the Streeties within the garden. Consequently, we conducted this research in a manner that respected and contributed positively to the *mauri* (life essence) of the research site through an emphasis on shared engagement, participation in communal work, and relationship building. Concurrently, we embraced the ethnographic turn in social research and developments in Indigenous psychologies that advocate for the use of case-based methods characterized by closer, more engaged, and reciprocal relationships between researchers and participants (Hodgetts et al. 2014; Hodgetts et al. 2010b). Figure 17.2 depicts our research in action with Māori men of a similar age caring for each other and their respective *whakapapa*.

As an older man, Tiniwai, a member of the research team, guided our interactions with the Streeties because he is of a similar age and is respected by them for his Māori cultural knowledge and expertise. His presence also assisted us to become accepted into the marae space where the Streeties and Tiniwai recognized each other's *mana* (authority, influence, status, spiritual power) (Walker 1992). To accompany an elder into a marae setting is seen as to be acting under their stewardship, which made this research project possible. This was important, as it was central to minimize the disruptions our research could have on the participants' everyday lives (Hodgetts et al. 2016). We drew less on our training as social scientists and relied more on our different yet overlapping personal and cultural skills as Māori men. We had all learned how to engage respectfully with older Māori men from childhood and knew not to pressure these men for recorded interviews.

Homelessness and Restraints on Māori Being

Considerable effort has gone into defining homelessness by researchers, governments, and service providers. This, in part, is a response to the importance of ascertaining the prevalence of homelessness, to allocate resources, and to target services (Hodgetts, Stolte, and Groot 2014). Underlying many definitions is a continuum of housing situations, ranging from insecure housing to the absence of a dwelling. Although arising from an appropriate concern for addressing homelessness, such definitions have been criticized for pigeonholing people into reified categories that can gloss over the lived nuances of homelessness (Illsley 2013; Lancione 2013). Such official definitions also, all but, ignore Indigenous world views and issues of culture. In order to appreciate the complexities of homelessness, some researchers have moved beyond overly rigid, Eurocentric, individualistic, and deficit-focused conceptualizations of homelessness (Lancione 2013; Hodgetts, Stolte, and Groot 2014). After all, homelessness constitutes much more than the presence or absence of particular forms of shelter, or personal economic hardship. Particularly for Indigenous people, homelessness also involves issues of colonialism, culture, spirituality, dislocation, socio-economic relations, belonging, and place. It denotes spiritual disruptions to ancestral affiliations to geo-cultural landscapes, knowledge, tradition, and kinship (Groot et al. 2011b; Memmott et al. 2003).

Therefore, many international scholars have tended to fixate on individual pathways into and out of homelessness (Hodgetts, Stolte, and Groot 2014). Researchers have demonstrated the influence of various interlinked structural (growing inequalities, unemployment, and housing unaffordability) and personal (familial traumas, psychological illness, substance misuse) risk factors for homelessness (Perreault et al. 2013). Correspondingly, generic responses to homelessness tend to focus on personal pathways out of homelessness by addressing issues of housing, mental health, and substance abuse, and by promoting participation in the labour market (Illsley 2013; Lancione 2013). This dominant focus can work for some people. However, it can also obscure group and culturally based experiences of homelessness that—as noted in the earlier quote from a representative of Ngāti Whātua—are associated with historical processes, including colonization and the structural violence that many Indigenous peoples experience at the hands of the institutions of settler societies (Hodgetts, Stolte, and Groot 2014). Studies of the everyday lives, socio-cultural practices, and relational experiences of homeless people (Borchard 2010; Hodgetts et al. 2008; Hodgetts et al. 2012; Lancione 2013) constitute a broader complementary research agenda to which our research contributes to in an effort to better understand how we might respond more effectively to the needs of Māori homeless people.

Our research is guided by the assertion that Māori are metaphysically orientated people whose being is constructed through connections and relationships to the natural and supernatural worlds (Marsden 2003) and that these relationships are lived out through everyday socio-cultural practices (Kawharu 1975). In contrast to the dominant Cartesian dualist model of existence, Marsden (2003) advocates the view that Māori traditionally distinguished between three levels of existence: Te Korekore (the world of potential being), Te Pō (the world of becoming), and Te Ao Mārama (the world of being). For Māori, being is made up of interwoven connections to place, social and spiritual relationships, systems of kinship or *whakapapa*, cultural practices, positioning within society, access to resources, cultural connectedness, and creation narratives that emphasize a fundamental *whakapapa* (genealogical) relationship between people, the natural world, and a pantheon of gods (Mead 2003).

The depth of understanding of being and one's place in the world comes to the fore for Māori through practical and emplaced practices (Kawharu 1975), such as growing food, eating communally, and conversing with others. To lose one's sense of these connections, through for example homelessness and displacement, is not simply a matter of losing sight of who you are. The experience also involves a loss of the many support structures that are crucial to the preservation of a person's sense of existence, self, and belonging within culturally collective structures and processes that comprise the Māori world. As we will demonstrate, it is in everyday practical activities such as gardening, storytelling, and sharing of food that a Māori sense of being, centralizing social, physical, and spiritual connections, can be regained and brought to the fore in everyday life (Kawharu 1975). We will show how the Ōrākei marae gardening project constitutes a response to Māori homelessness that embraces this world view and promotes taking part in everyday practices that sow our participants in this culturally textured place where, for regular moments at least, they are no longer culturally homeless.

Here, gardening is particularly culturally significant for Māori. After all, relationships between people and physical and metaphysical realms were central in pre-colonial Māori gardening practices, which wove people into particular home places (Moon 2005). Traditionally, gardens were a hub of activity within Māori communities (King 2003) with substantial plantings evident among *iwi* and *hapū* (subtribal) groups. In maintaining a garden, Māori people maintained their collective identities as a *hapū* and shared traditions and knowledge that was stimulated through the care and guardianship of particular places (see Walker 2014). Today, gardening on a marae still enacts the concept of *manawhenua* (territorial rights), where a group's *mana* is contingent on their ability to maintain tribal lands, knowledge, and resources (King 2012). Within the gardens, the constant togetherness and bonding of *iwi*, *hapū*, and *whānau* (family, including extended family) members can reinforce kinship (Moon 2005). Gardening continues to connect Māori with Papatūānuku (earth mother) as an eternal caregiver, and in caring for the *whenua*, people care for Papatūānuku, themselves, and others. As the *tohunga* (expert in traditional Māori cultural knowledge) Hohepa Kereopa (quoted in Moon 2005, 36) explains: "whatever you do to the land, you do to yourself. So the issue of how you treat the land is really about self-respect. What this means is that you have to respect yourself before you can respect the land." This interconnectedness refers to the concept of *mauri* (life force), which Marsden (2003, 44) describes as "the bonding element that knits all the diverse elements within the Universal 'Procession' giving creation its unity in diversity. It is the bonding element that holds the fabric of the universe together." Through gardening, Māori are able to acknowledge the *mauri* of all things (Moon 2005) and strengthen their connection with the *atua* (gods) and each other (Marsden 2003).

In many respects, this cultural orientation towards gardening and people enables us to approach the Ōrākei marae garden as involving the deceptively simple activity of preparing the ground, germinating, sowing, and caring for plants, while there are complex spiritual and relational practices that are rooted and remembered in the process. For us, Māori gardening on a marae refers to a site for basic human sustenance and aesthetic enjoyment, the growing of social ties, and cultivation of relationships that reproduce our traditions, knowledge, and connections (see Li, Hodgetts, and Ho 2010; Moon 2005). Māori gardens provide spaces to reconnect with the very essence of what it means to be Māori. Such gardens can manifest emplaced memories, histories, heritage, group identities, cooperation, and ways of being.

The Māori concept of *pūtahi* (confluence), whereby aspects of the world are interconnected and not broken down into smaller distinct components or categories, is central to our understanding of the Ōrākei marae garden project and its implications for the homeless men who participated in this research. Rather, asserting that everything must be viewed within the larger context in which it is situated (Ritchie 1992), at its core, *pūtahi* is about holism and totality. It necessitates us to suspend methods of atomization and reductionism that pervade our training in the Eurocentric social sciences. We embrace an approach to the Ōrākei marae garden and everyday practices of our participants as constitutive of not only local relations and a sense of place for these men, but also the reproduction of culture and Māori ways of being. As we will show, space and action cannot be meaningfully separated from each other, as they are interdependent (Tilley 1994). Spaces, such as gardens, are produced and reproduced through day-to-day practices of Māori cultural rituals and communal values that in turn offer occasions for being Māori (see Lefebvre [1974] 1991).

As a people who have undergone, and continue to experience, processes of colonization, Māori ways of being must not only contend with the development of physical spaces, but also intellectual spaces. Western institutions, such as universities and core cultural objects, including journal articles and chapters, are predominantly textured by the very philosophical world views that came to us with colonialism and which Indigenous peoples have resisted for centuries. However, by appropriating aspects of European philosophy within Māori cultural frameworks and concepts, such as *pūtahi*, we can find a more fitting place from which to speak.

For example, Mika (2015) argues that Heidegger's "metaphysics of presence" provides a critique of the Western philosophical thought that has also colonized Indigenous systems of thought and knowledge production. He outlines the problem of presence with the fixation of Western endeavours (dating back to the early post-Socratic philosophers) to pin down a single object into preconceived categories that are free of context and connections to other things. Consequently, when Indigenous scholars attempt to discuss Indigenous issues within broader relational contexts, we are metaphorically "backed into a corner" in terms of how we can discuss and present issues, such as homelessness, that affect us as interconnected human beings. Mika (2015, 6) explains: "If I am asked [by settler institutions] to provide evidence about a block of land, I am asked to do something even before I talk about land itself: I am asked to take on a notion of an object as utterly undistracted or uninformed by other objects.... Whenua [land] as a phenomenon then has no relationship with other entities for that short time." For Indigenous researchers for whom everything is relational, such processes of cultural interchange mean that even before we make our first utterance about an issue, we must first contend with the ways in which the subject is reduced by a Eurocentric metaphysics of presence that frames such conversations. The interconnected nature of our way of constructing knowledge and the intricate relationships that this implies are excluded from the totality of understanding specific objects, such as a block of land.

What dominates Western thought, and what we seek to resist through our research practice, is the reduction of an object of scrutiny (e.g., a particular piece of land) to its simplest form. Indigenous accounts that deviate from this Eurocentric presupposition are often viewed by institutions of settler societies as extraneous, and so rendered mute in the knowledge production process. As Mika (2015, 9) continues: "Ways of expression have to agree with the highly visible: one is questioned in a court, is asked to provide information about one's tribe in government departments, and is asked to write an essay, and is only acknowledged if one's answers are [perceived to be] logical. In that light, answers correspond directly to questions, one's tribe is brought into glaring focus, and the writing of an essay has to draw on what was established truth and must be on guard against irrational representations of phenomena." To engage in international scholarly conversations about complex relational issues such as homelessness, Indigenous researchers are forced to provide accounts of things from within the framework provided by others. Such symbolic and colonial processes reflect what Teo (2010) recently referred to as epistemological violence within the empirical sciences. Despite being hindered by what the established colonial order already understands, and our training as researchers, we Indigenous scholars must find ways to articulate our own cultural ways of understanding homelessness. Our analysis demonstrates how to assert our own cultural ways of knowing in order for us to carve out physical, cultural, and intellectual spaces to be.

Our analysis involved extracting general arguments out of detailed considerations of specific relationally situated and emplaced events, such as planting and growing food, cooking, and conversing and reminiscing at lunchtime in the marae garden (de Certeau 1984; Simmel [1903] 1997). We treated such daily emplaced practices of reconnection as the starting point for an analysis of the hidden, invisible, and culturally textured relationships that are at play in shaping the marae garden and people who work there (see Lefebvre [1974] 1991). Our engagements with particular practices, material objects, and the marae garden space provided a basis for developing a theoretically informed interpretation of the centrality of Māori culture to the garden and Māori homeless men's ways of being in this particular place. In doing so, we note that this particular marae garden is also interwoven with other such places within which these men are also at home. Our analysis exemplifies the importance of Indigenous researchers drawing upon cultural concepts germane to participant groups in order to extend understandings of the everyday lives of Indigenous peoples. Using Māori cultural concepts as central theoretical elements in our research contributes to an interpretation more relevant to our participants and their sense of self, their place in the world, and their everyday lives (Pihama, Cram, and Walker 2002).

The Gift of the Marae as a Space of Care, Belonging, and Being Māori

Street homelessness is a harsh, socio-economically marginal, and unhealthy situation that involves the conduct of everyday life within what has been termed as a broader *landscape of despair* (Dear and Wolch 1987; Stolte and Hodgetts 2015). In this landscape, people who are homeless are often deemed to be out of place and their efforts to conduct everyday activities such as socializing, eating, and toileting are constantly being disrupted and subjected to official scrutiny. In contrast, Ōrākei marae offers our Māori homeless people a *space of care* and respite from the perils and disruptions of street life and the landscape of despair associated with the broader settler society. This marae also provides a culturally patterned *space of being* (Heidegger [1927] 1962; Tolia-Kelly 2006) in which our participants can engage in everyday activities without fear of disruption, and in doing so re-engage with Māori ways of being they experienced earlier in their lives. Below, we document how their actions contribute to the reconciliation of the *whenua* and the enactment of cultural traditions that belong on the marae.

Time spent at the marae involved more than simply planting, cultivating, or consuming food. It took the Streeties away from their daily struggles while living rough. The marae re-engaged them in aspects of Māori ways of being that are more difficult to re-enact of the settler society, which makes up their landscape of despair (Conradson 2003; Groot et al. 2011a). The following excerpt is taken from our reflections to demonstrate how the Streeties transition from being homeless within a landscape of despair, to being Māori emplaced within the marae space of care and being: "There was a transition of *reo* [language] across space. English was used in the city... but as they [the Streeties] got into the van to go to the garden, the language slowly changed to *te reo* Māori, and [they were] totally immersed in *te reo* Māori by the time they were working in the gardens" (Field note, Pita King, 21 February 2013). Changes in language along with changes in space, invoked in this quote, reflect how many Indigenous peoples transition between their cultural worlds and that of the settler society. The movement from the city (a space dominated and textured primarily by settler values, practices, and evidently language) to the marae (a traditional space where Māori culture, values, practices, and language dominates) is evident in several participants' accounts. This reflects Walker's (1990) proposition that marae function as sites of cultural revival for Māori where people can resist colonial domination over Māori ways of being. The marae allows the Streeties to reconnect with their heritage within the context of the broader landscape of despair. As Rātā (Streetie) remarks: "Marae are our rules. Outside here, is other people's rules." Ōrākei marae comprises a cultural enclave for the Streeties that allows them to re-enter the Māori world physically, spiritually, psychologically, and relationally.

Takaparawhau is not simply a location where the people of Ngāti Whātua happen to be. It is one of the last remaining spaces where a traditional cultural way of life is being practiced in central Auckland. As Miro (Streetie) reflects: "The gift of the marae. It's like being at home on the marae, any marae will comfort you and that's like being at home. It's normal. There's no tension. The thing about it it's being open with each other, it's being like that on the marae. It's the people themselves." Miro's account locates people as creators and shapers of spaces. Building on Conradson's (2003) notion of drop-in centres as spaces of care, the marae provides such space for more than just "dropping-in"; it is a place to "join-in," "belong-in," and "be-in." The culturally textured nature of the marae as a space offers the Streeties a more intimate and recognisable form of interaction than what they experience with traditional social services. Our observations here are informed by Heidegger's ([1927] 1962) use of the term *dwelling*, which speaks to the unique connection a person has with a particular place of familiarity and belonging. In light of this, the marae can be approached as not only a space for Māori Streeties to occupy in a spatial sense; it is a place in which they dwell, a place where they belong, a space of being.

The garden space is not open to the Streeties by chance. It is a space textured by Ngāti Whātua who have a strong tradition of extending *manaakitanga* (care/nurturing) to other groups. In continuing this practice through the gardening project and other initiatives, the *iwi* is able to also reaffirm their own collective identity, traditions, and ways of being. Matipo explains: "A good thing for us, I guess, think you've done right by your *tūpuna* [ancestors], that we're still doing it [keeping traditions of *manaakitanga* alive], nothing can beat us, we're still helping people that need our help." This quote reflects an understanding expressed by all three Ngāti Whātua representatives that their resilience as an *iwi* (tribe) does not reside solely in their ability to maintain themselves. It is also contained relationally within their tradition of *manaaki* (care/nurture) towards others. Karaka (marae representative) further reflects on the importance of maintaining Ngāti Whātua as an *iwi* that cares for others: "Coming back here [marae], it's reconnecting back to where they're [Streeties] from, and now, they're like *tangata whenua* [people of the land/hosts]... Yea, really just part of us, everybody knows them. I'm leaving [retiring from formal employment in the garden] in two weeks, and I was saying to everyone 'while I'm gone, you have to maintain that *manaakitanga* for all those who come through here.' That must be maintained when I leave." The *manaaki* that is passed down from the older generations to the younger exemplifies the *iwi*'s contribution and commitment to addressing structural and systemic histories of dislocation and disruption that Māori have endured through colonization.

The enactment of *manaakitanga* is central to the transformation of the people who interact there and continuation of this place as a space of care and being. Also central to the marae being a space of care is the autonomy the people who dwell within it have, in texturing the nature of the space on their own terms. This is contrary to the experiences of the Streeties who have spaces dictated to them within the settler society. Having a voice that is heard, respected, and admired complements the marae as a space of care for these men. As will be demonstrated throughout our analysis, the emphasis placed on *manaakitanga* by Ngāti Whātua has broader implications for responses to Māori homelessness. It foregrounds the importance of genuine care for homeless people, where they are not simply constructed as objects of pity or bodies to be "managed." Māori homeless people are treated just like other welcomed guests to the marae, as human beings of fundamental value to our collective humanity. Within the settler world, these men are homeless. However, on the marae these men are referred to as *koroua* (elderly men) and *kaumātua* (respected elders) who belong, a reflection of the cultural admiration and reverence the people of Ngāti Whātua have for these men.

Identity and Being

Maintaining a positive sense of self and one's value while living on the streets is often difficult. Homeless people are at risk of losing themselves to the streets (Snow and Anderson 1993). Navigating this risk to one's very sense of being is widely recognized as central to surviving street life (Hodgetts, Hodgetts, and Radley 2006). For Māori, one's traditional sense of belonging and self is anchored relationally in *whānau*, *hapū*, and *iwi* links, often centred around one or several marae, and reinforced through reciprocal acts of *manaakitanga* that speak to the collective caring of the social group (Mead 2003). For the Streeties participating in this project, such links have been ruptured. However, they preserve themselves by enacting their cultural knowledge of how to conduct themselves, as Māori, somewhere new. In doing so, they demonstrate the importance of their *knowing how to being*. We use this grammatically incorrect phrase here purposefully—to invoke the collective knowledge Māori obtain from childhood and drawn upon throughout life—to locate our participants' cultural identities relationally and purposefully in their conduct at Ōrākei marae (Rangihau 1992). The grammatically correct phrase, "to be," implies a completed state of knowledge and identity, whereas "how to being" invokes an aspirational and ongoing process consistent with a Māori world view. This phrasing also begins to challenge the metaphysics of presence outlined by Mika (2015) in terms of Western framework's tendency to pre-construct meaning prior to use. Due to the implications of "knowing how to be" we were forced to be ungrammatical in order to remain authentic in our analysis. How to being also summons processes central to how these homeless men become part of the marae and the marae becomes part of them through the enactment of everyday cultural practices in this space. The knowledge/practice nexus our participants take form through is central to the texturing of the marae as a space of being Māori.

Access to Ōrākei marae affords opportunities for our participants to enact their cultural knowledge of *how to being* within cultural practices that are familiar and comfortable to them (see Figure 17.3). In the process, the marae garden becomes a physical manifestation of ways of being Māori men, where through the act of gardening these participants can contemplate existential questions regarding who they are, where they are from, and where they are going:

> I get strength in knowing my *te reo* [Māori language] and in being here. To me it's very important… being able to be Māori here is important to my confidence. Know the differences between who I really am or who I am supposed to be in this world of ours. Half the time I am lost [on the streets]. Now, what is my purpose and I can find it here?… I miss the old days where everything was always set out, especially as a child, Māori way of growing up. Always take the lessons from our *korouas* [male elder] and *kuias* [female elder]. Just the structure in life that's hard to keep going. That's what I notice here is rebuilding that confidence in what you were taught back at home…And at least we know that we contribute to the *whenua* here. And I have faith in this marae and what they are trying to bring back that structure and we contribute to that, you know. (Miro)

With the marae come Māori ways of being and preserving of the self. Contained within participants' accounts is the importance of the passing down

Figure 17.3. Miro working away in the marae garden.

of cultural knowledge from elders, which locates these men as full participants within the Māori world. Such processes were not simply invoked through language and talked about in reflective terms. For example, during our time spent with the Streeties, Miro took a leaf from a tree and showed us how to make particular bird calls with it. This was something he learned from his elders and, in sharing this with us, he was able to continue a small aspect of the tradition that he was raised in, which constitutes his identity and being. It was a practice recognized by Tiniwai, Mohi, and Pita from their own childhoods and time with their children. Our engaging in the playful practice enabled us to demonstrate commonality in backgrounds.

Specifically, being on the marae for these men involves remembering or reconnecting with their familial traditions and heritage through material practices. Involving themselves in the day-to-day happenings of the marae—including planned events such as planting and mundane moments such as making bird calls—the Streeties are able to bridge the gap between the "then" (youth on the marae) and the "now" (current Māori self on the marae) that homelessness has disrupted. Gardening and associated activities at Ōrākei marae facilitates the manifestation of identity through self-reflection and cultural reconnection to place.

More broadly, the Streeties' involvement on Ōrākei marae demonstrates how people, places, and objects are fundamentally interwoven within the social fabric of everyday life through which we become ourselves (Hodgetts et al. 2010a). Meaning that in matters of identity, the concept of *pūtahi* enables us to grapple with just how various aspects of everyday life cannot be meaningfully separated from one another (Ritchie 1992). These processes of becoming are not only spatially located but, as in the example of the use of leaves in bird calling, they involve the use of material objects, particularly those that have taken on cultural significance within the enactment of everyday life. Regard for material objects and associated material practice permeates throughout all of our analysis sections and provides additional depth to our interpretation of participant engagements within the marae garden. We will consider how our interactions with everyday objects within such spaces reproduce cultural ways of being that reaffirm our participants' sense of self as Māori and locate them and us within a broader socio-cultural landscape (Heidegger [1927] 1962). Objects, such as carvings and other traditional forms of artistic expression, communicate various meanings, histories, connections, and relationships (Te Awekotuku et al. 2007). The often taken-for-granted presence of these objects (see Figure 17.4) in the garden adds to the texturing of this place, creating a familiar setting for the Streeties by marking this garden as a distinctively Māori garden. The garden takes on an identity as Māori in its own right.

The marae and the men's participation in the garden, amidst such material objects, adds cultural fibres to a thread that reaffirms the Streeties' identities as valuable Māori men who are interacting in the right place to reflect, grow, and heal themselves. Reflecting the broader relevance of this assertion, research by Boydell, Goering, and Morrell-Bellai (2000) found that people who are homeless tend to view their identities prior to being homeless with positive nostalgia, whereas their current identities as homeless persons are sometimes undervalued. These men remember a better time in their lives and have circumvented, to a certain degree, the devaluing of the current self through being involved in gardening and the associated use of tools. The threat of becoming disconnected and dislocated from the people, places, and objects that ground one's sense of identity can have negative implications for the overall health of people (Durie 1998; Stolte and Hodgetts 2015). By engaging with the marae garden and the objects that populate it, the men are able to fulfill their cultural needs and form interconnected networks of relatedness that locates the self within a complex socio-cultural world.

All our participants spoke to the need for Māori to maintain physical, emotional, and spiritual connections with the *whenua* (land) and, in the process,

Figure 17.4. Kaitiaki (guardian) of the garden.

portrayed themselves as emplaced beings who have been rendered out of place through homelessness. Gardening was also contextualized as aiding them in transcending the physical task of planting and nurturing plants to re-establish their frayed connections to Papatūānuku (primal Earth Mother) (Marsden 2003). They also gained a sense of being reimmersed in things Māori and contributing to enhancing the *mauri* (life essence) of the Ōrākei marae. In the process, they could be more than the recipients of the charity of others, which is how they are rendered by conventional "interventions" that attempt to address their homelessness. They became part of a place and a group of Māori people engaged in the spiritual, physical, and psychological care of the land and other people. They were engaged in sharing their knowledge of Māori culture with members of the local *iwi*, as well as growing food that went to the Auckland City Mission food bank to feed families living in poverty.

At Ōrākei marae, gardening serves as a medium for remembering cultural, familial, and spiritual connections that may have been lost while on the streets. These men were welcome to make such connections as is reflected in Ngāti Whātua affording them considerable autonomy in the garden due to their extensive cultural knowledge of *how to being* and act in this space. The Streeties planned their own patches within the garden and contributed to the space in its entirety in ways that were particularly meaningful for them. The reconnections and relational work that resulted was not lost on the marae staff who recognized the importance of the gardens in bringing these men back into the Māori world of the marae: "Probably reconnection…it's reminded them of *whanaungatanga* [process of maintaining relationships]. The practices that they used to do when they were young, what they thought, from their *tūpuna* [ancestors]. You know, I still garden the same way my mother did" (Karaka). As noted above, the actions that take place in the marae gardens constitute a continuation of actions that stem from the Streeties' earlier lives within their *whānau*. By joining in collective action in the marae garden, the Streeties re-form tribal-like links with one another and the people of Ngāti Whātua, which anchor their place on the marae. As Karaka notes, "They can be part of a *hapū* [subtribe] again where they can be cared for and care for others." This is an important statement as it captures how the Streeties are not simply recipients of care. Rather, they are able to sustain their *mana* (status/authority) as people who care for others through their contributions to sustaining the garden and providing food to the local food bank. In this regard, they receive and offer care simultaneously (Bowlby 2011). The Streeties make genuine and valuable contributions to the marae. Their actions contribute to the texturing of this already nationally significant site (Takaparawhau) as a Māori space of being. By becoming involved on the marae, the Streeties were able to re-anchor themselves to cultural traditions and ways of being that have been rarefied through processes of disconnection and dislocation, associated with colonization and homelessness (Groot et al. 2011b).

Food and the Enactment of Māori Culture

As noted in the previous section, participant accounts also illustrate how the Māori self is not confined to an individual's body. The self extends out into the world through spiritual connections to place and the use of everyday objects that relationships and culture are lived through (see Heidegger [1927] 1962). The role of everyday material objects such as the boil-up pot and the barbecue facility, created by Ngāti Whātua for the Streeties (Figure 17.5), offer important insights into how Māori ways of being are reproduced through the everyday practices of these men. Much attention has been given to Māori high cultural objects, such as traditional wooden and bone carvings, weaved objects, and other artworks (Te Awekotuku et al. 2007). We would argue that the use of everyday objects within the marae gardens is central to the enactment of *manaakitanga* (caring), *whanaungatanga* (relationship building), and cultural connectedness, and therefore these items deserve our attention. Below, we explore how identities, culture, and togetherness are lived through the use

Figure 17.5. Garden barbecue and black boil-up pot cooking lunch.

of everyday objects, such as the boil-up pot (Figure 17.5); the pot permits the reproduction of traditional Māori cultural values through food sharing during lunchtimes in the gardens.

For Māori, the sharing of food is part of many formal and informal meetings, where hosts demonstrate and build upon their already established *mana* (status/authority), by providing for others and strengthening bonds between people (Salmond 2004). Thus, the consumption of food is not simply the taking in of an inert substance. The food embodies expressions of identity, gift giving practices, and culture. The Streeties continue their traditions during lunch in the garden as a way of expressing their cultural connectedness and identities. Lunchtime at the marae is a time when bonds between people are created and maintained, and where culturally embedded ethical values, such as *manaakitanga* and *whanaungatanga*, manifest. Through a lifetime of navigating Māori spaces of being, our participants have built the capacity to knowing *how to being*, which in turn continues to reproduce such spaces and selves in the world.

Rimu (Ōrākei marae caretaker) constructed the barbecue (Figure 17.5) and subsequent lunch space for the Streeties and people of the marae. This barbecue and the surrounding area represent a physical manifestation of *manaakitanga* and *whanaungatanga* and embody the connection and the relationship Rimu has with the Streeties and the marae. This gesture of caring for others has facilitated the Streeties in reproducing further acts of care towards others, such as our research group, through the medium of food. The connections and relationships between people on the marae are lived out through mundane objects, making the barbecue and boil-up pot a part of the people who are connected to it (Heidegger [1927] 1962). The following is taken from our field notes: "We broke for lunch. The *kai* [food] came from the garden and was cooked on the barbecue Rimu had built. Miro [Streetie] was head chef and had brought a few sausages along. He was saying that the people from the marae would come along and use the barbecue. He didn't say this in a way that came across as 'this is our BBQ!' but in more of a way to complement the facility that had become a socially shared space for anyone who wanted to come and cook a feed" (Field note, Pita King, 21 February 2013). As people on the marae congregate around the barbecue and take part in lunchtimes in the gardens, the Streeties are embedded within the marae's landscape. The preparing and sharing of foods familiar from a childhood provides a focal point for care and relationships and is a basis for extending hospitality, care, and connection.

Māori spirituality and cultural sustenance are also brought to the fore at lunchtime. It is through daily activities such as lunch breaks and the use of everyday objects that these men can realize themselves as interconnected within the physical, cultural, and spiritual world of Māori (see Heidegger [1927] 1962). As noted by Kauri (Auckland City Mission representative), the lunch setting facilitates the enactment of the heritage of the Streeties and is a culturally familiar and comforting mundane event. He remarked how at lunchtimes the Streeties re-embed themselves within marae's life away from the landscape of despair where preparing and sharing such meals is all but impossible: "To be able to come here, you know... Might do a *kai*, put the jug on, cleaned up afterwards. So they're playing a useful part and all of that's been washed with, I guess, the *aroha* [love/care] and the comfortableness of a marae setting. It's all in that context, which is healing, it's soothing, it's strengthening" (Kauri). Within the Māori world, the sharing of food comes second to the strengthening of relationships. As Hohepa (quoted in Moon 2005, 24–25) observes, "it was the joining together that was more important than the food... it was more than just about what we were eating. It was one of the ways we connected with each other." These cultural practices are epitomized by the Streeties' actions in the way in which we, the *manuhiri* (visitors), are invited to eat first. In the process, cultural needs take precedence over personal hunger.

The formation and continuity of these relationships centre around material objects that provide the opportunities to enact cultural and spiritual practices surrounding food and its consumption. Figure 17.6 presents a photograph

Figure 17.6. Miro cooking lunch for the Streeties and the research team.

taken during a group fishing trip and exemplifies how we, the researchers, were cared for, through food, by the Streeties. As earlier in the shift from the city to the marae, the transition from the marae to the open water, towards the end of our time spent with the Streeties, provided additional opportunities to develop our relationships, further trust, and to learn from each other.

Lunchtime in this setting reflects how mundane moments in the garden have broader cultural significance for our participants and their sense of belonging. While they are homeless on the streets, the kinds of food available and the lack of facilities required to prepare food can disconnect Māori from reproducing their cultural traditions. However, on the marae, these cultural practices are observed in the gardens on a daily basis. Participants can take their time in preparing their food, free from the fear of being told to move on. Their sense of self is strengthened through rejoining the traditions of the marae, and is lived through people, places, and objects. Lunchtime for these men also provides opportunities to re-enact and reproduce Māori spiritual practices surrounding the consumption of food. These include *karakia* (ritualized chant) that connect these men back to and strengthens their relationship with the *atua* (gods) (Marsden 2003). Within the Māori world, the sharing of food fulfills "social obligations to the gods and the manuhiri" (Marsden

2003, 9), meaning that no expense is spared in extending hospitality through food to people. As articulated by Karaka (marae representative) when pointing across to the barbecue, "That there that is for them. It's there so they can have their *kai* and share their *kai* and get to know everyone. It's important to do that cos they're Māori and there's a lot to sharing food for Māori." Through such cultural practices, we see the broader reproduction of Māori culture, and the cultivation of a place for these displaced men within their own traditions and cultural heritage.

Discussion

Ngāti Whātua's tribal efforts to reclaim their land, re-texture it as distinctively Māori, and invite Māori homeless people from other places to be a part of the process has wider implications for how we understand and respond to Indigenous homelessness. Traditionally, the success of Māori gardens was not only measured in practical terms of feeding people, but also in terms of the social development and nurturing of human connectedness (Kawharu 1975). Culturally patterned relationships and material acts documented through our analysis constitute processes through which the marae garden is reproduced as a Māori space of being. In this place, our homeless participants can cultivate a sense of connection and self as Māori men who belong. Gardening provided a vehicle for our participants to weave themselves back into the material, social, and cultural space of the marae. Gardening also brought normality and flow to these men's lives, and aided them in the processes of remembering cultural traditions and ways of being that can be forgotten when they are living on the streets. The marae is a place for our homeless participants to belong, where respite from street life is gained, and where pride is taken in being able to contribute to the reconciliation of the land. As a judgement free space (Trussell and Mair 2010), the Ōrākei marae allows the homeless participants to have some control over their daily activities and to be treated with respect and dignity. In short, the men were able to contribute back to the Auckland City Mission food bank, find respite from the cityscape, reproduce cultural values, and spend time just being Māori.

We have explored homeless men's gardening activities on a marae to shed new light on the reproduction of culturally patterned ways of being, through emplaced day-to-day practices. Our research demonstrates how pre-existing cultural resources, including the marae and associated ways of being and acting as Māori, can provide culturally nurturing, compassionate, and effective responses to Indigenous homelessness. Such responses build genuine, meaningful, and ongoing relationships between Māori homeless people, local *iwi*, and homeless service providers. By helping to craft a garden space, our participants are able to re-enter the Māori world and mutually benefit from engaging in reciprocal acts of care that support their well-being and the well-being of others. The creation of a sense of participation and reciprocity in this place is important in addressing our participants' homelessness (Johnson, Hodgetts, and Nikora 2013).

For far too long services designed to help homeless people have been overly Eurocentric in nature, and agencies have been reluctant to draw upon Māori cultural concepts and practices in any meaningful way. Such services are less effective for Māori and in many respects are simply designed to "manage" Streeties and to "get them off the streets" (Hodgetts, Stolte, and Groot 2014). The marae garden exemplifies the benefits of responses to homelessness that are driven by Māori, informed by our cultural concepts and relational practices, and which promote care and inclusion. In terms of our own practice as researchers, this project has taught us the importance of moving beyond Eurocentric approaches to service provision and research that disturb and impose settler world views on Māori homeless people. We have made a conscious effort to address issues of epistemological violence associated with generic approaches to social research (Teo 2010), which often silence Māori ways of knowing, interacting, and being (Mika 2015). As Indigenous scholars, it is important that we consider how the efforts of Ngāti Whātua as a tribe, the Auckland City Mission, and the homeless men who garden might be appropriated and replicated to some extent in other settings with other groups of homeless people.

Acknowledgements

This research was funded by Ngā Pae o te Māramatanga and this chapter is a substantial redevelopment of a journal article originally published in *AlterNative:* http://www.alternative.ac.nz/content/older-men-marae-everyday-practices-being-m%C4%81ori. We would also like to acknowledge Ngāti Whātua and the gardening project for making this research possible, Wilf Holt for facilitating contact between the research team, Ngāti Whātua and the Streeties, and the contributions of Dr. Carl Mika to our philosophical considerations of Māori ways of being.

References

Borchard, Kurt. 2010. "Between Poverty and a Lifestyle: The Leisure Activities of Homeless People in Las Vegas." *Journal of Contemporary Ethnography* 39 (4): 441–66.

Bowlby, Sophie. 2011. "Friendship, Co-Presence and Care: Neglected Spaces." *Social and Cultural Geography* 12 (6): 605–22.

Boydell, Katherine M., Paula Goering, and Tammy L. Morrell-Bellai. 2000. "Narratives of Identity: Re-Presentation of Self in People Who Are Homeless." *Qualitative Health Research* 10 (1): 26–38.

Conradson, David. 2003. "Spaces of Care in the City: The Place of a Community Drop-In Centre." *Social and Cultural Geography* 4 (4): 507–25.

de Certeau, Michel. 1984. *The Practice of Everyday Life*. Translated by Steven Rendall. Berkeley: University of California Press.

Dear, Michael J., and Jennifer R. Wolch. 1987. *Landscapes of Despair: From Deinstitutionalization to Homelessness*. Princeton: Princeton University Press.

Durie, Mason. 1998. *Whaiora: Māori Health Development*. Auckland, New Zealand: Oxford University Press.

Groot, Shiloh, Darrin Hodgetts, Linda Waimarie Nikora, and Chez Leggatt-Cook. 2011a. "A Māori Homeless Woman." *Ethnography* 12 (3): 375–97.

Groot, Shiloh, Darrin Hodgetts, Linda Waimarie Nikora, and Mohi Rua. 2011b. "Māori and Homelessness." In *Māori and Social Issues*, edited by Tracey McIntosh and Malcolm Mulholland, 235–48. Wellington, New Zealand: Huia Publishers.

Heidegger, Martin. (1927) 1962. *Being and Time*. Translated by John Macquarrie and Edward Robinson. London: SCM Press.

Hodgetts, Darrin, Kerry Chamberlain, Shiloh Groot, and Yardena Tankel. 2014. "Urban Poverty, Structural Violence and Welfare Provision for 100 Families in Auckland." *Urban Studies* 51 (10): 2036–51.

Hodgetts, Darrin, Neil Drew, Christopher Sonn, Ottilie Stolte, Linda Waimarie Nikora, and Cate Curtis. 2010a. *Social Psychology and Everyday Life*. Basingstoke; New York: Palgrave Macmillan.

Hodgetts, Darrin, Andrea Hodgetts, and Alan Radley. 2006. "Life in the Shadow of the Media: Imaging Street Homelessness in London." *European Journal of Cultural Studies* 9 (4): 497–516.

Hodgetts, Darrin, Mohi Rua, Pita King, and Tiniwai Te Whetu. 2016. "The Ordinary in the Extraordinary: Everyday Living Textured by Homelessness." In *Psychology and the Conduct of Everyday Life*, edited by Ernst Schraube and Charlotte Højholt, 124–44 . London: Routledge.

Hodgetts, Darrin, Ottilie Stolte, Kerry Chamberlain, Alan Radley, Shiloh Groot, and Linda Waimarie Nikora. 2010b. "The Mobile Hermit and the City: Considering Links between Places, Objects, and Identities in Social Psychological Research on Homelessness." *British Journal of Social Psychology* 49 (2): 285–303.

Hodgetts, Darrin, Ottilie Stolte, Kerry Chamberlain, Alan Radley, Linda Waimarie Nikora, Eci Nabalarua, and Shiloh Groot. 2008. "A Trip to the Library: Homelessness and Social Inclusion." *Social and Cultural Geography* 9 (8): 933–53.

Hodgetts, Darrin, Ottilie Stolte, and Shiloh Groot. 2014. "Towards a Relationally and Action-Orientated Social Psychology of Homelessness." *Social and Personality Psychology Compass* 8 (4): 156–64.

Hodgetts, Darrin, Ottilie Stolte, Linda Waimarie Nikora, and Shiloh Groot. 2012. "Drifting Along or Dropping into Homelessness: A Class Analysis of Responses to Homelessness." *Antipode* 44 (4): 1209–26.

Illsley, Barbara. 2013. "Promoting Cohesion in Measuring Homelessness within the European Union." *International Journal of Society Systems Science* 5 (2): 173–91.

Jackson, Moana. 1992. "The Treaty and the World: The Colonisation of Māori Philosophy." In *Justice, Ethics and New Zealand Society* edited by Graham Oddie and Roy W. Perrett, 1–10. Auckland, New Zealand: Oxford University Press.

Johnson, Diana, Darrin Hodgetts, and Linda Waimarie Nikora. 2013. "A Humanistic Approach to Addressing the Needs of Homeless People with Mental Concerns." *Journal of Humanistic Psychology* 53 (1): 94–113.

Kawharu, Ian Hugh. 1975. *Orakei: A Ngati Whatua Community*. Wellington, New Zealand: New Zealand Council for Educational Research.

King, Michael. 2003. *The Penguin History of New Zealand*: Auckland, New Zealand: Penguin Books.

Lancione, Michele. 2013. "How is Homelessness?" *European Journal of Homelessness* 7 (2): 237–48.

Lefebvre, Henri. (1974) 1991. *The Production of Space*. Translated by Donald Nicholson-Smith. Oxford, UK; Cambridge, Mass.: Blackwell.

Li, Wendy Wen, Darrin Hodgetts, and Elsie Ho. 2010. "Gardens, Transitions and Identity Reconstruction among Older Chinese Immigrants to New Zealand." *Journal of Health Psychology* 15 (5): 786–96.

Marsden, Maori. 2003. *The Woven Universe: Selected Writings of Rev. Māori Marsden*. Edited by Charles Royal. Otaki, New Zealand: Estate of Rev. Māori Marsden

Mead, Hirini Moko. 2003. *Tikanga Māori: Living by Māori Values*. Wellington, New Zealand: Huia Publishers.

Memmot, Paul, Stephen Long, Catherine Chambers, and Frederick Spring. 2003. *Categories of Indigenous 'Homelessness' People and Good Practice Responses to Their Needs*, AHURI Final Report No. 49. St. Lucia: Australian Housing and Urban Research Institute, Queensland Research Centre.

Mika, Carl, T. 2015. "'Thereness:' Implications of Heidegger's 'Presence' for Māori." *AlterNative* 11 (1): 3–13.

Moon, Paul. 2005. *A Tohunga's Natural World: Plants, Gardening and Food*. Auckland, New Zealand: David Ling Publishing.

Perreault, Michel, Annie Jaimes, Daniel Rabouin, Noé. D White, and Diana Milton. 2013. "A Vacation for the Homeless: Evaluating a Collaborative Community Respite Programme in Canada through Clients' Perspectives." *Health and Social Care in the Community* 21 (2): 159–70.

Pihama, Leonie, Fiona Cram, and Sheila Walker. 2002. "Creating Methodological Space: A Literature Review of Kaupapa Maori Research." *Canadian Journal of Native Education* 26 (1): 30–43.

Rangihau, John. 1992. "Being Maori." In *Te Ao Hurihuri: Aspects of Maoritanga*, edited by Michael King, 185–190. Auckland: Reed Books.

Ritchie, James E. 1992. *Becoming Bicultural*. Wellington, New Zealand: Huia Publishers and Daphne Brasell Associates Press.

Salmond, Anne. 2004. *Hui: A Study of Māori Ceremonial Gatherings*. Auckland, New Zealand: Reed.

Simmel, Georg. (1903) 1997. "The Metropolis and Mental Life." In *Simmel on Culture*, edited by David Frisby and Mike Featherstone, 174–185. London: Sage.

Snow, David A., and Leon Anderson. 1993. *Down on Their Luck: A Study of Homeless Street People*. Berkeley, CA: University of California Press.

Stolte, Ottilie, and Darrin Hodgetts. 2015. "Being Healthy in Unhealthy Places: Health Tactics in a Homeless Lifeworld." *Journal of Health Psychology* 20 (2): 144–53.

Te Awekotuku, Ngahuia with Linda Waimarie Nikora, Mohi Rua, and Rolina Karapu. 2007. *Mau Moko: The World of Maōri Tatto*. Auckland, New Zealand: Penguin Publishing.

Teo, Thomas. 2010. "What is Epistemological Violence in the Empirical Social Sciences?" *Social and Personality Psychology Compass* 4 (5): 295–303.

Tilley, Christopher Y. 1994. *A Phenomenology of Landscape: Places, Paths, and Monuments*. Oxford, UK; Providence, RI: Berg.

Tolia-Kelly, Divya P. 2006. "Affect: An Ethnocentric Encounter? Exploring the 'Universalist' Imperative of Emotional/Affectual Geographies." *Area* 38 (2): 213–17.

Trussell, Dawn E., and Heather Mair. 2010. "Seeking Judgment Free Spaces: Poverty, Leisure, and Social Inclusion." *Journal of Leisure Research* 42 (4): 513–33.

Walker, Ranginui. 1990. *Ka Whawhai Tonu Mātou: Struggle Without End*. Auckland, New Zealand: Penguin.

_____. 1992. "Marae: A Place to Stand." In *Te Ao Hurihuri: Aspects of Maoritanga*, edited by Michael King, 15–28. Auckland, New Zealand: Reed Books.

Conclusion

EVELYN J. PETERS

The chapters in this volume have sought to explore the cultural and geographic distinctiveness of Indigenous homelessness in Canada, Australia, and New Zealand. While Indigenous homeless individuals are overrepresented in the homeless populations in all of these countries, relatively few studies have addressed their characteristics and the specific dimensions of their experiences. A deeper understanding of Indigenous homelessness provides a crucial framework for initiatives and successful solutions.

Although many Indigenous people experience social and economic success, many also share the personal characteristics of other marginalized groups that put them at risk of being homeless. However, there are additional factors identified in work on the situation of homeless Indigenous people and these factors must be recognized for the design and implementation of successful and supportive policy initiatives. The authors of the chapters in this collection all contribute to our understanding of the nature of Indigenous homelessness.

While the research presented in this volume emerges from three different countries and many distinct areas and while the researchers represent different disciplines, there are some broad themes that emerge from the papers. These themes are: the legacies of Western colonialisms, contemporary policy-driven homelessness, cultural survival and resistance, and the specificity of places and identities. This conclusion briefly summarizes these themes with the intent of identifying common threads connecting Indigenous experiences of homelessness across distinct geographies.

Legacies of Colonialism

All of the authors situate their analysis within the ongoing legacy of Western colonialisms that dispossessed people of their lands, waters and resources, attempted to destroy Indigenous cultures, and resulted in intergenerational individual and collective trauma. While specific initiatives varied in different countries, colonial practices in all of these states assaulted cultures, communities, and families. Demographic collapse, which occurred as a result of foreign diseases, lack of health care, and sometimes outright slaughter, led to the loss of community structures and knowledge of cultural traditions. Indigenous people were removed from their traditional lands and resettled in often unfamiliar territories. In each country there were numerous and varied assimilation initiatives through legislation, community control, and the seizure of children. Indigenous homelessness cannot be understood without recognition of this legacy.

Several authors explore the relationship between dispossession and Indigenous feelings of homelessness. According to Groot and Peters and King and colleagues, Māori experiences of homelessness include the loss of connection with family and tribe resulting in cultural and spiritual dislocation. Similarly Brown argues that Māori perceptions of homelessness are broader than "houselessness." *Tūrangawaewae*, or having an ancestral "place to stand," is central to individual and collective New Zealand Māori identities. Tūrangawaewae describes one's sense of belonging or attachment to a particular place and the ability to locate oneself there physically and spiritually. Having a place to stand is strongly associated with Māori notions of "home." Similar concepts are echoed in Christensen with Andrew's consideration of Indigenous homelessness in the Northwest Territories, Canada. They argue that land, community, and family are entwined in Indigenous concepts of home. A "home" is more than "house" and includes the idea of a secure place to be. Reconnection to land, community, and family, all damaged by the forces of colonialism, is integral to the process of regaining a secure place to be.

In addition, several papers link specific colonial policies and practices to the contemporary characteristics of Indigenous homelessness. In Canada, Lindstrom and Belanger describe the fragmentation of Niitsitapi (Blackfoot) territory with the creation of reserves for Niitsitapi communities. Because of the lack of education and employment opportunities on reserves, homeless Niitsitapi people in Lethbridge experience constant mobility as well as estrangement from families and traditional cultures, all of which contribute to feelings of homelessness in their own territories. In the Groot and Peters introduction as well as in the Brown paper, authors describe the history of legislation and practices of colonial dispossession of the Māori people and the colonial acquisition of Indigenous resources to support Pākehā (European) settlement that result in Māori homelessness. Brown argues that the imposition of Western style of housing challenged Māori protocols by dividing aspects of life that were usually shared such as family sleeping, and incorporated activities always kept separate, by putting living areas adjacent to the *noa* (common) activities of cooking and dining (and later washing and toileting). Buildings were also too small to accommodate large multi-generational families. In these ways, colonial practices undermined Māori family life, which is an important component of feeling "homed."

In the Australian context, Birdsall-Jones explores mobility and long-term visiting alongside colonial policies that moved individuals and communities from their traditional lands. As a result, individuals are forced to move across large areas to maintain cultural relationships with kin and family, resulting in what mainstream definitions consider homelessness. Prout Quicke and Green's study of the history of fringe dwelling near Geraldton in Western Australia describes how widespread ideas of the incompatibility of Indigenous cultures and successful urban living meant that Indigenous people living at the fringes of urban settlements were viewed as being spiritually, geographically, and culturally homeless. They were seen as no longer being a part of their original communities but also as being simultaneously unable or unwilling to assimilate to the socio-spatial systems and norms of settler society. Attempts to locate fringe dwellers away from the city, as well as records that show Indigenous people felt unwelcome in city spaces, reflected colonial perspectives that Indigenous cultures were out of place in urban life. Like the Niitsitapi studied by Lindstrom and Belanger, fringe dwellers were alienated from the spaces imposed by the colonizers over their traditional homelands.

Policy-Driven Homelessness

Several authors show how Indigenous homelessness results from the clash between continuing Indigenous cultural values and contemporary dominant social policy paradigms. Bonnycastle and Thurston and their colleagues note that the implementation of the current child welfare system in Canada increases the likelihood of becoming homeless both for children who have been apprehended and for their parents. Christensen with Andrew explain that in Canada's Northwest Territories most foster homes where children can be placed are in Yellowknife, and Indigenous parents moving to be near their children find it almost impossible to find public housing for single adults. Homeless shelters are their only option, but parents need secure housing before they can regain custody of their children. Also, parents who already live in public housing in Yellowknife lose that housing when their children are apprehended, because they no longer qualify for family housing. Several authors (Bonnycastle and co-authors, Lindstrom and Belanger, and Schiff and colleagues) explain that the lack of federal government investment in housing on reserves means that housing is often overcrowded, or not available. However, individuals who move to nearby urban areas because of the lack of investment in reserve housing often cannot find accommodation in these cities either.

The administration of public housing regulations helps to exacerbate the situation of Indigenous homelessness in cities. Christensen with Andrew describe how the two-week limit for visitors to families living in public housing creates homelessness in the Northwest Territories. While this policy can support efforts to remove undesirable guests, they argue that far more often it hinders a family by forcing the eviction (and subsequent absolute homelessness) of adult children. These evictions also create feelings of homelessness associated with disconnection from family. Birdsall-Jones's work on homelessness in Western Australia argues that, under the Department of Housing's Disruptive Behaviour Management policy, commonly referred to as the "'three strikes" model, the majority of public housing evictions of Indigenous families have occurred as a result of minor disruptive behaviour such as noisy children, loud parties requiring police attendance, and domestic disputes.

In several chapters, authors show that apparently neutral definitions of crowding and housing adequacy actually reflect Western norms of how people should live together and share bedrooms, and do not currently capture the reality of what makes housing adequate for Indigenous people, nor reflect their cultural and social values. Peters and Kern demonstrate that what Canadian definitions identify as hidden homelessness is actually a significant part of the overall homeless experiences of urban First Nations people. Despite its importance as part of first Nations urban housing strategies, hidden homelessness is underemphasized in research and in policy initiatives. Greenop and Memmott show that official definitions, administration, and designs based on state policies fail to meet the needs of Indigenous households. Brown argues that extended family living is important to Māori well-being, and when family stress results from having too many people under one roof it is architecture that has failed Indigenous families not the other way around. Prout Quicke and Green argue that the legacy of colonial discourses about the "out-of-placeness" of Indigenous people in cities continues to be reflected in contemporary housing policies, increasing urban Indigenous people's vulnerability to homelessness. Various levels of government dispute their responsibility for providing housing to urban Indigenous people, and housing for Indigenous people is limited and the design does not reflect Indigenous kin relationships and obligations. Finally, Groot and Peters point out that the lack of a coordinated response to homelessness in New Zealand exacerbates the situation for Māori people.

Cultural Survival and Resistance

Despite these challenges, Indigenous individuals, organizations, and families struggle to maintain individual dignity, preserve cultural values that underpin kinship and family relationships, and find culturally appropriate ways of responding to homelessness. In Canada, Christensen with Andrew introduce the idea of "home-journeying" as a way of conceptualizing resistance to northern social policy. Home-journeying refers to the strategies individuals use to find safe and secure places to live. These strategies may include occupying places that would not officially be defined as dwellings, for example, camping outside of town in order to avoid the atmosphere of a homeless shelter. An important component of home-journeying refers to the steps individuals take to reconnect to family, community, and land. King and colleagues describe how gardening on a marae creates a "space of care" for homeless men in Auckland, allowing them to reconnect with land, culture, community, and traditions.

In a New Zealand context, Brown writes that Māori were not passive victims in the process of land alienation which underpins contemporary homelessness. They not only resisted encroachment on their lands during the New Zealand Wars, but they continue to fight against it through political, spiritual, and social action to the present day. Similarly in Australia, Prout Quicke and Green found that Geraldton's Indigenous residents resisted attempts to move or remove them through evasion and sometimes confrontation, and asserted their rights to decent and self-determined living conditions, eventually gaining access to housing as citizens with equal rights.

Birdsall-Jones found that, despite centuries of colonizers' attempts to undermine Indigenous cultures in Australia, the cultural norms governing visiting patterns and mobility persist. She argues that household crowding is a rule-driven phenomenon. Individuals engage in visiting practices in order to support kin relationships and rights, individuals and households have an obligation to support visiting kin, and there are culturally accepted times when men in their late teens and early twenties travel to visit extended family. Similar to Birdsall-Jones, Greenop and Memmott found that cultural values particular to Indigenous households persist in contemporary areas and vary greatly from non-Indigenous households in Australia. They argue that extended family households typify sharing and kin obligations that reflect Indigenous values of "living properly." These obligations are seen as part of Indigeneity in contrast to non-Indigenous values which are viewed as preferring privacy and showing a lack of generosity. Greenop and Memmott found that Indigenous people had a number of cultural strategies for alleviating the stresses created by crowding and these included: enforcing strict household rules and thus controlling the household; ensuring avoidance and companionship protocols to avoid shaming people or putting them at risk; managing neighbourhood crowding through diplomacy and the judicious use of police; and withdrawing from crowded households or diverting visitors to other houses nearby.

Because of the persistence of Indigenous cultural values of "how to live properly," Canadians Bonnycastle and co-authors and Thurston and colleagues argue that the research process and the process of designing solutions must be rooted in close relationships with Indigenous people. Thurston, Turner, and Bird found that cultural healing and developing a strong identity can restore balance for Indigenous peoples and provide them with the capacity to address other challenges which lead to homelessness. They argue that the homelessness sector has been resistant to acknowledging that Indigenous people might need programs that differ from those needed by non-Indigenous counterparts. They use the example of the Calgary Alpha House Society, which attempted to build cultural competency by connecting with the homeless outreach project at the Aboriginal Friendship Centre in Calgary, to show how mainstream organizations can build the spaces of cultural safety needed by urban Indigenous homeless individuals. Bonnycastle, Simpkins, and Siddle describe the Aboriginal Accord, in Thompson, Manitoba, which recognizes the role of Indigenous people in the region's history and affirms the city's commitment to strengthening relationships with Indigenous governments and peoples. Thompson has also developed a number of Housing First initiatives and has included homeless people (Indigenous individuals as well) in advising organizations about appropriate strategies. In their study of two regions in northern Australia, Memmott and Nash have pointed out the importance of having Indigenous organizations and staff. They argue that Indigenous networks of the management and the staff facilitated the movement of some Indigenous people out of homelessness. Indigenous staff contacted individuals who would otherwise not have accessed these organizations and provided links to other non-Indigenous NGOs who could provide services. Part of the best practices of Indigenous staff included promoting cultural preservation and building family connections.

Specificity of Places and Identities

While we have argued in this book that it is important to acknowledge the uniqueness of Indigenous experiences of homelessness, a number of chapter authors also remind us that Indigenous people and the places where they experience homelessness are not homogeneous. It is important to recognize that subgroups with Indigenous homeless populations may have particular needs and experiences, and explore the specific geographic contexts in which homelessness takes place.

Several chapters explore or mention different gendered experiences. In Canada, Klodawsky and colleagues' panel study of a large number of homeless people in three large Canadian cities highlighted the unique health issues of Indigenous women compared to other homeless individuals, with Indigenous women experiencing particularly poor mental and physical health status. They urge us to increasingly acknowledge that social identities relating to gender, race/ethnicity, class, age, and so on are not "additive or independent characteristics but integrally implicated in each person's life chances and circumstances" (92). Thurston, Turner, and Bird's work in Calgary, Alberta, found that Indigenous women are more likely than Indigenous men to be homeless because of domestic violence and as a result are also more likely to be in homeless shelters created for individuals escaping partner abuse. Bonnycastle and colleagues also note that pathways to homelessness for women often include domestic violence. In Australia, Birdsall-Jones describes the gendered nature of visiting with women visiting mothers, sisters, and children to maintain kin relationships and rights, and men travelling widely during a period in their youth.

Several researchers addressed the specific issues facing small towns in their attempts to meet the needs of Indigenous homeless individuals. Schiff, Turner, and Waegemakers Schiff's research on challenges facing small centres fills in an important gap in the literature which has focused mainly on homelessness in large urban places. They note that many small centres, particularly in northern Canada, attempt to accommodate First Nations people forced off reserves because of a lack of housing, services, and employment (see also Lindstrom and Belanger). Schiff and colleagues highlight a number of common characteristics with respect to providing housing and services to homeless urban Indigenous people, including the lack of shelters and social housing in many small centres. This scarcity of services to meet complex needs results in hidden homelessness and crowding as well as camping, and goes along with a lack of stated acknowledgement of homelessness as an important issue in these centres. Bonnycastle, Simpkins, and Siddle note that limited shelter beds in small northern towns lead to camping even in very cold weather. Similarly, Memmott and Nash describe the lack of housing providers in more isolated Australian urban centres and the challenges small centres face in providing services for multiple-need homeless individuals.

Finally, several chapter authors comment on the alienation that homeless Indigenous people experience in cities. The city represented estrangement from family and community for the homeless individuals who were part of Belanger and Lindstrom's southern Alberta study. The city also represented an environment of racism and discrimination, as homeless people faced cat calls as they walked to and from the homeless shelter, and faced difficulty renting apartments from landlords. Prout Quicke and Green also mentioned landlord discrimination in Geraldton, Australia.

Freistadt's analysis of the policing of homeless individuals in Edmonton uncovers the social geography of ideas as to where Indigenous people belong in the city. His interviews showed that police interacted differently with Indigenous and non-Indigenous homeless people present on a major com-mercial street. Indigenous people were much more likely to be picked up and moved to a more dangerous inner-city neighbourhood where the homeless shelter was located. Freistadt argues that this racialized policing shows that police see consumer spaces as white places and dangerous inner-city spaces as Indigenous. The removal of Indigenous people from these consumer spaces then reinforces their assumed whiteness.

Conclusion

Indigenous homelessness presents complex challenges for each of the countries in this volume. The sources of homelessness are complicated and have long histories that continue to have implications for Indigenous individuals and communities today. Finding solutions requires an understanding of the unique aspects driving Indigenous homelessness. It also requires an examination of the cultural assumptions and structural racism embedded in policies and prac-tices, as well as these policies' often unintended or unheeded consequences. The process of designing appropriate responses will require the involvement of Indigenous people in a variety of roles from designing research initiatives to creating and delivering services. Clearly there are many areas of research that still require fleshing out, for example, the specific homeless experiences of different Indigenous identity groups. This volume, however, represents the first of what we hope to be many new contributions to the topic of Indigenous homelessness.

Contributors

Paul Andrew was the Chair of 2012 Minister's Forum on Addictions and Community Wellness in the Department of Health and Social Services, Government of the Northwest Territories. Prior to his retirement in 2012, Paul had a long and storied career as a broadcaster with CBC North, including eleven years as host of CBC *Northbeat*.

Tim Aubry is a Professor in the School of Psychology, Senior Researcher at the Centre for Research on Educational and Community Services, and holder of the Faculty Research Chair on Community Mental Health and Homelessness in the Faculty of Social Sciences at the University of Ottawa.

Yale Belanger is a Professor of Political Science, University of Lethbridge.

Cynthia Bird is an independent researcher and senior education consultant with over thirty years of experience in Indigenous and mainstream education working with First Nations, urban Indigenous, mainstream education institutions, and non-profit organizations. She focuses on community-based research, women, education, health, and homelessness.

Christina Birdsall-Jones is a Senior Research Fellow at the John Curtin Institute of Public Policy at Curtin University in Perth, Western Australia. She is an anthropologist with research interests in Indigenous housing and homelessness issues.

Marleny M. Bonnycastle is an Assistant Professor in the Faculty of Social Work at the University of Manitoba in Thompson, Manitoba, Canada. Her areas of interest are homelessness, gender and women, including post-secondary students, refugee and immigrant women, and violence against women and girls.

Deidre Brown is an Associate Professor in Architecture at the School of Architecture and Planning at the University of Auckland, New Zealand. She is a member of the Ngāpuhi and Ngāti Kahu tribes of Northland.

Rebecca Cherner is a Postdoctoral Fellow with the Centre for Research on Educational and Community Services and the School of Psychology at the University of Ottawa.

Julia Christensen is an Assistant Professor in Geography and Planning Studies at Roskilde University in Roskilde, Denmark. Julia was born and raised on Chief Drygeese Territory in Yellowknife, Northwest Territories and has written extensively on home and homelessness in northern and Indigenous contexts.

Patricia Franks is an Indigenous Elder in Tennant Creek, Northern Territory, Australia and a leader of the Warumungu people.

Susan Farrell is a psychologist and the Clinical Director of the Community Mental Health Program at The Royal. She works directly with people who are homeless and vulnerably housed in community settings. She holds appointments in the Faculty of Medicine and the School of Psychology at the University of Ottawa.

Joshua Freistadt is a former Killam Scholar and SSHRC Postdoctoral Fellow who now works in the public sector.

Charmaine Green works for the Western Australian Centre for Rural Health at the University of Western Australia. Charmaine is from the Yamaji Nation in Western Australia. She is a researcher, community advocate, and artist based in Geraldton, Western Australia.

Kelly Greenop is a Lecturer at the School of Architecture at the University of Queensland, and is affiliated with the Aboriginal Environments Research Centre and the Centre for Architecture Theory Criticism History.

Shiloh Groot is a Lecturer in social psychology at the University of Auckland. She is the Co-Chair of the Māori Caucus of the New Zealand Coalition to End Homelessness.

Darrin Hodgetts (Ngai Tahu) is a Professor of Social Psychology at the School of Psychology, Massey University in New Zealand. His research interests focus on urban poverty.

Selena Kern is a member of the Brokenhead Ojibway Nation, and currently resides in Winnipeg, Manitoba. Selena started work at the Eagle Urban Transition Centre (EUTC) in 2012 as the Centre's first Housing Counsellor and she is now the Service Coordinator and Project Lead for housing and homelessness projects at EUTC.